EMPIRE

Niall Ferguson is Professor of International History at Harvard University, Senior Research Fellow of Jesus College, Oxford University, and a Senior Fellow of the Hoover Institution, Stanford University. He is the author of *Paper and Iron*, *The House of Rothschild* (two volumes), *The Pity of War*, *The Cash Nexus*, *Empire*, *Colossus* and *The War of the World*. He was also the editor of *Virtual History*. He lives in Oxfordshire with his wife and three children.

NIALL FERGUSON

Empire

How Britain Made the Modern World

Best wishes

[signature]

PENGUIN BOOKS

PENGUIN
CELEBRATIONS

For Ken and Vivienne

PENGUIN BOOKS

Published by the Penguin Group
Penguin Books Ltd, 80 Strand, London WC2R ORL, England
Penguin Group (USA) Inc., 375 Hudson Street, New York, New York 10014, USA
Penguin Group (Canada), 90 Eglinton Avenue East, Suite 700, Toronto, Ontario, Canada M4P 2Y3
(a division of Pearson Penguin Canada Inc.)
Penguin Ireland, 25 St Stephen's Green, Dublin 2, Ireland
(a division of Penguin Books Ltd)
Penguin Group (Australia), 250 Camberwell Road, Camberwell, Victoria 3124, Australia
(a division of Pearson Australia Group Pty Ltd)
Penguin Books India Pvt Ltd, 11 Community Centre, Panchsheel Park, New Delhi – 110 017, India
Penguin Group (NZ), 67 Apollo Drive, Rosedale, North Shore 0632, New Zealand
(a division of Pearson New Zealand Ltd)
Penguin Books (South Africa) (Pty) Ltd, 24 Sturdee Avenue, Rosebank, Johannesburg 2196, South Africa

Penguin Books Ltd, Registered Offices: 80 Strand, London WC2R ORL, England

www.penguin.com

First published by Allen Lane 2003
Published in Penguin Books 2004
Reissued in this edition 2007

1

Copyright © Niall Ferguson, 2003
All rights reserved

The moral right of the author has been asserted

Set in 9.5/12.75 pt Linotype Sabon
Typeset by Rowland Phototypesetting Ltd, Bury St Edmunds, Suffolk
Printed in England by Clays Ltd, St Ives plc

ISBN: 978-0-141-03526-0

The old river in its broad reach rested unruffled at the decline of day, after ages of good service done to the race that peopled its banks, spread out in the tranquil dignity of a waterway leading to the uttermost ends of the earth . . . The tidal current runs to and fro in its unceasing service, crowded with memories of men and ships it had borne to the rest of home or to the battles of the sea. It had known and served all the men of whom the nation is proud . . . It had borne all the ships whose names are like jewels flashing in the night of time . . . It had known the ships and the men. They had sailed from Deptford, from Greenwich, from Erith – the adventurers and the settlers; kings' ships and the ships of men on 'Change; captains, admirals, the dark 'interlopers' of the Eastern trade, and the commissioned 'generals' of East India fleets. Hunters for gold or pursuers of fame, they all had gone out on that stream, bearing the sword, and often the torch, messengers of the might within the land, bearers of a spark from the sacred fire. What greatness had not floated on the ebb of that river into the mystery of an unknown earth! . . . The dreams of men, the seed of commonwealths, the germs of empires . . .

Joseph Conrad, *Heart of Darkness*

Contents

Introduction   xi

1 Why Britain?   1
2 White Plague   53
3 The Mission   113
4 Heaven's Breed   163
5 Maxim Force   221
6 Empire For Sale   294

Conclusion   365

Acknowledgements   383
Illustration Acknowledgements   385
Bibliography   389
Index   406

Introduction

Once there was an Empire that governed roughly a quarter of the world's population, covered about the same proportion of the earth's land surface and dominated nearly all its oceans. The British Empire was the biggest Empire ever, bar none. How an archipelago of rainy islands off the north-west coast of Europe came to rule the world is one of the fundamental questions not just of British but of world history. It is one of the questions this book seeks to answer. The second and perhaps more difficult question it addresses is simply whether the Empire was a good or bad thing.

It is nowadays quite conventional to think that, on balance, it was bad. Probably the main reason for the Empire's fall into disrepute was its involvement in the Atlantic slave trade and slavery itself. This is no longer a question for historical judgement alone; it has become a political, and potentially a legal, issue. In August 1999 the African World Reparations and Repatriation Truth Commission, meeting in Accra, issued a demand for reparations from 'all those nations of Western Europe and the Americas and institutions, who participated and benefited from the slave trade and colonialism'. The sum suggested as adequate compensation – based on estimates of 'the number of human lives lost to Africa during the slave-trade, as well as an assessment of the worth of the gold, diamonds and other minerals taken from the continent during colonial rule' – was $777 trillion. Given that more than three million of the ten million or so Africans who crossed the Atlantic as slaves before 1850 were shipped in British vessels, the putative British reparations burden could be in the region of £150 trillion.

Such a claim may seem fantastic. But the idea was given some encouragement at the United Nations World Conference against Racism, Racial Discrimination, Xenophobia and Related Intolerance, held in Durban in the summer of 2001. The conference's final report 'acknowledged' that slavery and the slave trade were 'a crime against humanity' of which 'people of African descent, Asians and people of Asian and indigenous peoples' were 'victims'. In another of the conference's declarations, 'colonialism' was casually lumped together with 'slavery, the slave trade . . . apartheid . . . and genocide' in a blanket call to UN member states 'to honour the memory of the victims of past tragedies'. Noting that 'some States have taken the initiative to apologize and have paid reparation, where appropriate, for grave and massive violations committed', the conference 'called on all those who have not yet contributed to restoring the dignity of the victims to find appropriate ways to do so'.

These calls have not gone unheeded in Britain itself. In May 2002 the director of the London-based 'think tank' Demos, which may be regarded as the avant-garde of New Labour, suggested that the Queen should embark on 'a world tour to apologize for the past sins of Empire as a first step to making the Commonwealth more effective and relevant'. The news agency that reported this remarkable suggestion added the helpful gloss: 'Critics of the British Empire, which at its peak in 1918 covered a quarter of the world's population and area, say its huge wealth was built on oppression and exploitation.'

At the time of writing, one BBC website (apparently aimed at school-children) offered the following equally incisive overview of imperial history:

The Empire came to greatness by killing lots of people less sharply armed than themselves and stealing their countries, although their methods later changed: killing lots of people with machine guns came to prominence as the army's tactic of choice . . . [It] . . . fell to pieces because of various people like Mahatma Gandhi, heroic revolutionary protester, sensitive to the needs of his people.

The questions recently posed by an eminent historian on BBC television may be said to encapsulate the current conventional wisdom. 'How', he asked, 'did a people who thought themselves free end up subjugating so much of the world . . . How did an empire of the free become an empire of slaves?' How, despite their 'good intentions', did the British sacrifice 'common humanity' to 'the fetish of the market'?

Beneficiaries

Thanks to the British Empire, I have relatives scattered all over the world – in Alberta, Ontario, Philadelphia and Perth, Australia. Because of the Empire, my paternal grandfather John spent his early twenties selling hardware and hooch to Indians in Ecuador.* I grew up marvelling at the two large oil paintings he brought back of the Andean landscape, which hung luminously on my

---

* Not a colony, of course, but part of Britain's 'informal' economic empire in Latin America.

grandmother's living room wall; and the two Indian dolls, grim faced and weighed down with firewood, incongruous beside the china figurines in her display cabinet. Thanks to the Empire, my other grandfather Tom Hamilton spent more than three years as an RAF officer fighting the Japanese in India and Burma. His letters home, lovingly preserved by my grandmother, are a wonderfully observant and eloquent account of the Raj in wartime, shot through with that sceptical liberalism which was the core of his philosophy. I can still recall the joy of leafing through the photographs he took while stationed in India, and the thrill of hearing his stories about swooping kites and sweltering heat. Thanks to the Empire, my Uncle Ian Ferguson's first job after he qualified as an architect was with the Calcutta firm of McIntosh Burn, a subsidiary of the Gillanders managing agency. Ian had started his working life in the Royal Navy; he spent the rest of his life abroad, first in Africa, then in the Gulf states. To me he seemed the very essence of the expatriate adventurer: sun-darkened, hard-drinking and fiercely cynical – the only adult who always, from my earliest childhood, addressed me as a fellow-adult, profanities, black humour and all.

His brother – my father – also had his moment of *Wanderlust*. In 1966, having completed his medical studies in Glasgow, he defied the advice of friends and relatives by taking his wife and two infant children to Kenya, where he worked for two years teaching and practising medicine in Nairobi. Thus, thanks to the British Empire, my earliest childhood memories are of colonial Africa; for although Kenya had been independent for three years, and the radio constantly played Jomo Kenyatta's signature tune 'Harambe, Harambe' ('Let's all pull together'), scarcely anything had changed since the days of White Mischief. We had our bungalow, our maid, our smattering of Swahili – and our sense of unshakeable security. It was a magical time, which indelibly impressed on my consciousness the sight of the hunting cheetah, the sound of Kikuyu women singing, the smell of the first rains and the taste of ripe mango. I suspect my mother was never happier. And although we finally came back to the grey skies and the winter slush of Glasgow, our house was always filled with Kenyan memorabilia. There was the antelope skin on the sofa; the Masai warrior's portrait on the wall; the crudely carved but exquisitely decorated footstool that my sister and I liked to perch on. Each of us had a zebra skin drum; a gaudy basket from Mombasa; a wildebeest-hair fly-whisk; a Kikuyu doll. We did not know it, but we grew up in a little post-colonial museum. I still have the carved wooden hippopotamus, warthog, elephant and lion which were once my most treasured possessions.

Still, we had come home – and we never went back. One who did not return to Scotland was my great-aunt Agnes Ferguson (Aggie to all who knew her). Born in 1888, the daughter of my great-grandfather James Ferguson, a garden labourer, and his first wife Mary, Aggie personified the transforming power of the imperial dream. In 1911, enticed by alluring pictures of the Canadian prairies, she and her new husband Ernest Brown decided to follow his brother's example: to leave their home, their family and friends in Fife, and head west. The lure was the offer of 160 acres of virgin real estate in Saskatchewan, free of charge. The only stipulation was that they had to build a dwelling there and cultivate the land. According to family legend, Aggie and Ernest were supposed to sail on the *Titanic*; by chance, only their luggage was on board when the ship went down. That was luck of a sort, but it meant that they had to start their new life from scratch. And if Aggie and Ernest thought they were getting away from the nasty Scottish winter, they were swiftly disillusioned. What they found in Glenrock was a windswept wilderness where temperatures could plunge far lower than in drizzly Fife. It was, as Ernest wrote to his sister-in-law Nellie, 'sure terriabl [*sic*] cold'. The first shelter they were able to build for themselves was so primitive they called it a chicken shack. The nearest town, Moose Jaw, was ninety-five miles away. To begin with, their nearest neighbours were Indians; friendly ones, fortunately.

Yet the black and white photographs they sent back to their relatives every Christmas of themselves and 'our prairie home' tell a story of success and fulfilment; of hard-won happiness. As the mother of three healthy children, Aggie lost the pinched look she had worn as an emigrant bride. Ernest grew tanned and broad-shouldered working the prairie soil; shaved off his moustache; became handsome where once he had been hangdog. The chicken shack was supplanted by a clapboard farmhouse. Gradually, their sense of isolation diminished as more Scots settled in the area. It was reassuring to be able to celebrate Hogmanay with fellow countrymen so far from home, since 'they don't hold New Year out here very much just the Scotch folk'. Today their ten grandchildren live all over Canada, a country whose annual income per capita is not merely 10 per cent higher than Britain's but second only to that of the United States. All thanks to the British Empire.

So to say that I grew up in the Empire's shadow would be to conjure up too tenebrous an image. To the Scots, the Empire stood for bright sunlight. Little may have been left of it on the map by the 1970s, but my family was so completely imbued with the imperial ethos that its importance went unquestioned. Indeed, the legacy of the Empire was so ubiquitous and omnipresent that we regarded it as part of the normal human condition. Holidays in Canada did nothing to alter this impression. Nor did that systematic defamation of Catholic Ireland which in those days was such an integral part of life on the south side of the Clyde. I grew up still thinking complacently of Glasgow as the 'Second City' (of the Empire); reading quite uncritically the novels of H. Rider Haggard and John Buchan; relishing all the quintessentially imperial sporting clashes – best of all the rugby tours by the 'British Lions' to Australia, New Zealand and (until they were regrettably interrupted) South Africa.* At home we ate 'Empire biscuits'. At school we did 'Empire shooting'.

---

* The ban on sporting tours of Africa was in fact quite easy to reconcile with the liberal imperialist assumptions of my youth. It seemed obvious that in denying black South Africans civil and political rights, the Afrikaners were merely showing their true colours and vindicating earlier (but sadly unsuccessful) efforts by the enlightened British to break their dominance. I am afraid the possibility that the apartheid system might have anything to do with British rule – or that the British had ever practised their own tacit systems of apartheid – never occurred to me.

Cases Against

Admittedly, by the time I reached my teens, the idea of a world ruled by chaps with red coats, stiff upper lips and pith helmets had become something of a joke, the raw material for *Carry On Up the Khyber*, *It Ain't Half Hot Mum* and *Monty Python's Flying Circus*. Perhaps the archetypal line in the genre is in the Monty Python film *The Meaning of Life*, when a blood-spattered 'Tommy', fatally wounded in a battle with the Zulus, exclaims ecstatically: 'I mean, I killed fifteen of those buggers, sir. Now, at home, they'd hang me! Here, they'll give me a fucking medal, sir!'

When I got to Oxford in 1982 the Empire was no longer even funny. In those days the Oxford Union still debated solemn motions like 'This House Regrets Colonization'. Young and foolish, I rashly opposed this motion and in doing so prematurely ended my career as a student politician. I suppose that was the moment the penny dropped: clearly not everyone shared my confidently rosy view of Britain's imperial past. Indeed, some of my contemporaries appeared quite scandalized that I should be prepared to defend it. As I began to study the subject in earnest, I came to realize that I and my family had been woefully misinformed: the costs of the British Empire had, in fact, substantially outweighed its benefits. The Empire had, after all, been one of history's Bad Things.

There is no need here to recapitulate in any detail the arguments against imperialism. They can be summarized, I think, under two headings: those that stress the negative consequences for the colonized; and those that stress the negative consequences for the colonizers. In the former category belong both the nationalists and the Marxists, from the Mughal historian Gholam Hossein Khan, author of the *Seir Mutaqherin* (1789) to the Palestinian academic Edward Said, author of *Orientalism* (1978), by way of Lenin and a thousand others in between. In the latter camp belong the liberals, from Adam Smith onwards, who have maintained for almost as many years that the British Empire was, even from Britain's point of view, 'a waste of money'.

The central nationalist/Marxist assumption is, of course, that imperialism was economically exploitative; every facet of colonial rule, including even the apparently sincere efforts of Europeans to study and understand indigenous cultures, was at root designed to maximize the 'surplus value' that could be extracted from the subject peoples. The central liberal assumption is more paradoxical. It is that precisely because imperialism distorted market forces – using everything from military force to preferential tariffs to rig business in the favour of the metropolis – it was not in the long-term interests of the metropolitan economy either. In this view, it was free economic integration with the rest of the world economy that mattered, not the coercive integration of imperialism. Thus, investment in domestic industry would have been better for Britain than investment in far-flung colonies, while the cost of defending the Empire was a burden on taxpayers, who might otherwise have spent their money on the products of a modern consumer goods sector. One historian, writing in the new *Oxford History of the British Empire*, has gone so far as to speculate that if Britain had got rid of the Empire in the mid 1840s she could have reaped a 'decolonization dividend' in the form of a 25 per cent tax cut. The money taxpayers would have saved as a result of this could have been spent on electricity, cars and consumer durables, thus encouraging industrial modernization at home.

Nearly a century ago, the likes of J. A. Hobson and Leonard Hobhouse were arguing along very similar lines; they in turn were in some measure the heirs of Richard Cobden and John Bright in the 1840s and 1850s. In *The Wealth of Nations* (1776), Adam Smith had expressed his doubts about the wisdom of 'raising up a nation of customers who should be obliged to buy from the shops of our different producers, all the goods with which these could supply them'. But it was Cobden who had originally insisted that the expansion of British trade should go hand in hand with a foreign policy of complete non-intervention. Commerce alone, he maintained, was 'the grand panacea', which, like a beneficent medical discovery, will serve to inoculate with the healthy and saving taste for civilization all the nations of the world. Not a bale of merchandise leaves our shores, but it bears the seeds of intelligence and fruitful thought to the members of some less enlightened community; not a merchant visits our seats of manufacturing industry, but he returns to his own country the missionary of freedom, peace, and good government – whilst our steamboats, that now visit every port of Europe, and our miraculous railroads, that are the talk of all nations, are the advertisements and vouchers for the value of our enlightened institutions.

The critical point for Cobden was that neither trade nor even the spread of British 'civilization' needed to be *enforced* by imperial structures. Indeed, the use of force could achieve nothing if it sought to run counter to the benign laws of the global free market:

So far as our commerce is concerned, it can neither be sustained nor greatly injured abroad by force or violence. The foreign customers who visit our markets are not brought hither through fear of the power or the influence of British diplomatists: they are not captured by our fleets and armies: and as little are they attracted by feelings of love for us; for that 'there is no friendship in trade' is a maxim equally applicable to nations and to individuals. It is solely from the promptings of self interest that the merchants of Europe, as of the rest of the world, send their ships to our ports to be freighted with the products of our labour. The self-same impulse drew all nations, at different periods of history, to Tyre, to Venice, and to Amsterdam; and if, in the revolution of time and events, a country should be found (which is probable) whose cottons and woollens shall be cheaper than those of England and the rest of the world, then to that spot – even should it, by supposition, be buried in the remotest nook of the globe – will all the traders of the earth flock; and no human power, no fleets or armies, will prevent Manchester, Liverpool, and Leeds, from sharing the fate of their once proud predecessors in Holland, Italy, and Phoenicia . . .

Thus there was no need for an Empire; trade would take care of itself – and everything else too, including world peace. In May 1856 Cobden went so far as to say that it would 'be a happy day when England has not an acre of territory in Continental Asia'.

The common factor in all such arguments was and remains, however, the assumption that the benefits of international exchange could have been and can be reaped without the costs of empire. To put it more concisely, can you have globalization without gunboats?

Empire and Globalization

It has become almost a commonplace that globalization today has much in common with the integration of the world economy in the decades before 1914. But what exactly does this overused word mean? Is it, as Cobden implied, an economically determined phenomenon, in which the free exchange of commodities and manufactures tends 'to unite mankind in the bonds of peace'? Or might free trade require a political framework within which to work?

The Leftist opponents of globalization naturally regard it as no more than the latest manifestation of a damnably resilient international capitalism. By contrast, the modern consensus among liberal economists is that increasing economic openness raises living standards, even if there will always be some net losers as hitherto privileged or protected social groups are exposed to international competition. But economists and economic historians alike prefer to focus their attention on flows of commodities, capital and labour. They say less about flows of knowledge, culture and institutions. They also tend to pay more attention to the ways government can *facilitate* globalization by various kinds of deregulation than to the ways it can actively promote and indeed *impose* it. There is a growing appreciation of the importance of legal, financial and administrative institutions such as the rule of law, credible monetary regimes, transparent fiscal systems and incorrupt bureaucracies in encouraging cross-border capital flows. But how did the West European versions of such institutions spread as far and wide as they did?

In a few rare cases – the most obvious being that of Japan – there was a process of conscious, voluntary imitation. But more often than not, European institutions were imposed by main force, often literally at gunpoint. In theory, globalization may be possible in an international system of multilateral cooperation, spontaneously arising as Cobden envisaged. But it may equally well be possible as a result of coercion if the dominant power in the world favours economic liberalism. Empire – and specifically the British Empire – is the instance that springs to mind.

Today, the principal barriers to the optimal allocation of labour, capital and goods in the world are, on the one hand, civil wars and lawless, corrupt governments, which together have condemned so many countries in sub-Saharan Africa and parts of Asia to decades of impoverishment; and, on the other, the reluctance of the United States and her allies to practise as well as preach free trade, or to devote more than a trifling share of their vast resources to programmes of economic aid. By contrast, for much (though certainly, as we shall see, not all) of its history, the British Empire acted as an agency for imposing free markets, the rule of law, investor protection and relatively incorrupt government on roughly a quarter of the world. The Empire also did a good deal to encourage those things in countries which were outside its formal imperial domain but under its economic influence through the 'imperialism of free trade'. *Prima facie*, there therefore seems a plausible case that empire enhanced global welfare – in other words, was a Good Thing.

Many charges can of course be levelled against the British Empire; they will not be dropped in what follows. I do not claim, as John Stuart Mill did, that British rule in India was 'not only the purest in intention but one of the most beneficent in act ever known to mankind'; nor, as Lord Curzon did, that 'the British Empire is under Providence the greatest instrument for good that the world has seen'; nor, as General Smuts claimed, that it was 'the widest system of organized human freedom which has ever existed in human history'. The Empire was never so altruistic. In the eighteenth century the British were indeed as zealous in the acquisition and exploitation of slaves as they were subsequently zealous in trying to stamp slavery out; and for much longer they practised forms of racial discrimination and segregation that we today consider abhorrent. When imperial authority was challenged – in India in 1857, in Jamaica in 1831 or 1865, in South Africa in 1899 – the British response was brutal. When famine struck (in Ireland in the 1840s, in India in the 1870s) their response was negligent, in some measure positively culpable. Even when they took a scholarly interest in oriental cultures, perhaps they did subtly denigrate them in the process.

Yet the fact remains that no organization in history has done more to promote the free movement of goods, capital and labour than the British Empire in the nineteenth and early twentieth centuries. And no organization has done more to impose Western norms of law, order and governance around the world. To characterize all this as 'gentlemanly capitalism' risks underselling the scale – and modernity – of the achievement in the sphere of economics; just as criticism of the 'ornamental' (meaning hierarchical) character of British rule overseas tends to overlook the signal virtues of what were remarkably non-venal administrations. It was not just my family that benefited from these things.

The difficulty with the achievements of empire is that they are much more likely to be taken for granted than the sins of empire. It is, however, instructive to try to imagine a world without the Empire. But while it is just about possible to imagine what the world would have been like without the French Revolution or the First World War, the imagination reels from the counter-factual of modern history without the British Empire.

As I travelled around that Empire's remains in the first half of 2002, I was constantly struck by its ubiquitous creativity. To imagine the world without the Empire would be to expunge from the map the elegant boulevards of Williamsburg and old Philadelphia; to sweep into the sea the squat battlements of Port Royal, Jamaica; to return to the bush the glorious skyline of Sydney; to level the steamy seaside slum that is Freetown, Sierra Leone; to fill in the Big Hole at Kimberley; to demolish the mission at Kuruman; to send the town of Livingstone hurtling over the Victoria Falls – which would of course revert to their original name of Mosioatunya. Without the British Empire, there would be no Calcutta; no Bombay; no Madras. Indians may rename them as many times as they like, but they remain cities founded and built by the British.

It is of course tempting to argue that it would all have happened anyway, albeit with different names. Perhaps the railways would have been invented and exported by another European power; perhaps the telegraph cables would have been laid across the sea by someone else. Maybe, as Cobden claimed, the same volumes of trade would have gone on without bellicose empires meddling in peaceful commerce. Maybe too the great movements of population which transformed the cultures and complexions of whole continents would have happened anyway.

Yet there is reason to doubt that the world would have been the same or even similar in the absence of the Empire. Even if we allow for the possibility that trade, capital flows and migration could have been 'naturally occurring' in the past 300 years, there remain the flows of culture and institutions. And here the fingerprints of empire seem more readily discernible and less easy to expunge.

When the British governed a country – even when they only influenced its government by flexing their military and financial muscles – there were certain distinctive features of their own society that they tended to disseminate. A list of the more important of these would run:

1 The English language
2 English forms of land tenure
3 Scottish and English banking
4 The Common Law
5 Protestantism
6 Team sports
7 The limited or 'night watchman' state
8 Representative assemblies
9 The idea of liberty

The last of these is perhaps the most important because it remains the most distinctive feature of the Empire, the thing that sets it apart from its continental European rivals. I do not mean to claim that all British imperialists were liberals: some were very far from it. But what is very striking about the history of the Empire is that whenever the British were behaving despotically, there was almost always a liberal critique of that behaviour from within British society. Indeed, so powerful and consistent was this tendency to judge Britain's imperial conduct by the yardstick of liberty that it gave the British Empire something of a self-liquidating character. Once a colonized society had sufficiently adopted the other institutions the British brought with them, it became very hard for the British to prohibit that political liberty to which they attached so much significance for themselves.

Would other empires have produced the same effects? It seems doubtful. In my travels I caught many glimpses of world empires that might have been. In dilapidated Chinsura, a vision of how all Asia might look if the Dutch empire had not declined and fallen; in whitewashed Pondicherry, which all India might resemble if the French had won the Seven Years War; in dusty Delhi, where the Mughal Empire might have been restored if the Indian Mutiny had not been crushed; in humid Kanchanaburi, where the Japanese empire built its bridge on the River Kwai with British slave labour. Would New Amsterdam be the New York we know today if the Dutch had not surrendered it to the British in 1664? Might it not resemble more closely Bloemfontein, an authentic survivor of Dutch colonization?

Anglobalization

There are already several good general histories of the British Empire in print. My aim has not been to replicate these but to write the history of globalization as it was promoted by Great Britain and her colonies – 'Anglobalization', if you like. The structure is broadly chronological, but each of the six chapters has a distinct theme. For simplicity's sake the contents may be summarized as the globalization of:

1 Commodity markets
2 Labour markets
3 Culture
4 Government
5 Capital markets
6 Warfare

Or, in rather more human terms, the role of:

1 Pirates
2 Planters
3 Missionaries
4 Mandarins
5 Bankers
6 Bankrupts

The first chapter emphasizes that the British Empire began as a primarily economic phenomenon, its growth powered by commerce and consumerism. The demand for sugar drew merchants to the Caribbean. The demand for spices, tea and textiles drew them to Asia. But this was from the outset globalization with gunboats. For the British were not the first empire-builders, but the pirates who scavenged from the earlier empires of Portugal, Spain, Holland and France. They were imperial imitators.

The second chapter describes the role of migration. British colonization was a vast movement of peoples, a *Völkerwanderung* unlike anything before or since. Some quit the British Isles in pursuit of religious freedom, some in pursuit of political liberty, some in pursuit of profit. Others had no choice, but went as slaves or as convicted criminals. The central theme of this chapter, therefore, is the tension between British theories of liberty and the practice of imperial government; and how that tension came to be resolved.

Chapter Three emphasizes the voluntary, non-governmental character of Empire-building, focusing in particular on the increasingly important role played by Evangelical religious sects and missionary societies in the expansion of British influence. A critical point here is the self-consciously modernizing project that emanated from these organizations – the Victorian 'NGOs'. The paradox is that it was precisely the belief that indigenous cultures could be Anglicized which provoked the most violent nineteenth-century revolt against imperial rule.

The British Empire was the nearest thing there has ever been to a world government. Yet its mode of operation was a triumph of minimalism. To govern a population numbering hundreds of millions, the Indian Civil Service had a maximum strength of little more than 1,000. Chapter Four asks how it was possible for such a tiny bureaucracy to govern so huge an empire, and explores the symbiotic but ultimately unsustainable collaboration between British rulers and indigenous elites, both traditional and new.

Chapter Five deals primarily with the role of military force in the period of the 'Scramble for Africa', exploring the interaction between financial globalization and the armaments race between the European powers. Though they had been anticipated before, this was the era when three critical modern phenomena were born: the truly global bond market, the military-industrial complex and the mass media. Their influence was crucial in pushing the Empire towards its zenith. The press, above all, led the Empire into the temptation the Greeks called hubris: the pride that precedes a fall.

Finally, Chapter Six considers the role of the Empire in the twentieth century, when it found itself challenged not so much by nationalist insurgency – it could deal with that – but by rival, and far more ruthless, empires. The year 1940 was the moment when the Empire was weighed in the historical balance; when it faced the choice between compromise with Hitler's evil empire and fighting on for, at best, a Pyrrhic victory. In my view, the right choice was made.

In a single volume covering what is, in effect, 400 years of global history, there must necessarily be omissions; I am all too painfully aware of these. I have tried, however, not to select so as to flatter. Slavery and the slave trade cannot be and are not disclaimed; any more than the Irish potato famine, the expropriation of the Matabele or the Amritsar massacre. But this balance sheet of the

British imperial achievement does not omit the credit side either. It seeks to show that the legacy of Empire is not just 'racism, racial discrimination, xenophobia and related intolerance' – which in any case existed long before colonialism – but

- the triumph of capitalism as the optimal system of economic organization;
- the Anglicization of North America and Australasia;
- the internationalization of the English language;
- the enduring influence of the Protestant version of Christianity; and, above all
- the survival of parliamentary institutions, which far worse empires were poised to extinguish in the 1940s.

As a young man, fresh from his first colonial war, Winston Churchill asked a good question:

What enterprise that an enlightened community may attempt is more noble and more profitable than the reclamation from barbarism of fertile regions and large populations? To give peace to warring tribes, to administer justice where all was violence, to strike the chains off the slave, to draw the richness from the soil, to plant the earliest seeds of commerce and learning, to increase in whole peoples their capacities for pleasure and diminish their chances of pain – what more beautiful ideal or more valuable reward can inspire human effort?

But Churchill recognized that, even with such aspirations, the practicalities of empire were seldom edifying.

Yet as the mind turns from the wonderful cloudland of aspiration to the ugly scaffolding of attempt and achievement, a succession of opposite ideas arise . . . The inevitable gap between conquest and dominion becomes filled with the figures of the greedy trader, the inopportune missionary, the ambitious soldier, and the lying speculator, who disquiet the minds of the conquered and excite the sordid appetites of the conquerors. And as the eye of thought rests on these sinister features, it hardly seems possible for us to believe that any fair prospect is approached by so foul a path.

For better for worse – fair and foul – the world we know today is in large measure the product of Britain's age of Empire. The question is not whether British imperialism was without a blemish. It was not. The question is whether there could have been a less bloody path to modernity. Perhaps in theory there could have been. But in practice? What follows will, I hope, enable the reader to decide.

I

Why Britain?

*By what means are the Europeans thus powerful; or why,
since they can so easily visit Asia and Africa for trade or conquest, cannot the Asiaticks and Africans invade their coasts,
plant colonies in their ports, and give laws to their natural
princes? The same wind that carries them back would bring us
thither.*

Samuel Johnson, *Rasselas*

In December 1663 a Welshman called Henry Morgan sailed five
hundred miles across the Caribbean to mount a spectacular raid
on a Spanish outpost called Gran Grenada, to the north of Lago de
Nicaragua. The aim of the expedition was simple: to find and steal
Spanish gold – or any other movable property. When Morgan and
his men got to Gran Grenada, as the Governor of Jamaica reported
in a despatch to London, '[They] fired a volley, overturned eighteen
great guns . . . took the serjeant-major's house wherein were all their
arms and ammunition, secured in the great Church 300 of the best
men prisoners . . . plundered for 16 hours, discharged the prisoners,
sunk all the boats and so came away.' It was the beginning of one
of the seventeenth century's most extraordinary smash-and-grab
sprees.

It should never be forgotten that this was how the British Empire
began: in a maelstrom of seaborne violence and theft. It was not
conceived by self-conscious imperialists, aiming to establish English rule over foreign lands, or colonists hoping to build a new life

overseas. Morgan and his fellow 'buccaneers'* were thieves, trying to steal the proceeds of someone else's Empire.

The buccaneers called themselves the 'Brethren of the Coast' and had a complex system of profit-sharing, including insurance policies for injury. Essentially, however, they were engaged in organized crime. When Morgan led another raid against the Spanish town of Portobelo in Panama, in 1668, he came back with so much plunder – in all, a quarter of a million pieces of eight – that the coins became legal tender in Jamaica. That amounted to £60,000 from just one raid. The English government not only winked at Morgan's activity; it positively encouraged him. Viewed from London, buccaneering was a low-budget way of waging war against England's principal European foe, Spain. In effect, the Crown licensed the pirates as 'privateers', legalizing their operations in return for a share of the proceeds. Morgan's career was a classic example of the way the British Empire started out, using enterprising freelances as much as official forces.

Pirates

It used to be thought that the British Empire was acquired 'in a fit of absence of mind'. In reality the expansion of England was far from inadvertent: it was a conscious act of imitation. Economic historians often think of England as the 'first industrial nation'. But in the European race for empire, the English were late beginners. It was only in 1655, for example, that England acquired Jamaica. At that time, the British Empire amounted to little more than a handful of Caribbean islands, five North American 'plantations' and a couple of Indian ports. But Christopher Columbus had laid the foundations of Spain's American empire more than a century and a half before. That empire was the envy of the world, stretching as it did from Madrid to Manila and encompassing Peru

---

* The original *boucaniers* were marooned seamen or escaped slaves who cured strips of meat on a simple barbecue known as a boucan.

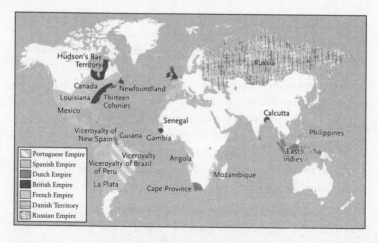

European colonial empires *c.* 1750

and Mexico, the wealthiest and most populous territories on the American continent. Even more extensive and no less profitable was Portugal's empire, which spread outwards from the Atlantic islands of Madeira and São Tomé to include the vast territory of Brazil and numerous trading outposts in West Africa, Indonesia, India and even China. In 1493 the Pope had issued a bull allocating trade in the Americas to Spain and trade in Asia to Portugal. In this division of the world, the Portuguese had got the sugar, spices and slaves. But what the English envied most was what the Spanish discovered in America: gold and silver.

Since the time of Henry VII, Englishmen had dreamt of finding an 'El Dorado' of their own, in the hope that England too could become rich on American metals. Time and again they had drawn a blank. The best they could ever manage was to exploit their skills as sailors to steal gold from Spanish ships and settlements. As early as March 1496, in a move clearly inspired by Columbus's discovery of America on behalf of the Spanish crown three years before, Henry VII granted letters patent to the Venetian navigator John Cabot, giving him and his sons full and free authority, faculty and power to sail to all parts, regions and coasts of the eastern, western and northern sea [not the southern sea, to avoid conflict with Spanish discoveries], under our banners, flags and ensigns . . . to find discover and investigate whatsoever islands, countries, regions or provinces of heathens or infidels, in whatsoever part of the world placed, which before this time were unknown to all Christians . . . [and to] conquer, occupy and possess whatsoever such towns, castles, cities and islands by them thus discovered that they may be able to conquer, occupy and possess, as our vassals and governors lieutenants and deputies therein, acquiring for us the dominion, title and jurisdiction of the same towns, castles, cities, islands and mainlands so discovered . . .

The English sense of empire envy only grew more acute after the Reformation, when proponents of war against Catholic Spain began to argue that England had a religious duty to build a Protestant empire to match the 'Popish' empires of the Spanish and Portuguese. The Elizabethan scholar Richard Hakluyt argued that if the Pope could give Ferdinand and Isabella the right to occupy 'such island and lands . . . as you may have discovered or are about to discover' outside Christendom, the English crown had a duty to 'enlarge and advance . . . the faith of Christ' on behalf of Protestantism. The English conception of empire was thus formed in reaction to that of her Spanish rival. England's empire was to be based on Protestantism; Spain's rested on Popery.

There was a political distinction too. The Spanish empire was an autocracy, governed from the centre. With his treasury overflowing with American silver, the King of Spain could credibly aspire to world domination. What else was all that money for, but to enhance his glory? In England, by comparison, the power of the monarch never became absolute; it was always limited, first by the country's wealthy aristocracy and later by the two houses of Parliament. In 1649 an English king was even executed for daring to resist the political claims of Parliament. Financially dependent on Parliament, the English monarchs often had little option but to rely on freelances to fight their wars. Yet the weakness of the English crown concealed a future strength. Precisely because political power was spread more widely, so was wealth. Taxation could only be levied with the approval of Parliament. People with money could therefore be reasonably confident that it would not simply be appropriated by an absolute ruler. That was to prove an important incentive for entrepreneurs.

The crucial question was, where should England build her anti-Spanish imperium? Hakluyt had been given a glimpse of infinite possibilities by his cousin and namesake in 1589:

. . . I found lying upon [my cousin's] board . . . an universall Mappe: he seeing me somewat curious in the view thereof began to instruct my ignorance, by shewing me the division of the earth into three parts after the olde account, and then according to the later & better distribution, into more: he pointed with his wand to all the knowen Seas, Gulfs, Bays, Straights, Capes, Rivers, Empires, Kingdomes, Dukedomes and Territories of ech part, with declaration also of their special commodities, & particular wants, which by the benefit of traffike and entercourse of merchants, are plentifully supplied. From the Mappe he brought me to the Bible, and turning to the 107th Psalm, directed mee to the 23rd & 24th verses, where I read, that they which go downe to the sea in ships, and occupy by the great waters, they see the works of the Lord, and his wonders in the deepe, &c.

But what his cousin could not show him was where else in the world there might be unclaimed supplies of silver and gold.

The first recorded voyage from England to this end was in 1480, when a shipload of optimists set sail from Bristol to look for 'the island of Brasylle in the west part of Ireland'. The success of the undertaking is not recorded; it seems doubtful. The Venetian navigator John Cabot (Zuan Caboto) made a successful crossing of the Atlantic from Bristol in 1497, but he was lost at sea the following year and few in England seem to have been persuaded by his Columbus-like belief that he had discovered a new route to Asia (the intended destination of his fatal second expedition was Japan, known then as 'Cipango'). It is possible that earlier Bristol ships had reached America. Certainly, as early as 1501 the Spanish government was fretting that English conquistadors might beat them to any riches in the Gulf of Mexico – they even commissioned an expedition to 'stop the exploration of the English in that direction'. But if Bristol sailors like Hugh Elyot did indeed cross the Atlantic so early, it was Newfoundland they reached, and what they found was not gold. In 1503 Henry VII's Household Book records payments for 'hawks from Newfoundland Island'. Of more interest to the Bristol merchant community were the immense cod fisheries off the Newfoundland coast.

It was gold that drew Sir Richard Grenville to the southernmost tip of South America – or, as he put it in his 1574 petition, 'the likelihood of bringing in great treasure of gold, silver and pearl into this realm from those countries, as other princes have out of like regions.' Three years later, it was the same 'great hope of gold [and] silver' – not to mention 'spices, drugs, cochineal' – that inspired Sir Francis Drake's expedition to South America. ('There is no doubt', Hakluyt declared enthusiastically, 'that we shall make subject to England all the golden mines of Peru . . .') The expeditions of Martin Frobisher in 1576, 1577 and 1578 were likewise all in pursuit of precious metals. The discovery and exploitation of 'Mynes of Goulde, Silver and Copper' were also among the objects of the colonization of Virginia, according to the letters patent granted to Sir Thomas Gates and others in 1606. (As late as 1607 there was still a glimmer of hope that Virginia was 'verie Riche in gold and Copper'.) It was the *ideé fixe* of the age. The greatness of Spain, declared Sir Walter Ralegh in *The Discoverie of the large, rich, and beautifull Empire of Guiana, with a relation of the great and golden citie of Manoa (which the Spaniards call El Dorado)* (1596), had nothing to do with 'the trade of sacks of Seville oranges . . . It is his Indian Gold that . . . endangereth and disturbeth all the nations of Europe'. Ralegh duly sailed to Trinidad where in 1595 he raided the Spanish base at San José de Oruña and captured Antonio de Berrio, the man he believed knew the whereabouts of El Dorado. Sitting in a stinking ship in the Orinoco delta, Ralegh lamented: 'I will undertake that there was never any prison in England, that could be found more unsavoury and loathsome – especially to my selfe, who had for many yeeres before bene dieted and cared for in a sort farre more difering.'

It would all have been worth it if someone had found the yellow metal. No one did. All Frobisher came home with was one Eskimo; and Ralegh's dream of discovering the 'Large, Rich and Beautiful Empire of Guiana' was never fulfilled. The most pleasing thing he encountered up the Orinoco was not gold but a native woman ('In all my life I have never seene a better favoured woman: she was of good stature, with blacke eyes, fat of body, of an excellent countenance . . . I have seene a Lady in England so like to her, as but for the difference of colour, I would have sworne might have been the same'). Near the mouth of the River Caroní they picked up some ore, but it was not gold. As his wife reported, he returned to Plymouth 'with as gret honnor as ever man can, but with littell riches'. The Queen was unimpressed. Meanwhile, analysis of the ore found in Virginia by an excited Christopher Newport dashed his hopes. As Sir Walter Cope reported to Lord Salisbury on 13 August 1607: 'Thys other daye we sent you newes of golde/And thys daye, we cannot returne yow so much as Copper/Oure newe dyscovery is more Lyke to prove the Lande of Canaan then the Lande of ophir . . . In the ende all turned to vapore.' In the same way, three voyages to Gambia between 1618 and 1621 in search of gold yielded nothing; indeed, they lost around £5,600.

The Spaniards had found vast quantities of silver when they had conquered Peru and Mexico. The English had tried Canada, Guiana, Virginia and the Gambia, and found nothing. There was only one thing for it: the luckless English would simply have to rob the Spaniards. That was how Drake had made money in the Caribbean and Panama in the 1570s. It was also Hawkins's rationale for attacking the Azores in 1581. And it was the primary purpose of Drake's attack on Cartagena and Santo Domingo four years later. Generally, when an expedition went wrong – as when Sir Humphrey Gilbert's expedition to the West Indies foundered off Ireland in 1578 – the survivors resorted to piracy to cover their expenses. That was also the way Ralegh sought to finance his expedition in search of El Dorado – by sending his captain Amyas to sack Caracas, Río de la Hacha and Santa Marta. It was a similar story when Ralegh tried again in 1617, having persuaded James I to release him from the Tower, where he had been imprisoned for high treason since 1603. With difficulty Ralegh raised £30,000 and with it assembled a fleet. But by that time Spanish control of the region was far more advanced and the expedition ended in disaster when his son Wat attacked the Spanish-controlled town of Santo Tomé, at the cost of his own life and in defiance of his pledge to James I not to create any friction with the Spaniards. The only fruits of this ill-starred voyage took the form of two gold ingots (from the Governor of Santo Tomé's strongbox), as well as some silver plate, some emeralds and a quantity of tobacco – not to mention a captive Indian, who Ralegh hoped would know the location of the elusive gold mines. He and his men having been denounced (quite justly) as 'Pirates, pirates, pirates!' by the Spanish ambassador, Ralegh was duly executed on his return. He died still believing firmly that there was 'a Mine of Gold . . . within three miles of St Tomé'. As he declared on the scaffold: 'It was my full intent to go for Gold, for the benefit of his Majesty and those that went with me, with the rest of my Country men.'

Even when English ships went in search of goods less precious than gold, collisions with other powers seemed unavoidable. When John Hawkins sought to break into the West African slave trade in the 1560s he very quickly found himself in conflict with Spanish interests.

From such shamelessly piratical origins arose the system of 'privateering' or privatized naval warfare. Faced with a direct threat from Spain – culminating in but not ending with the Armada – Elizabeth I took the eminently sensible decision to license what was happening anyway. Robbing the Spaniard thus became a matter of strategy. In the period of recurrent war with Spain from 1585 to 1604, between 100 and 200 ships a year set off to harass Spanish vessels in the Caribbean and the value of prize money brought back amounted to at least £200,000 a year. This was a complete naval free-for-all, with English 'ships of reprisal' also attacking any and every vessel entering or leaving Iberian ports.

'The sea is the only empire which can naturally belong to us,' Andrew Fletcher of Saltoun had written at the end of the seventeenth century. In the early eighteenth century, James Thomson wrote of Britain's 'well earned empire of the deep'. The key to the rise of the British Empire is the fact that, in the space of around a century after the Armada, this maritime empire went from aspiration to reality.

Why were the British such good pirates? They had to overcome some real disadvantages. For one thing, the clockwise pattern of Atlantic winds and currents meant that Portuguese and Spanish vessels enjoyed relatively easy passage between the Iberian Peninsula and Central America. By comparison, the winds in the North-East Atlantic tend to be south-westerly (that is, they come from the south-west) for most of the year, blowing against English ships heading for North America. It was much easier to head for the Caribbean, following the prevailing north-easterly winds in the South Atlantic. Traditionally coast-hugging English seamen took time to learn the arts of oceanic navigation, which the Portuguese had done much to refine. Even Drake's West Indian expedition in 1586 set off from Cartagena to Cuba only to return to Cartagena sixteen days later as a result of errors in navigation and the cumulative effect of compass variation.

In naval technology too the English were laggards. The Portuguese were the initial leaders when it came to speed. By the end of the fifteenth century, they had developed a three-masted ship, which generally set square sails on the fore and main masts and a triangular lateen sail on the mizzen mast, allowing the ship to tack more easily. They were also pioneers of the carvel, which was constructed around a strong internal frame rather than clinker-built. This was not only cheaper; it was also able to accommodate watertight gunports. The difficulty was that there was a clear trade-off between manoeuvrability and firepower. The Iberian carvel was no match for a Venetian galley when it came to a shooting match, because the latter could carry far heavier artillery, as Henry VIII discovered off Brittany in 1513, when Mediterranean galleys sank one of his ships outright, damaged another and killed his Lord Admiral. By the 1530s Venetian galleys could fire cannonballs weighing up to 60 pounds. It was not until the 1540s that both the

English and Scottish navies were able to launch carvel-style ships with load-bearing decks capable of carrying anything like as much firepower.

But the English were catching up. By the time of Elizabeth I, the hybrid 'sailing-galley' or galleon, capable of mounting four forward-firing guns, had emerged as the key British vessel. It still lacked the punch of a galley, but made up for that in speed and manoeuvrability. At the same time as ship design was evolving, English artillery was improving thanks to advances in iron founding. Henry VIII had needed to import bronze cannons from the continent. But home-made iron cannons, though harder to cast, were far cheaper (almost one-fifth the price). This meant significantly more 'bangs per buck' – a technical advantage that was to endure for centuries. English sailors were also becoming better navigators thanks to the reorganization of Trinity House at Deptford, the adoption of Euclidian geometry, better understanding of the variation of the compass and its dip, the translation of Dutch charts and tables in books like *The Mariners Mirrour* (1588) and the publication of improved maps like the 'new map with the augmentation of the Indies' mentioned in Shakespeare's *Twelfth Night*.

The English were also pioneers in improving the health of crews at sea. Sickness and disease had in many ways proved the most persistent of all the obstacles to European expansion. In 1635 Luke Fox described the seaman's lot as 'but to endure and suffer; as a hard Cabbin, cold and salt Meate, broken sleepes, mould[y] bread, dead beere, wet Cloathes, want of fire'. Scurvy was a major problem on long voyages because the traditional naval diet lacked vitamin C; crews were also vulnerable to wet beriberi and food poisoning, plague, typhus, malaria, yellow fever and dysentery (the dreaded 'bloody flux'). George Wateson's *The Cures of the Diseased in Remote Regions* (1598) was the first textbook on the subject, though it did not help much (since treatment revolved around bleeding and changes of diet). It was not until the latter part of the eighteenth century that real headway began to be made in this area. Still, the British Isles seemed to have an endless supply of men tough enough to withstand the hardships of life at sea – men like Christopher Newport of Limehouse, who rose from being a common seaman to become a wealthy shipowner. Newport made his fortune as a privateer in the West Indies, losing an arm in a fight with Spaniards and ransacking the town of Tabasco in Mexico in 1599. Henry Morgan was far from unique.

Morgan's raid on Gran Grenada was one of many such incursions into the Spanish Empire. In 1668 he attacked El Puerto del Principe in Cuba, Portobelo in present-day Panama, the island of Curaçao and Maracaibo in what is now Venezuela. In 1670 he captured the island of Old Providence, crossed to the mainland coast and traversed the isthmus to capture Panama itself.* The scale of such operations should not be exaggerated. Often the vessels involved were little more than rowing boats; the biggest ship Morgan had at his disposal in 1668 was no more than fifty feet long and had just eight guns. At most, they were disruptive to Spanish commerce. Yet they made him a rich man.

The striking point, however, is what Morgan did with his plundered pieces of eight. He might have opted for a comfortable retirement back in Monmouthshire, like the 'gentleman's son of good quality' he claimed to be. Instead he invested in Jamaican real estate, acquiring 836 acres of land in the Rio Minho valley (Morgan's Valley today). Later, he added 4,000 acres in the parish of St Elizabeth. The point about this land was that it was ideal for growing sugar cane. And this provides the key to a more general change in the nature of British overseas expansion. The Empire had begun with the stealing of gold; it progressed with the cultivation of sugar.

In the 1670s the British crown spent thousands of pounds

---

* The detailed descriptions of Morgan's famous raids on Spanish possessions are based on the writings of a Dutchman named Exquemlin who apparently took part in some of the raids. His book *De Americaensche Zee-Rovers* (c. 1684) was translated as *The History of the Bucaniers*. Morgan sued the English publishers not so much because Exquemlin accused him of sanctioning atrocities by his men but because he implied that Morgan was an indentured servant when he arrived in the Caribbean.

constructing fortifications to protect the harbour at Port Royal in Jamaica. The walls still stand (though much further from the sea because an earthquake shifted the coastline). This investment was deemed necessary because Jamaica was fast becoming something much more than a buccaneer base. Already, the crown was earning substantial sums from the duties on imports of Jamaican sugar. The island had become a prime economic asset, to be defended at all costs. Significantly, the construction work at Port Royal was supervised by none other than Henry Morgan – now Sir Henry. Just a few years after his pirate raid on Gran Grenada, Morgan was now not merely a substantial planter, but also Vice-Admiral, Commandant of the Port Royal Regiment, Judge of the Admiralty Court, Justice of the Peace and even Acting Governor of Jamaica. Once a licensed pirate, the freelance was now being employed to govern a colony. Admittedly, Morgan lost all his official posts in 1681 after making 'repeated divers extravagant expressions ... in his wine'. But his was an honourable retirement. When he died in August 1688 the ships in Port Royal harbour took turns to fire twenty-two gun salutes.

Morgan's career perfectly illustrates the way the empire-building process worked. It was a transition from piracy to political power that would change the world forever. But it was possible only because something quite revolutionary was happening back home.

Sugar Rush

The son of a London merchant and author of the best-selling novels *Robinson Crusoe* and *Moll Flanders*, Daniel Defoe was also an acute observer of contemporary British life. What he saw happening in early eighteenth-century England was the birth of a new kind of economy: the world's first mass consumer society. As Defoe noted in *The Complete English Tradesman* (1725):

England consumes within itself more goods of foreign growth, imported from the several countries where they are produced or wrought, than any other nation in the world ... This importation consists chiefly of sugars and tobacco, of which the consumption in Great Britain is scarcely to be conceived of, besides the consumption of cotton, indigo, rice, ginger, pimento or Jamaica pepper, cocoa or chocolate, rum and molasses ...

The rise of the British Empire, it might be said, had less to do with the Protestant work ethic or English individualism than with the British sweet tooth. Annual imports of sugar doubled in Defoe's lifetime, and this was only the biggest part of an enormous consumer boom. As time went on, articles that had once been the preserve of the wealthy elite became staples of daily life. Sugar remained Britain's largest single import from the 1750s, when it overtook foreign linen, until the 1820s, when it was surpassed by raw cotton. By the end of the eighteenth century, per capita sugar consumption was ten times what it was in France (20 lbs. per head per year compared with just two). More than anyone else in Europe, the English developed an insatiable appetite for imported commodities.

In particular, what the English consumer liked was to mix his sugar with an orally administered and highly addictive drug, caffeine, supplemented with an inhaled but equally addictive substance, nicotine. In Defoe's time, tea, coffee, tobacco and sugar were the new, new things. And all of them had to be imported.

The first recorded English request for a pot of tea is in a letter dated 27 June 1615 from Mr R. Wickham, agent of the East India Company on the Japanese island of Hirado, to his colleague Mr Eaton at Macao, asking him to send on only 'the best sort of chaw'. However, it was not until 1658 that the first advertisement appeared in England for what was to become the national drink. It was published in the officially subsidized weekly, *Mercurius Politicus*, for the week ending 30 September and offered: 'That Excellent, and by all Physicians approved, *China* Drink, called by the *Chineans*, *Tcha*, by other Nations *Tay alias Tee* ... sold at the *Sultaness-head*, 2 *Cophee-house* in *Sweetings* Rents by the Royal Exchange, *London*.' At around the same time, the coffee house owner Thomas Garraway published a broadsheet entitled 'An Exact Description of the Growth, Quality and Vertues of the Leaf TEA', in which he claimed that it could cure 'Headache, Stone, Gravel, Dropsy, Liptitude Distillations, Scurvy, Sleepiness, Loss of Memory, Looseness or Griping of the Guts, Heavy Dreams and Collick proceeding from Wind'. 'Taken with Virgin's Honey instead of Sugar', he assured potential consumers, 'tea cleanses the Kidneys and Ureters, & with Milk and water it prevents Consumption. If you are of corpulent body it ensures good appetite, & if you have a surfeit it is just the thing to give you a gentle Vomit.' For whatever reason, Charles II's Portuguese Queen was also a tea-drinker: Edmund Waller's poem dedicated to her on her birthday praised 'The Muses's friend, tea [which] does our fancy aid, / Repress those vapours which the head invade, / And keep the palace of the soul serene.' On 25 September 1660 Samuel Pepys drank his first 'cup of tee (a China drink)'.

However, it was only in the early eighteenth century that tea began to be imported in sufficient quantities – and at sufficiently low prices – to create a mass market. In 1703 the *Kent* arrived in London with a cargo of 65,000 lbs. of tea, not far off the entire annual importation in previous years. The real breakthrough came when the figure for tea 'retained for home consumption' leapt from an average of under 800,000 lbs. in the early 1740s to over 2.5 million lbs. between 1746 and 1750. By 1756 the habit was far enough spread to prompt a denunciation in Hanway's *Essay on Tea*: 'The very chambermaids have lost their bloom by drinking tea.' (Samuel Johnson retorted with an ambivalent review, written – as he put it – by a 'hardened and shameless tea-drinker'.)

Even more controversial was tobacco, introduced by Walter Ralegh and one of the few enduring legacies of the abortive Roanoke settlement in Virginia (see Chapter 2). As with tea, the purveyors of tobacco insisted on its medicinal properties. In 1587 Ralegh's servant Thomas Heriot reported that the 'herbe', when dried and smoked, 'purgeth superfluous fleame and other grosse humours, and openeth all the pores and passages of the body: by which means the use thereof not onely preserveth the body from obstructions, but also . . . in short time breake them: whereby their bodies are notably preserved in health, and know not many griev-

ous diseases, wherewithall we in England are often times afflicted.'
One early advertisement proclaimed tobacco's ability 'Health to
preserve, or to deceive our Pein, / Regale thy Sense, & aid the
Lab'ring Brain'. Not everyone was persuaded. To James I – a man
ahead of his times in other respects too – the burning weed was
'loathesome to the eye, hateful to the nose, harmful to the brain
[and] dangerous to the lungs'. But as the cultivation of tobacco
exploded in Virginia and Maryland, there was a dramatic slide in
prices (from between 4 and 36 pence per pound in the 1620s and
1630s to around 1 penny per pound from the 1660s onwards)
and a corresponding shift towards mass consumption. While in the
1620s only gentlemen had taken tobacco, by the 1690s it was 'a
custom, the fashion, all the mode – so that every plow-man had
his pipe'. In 1624 James put aside his scruples and established a
royal monopoly; the revenue to be gained as imports soared was
clearly worth the 'hateful' fumes, though the monopoly proved as
unenforceable as a blanket ban.

The new imports transformed not just the economy but the
national lifestyle. As Defoe observed in his *Complete English
Tradesman*: 'The tea-table among the ladies and the coffee house
among the men seem to be the places of new invention . . .' What
people liked most about these new drugs was that they offered a
very different kind of stimulus from the traditional European drug,
alcohol. Alcohol is, technically, a depressant. Glucose, caffeine and
nicotine, by contrast, were the eighteenth-century equivalent of
uppers. Taken together, the new drugs gave English society an
almighty hit; the Empire, it might be said, was built on a huge
sugar, caffeine and nicotine rush – a rush nearly everyone could
experience.

At the same time, England, and especially London, became
Europe's emporium for these new stimulants. By the 1770s about
85 per cent of British tobacco imports were in fact re-exported and
almost 94 per cent of imported coffee was re-exported, mainly to
northern Europe. This was partly a reflection of differential tariffs:
heavy import duties restricted domestic coffee consumption to
the benefit of the burgeoning tea industry. Like so many national

characteristics, the English preference for tea over coffee had its origins in the realm of fiscal policy.

By selling a portion of their imports from the West and East Indies to continental markets, the British were making enough money to satisfy another long-dormant appetite, for a crucial component of the new consumerism was a sartorial revolution. Writing in 1595, Peter Stubbs remarked that 'no people in the world are so curious in new fangles as they of England be'. He had in mind the growing appetite of English consumers for new styles of textile, an appetite which by the early 1600s had swept aside a whole genre of legislation: the sumptuary laws that had traditionally regulated what Englishmen and women could wear according to their social rank. Once again Defoe spotted the trend, in his *Everybody's Business is Nobody's Business*:

. . . plain country Joan is now turned into a fine London madam, can drink tea, take snuff, and carry herself as high as the best. She must have a hoop too, as well as her mistress; and her poor scanty linsey-woolsey petticoat is changed into a good silk one, four or five yards wide at the least.

In the seventeenth century, however, there was only one outlet the discerning English shopper would buy her clothes from. For sheer quality, Indian fabrics, designs, workmanship and technology were in a league of their own. When English merchants began to buy Indian silks and calicoes and bring them back home, the result was nothing less than a national makeover. In 1663 Pepys took his wife Elizabeth shopping in Cornhill, one of the most fashionable shopping districts of London, where he, 'after many tryalls bought my wife a Chinke [chintz]; that is, a paynted Indian Callico for to line her new Study, which is very pretty'. When Pepys himself sat for the artist John Hayls he went to the trouble of hiring a fashionable Indian silk morning gown, or *banyan*. In 1664 over a quarter of a million pieces of calico were imported into England. There was almost as big a demand for Bengal silk, silk cloth taffeta and plain white cotton muslins. As Defoe recalled in the *Weekly Review* of 31 January 1708: 'It crept into our houses, our closets, our bedchambers; curtains, cushion, chairs, and at last beds themselves were nothing but Callicoes or Indian stuffs.'

The beauty of imported textiles was that the market for them was practically inexhaustible. Ultimately, there is only so much tea or sugar a human being can consume. But people's appetite for new clothes had, and has, no such natural limit. Indian textiles – which even a servant like Defoe's 'plain country Joan' could afford – meant that the tea-swilling English not only felt better; they looked better too.

The economics of this early import trade were relatively simple. Seventeenth-century English merchants had little they could offer Indians that the Indians did not already make themselves. They therefore paid for their purchases in cash, using bullion earned from trade elsewhere rather than exchanging English goods for Indian. Today we call the spread of this process globalization, by which we mean the integration of the world as a single market. But in one important respect seventeenth-century globalization was different. Getting the bullion out to India and the goods home again, even the transmission of orders to buy and sell, meant round trips of some twelve thousand miles, every mile made hazardous by the chance of storms, shipwrecks and pirates.

The biggest threat of all, however, came not from ships flying the Jolly Roger. It came from other Europeans who were trying to do exactly the same thing. Asia was about to become the scene of a ruthless battle for market share.

This was to be globalization with gunboats.

Going Dutch

The wide, brown Hugli River is the biggest branch of the Great Ganges Delta in Bengal. It is one of India's historic trading arteries. From its mouth at Calcutta you can sail upstream to the Ganges itself and then on to Patna, Varanasi, Allahabad, Kanpur, Agra and Delhi. In the other direction lie the Bay of Bengal, the monsoon trade winds and the sea lanes leading to Europe. So when Europeans came to trade in India, the Hugli was one of their preferred destinations. It was the economic gateway to the subcontinent.

Today, a few crumbling buildings in the town of Chinsura, north of Calcutta, are all that remain of the first Indian outpost of one of the world's greatest trading companies, the East India Company. For more than a hundred years it dominated the Asian trade routes, all but monopolizing trade in a whole range of commodities ranging from spices to silks.

But this was the Dutch East India Company – the Vereenigde Oostindische Compagnie – not the English one. The dilapidated villas and warehouses of Chinsura were built not for Englishmen, but for merchants from Amsterdam, who were making money in Asia long before the English turned up.

The Dutch East India Company was founded in 1602. It was part of a full-scale financial revolution that made Amsterdam the most sophisticated and dynamic of European cities. Ever since they had thrown off Spanish rule in 1579, the Dutch had been at the cutting edge of European capitalism. They had created a system of public debt that allowed their government to borrow from its citizens at low interest rates. They had founded something like a modern central bank. Their money was sound. Their tax system – based on the excise tax – was simple and efficient. The Dutch East India Company represented a milestone in corporate organization too. By the time it was wound up in 1796 it had paid on average an annual return of 18 per cent on the original capital subscribed, an impressive performance over such a long period.

It is true that a group of London-based merchants had already subscribed £30,000 to 'set forthe a vyage . . . to the Est Indies and other ilandes and countries thereabout' provided they could secure a royal monopoly; that in September 1600 Elizabeth I duly gave 'The Company of Merchants of London trading into the East Indies' a fifteen-year monopoly over East Indian trade; and that the following year their first fleet of four ships sailed for Sumatra. But Dutch merchants had been trading with India via the Cape of Good Hope since 1595. By 1596 they had firmly established themselves at Bantam, on the island of Java, from where the first consignments of Chinese tea destined for the European market were shipped in 1606. Moreover, their company was a permanent joint stock company, unlike the English company, which did not become permanent until 1650. Despite being founded two years after the English one, the Dutch company was swiftly able to dominate the lucrative spice trade with the Moluccan islands of Indonesia, once a Portuguese monopoly. The Dutch scale of business was simply bigger: they were able to send out nearly five times as many ships to Asia as the Portuguese and twice as many as the English. This was partly because, unlike the English company, the Dutch company rewarded its managers on the basis of gross revenue rather than net profits, encouraging them to maximize the volume of their business. In the course of the seventeenth century the Dutch expanded rapidly, establishing bases at Masulipatnam on the east coast of India, at Surat in the north-west and at Jaffna in Ceylon. But by the 1680s it was textiles from Bengal that accounted for the bulk of its shipments home. Chinsura seemed well on its way to becoming the future capital of a Dutch India.

In other respects, however, the two East India companies had much in common. They should not be equated naively with modern multinational corporations, since they were much more like state-licensed monopolies, but on the other hand they were a great deal more sophisticated than the associations of buccaneers in the Caribbean. The Dutch and English merchants who founded them were able to pool their resources for what were large and very risky ventures under the protection of government monopolies. At the same time, the companies allowed governments to privatize overseas expansion, passing on the substantial risks involved. If they made money, the companies could also be tapped for revenue or, more commonly, loans, in return for the renewal of their charters. Private investors, meanwhile, could rest assured that their company had a guaranteed market share of 100 per cent.

The companies were not the first such organizations; nor were they by any means the last. One had been founded in 1555 (as 'The Mysterie and Companie of the Merchants Adventurers for the discoverie of Regions, Dominions, Islands and places unknown'); it ended up as the Muscovy Company trading with Russia. In 1592 a Levant Company was formed when the Venice and Turkey Companies merged. Licences were granted in 1588 and 1592 to companies wishing to monopolize respectively the Senegambian and Sierra Leonese trade in West Africa. These were succeeded in 1618 by the Guinea Company ('Company of Adventurers of London Trading to the Ports of Africa'), which in 1631 was re-chartered with a thirty-one-year monopoly on all trade with West Africa. By the 1660s a new and powerful company, the Company of Royal Adventurers into Africa, had come into being with a monopoly intended to last no less than a thousand years. This was an especially lucrative enterprise, since it was here – at last – that the English found gold; though slaves would ultimately prove the region's biggest export. At the other climatic extreme was the Hudson Bay Company (the 'Honourable Company of Adventurers of England Trading Into Hudson's Bay') founded in 1670 to monopolize the trade in Canadian furs. In 1695 the Scots sought to emulate the English by establishing their own Company of Scotland Trading to Africa and the Indies. The South Sea Company, intended to monopolize trade with Spanish America, came later, in 1710.

But were the monopolies granted to these companies actually enforceable? To take the case of the two East India companies, the trouble was that they could not both have a monopoly on Asian trade with Europe. The idea that flows of goods to London were somehow distinct from flows of goods to Amsterdam was absurd, given the proximity of the Dutch and English markets to one another. In establishing itself at Surat on the north-west coast of India in 1613, the English East India Company was very obviously trying to win a share of the lucrative spice trade. If the volume of spice exports was inelastic, then it could only succeed by taking business away from the Dutch company. This was indeed the assumption: in the words of the contemporary political economist William Petty, there was 'but a certain proportion of trade in the world'. The hope of the East India Company director Josiah Child was 'that other Nations who are in competition with us for the same [business], may not wrest it from us, but that ours may continue and increase, to the diminution of theirs.' It was economics as a zero sum game – the essence of what came to be called mercantilism. If, on the other hand, the volume of spice exports proved to be elastic, then the increased supply going to England would depress the European spice price. The English company's initial voyages from Surat were exceedingly profitable, with profits as high as 200 per cent. But thereafter the predictable effect of Anglo-Dutch competition was to drive down prices. Those who contributed to the second East India joint stock of £1.6 million (between 1617 and 1632) ended up losing money.

It was therefore all but inevitable that English attempts to muscle in on the Eastern trade would lead to conflict, especially since spices accounted for three-quarters of the value of the Dutch company's business at this time. Violence flared as early as 1623, when the Dutch murdered ten English merchants at Amboina in Indonesia. Between 1652 and 1674 the English fought three wars against the Dutch, the main aim of which was to wrest control of the main sea routes out of Western Europe – not only to the East Indies, but also to the Baltic, the Mediterranean, North America and West Africa. Seldom have wars been fought for such nakedly commercial reasons. Determined to achieve naval mastery, the English more than doubled the size of their merchant navy and, in the space of just eleven years (1649 to 1660) added no fewer than 216 ships to the navy proper. Navigation Acts were passed in 1651 and 1660 to promote English shipping at the expense of the Dutch merchants who dominated the oceanic carrying trade by insisting that goods from English colonies come in English ships.

Yet despite some initial English successes, the Dutch came out on top. The English trading posts on the West African coast were almost wholly wiped out. In June 1667 a Dutch fleet even sailed up the Thames, occupied Sheerness and forced the Medway boom, destroying the docks and ships at Chatham and Rochester. At the end of the second Dutch War, the British found themselves driven out of Surinam and Polaroon; in 1673 they temporarily lost New York too. This came as a surprise to many. After all, the English population was two and a half times bigger than the Dutch; the English economy was bigger too. In the third Dutch War the English had the additional benefit of French support. Yet the superior Dutch financial system enabled them to punch well above their economic weight.

By contrast, the cost of these unsuccessful wars placed a severe strain on England's antiquated financial system. The government itself teetered on the brink of bankruptcy: in 1671 Charles II was forced to impose a moratorium on certain government debts – the so-called 'Stop of the Exchequer'. This financial upheaval had profound political consequences; for the links between the City and the political elite in Britain had never been closer than they were in the reign of Charles II. Not only in the boardrooms of the City but in the royal palaces and stately homes of the aristocracy, the Anglo-Dutch Wars caused consternation. The Duke of Cumberland was one of the founders of the Royal African Company and later governor of the Hudson's Bay Company. The Duke of York, the future James II, was governor of the New Royal African Company, founded in 1672 after the Dutch had ruined its predecessor. Between 1660 and 1683 Charles II was given 'voluntary contributions' of £324,150 by the East India Company. Literally cut-throat competition with the Dutch was spoiling the Restoration party. There had to be an alternative. The solution turned out to be (as so often in business history) a merger – but not a merger between the two East India companies. What was required was a political merger.

In the summer of 1688, suspicious of James II's Catholic faith and fearful of his political ambitions, a powerful oligarchy of English aristocrats staged a coup against him. Significantly, they were backed by the merchants of the City of London. They invited the Dutch Stadholder William of Orange to invade England, and in an almost bloodless operation James was ousted. This 'Glorious Revolution' is usually portrayed as a political event, the decisive confirmation of British liberties and the system of parliamentary monarchy. But it also had the character of an Anglo-Dutch business merger. While the Dutch Prince William of Orange became, in effect, England's new Chief Executive, Dutch businessmen became major shareholders in the English East India Company. The men who organized the Glorious Revolution felt they needed no lessons from a Dutchman about religion or politics. Like the Dutch, England already had Protestantism and parliamentary government. But what they could learn from the Dutch was modern finance.

In particular, the Anglo-Dutch merger of 1688 introduced the British to a number of crucial financial institutions that the Dutch had pioneered. In 1694 the Bank of England was founded to manage the government's borrowings as well as the national currency, similar (though not identical) to the successful Amsterdam Wisselbank founded eighty-five years before. London was also able to import the Dutch system of a national public debt, funded through a Stock Exchange, where long-term bonds could easily be bought and sold. The fact that this allowed the government to borrow at significantly reduced interest rates made large-scale projects – like wars – far easier to afford. Perceptive as ever, Daniel Defoe was quick to see what cheap credit could do for a country:

Credit makes war, and makes peace; raises armies, fits out navies, fights battles, besieges towns; and, in a word, it is more justly called the sinews of war than the money itself . . . Credit makes the soldier fight without pay, the armies march without provisions . . . it is an impregnable fortification . . . it makes paper pass for money . . . and fills the Exchequer and the banks with as many millions as it pleases, upon demand.

Sophisticated financial institutions had made it possible for Holland not only to fund its worldwide trade, but also to protect it with first-class naval power. Now these institutions were to be put to use in England on a much larger scale.

The Anglo-Dutch merger meant that the English could operate far more freely in the East. A deal was done which effectively gave Indonesia and the spice trade to the Dutch, leaving the English to develop the newer Indian textiles trade. That turned out to be a good deal for the English company, because the market for textiles swiftly outgrew the market for spices. It turned out that the demand for pepper, nutmeg, mace, cloves and cinnamon – the spices on which the Dutch company's fortunes depended – was significantly less elastic than the demand for calicoes, chintz and cotton. This was one reason why, by the 1720s, the English company was overtaking its Dutch rival in terms of sales; and why the former made a loss in only two years between 1710 and 1745, while the latter's profits declined. The English East India Company's head office was now in Leadenhall Street. This was where the meetings took place of the company's two governing bodies – the Court of Directors (shareholders with £2,000 or more of East India stock) and the Court of Proprietors (shareholders with £1,000 or more). But the real symbols of its growing profitability were the immense warehouses in Bishopsgate built to house the growing volume of imported cloth the company was bringing to Europe from India.

The shift from spices to cloth also implied a relocation of the East India Company's Asian base. Surat was now gradually wound down. In its stead three new 'factories' (as they were sometimes known) were established – fortified trading posts which today are among Asia's most populous cities. The first of these was on the south-east coast of India, the fabled shore of Coromandel. There, on a shore site acquired in 1630, the company built a fort which, as if to advertise its Englishness, was christened Fort St George. Around it would spring up the city of Madras. Just over thirty years later, in 1661, England acquired Bombay from Portugal as part of Charles II's dowry when he married Catherine of Braganza. Finally, in 1690, the company established a fort at Sutanuti on the east bank of the River Hugli. This was then amalgamated with two other villages to form a larger town renamed Calcutta.

Today, it is still possible to discern the remains of these British 'factories', which were in many ways the enterprise zones of early empire. The fort at Madras is still more or less intact, complete with its church, a parade ground, houses and warehouses. There was nothing original in this layout. The earlier Portuguese, Spanish and Dutch trading posts had been built along much the same lines. But under the new Anglo-Dutch arrangement, places like Chinsura belonged to the past. Calcutta was the future.

*

Yet no sooner had the East India Company solved the problem of Dutch competition than it ran into another, far more insidious source of competition, its own employees. This is what economists call the 'agency problem': the fundamental difficulty the proprietors of a company have in controlling their employees. It is a difficulty which grows in proportion to the distance between those who own the shares and those on the payroll.

Here a word needs to be said not just about distance but about the wind. By 1700 it was possible to sail from Boston to England in four to five weeks (in the other direction the journey took five to seven weeks).* To reach Barbados generally took around nine weeks. Because of the direction of the Atlantic winds, trade had a seasonal rhythm: ships left for the West Indies between November and January; ships for North America, by contrast, left from midsummer until the end of September. But journey times were much longer for those heading to and from India; to reach Calcutta from England via Cape Town took, on average, around six months. The prevailing winds in the Indian Ocean are south-westerly from April to September, but north-easterly from October to March. To sail for India meant leaving in the spring; you could only return home in the autumn.

The much longer journey times between Asia and Europe made the East India Company's monopoly at once easy and hard to enforce. Compared with the North American trade, it was hard for smaller rival companies to compete for the same business; whereas hundreds of companies carried goods to and from America and the Caribbean by the 1680s, the costs and risks of the six-month voyage to India encouraged the concentration of trade in the hands of one big operator. But that big operator could only with the utmost difficulty control its own staff when it took them half a year just to reach their place of work. Letters of instruction to them took just as long. East India Company employees therefore enjoyed a good deal of latitude – indeed, most of them were wholly beyond the

* Some readers may find it helpful to think of modern flight times, but replace the word 'hours' with 'weeks'.

control of their London paymasters. And since the salaries they were paid were relatively modest (a 'writer' or clerk got a basic £5 a year, not much more than a domestic servant back in England) most company employees did not hesitate to conduct business on the side, on their own account. This was what would later be lampooned as 'the good old principles of Leadenhall Street economy – small salaries and immense perquisites'. Others went further, leaving the company's employ altogether and doing business exclusively for themselves. These were the bane of the directors' existence: the interlopers.

The supreme interloper was Thomas Pitt, the son of a Dorset clergyman, who entered the service of the East India Company in 1673. On reaching India, Pitt simply absconded and began buying goods from Indian merchants, shipping them back to England on his own account. The Court of the company insisted that Pitt return home, denouncing him as 'a desperate young fellow of a haughty, huffing, daring temper that would not stick at doing any mischief that lay in his power'. But Pitt blithely ignored these requests. Indeed, he went into business with the company's chief officer in the Bay of Bengal, Matthias Vincent, whose niece he married. Faced with a lawsuit, Pitt settled with the company by paying a fine of £400, which by now was small beer to him.

Men like Pitt were crucial in the growth of the East India trade. Alongside the official trade of the company, an enormous private business was developing. What this meant was that the monopoly over Anglo-Asian trade, which the crown had granted to the East India Company, was crumbling. But this was probably just as well, since a monopoly company could not have expanded trade between Britain and India as rapidly without the interlopers. Indeed, the company itself gradually began to realize that the interlopers – even the wayward Pitt – could be a help rather than a hindrance to its business.

It would be quite wrong to imagine that the Anglo-Dutch merger handed India over to the English East India Company. The fact remained that both Dutch and English traders were minor players in a vast Asian empire. Madras, Bombay and Calcutta were no more than tiny outposts on the edge of a vast and economically advanced subcontinent. The English at this stage were merely parasites on the periphery, reliant on partnerships with Indian businessmen: *dubashes* in Madras, *banyans* in Bengal. And political power continued to be centred in the Red Fort in Delhi, the principal residence of the Mughal Emperor, the Muslim 'Lord of the Universe' whose ancestors had swept into India from the north in the sixteenth century and had ruled the greater part of the subcontinent ever since. English visitors like Sir Thomas Roe might attempt to disparage what they saw when they visited Delhi ('Religions infinite; laws none. In that confusion what can be expected?' was Roe's verdict in 1615), but the Mughals' was a wealthy and mighty empire, which dwarfed the European nation states. In 1700 the population of India was twenty times that of the United Kingdom. India's share of total world output at that time has been estimated at 24 per cent – nearly a quarter; Britain's share was just 3 per cent. The idea that Britain might one day rule India would have struck a visitor to Delhi in the late seventeenth century as simply preposterous.

It was only by the Mughal Emperor's permission – and with the consent of his local subordinates – that the East India Company was able to trade at all. These were not always forthcoming. As the company's Court of Directors complained:

These [native] governors have ... the knack of trampling upon us, and extorting what they please of our estate from us, by the besieging of our factorys* [sic] and stopping of our boats upon the Ganges, they will never forbear doing so till we had made them sensible of our power as we have of our truth and justice ...

But that was more easily said than done. For the time being, appeasing the Mughal Emperor was a crucial part of the East India Company's business, since loss of favour meant loss of money.

---

* By a 'factory' the directors simply meant a warehouse; the company was not itself engaged in industrial production.

Visits had to be paid to the Mughal court. Company representatives had to prostrate themselves before the Peacock Throne in the Red Fort's inner court, the Diwan-i-am. Complex treaties had to be negotiated. Bribes had to be paid to Mughal officials. All this called for men who were as adept at wheeling and dealing as they were at buying and selling.

In 1698, despite their previous misgivings, the company decided to send none other than the interloper Thomas Pitt to Madras as Governor of Fort St George. His salary was just £200 a year, but his contract now explicitly acknowledged that he could do business on his own account as well. A fine specimen of the poacher turned gamekeeper (who could still do a bit of poaching on the side), Pitt almost immediately had to contend with an acute diplomatic crisis when the Emperor, Aurungzeb, announced not only a ban on trade with Europeans but their arrest and the immediate confiscation of their goods. Even as he was negotiating with Aurungzeb to have the edict revoked, Pitt had to defend Fort St George against Duad Khan, the Nawab of the Carnatic, who hastened to execute the Emperor's edict.

By the 1740s, however, the Emperor was losing his grip over India. The Persian Nadir Shah Afshar sacked Delhi in 1739 at the head of an Afghan–Turkic army; Afghans led by Ahmed Shah Abdali invaded northern India repeatedly after 1747. In addition to these 'tribal breakouts', the Mughals' erstwhile deputies in the provinces – men like the Nawab of Arcot and the Nizam of Hyderabad – were carving out kingdoms for themselves. To the west the Marathas ruled without reference or regard to Delhi. India was entering a phase of internecine warfare that the British would later characterize dismissively as 'anarchy' – proof that the Indians were unfit to govern themselves. In truth, this was a struggle for mastery in India no different from the struggle for mastery in Habsburg-dominated Europe that had been raging since the seventeenth century. Precisely the threats from the north forced Indian rulers to govern more effectively, modernizing their tax systems to pay for large standing armies, much as their counterparts in Europe were doing at the same time.

The European settlements in India had always been fortified. Now, in these dangerous times, they had to be garrisoned in earnest. Unable to muster enough manpower from its English staff, the East India Company began to raise its own regiments from among the subcontinent's warrior castes – Telugu peasants in the south, Kunbis in the west and Rajputs and Brahmins from the central Ganges valley – equipping them with European weapons and subordinating them to English officers. In theory, this was simply the company's security division, intended to protect its assets in time of war. In practice, it was a private army, and one that would soon become crucial to its business. Having begun as a trading operation, the East India Company now had its own settlements, its own diplomats, even its own army. It was beginning to look more and more like a kingdom in its own right. And here was the key difference between Asia and Europe. The European powers could fight one another to their hearts' content: the winner could only be European. But when the Indian powers went to war, the possibility existed that a non-Indian power might emerge as victor.

The only question was, which one?

Men of War

Gingee is one of the most spectacular forts in the Carnatic. Perched on a steep hill that rises abruptly out of the haze of the plains, it dominates the hinterland of the Coromandel coast. But by the middle of the eighteenth century it was garrisoned not by the British, nor by the area's local rulers. Gingee was in the hands of the French.

The English conflict with the Dutch had been commercial. At root, it had been strictly business, a competition for market share. The struggle with France – which was to rage in every corner of the globe like a worldwide version of the Hundred Years War – would decide who would *govern* the world. The outcome was far from a foregone conclusion.

*

They say that on any given morning the French Minister of Education knows exactly what is being taught in every school under his control. Every French pupil is taught the same syllabus: the same maths, the same literature, the same history, the same philosophy. It is a truly imperial approach to education. And it applies as much to the French *lycée* at Pondicherry as to its counterparts in Paris. Had things gone differently in the 1750s, schools all across India might have been the same – and French, not English, might have become the world's *lingua franca*.

The counterfactual is far from fanciful. To be sure, the Anglo-Dutch merger had greatly strengthened England. And, with the union of the Parliaments in 1707, a second merger had produced a redoubtable new entity: the United Kingdom of Great Britain, a term originally propagated by James I to reconcile Scotland to being annexed by England – and the English to being ruled by a Scot. By the end of the War of the Spanish Succession (1713), this new state was now unquestionably Europe's dominant naval power. Having acquired Gibraltar and Port Mahon (Minorca), Britain was in a position to control access to and from the Mediterranean. Yet France remained the predominant power on the continent of Europe itself. In 1700 France had an economy twice the size of Britain's and a population almost three times as large. And, like Britain, France had reached out across the seas to the world beyond Europe. There were French colonies in America in Louisiana and Quebec – 'New France'. The French sugar islands like Martinique and Guadaloupe were among the richest in the Caribbean. And in 1664 the French had set up their own East India Company, the Compagnie des Indes Orientales, with its base at Pondicherry, not far south of the British settlement at Madras. The danger that France would win a struggle for global mastery against Britain was a real one, and remained real for the better part of a century. In the words of the *Critical Review* in 1756:

Every Briton ought to be acquainted with the ambitious views of France, her eternal thirst after universal dominion, and her continual encroachments on the properties of her neighbours . . . [O]ur trade, our liberties, our country, nay all the rest of Europe, [are] in a continual danger of falling prey to the common Enemy, the universal Cormorant, that would, if possible, swallow up the whole globe itself.

Commercially, it is true, the Compagnie des Indes posed a relatively modest threat to the East India Company. Its first incarnation lost substantial amounts of money despite government subsidies, and it had to be refounded in 1719. Unlike its English counterpart, the French company was under firm government control. It was run by aristocrats, who cared little for trade but a lot for power politics. The form the French threat took was thus quite unlike that of the Dutch. The Dutch had wanted market share. The French wanted territory.

In 1746 the French Governor at Pondicherry, Joseph François Dupleix, resolved to strike a blow against the English presence in India. The diary of Ananda Ranga Pillai, his Indian *dubash*, gives a flavour of the mood in the French fort on the eve of Dupleix's coup. According to Pillai, 'public opinion now says that the tide of victory will henceforth turn in favour of the French ... The people ... assert that the Goddess of Fortune has departed from Madras to take up her residence at Pondicherry.' Dupleix assured him that 'the English Company is bound to die out. It has long been in an impecunious condition, and what it had to its credit has been lent to the King, whose overthrow is certain. The loss of the capital is therefore inevitable, and this must lead to collapse. Mark my words. The truth of them will be brought home to you when you, ere long, find that my prophecy has been realised.' On 26 February 1747, as Pillai recorded, the French

hurled themselves against Madras ... as a lion rushes into a herd of elephants ... surrounded the fort, and in one day astonished and bewildered the Governor ... and all the people who were there ... They captured the fort, planted their flag on the ramparts, took possession of the whole city, and shone in Madras like the sun, which spreads its beams over the whole world.

Dismayed, the East India Company feared that it would be 'utterly destroyed' by its French rival. According to one report received by the directors in London, the French aimed 'at nothing less than to exclude us from the trade of this coast [Madras area], and by degrees from that of India'.

In fact, Dupleix had mistimed his move. The ending of the War of Austrian Succession in Europe with the Peace of Aix-la-Chapelle in 1748 forced him to relinquish Madras. But then, in 1757, hostilities between Britain and France resumed – this time on an unprecedented scale.

The Seven Years War was the nearest thing the eighteenth century had to a world war. Like the global conflicts of the twentieth century, it was at root a European war. Britain, France, Prussia, Austria, Portugal, Spain, Saxony, Hanover, Russia and Sweden were all combatants. But the fighting raged from Coromandel to Canada, from Guinea to Guadeloupe, from Madras to Manila. Indians, native Americans, African slaves and American colonists all became involved. At stake was the future of empire itself. The question was simply this: Would the world be French or British?

The man who came to dominate British policy in this Hanoverian Armageddon was William Pitt. Not surprisingly, a man whose family's fortune rested on Anglo-Indian trade had no intention of yielding Britain's global position to her oldest European rival. As Thomas Pitt's grandson, Pitt instinctively thought of the war in global terms. His strategy was to rely on the one superior force the British possessed: their fleet and behind it their shipyards. While Britain's Prussian ally contained the French and their allies in Europe, the Royal Navy would carve up their empire on the high seas, leaving the scattered British armies to finish the job off in the colonies. The key, then, was to establish a clear maritime advantage. As Pitt put it to the House of Commons in December 1755, before war had formally been declared, but well after the fighting had begun in the colonies:

We ought to have our Navy as fully and as well manned as possible before we declare war ... Is it not then now necessary for us, as we are upon the very brink of a war, to take every method that can be thought of for encouraging able and expert seamen into His Majesty's service? ... An open war is already begun: the French have attacked His Majesty's troops in America, and in return His Majesty's ships have attacked the French king's ships in that part of the world. Is this not an open war? ... If we do not deliver the territories of all our Indian allies, as well as our own in America, from every French fort, and every French garrison, we may give up our plantations.

Pitt secured a commitment from Parliament to recruit 55,000 seamen. He increased the fleet so that it numbered 105 ships of the line, compared with just 70 on the French side. In the process, the Royal Dockyards became the largest industrial enterprise in the world, building and repairing ships and employing thousands of men.

Pitt's was a policy that partly depended on Britain's nascent economic pre-eminence: in shipbuilding, metallurgy and gun founding she now enjoyed a discernible lead. The British were using not only technology but also science to rule the waves. When George Anson circumnavigated the globe with his six vessels in the 1740s, the cure for scurvy was unknown and John Harrison was still working on the third version of his chronometer for determining longitude at sea. The seamen died in droves; the ships frequently got lost. By the time Captain James Cook's *Endeavour* sailed for the South Pacific in 1768, Harrison had won the Board of Longitude's prize and Cook's crew were being fed sauerkraut as an anti-scorbutic. It epitomized the new alliance between science and strategy that on board the *Endeavour* there was a group of naturalists, notably the botanist Joseph Banks, and that Cook's voyage had a dual mission: to 'maintain the power, dominion, and sovereignty of BRITAIN' by laying claim to Australasia for the Admiralty and to record the transit of Venus for the Royal Society.

Only naval discipline remained unchangingly harsh. Famously, Admiral John Byng was shot early in the war for failing to destroy a French force off Minorca, in breach of the 12th Article of War, which stated:

Every person in the fleet, who through cowardice, negligence or disaffection . . . shall not do his utmost to take or destroy every ship which it shall be his duty to engage; every such person so offending, and being convicted thereof by the sentence of a court-martial, shall suffer death.*

Harder men, like Byng's cousin Sir George Pocock, beat the French fleet off India. Harder men, like James Cook, carried General Wolfe and his troops along the St Lawrence River to attack Quebec. And harder men, like George Anson – now First Lord of the Admiralty – masterminded the blockade of France, perhaps the clearest demonstration the war afforded of British naval superiority.

In November 1759 the French fleet finally emerged in a desperate bid to mount an invasion of England. Sir Edward Hawke was waiting for them. In a rising storm, they pursued the French fleet deep into Quiberon Bay on the south coast of Brittany, where it was shattered – two-thirds of it wrecked, burned or captured. The invasion was abandoned. British naval supremacy was now complete, making victory in the French colonies all but certain, for by cutting communications between France and her empire the Navy gave British ground forces a decisive advantage. The capture of Quebec and Montreal ended French rule in Canada. The rich Caribbean sugar islands – Guadeloupe, Marie Galante and Dominica – fell too. And in 1762 France's Spanish allies were bundled out of Cuba and the Philippines. That same year the French garrison vacated the fort at Gingee. By then all their bases in India – including Pondicherry itself – had been captured.

It was a victory based on naval superiority. But this in turn was possible only because Britain had one crucial advantage over France: the ability to borrow money. More than a third of all Britain's war expenditure was financed by loans. The institutions copied from the Dutch in the time of William III had now come into their own, allowing Pitt's government to spread the cost of war by selling low-interest bonds to the investing public. The French, by contrast, were reduced to begging or stealing. As Bishop Berkeley

---

* Byng's fate inspired Voltaire's famous one-liner: 'In this country it is thought well to kill an admiral from time to time to encourage the others.'

put it, credit was 'the principal advantage which England hath over France'. The French economist Isaac de Pinto agreed: 'It was the failure of credit in time of need that did the mischief, and probably was the chief cause of the late disasters.' Behind every British naval victory stood the National Debt; its growth – from £74 million to £133 million during the Seven Years War – was the measure of Britain's financial might.

In the 1680s a distinction had still existed between England and 'the English Empire in America'. By 1743 it had been possible to speak of 'the British Empire, taking together as one body, viz. Great Britain, Ireland, the Plantations and Fishery in America, besides its Possessions in the East Indies and Africa'. But now Sir George Macartney could write of 'this vast empire on which the sun never sets and whose bounds nature has not yet ascertained'. Pitt's only regret (peace was not concluded until after he had left office) was that the French were allowed to retain any of their overseas possessions, particularly the islands that had been returned to her in the Caribbean. The new government, he complained in the Commons in December 1762, had

lost sight of the great fundamental principle, that France is chiefly, if not solely, to be dreaded by us in the light of a commercial and maritime power . . . and by restoring to her all the valuable West-India islands . . . we have given her the means of recovering her prodigious losses . . . The trade with these conquests is of the most lucrative nature . . . [and] all that we gain . . . is made fourfold to us by the loss which ensues to France.

As Pitt correctly divined, the 'seeds of war' were already germinating in the peace terms. The struggle for world mastery between Britain and France would rage on with only brief respites until 1815. But the Seven Years War decided one thing irrevocably. India would be British, not French. And that gave Britain what for nearly two hundred years would be both a huge market for British trade and an inexhaustible reservoir of military manpower. India was much more than the 'jewel in the crown'. Literally and metaphorically, it was a whole diamond mine.

*

And the Indians themselves? The answer is that they allowed themselves to be divided – and, ultimately, ruled. Even before the Seven Years War, the British and French were meddling in Indian politics, trying to determine the successors to the Subahdar of the Deccan and the Nawab of the Carnatic. Robert Clive, that most mercurial of East India Company men, first came to the fore when he sought to raise the siege of Trichinopoly, where the British candidate for the Deccan, Mahomed Ali, was trapped; then seized Arcot, the capital of the Carnatic, and held it against the besieging forces of Mahomed Ali's rival Chanda Sahib.

When the Seven Years War broke out, the Nawab of Bengal, Siraj-ud-Daula, attacked the British settlement of Calcutta, imprisoning between sixty and 150* British prisoners in what became known as the 'Black Hole' in Fort William. Siraj had French backing. But his rivals, the Jaget Seth banking family, subsidized the British counter-attack. And Clive was able to persuade the supporters of a rival Nawab, Mir Jafar, to defect from Siraj's side on 22 June 1757, at the Battle of Plassey. Having won the battle and secured the Governorship of Bengal, Clive then deposed Mir Jafar, appointing his son-in-law Mir Kasim; when the latter proved insufficiently malleable, he in turn was expelled and Mir Jafar restored. Once again Indian feuds were being exploited for European ends. It was entirely characteristic of the age that more than two-thirds of Clive's 2,900 troops at Plassey were Indians. In the words of the Indian historian, Gholam Hossein Khan, author of the *Seir Mutaqherin, or Review of Modern Times* (1789):

It is in consequence of such and the like divisions [between Indian rulers] that most of the strongholds, nay, almost the whole of Hindostan, have come into the possession of the English ... Two princes contend for the same country, one of them applies to the English, and informs them of the way and method of becoming masters of it. By his insinuations and by their

* Contemporary reports spoke of 146 prisoners, most of whom suffocated to death. It seems likely that the number was smaller, but there is no doubt that a large proportion of them died. It was the height of the Indian summer and the 'hole' was a cell just eighteen feet by fourteen.

assistance, he draws to himself some of the leading men of the country who being his friends, are already fast attached to his person; and meanwhile the English have concluded to their own mind some treaty and agreement with him, they for some time abide by those terms, until they have a good insight into the government and customs of the country, as well as thorough acquaintance with the several parties in it; and then they discipline an army, and getting themselves supported by one party, they soon overcome the other, and little by little introduce themselves into the country, and make a conquest of it . . . The English who seem quite passive, as if suffering themselves to be led, are in fact giving motion to the machine.

There was, he concluded, 'nothing strange in those merchants having found the means of becoming masters of this country'; they had simply 'availed themselves of the imbecility of some Hindostany Sovereigns, equally proud and ignorant'.

By the time of Clive's victory over his remaining Indian foes at Buxar in 1764, he had reached a radical conclusion about the East India Company's future. Doing business on Indian sufferance was no longer enough. As he himself put it in a letter to the company's directors in London:

I can assert with some degree of confidence that this rich and flourishing kingdom may be totally subdued by so small a force as two thousand Europeans . . . [The Indians are] indolent, luxurious, ignorant and cowardly beyond all conception . . . [They] attempt everything by treachery rather than force . . . What is it, then, can enable us to secure our present acquisitions or improve upon them but such a force as leaves nothing to the power of treachery or ingratitude?

Under the Treaty of Allahabad, the Mughal Emperor granted the East India Company the civil administration – known as the *diwani* – of Bengal, Bihar and Orissa. It was a licence not to print money but the next best thing: to raise it in taxation. The *diwani* gave the company the right to tax over 20 million people. Assuming that at least a third of their produce could be appropriated this way, that implied a revenue of between £2 million and £3 million a year. It was now in what seemed like the biggest business of all in India: the business of government. As the company's Bengal Council put it in a letter to the directors in 1769: 'Your trade from hence may be considered more as a channel for conveying your revenues to Britain.'

Once pirates, then traders, the British were now the rulers of millions of people overseas – and not just in India. Thanks to a combination of naval and financial muscle they had become the winners in the European race for empire. What had begun as a business proposition had now become a matter of government.

The question the British now had to ask themselves was: How should the government of India be carried out? The impulse of a man like Clive was simply to plunder – and plunder he did, though he later insisted that he had been 'astonished at his own moderation'. A man so violent in his disposition that in the absence of foes he thought at once of self-destruction, Clive was the forerunner of Kipling's dissolute empire-builders in his story 'The Man Who Would Be King':

We will . . . go away to some other place where a man isn't crowded and can come into his own . . . in any place where they fight, a man who knows how to drill men can always be a King. We shall go to those parts and say to any King we find – 'D'you want to vanquish your foes?' and we will show him how to drill men; for that we know better than anything else. Then we will subvert that King and seize his Throne and establish a Dy-nasty [sic].

But if British rule in Bengal was to be more than a continuation of the smash-and-grab tactics of the buccaneers, a more subtle approach was needed. The appointment of Warren Hastings as the first Governor-General by the 1773 Regulating Act seemed to inaugurate such an approach.

A clever little man, as much a brain as Clive was a brute, Hastings was a former King's Scholar at Westminster and joined the East India Company as a writer at the age of seventeen. He was soon fluent in Persian and Hindi; and the more he studied Indian culture, the more respectful he became. The study of Persian, he wrote in 1769, 'cannot fail to open our minds, and to inspire us with that benevolence which our religion inculcates, for the whole race of mankind'. As he remarked in his preface to the translation he commissioned of the *Bhagavadgītā*:

Every instance which brings [the Indians'] real character home to observation will impress us with a more generous sense of feeling for their natural rights, and teach us to estimate them by the measure of our own. But such instances can only be obtained by their writings; and these will survive, when the British dominion of India shall have long ceased to exist, and when the sources which it once yielded of wealth and power are lost to remembrance.

Hastings sponsored translations of the Islamic texts *Fatāwā al-'Ālamgiri* and the *Hidayā*, as well as founding the Calcutta Madrassa, an Islamic law school. 'Muslim law,' he told Lord Mansfield, 'is as comprehensive, and as well defined, as that of most states in Europe.' He was no less assiduous in encouraging the study of India's geography and botany.

Under Hastings's auspices, a new, hybrid society began to develop in Bengal. Not only did British scholars translate Indian laws and literature; company employees also married Indian women and adopted Indian customs. This extraordinary time of cultural fusion appeals to our modern sensibilities, suggesting as it does that the Empire was not born with the 'original sin' of racism. But is that its true significance? A crucial aspect of the Hastings era which is easily overlooked is that most of the East India Company men who 'went native' wholly or partially were themselves drawn from one of Britain's ethnic minorities. They were Scots.

In the 1750s little more than a tenth of the population of the British Isles lived in Scotland. Yet the East India Company was at the very least half-Scottish. Of 249 writers appointed by the Directors to serve in Bengal in the last decade of Hastings's administration, 119 were Scots. Of 116 candidates for the officer corps of the company's Bengal army recruited in 1782, fifty-six were Scots.*

* By contrast, Irishmen were over-represented in the lower ranks. In the early nineteenth century, the Bengal army was 34 per cent English, 11 per cent Scottish and 48 per cent Irish.

Of 371 men admitted to work as 'free merchants' by the directors, 211 were Scots. Of 254 assistant surgeon recruits to the company, 132 were Scots. Hastings himself referred to his closest advisers as his 'Scotch guardians': men like Alexander Elliot of Minto, John Sumner of Peterhead and George Bogle of Bothwell. Of thirty-five individuals entrusted by Hastings with important missions during his time as Governor-General, at least twenty-two were Scotsmen. Back in London, Hastings also relied on Scots shareholders to support his conduct in the company's Court of Proprietors, notably the Johnstones of Westerhall. In March 1787 Henry Dundas, the Scottish Solicitor-General, jokingly told his nominee for the governorship of Madras, Sir Archibald Campbell, that 'all India will be soon in [our] hands, and ... the county of Argyll will be depopulated by the emigration of Campbells to be provided for at Madras'. (Even Hastings's first wife was a Scot: Mary née Elliot of Cambuslang, widow of a Captain Buchanan who had perished in the Black Hole.)

Much of the explanation for this disproportion lay in the greater readiness of Scotsmen to try their luck abroad. That luck had been in short supply in the 1690s when the Company of Scotland had tried to establish a colony at Darien on the east coast of Panama, a location so unhealthy that the venture stood little chance of success, though Spanish and English hostility hastened its collapse. Happily, the Union of Parliaments of 1707 was also a union of economies – and a union of imperial ambitions. Now Scotland's surplus entrepreneurs and engineers, medics and musketeers could deploy their skills and energies ever further afield in the service of English capital and under the protection of England's navy.

The Scots may also have been more ready than the Britons of the south to be assimilated into indigenous societies. George Bogle, sent by Hastings to explore Bhutan and Tibet, had two daughters by a Tibetan wife and wrote admiringly of the distinctive Tibetan style of polygamy (in which one woman could take multiple husbands). John Maxwell, a minister's son from New Machar near Aberdeen who became editor of the *India Gazette*, was no less intrigued by the (to his eyes) luxurious and effeminate ways of Indian life; he had at least three children by Indian women. William Fraser, one of five brothers from Inverness who came to India in the early 1800s, played a crucial part in subjugating the Ghurkas; he collected both Mughal manuscripts and Indian wives. According to one account, he had six or seven of the latter and numberless children, who were 'Hindus and Muslims according to the religion and caste of their mamas'. Among the products of such unions was Fraser's friend and comrade-in-arms James Skinner, the son of a Scotsman from Montrose and a Rajput princess, and the founder of the cavalry regiment Skinner's Horse. Skinner had at least seven wives and was credited with siring eighty children: 'Black or white will not make much difference before His presence,' he once remarked. Though he dressed his men in scarlet turbans, silver-edged girdles and bright yellow tunics and wrote his memoirs in Persian, Skinner was a devout Christian who erected one of the most splendid churches in Delhi, St James's, in gratitude for surviving an especially bloody battle.

Not everyone was so multicultural, of course. Indeed, in his history of modern India, Gholam Hossain Khan complained about the very opposite tendency:

The gates of communication and intercourse are shut up betwixt the men of this land and those strangers, who are become their masters; and these latter constantly express an aversion to the society of Indians, and a disdain against conversing with them . . . Not one of the English Gentlemen shews any inclination or any relish for the company of the Gentlemen of this country . . . Such is the aversion which the English openly shew for the company of the natives, and such the disdain which they betray for them, that no love, and no coalition (two articles, which, by the bye, are the principle of all union and attachment, and the source of all regulation and settlement) can take root between the conquerors and the conquered.

Nor should we let the many appealing aspects of eighteenth-century Indo-Celtic fusion blind us to the fact that the East India Company existed not for the sake of scholarship or miscegenation but to make money. Hastings and his contemporaries became very rich men. They did so despite the fact that the key market for their core product, Indian textiles, was being restricted by various protectionist measures designed to stimulate British manufactures. And no matter how devoted they might be to Indian culture, their aim was always to transfer their profits back home to Britain. The notorious 'drain' of capital from India to Britain had begun.

It was a tradition that went back to the days of Thomas Pitt and before. In 1701, while Governor of Madras, Pitt had come across the perfect way to remit his gains to England. 'My grand affair,' he called it, 'my great concern, my all, the finest jewell in the world.' At the time, the Pitt Diamond was the largest the world had ever seen, weighing some 410 carats; when cut it was valued at £125,000. Pitt never revealed the full story of how he came by it (almost certainly it came from the Mughal Emperor's mines at Golconda, though Pitt denied this). In any event, he later sold it to the Prince Regent of France, who incorporated it into the French crown. But the jewel literally made his name: henceforth he was known as 'Diamond' Pitt. There was no more powerful symbol of the wealth an ambitious and able Englishman could make in India, and where Pitt led many others hastened to follow. Clive too sent his gains back to England in the form of diamonds. Altogether around £18 million was transferred to Britain from India by such means. In the decade from 1783 the drain totalled £1.3 million. As Gholam Hossein Khan put it:

The English have besides a custom of coming for a number of years, and then going away to pay a visit to their native country, without any one of them shewing any inclination to fix himself in this land . . . And as they join to that custom that other one of theirs, which every one of those emigrants holds to be of Divine obligation, I mean, that of scraping together as much money in this country as they can, and carrying it in immense sums to the kingdom of England; so it is not surprising that these two customs, blended together, should be ever undermining and ruining this country, and should be an eternal bar to it ever flourishing again.

Of course, not every East India Company writer became a Clive. Of a sample of 645 civil servants who went to Bengal, more than half died in India. Of the 178 who returned to Britain, a fair number –

around a quarter – were not especially wealthy. As Samuel Johnson said to Boswell: 'A man had better have ten thousand pounds at the end of ten years passed in England, than twenty thousand pounds at the end of ten years passed in India, because you must compute what you *give* for money; and a man who has lived ten years in India, has given up ten years of social comfort and all those advantages which arise from living in England.'

Nevertheless, a new word was about to enter the English language: the 'nabob', a corruption of the Indian princely title of *nawab*. The nabobs were men like Pitt, Clive and Hastings, who brought their Indian fortunes back home and converted them into imposing stately homes like Pitt's at Swallowfield, Clive's at Claremont or Hastings's at Daylesford. Nor did they confine themselves to buying real estate. It was with money he had made in India that Thomas Pitt bought the Parliamentary seat of Old Sarum, that notorious 'rotten borough' which his more famous grandson later represented in the House of Commons. It was magnificent hypocrisy on William Pitt's part when he complained in January 1770:

The riches of Asia have been poured in upon us, and brought with them not only Asiatic luxury, but, I fear, Asiatic principles of government . . . The importers of foreign gold have forced their way into Parliament, by such a torrent of private corruption, as no private hereditary fortune could resist.

'We have sitting among us', he grumbled twelve years later, 'the members of the Rajah of Tangore and the Nawab of Arcot, the representatives of petty Eastern despots.'

In Thackeray's *Vanity Fair*, Becky Sharp imagines herself – as the wife of the collector of Boggley Wollah – 'arrayed . . . in an infinity of shawls, turbans, and diamond necklaces, and . . . mounted upon an elephant', since 'they say all Indian nabobs are enormously rich'. Having returned to London on account of a 'liver complaint', the nabob in question

drove his horses in the Park; he dined at the fashionable taverns . . . he frequented the theatres, as the mode was in those days, or made his appearance at the opera, laboriously attired in tights and a cocked hat . . . He was

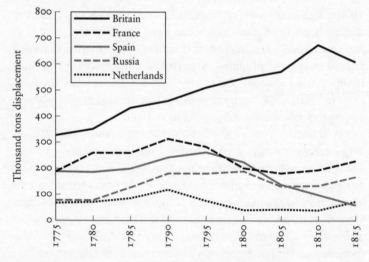

European navies: total tonnage of vessels above 500 tons, 1775–1815. By the end of the eighteenth century, Britannia truly ruled the waves

very witty regarding the number of Scotchmen whom ... the Governor-General, patronized ... How delighted Miss Rebecca was at ... the stories of the Scotch aides-de-camp.

A more timorous and unmartial figure than Jos Sedley it would be hard to imagine. Yet in truth the profits of the nabobs were increasingly underwritten by an enormous military establishment in India. By the time of Warren Hastings, the East India Company had more than 100,000 men under arms, and was in a state of near perpetual warfare. In 1767 the first shots were fired in what would prove a protracted struggle with the state of Mysore. The following year, the Northern Sarkars – the states of the east coast – were won from the Nizam of Hyderabad. And seven years after that, Benares and Ghazipur were seized from the Nawab of Oudh. What had started as an informal security force to protect the company's trade had now become the company's *raison d'être*: fighting new battles, conquering new territory, to pay for the previous battles. The British presence in India also depended on the Navy's ability to defeat the French when they returned to the fray, as they did in the 1770s. And that cost even more money.

It was easy to see who got rich from the Empire. The question was, who exactly was going to pay for it?

The Taxman

Robert Burns was just the sort of man who might have been tempted to seek his fortune in the Empire. Indeed, when his love life went awry in 1786 he thought seriously of taking himself off to Jamaica. In the end he missed his intended ship and elected, on reflection, to stay in Scotland. But his poems, songs and letters can still give us an invaluable insight into the political economy of the eighteenth-century Empire.

Burns was born in 1759, at the height of the Seven Years War, the son of a poor Alloway gardener. His early literary success, though gratifying, paid no bills. He tried his hand at farming, but that was little better. There was, however, a third possibility open to him. In 1788 he applied to one of the Commissioners of Excise to become, in effect, a taxman. It was something that embarrassed him a great deal more than his celebrated drinking and wenching. As he confided in a friend: 'I will make no excuses . . . that I have sat down to write you on this vile paper, stained with the sanguinary scores of "thae curst horse leeches o' th' Excise" . . . For the glorious cause of LUCRE I will do any thing, be any thing.' But 'five and thirty pounds a year was no bad dernier resort for a poor Poet'. 'There is', he admitted, 'a certain stigma affixed to the character of an Excise-Officer, but I do not intend to borrow honour from any profession; and though the Salary be comparatively small, it is luxury to any thing that the first twenty-five years of my life taught me to expect.' 'People may talk as they please of the ignominy of the Excise, but what will support my family and keep me independant [sic] of the world is to me a very important matter.'

In swallowing his pride for the sake of a taxman's salary, Burns became a link in the great chain of imperial finance. Britain's wars against France had been funded by borrowing and yet more borrowing, and the magic mountain atop which British power stood, the National Debt, had grown in proportion with the new territories acquired. When Burns started work for the Excise it stood at £244 million. A crucial function of the Excise was therefore to raise the money necessary to pay the interest on this debt.

Who paid the Excise? The main dutiable articles were spirits, wines, silks and tobacco, as well as beer, candles, soap, starch, leather, windows, houses, horses and carriages. Notionally the tax was levied on the producers of liable commodities. But in practice it fell on consumers, since producers simply added the excise to their prices. Every glass of beer or whisky a man drank was taxed, and every pipe he smoked. As Burns said, his business was 'grinding the faces of the Publican & the Sinner on the merciless wheels of the Excise'. But the virtuous also had to pay. Every candle a man lit to read by, even the soap he washed with, was taxed. For the nabobs, of course, these taxes were scarcely noticeable. But they ate up a substantial proportion of an ordinary family's income. In effect, then, the costs of overseas expansion – or to be precise of the interest on the National Debt – were met by the impoverished majority at home. And who received that interest? The answer was a tiny elite of mainly southern bondholders, somewhere around 200,000 families, who had invested a part of their wealth in 'the Funds'.

One of the great puzzles of the 1780s is therefore why it was to France – where taxes were much lighter and less regressive – rather than to Britain that political revolution finally came in the 1780s. Burns himself was one of those Britons to whom the idea of revolution appealed. It was he, after all, who gave the revolutionary era one of its most enduring anthems in 'A Man's a Man for a' that'. An instinctive meritocrat, Burns bitterly resented 'the stately stupidity of self-sufficient Squires, or the luxuriant insolence of upstart Nabobs'. Despite his own complicity as a taxman, he even wrote a populist attack on the excise tax, 'The De'il's awa' wi' th' Exciseman'. But Burns had to abandon his political principles in order to keep his job. After he was spotted singing a revolutionary anthem in a Dumfries theatre, he had to write an obsequious exculpatory letter to the Commissioner of the Scottish Board of Excise, pledging to 'seal up [his] lips' on the subject of revolution.

The poor drinkers and smokers of Ayrshire were far from the worst-off subjects of the British Empire, however. In India the impact of British taxes was even greater, for the spiralling cost of the Indian Army was the one item of imperial expenditure the British taxpayer never had to pay. Disastrously, the ratcheting up of taxes in Bengal coincided with a huge famine, which killed as many as a third of the population of Bengal – some five million people. To Gholam Hossein Khan, there was a clear connection between 'the vast exportation of coin which is carried every year to the country of England' and the plight of his country:

The decrease of products in each District, added to the innumerable multitudes swept away by famine and mortality still go on augmenting the depopulation of the country . . . For as the English are now the rulers and the masters of this country, as well as the only rich men, to whom can those poor people look up to for offering the productions of their art, so as to benefit by their expenses? . . . Numerous artificers . . . have no other

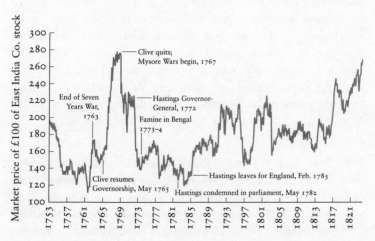

East India Company's share price, 1753–1823.

resource left than that of begging or thieving. Numbers, therefore, have already quitted their homes and countries; and numbers unwilling to leave their abodes, have made covenant with hunger and distress, and ended their lives in the corner of their cottages.

It was not just that the British repatriated so much of the money they made in India. Increasingly, even the money they spent while there tended to go on British goods, not Indian. Nor did the bad times end there. Another famine in 1783–4 killed more than a fifth of the population of the Indian plains; this was followed by severe scarcities in 1791, 1801 and 1805.

Back in London, the shareholders were feeling uneasy, and the East India Company's share price in this period makes it clear why. Having soared under Clive's Governor-Generalship, it slumped under Hastings. If the cash cow of Bengal were to starve to death, the company's prospective earnings would collapse. Nor could Hastings any longer rely on military operations to replenish the company's coffers. In 1773 he accepted the offer of 40 million rupees from the Nawab of Oudh to fight the Rohillas, an Afghan people who had settled in Rohilkund, but the costs of this mercenary operation were not much less than the fee, which was in any case never paid. In 1779 the Marathas defeated a British army sent to challenge their dominance of Western India. A year later Haider Ali of Mysore and his son Tipu Sultan attacked Madras. As revenue imploded and costs exploded, the company had to rely on bond sales and short-term borrowing to remain afloat. Finally, the directors were forced not only to reduce the annual dividend but to turn to the government for assistance – to the disgust of the free market economist, Adam Smith. As Smith noted contemptuously in *The Wealth of Nations* (1776):

Their debts, instead of being reduced, were augmented by an arrear to the treasury . . . of . . . four hundred thousand pounds, by another to the custom-house for duties unpaid, by a large debt to the bank for money borrowed, and by a fourth for bills drawn upon them from India, and wantonly accepted, to the amount of upwards of twelve hundred thousand pounds.

By 1784 the company's debt stood at £8.4 million and Hastings's critics now included a powerful array of politicians, among them Henry Dundas and Edmund Burke – the former a hard-nosed Scottish power-broker, the latter a tremendous Irish orator. When Hastings resigned as Governor-General and returned home in 1785, they secured his impeachment.

Hastings's trial, which ended up lasting an exhausting seven years, was more than the public humiliation of a chief executive before a meeting of disgruntled shareholders. In truth, it was the whole basis of the company's rule in India that was on trial. The original grounds of impeachment debated in the Commons charged Hastings

With gross injustice, cruelty and treachery against the faith of nations, in hiring British soldiers for the purpose of extirpating the innocent and helpless people . . . the Rohillas . . .

With various instances of extortion and other deeds of maladministration against the Rajah of Benares . . .

[With] The numerous and insupportable hardships to which the Royal Family of Oude [Oudh] had been reduced . . .

With impoverishing and depopulating the whole country of Oude [Oudh], rendering that country, which was once a garden, an uninhabited desert . . .

With a wanton, and unjust, and pernicious exercise of his powers, and the great situation of trust which he occupied in India, in overturning the ancient establishments of the country, and extending an undue influence by conniving extravagant contracts, and appointing inordinate salaries . . .

With receiving money against the orders of the Company, the Act of Parliament and his own sacred engagements; and applying the money to purposes totally improper and unauthorized [and with] enormous extravagances and bribery in various contracts with a view to enrich his dependants and favourites.

Though not all the charges were approved, the list was enough to get Hastings arrested and charged with 'high crimes and misdemeanours'. On 13 February 1788 the most celebrated – and certainly the most protracted – trial in the history of the British Empire began in an atmosphere like that of a West End opening night. Before a glittering audience, Burke and the playwright Richard Sheridan opened the prosecution with virtuoso hyperbole:

BURKE: I impeach him in the name of the English nation, whose ancient honour he has sullied. I impeach him in the name of the people of India, whose rights he has trodden under foot, and whose country he has turned into a desert. Lastly, in the name of human nature itself, in the name of both sexes, in the name of every age, in the name of every rank, I impeach the common enemy and oppressor of all.

SHERIDAN: In his mind all is shuffling, ambiguous, dark insidious, and little; all affected plainness, and actual dissimulation; – a heterogeneous mass of contradictory qualities; with nothing great but his crimes, and even those contrasted by the littleness of his motives, which at once denote both his baseness and his meanness, and mark him for a traitor and a trickster.

Hastings could not match this; he fluffed his lines. On the other hand, the hallmark of a successful play, a long run, is not the hallmark of a successful trial. In the end, Hastings was acquitted by an exhausted and substantially altered House of Lords.

Still, British India would never be the same again. Even before the trial began, a new India Act had been steered through Parliament by another William Pitt, son of the hero of the Seven Years War and great-grandson of 'Diamond' Pitt. The aim of the Act was to clean up the East India Company and to bring to an end the day of the freebooting nabob. From now on the Governor-Generals in India would not be company officers but grandees, appointed directly by the crown. When the first of them, the Earl of Cornwallis, arrived in India (fresh from defeat in America), he took immediate steps to change the ethos of company administration, increasing salaries and reducing perquisites in a deliberate inversion of 'the old principles of Leadenhall Street economy'. This marked the beginning of what would become an institution celebrated for its sea-green incorruptibility – the Indian Civil Service. In place of the arbitrary taxation of the Hastings era, Cornwallis's Permanent Settlement of 1793 introduced English-style private property rights in land and fixed landowners' tax obligations in perpetuity; the effect of this was to reduce peasants to mere tenants and strengthen the position of a rising Bengali gentry.

The Governor-General's new palace built in Calcutta by Cornwallis's successor, Richard, Earl of Mornington (later Marquess Wellesley) – brother of the future Duke of Wellington – was a telling symbol of what the British in India aspired to in the years after Warren Hastings. Oriental corruption was out; classical virtue was in, though despotism remained the preferred political order. As Horace Walpole somewhat disingenuously put it, a 'peaceable, quiet set of tradesfolks' had become the 'heir-apparent to the Romans'.

One thing did not change, however. Under Cornwallis and Wellesley, British power in India continued to be based on the sword. War after war extended British rule ever further beyond Bengal – against the Marathas, against Mysore, against the Sikhs in the Punjab. In 1799 Tipu Sultan was killed when his capital Seringapatam fell. In 1803, following the defeat of the Marathas at Delhi, the Mughal Emperor himself finally accepted British 'protection'. By 1815, around 40 million Indians were under British rule. Nominally, it was still a company that was in charge. But the East India Company was now much more than its name implied. It was the heir to the Mughals, and the Governor-General was the *de facto* Emperor of a subcontinent.

In 1615 the British Isles had been an economically unremarkable, politically fractious and strategically second-class entity. Two hundred years later Great Britain had acquired the largest empire the world had ever seen, encompassing forty-three colonies in five continents. The title of Patrick Colquhoun's *Treatise on the Wealth, Power and Resources of the British Empire in Every Quarter of the Globe* (1814) said it all. They had robbed the Spaniards, copied the Dutch, beaten the French and plundered the Indians. Now they ruled supreme.

Was all this done 'in a fit of absence of mind'? Plainly not. From the reign of Elizabeth I onwards, there had been a sustained campaign to take over the empires of others.

Yet commerce and conquest by themselves would not have sufficed to achieve this, no matter what the strength of British financial and naval power. There had also to be colonization.

2

White Plague

What should we do but sing his praise
That led us through the wat'ry maze
Unto an isle so long unknown,
And yet far kinder than our own?
Where he the huge sea-monsters wracks,
That lift the deep upon their backs,
He lands us on a grassy stage,
Safe from the storm's and prelates' rage.
He gave us this eternal spring
Which here enamels everything . . .

Andrew Marvell,
'Song of the Emigrants in Bermuda' (1653)

We [saw] a Set of Men . . . under the Auspices of the English
Government; & protected by it . . . for a long Series of Years
. . . rising, by easy Gradations, to such a State of Prosperity &
Happiness as was almost enviable, but we [saw] them also
run mad with too much Happiness, & burst into an open
Rebellion against that Parent, who protected them against the
Ravages of their Enemies.

Peter Oliver, *The Origin and Progress of*
the American Revolution (1781)

Between the early 1600s and the 1950s, more than 20 million people left the British Isles to begin new lives across the seas. Only a minority ever returned. No other country in the world came close to exporting so many of its inhabitants. In leaving Britain, the early emigrants risked not merely their life savings but their very lives.

Their voyages were never without hazard; their destinations were often unhealthy and inhospitable. To us, their decision to gamble everything on a one-way ticket seems baffling. Yet without millions of such tickets – some purchased voluntarily, some not – there could have been no British Empire. For the indispensable foundation of the Empire was mass migration: the biggest in human history. This Britannic exodus changed the world. It turned whole continents white.

For most of the emigrants, the New World spelt liberty – religious freedom in some cases, but above all economic freedom. Indeed, the British liked to think of this freedom as the thing that made their empire different from – and of course better than – the Spanish, the Portuguese and the Dutch. 'Without freedom', Edmund Burke declared in 1766, it 'would not be the British Empire.' But could an empire, implying as it did British rule over foreign lands, be based on liberty? Was that not a contradiction in terms? Certainly, not all those who crossed the oceans did so of their own free will. Moreover, all were still subjects of the British monarch; and just how politically free did that make them? It was precisely this question that sparked the first great war of independence against the Empire.

Since the 1950s flows of migration have of course reversed themselves. More than a million people from all over Britain's former Empire have come as immigrants to Britain. So controversial has this 'reverse colonization' been that successive governments have severely restricted it. But in the seventeenth and eighteenth centuries it was the British themselves who were the unwanted immigrants, at least in the eyes of those who already inhabited the New World. To those on the receiving end of Britain's empire of liberty, these millions of migrants seemed little better than a white plague.

Plantation

In the early 1600s, a group of intrepid pioneers sailed across the sea to settle and, they hoped, civilize a primitive country inhabited by – as they saw it – a 'barbarous people': Ireland.

It was the Tudor queens, Mary and Elizabeth, who authorized the systematic colonization of Ireland, first in Munster in the south and then, most ambitiously, in Ulster in the north. Nowadays we tend to think of this as the start of Ireland's troubles. But colonization was intended as the answer to the country's chronic instability.

Since Henry VIII's proclamation of himself as King of Ireland in 1541, English power had been limited to the so-called 'Pale' of earlier English settlement around Dublin and the beleaguered Scottish fort of Carrickfergus. In language, religion, land tenure and social structure, the rest of Ireland was another world. There was, however, a danger: Roman Catholic Ireland might be used by Spain as a back door into Protestant England. Systematic colonization was adopted as the remedy. In 1556 Mary allocated confiscated estates in Leix and Offaly in Leinster to settlers who established Philipstown and Maryborough there, but these were little more than military outposts. It was under her half-sister Elizabeth that the idea of English settlements took shape. In 1569 Sir Warham St Leger proposed a colony in south-west Munster; two years later Sir Henry Sydney and the Earl of Leicester persuaded the Queen to undertake a similar scheme in Ulster following the confiscation of the estates of Shane O'Neill.

The idea was that 'haven townes' would be established through merchants 'intrenchying themselves' and the settlement of 'good husband men, plow wryghtes, kart wryghtes and smythes ... eyther to take habitation yf they be hable, or else to staye and serve there under sotche gentlemen as shall inhabyte there.' Land that was now 'waste', 'desolate' and 'uninhabited' would flow with 'milk and honey', according to Walter Devereux, Earl of Essex, who mortgaged his estates in England and Wales to finance the 'enterprise of Ulster'.

But the would-be colonists did not fare well; many returned home, 'not having forgotten the delicacies of England, and wanting the resolute minds to endure the travail of a year or two in this waste country'. In 1575 an English expedition took Carrickfergus from the Scots, but Essex soon found himself pitted against the Gaelic Lords, under the leadership of the O'Neill (Turlough Luineach). A year later Essex died of dysentery in Dublin, still believing that the future lay in 'the introduction of collonys of English'. By 1595 power in Ulster was in the hands of Hugh O'Neill, Earl of Tyrone, who proclaimed himself Prince of Ulster after securing backing from Spain. In August 1598 O'Neill defeated an English army at Yellow Ford. It was a similar story in Munster. Following the suppression of Catholic revolts a scheme was launched for a settlement there. Lands were to be divided into estates of 12,000 acres for English-men who would undertake to populate them with English tenants. Among those who acquired estates in Munster were Sir Walter Ralegh and Edmund Spenser, who wrote *The Faerie Queene* in his house at Kilcolman, County Cork. But in October 1598 the settlers were massacred; Spenser's house was razed to the ground.

Only the failure of Spain to send an adequate force to Kinsale and the defeat of O'Neill's army when he attempted to relieve the siege there prevented the complete abandonment of the Elizabethan colonization strategy. After O'Neill's submission and flight to the continent in 1607, the strategy was nevertheless revived by Eliza-beth's successor, James VI of Scotland, now James I of England.

As any reader of the poetry of John Donne knows, the Jacobeans were inordinately fond of metaphors. Their term for coloniza-tion was 'plantation'; in the words of Sir John Davies, the settlers were 'good corn'; the natives were 'weeds'. But this was more than mere social gardening. In theory, plantation was just another word for colonization, the ancient Greek practice of establishing settlements of loyal subjects out on the political margins. In reality plantation meant what today is known as 'ethnic cleansing'. The lands of the rebel Earl and his associates – in practice, most of the six counties of Armagh, Coleraine, Fermanagh, Tyrone, Cavan and Donegal – would be confiscated. The most strategically and agriculturally valuable land would be given to what the Lord Deputy Chichester called 'colonies of civil people of England and Scotland'. Plant enough good English and Scottish corn, James's advisers argued, 'and the country will ever after be happily settled'. Where possible, as the King himself made clear, the natives would be 'removed'.

The so-called 'Printed Book', published in April 1610, spelt out in detail how plantation would work. The land would be reallocated in neat parcels ranging from 1,000 to 3,000 acres. The biggest plots would go to the ominously named 'undertakers', whose job it was to build Protestant churches and fortifications. Symbolically, the walls of Derry (or 'Londonderry' as it was renamed in 1610) were shaped like a shield, protecting the new Protestant community planted there by the City of London. Catholics had to live outside the walls, down in the Bogside. Nothing illustrates better the ethnic and religious segregation implicit in the policy of plantation.

It is hard to believe anyone thought this would 'settle' Ireland. It did nothing of the kind. On 22 October 1641 the Ulster Catholics rose up against the newcomers. In what one contemporary called a 'fearful tempest of blood', around 2,000 Protestants were killed. Not for the last time, colonization turned out to mean conflict, not coexistence. Yet by this time the plantation had taken hold. Even before the 1641 rising, there were more than 13,000 Englishmen and women established in the six counties of the Jacobean plantation, and more than 40,000 Scots throughout Northern Ireland. Munster too had revived: by 1641 the 'New English' population was 22,000. And this was just the beginning. By 1673 an anonymous pamphleteer could confidently describe Ireland as 'one of the chiefest members of the British Empire'.

So Ireland was the experimental laboratory of British colonization and Ulster was the prototype plantation. What it seemed to show was that empire could be built not only by commerce and conquest but by migration and settlement. Now the challenge was to export the model further afield – not just across the Irish Sea, but across the Atlantic.

*

Like the idea of Irish plantation, the idea of an American plantation was an Elizabethan one. As usual, it was a desire to emulate Spain – and a fear of being pre-empted by France* – that persuaded the crown to give its backing. In 1578 a Devon gentleman named Humphrey Gilbert, half-brother of Sir Walter Ralegh, secured a patent from the Queen to colonize the unoccupied lands north of Spanish Florida. Nine years later an expedition established the first British settlement in North America on Roanoke Island, south of the Chesapeake Bay at what is now Kitty Hawk. By this time, Spanish and Portuguese colonization of Central and South America had been going on for almost a century.

One of the most important questions of modern history is why the North European settlement of North America had such different results from the South European settlement of South America. It is worth first recalling how much the two processes had in common. What began as a hunt for gold and silver quickly acquired an agricultural dimension. Crops from the New World could be exported, including maize, potatoes, sweet potatoes, tomatoes, pineapples, cocoa and tobacco; while crops from elsewhere – wheat, rice, sugar cane, bananas and coffee – could be transferred to the Americas. Even more importantly, the introduction there of hitherto unknown domesticated animals (cattle, pigs, chickens, sheep, goats and horses) greatly enhanced agricultural productivity. Yet the wiping out of – in the Latin American case – around three-quarters of the indigenous population by European diseases (smallpox, measles, influenza and typhus) and then by diseases brought from Africa (particularly yellow fever) created not just a convenient power vacuum but also a chronic shortage of labour. This made large-scale immigration not only possible but desirable. It also meant that even after a hundred years of Iberian imperialism most of the American continent was still unsettled by Europeans. It was not just as a compliment to his celibate Queen that Ralegh named the country around Chesapeake Bay 'Virginia'.

---

* French Huguenots had already established settlements in what became South Carolina and in northern Florida in the 1560s.

Expectations of Virginia were high, with predictions that it would yield 'all the commodities of Europe, Affrica, and Asia'. According to one enthusiast, 'The earth [there] bringeth foorth all things in abundance, as in the first creation, without toile or labour.' The poet Michael Drayton called it 'Earth's only paradise'. Once again, there were assurances that the land would flow with milk and honey. Virginia would prove to be, according to another booster,

Tyrus for colours, Basan for woods, Persia for oils, Arabia for spices, Spain for silks, Narcis for shiping, Netherlands for fish, Pomona for fruit, and by tillage, Babylon for corn, besides the abundance of mulberries, minerals, rubies, pearls, gems, grapes, deer, fowls, drugs for physic, herbs for food, roots for colours, ashes for soap, timber for building, pastures for feeding, rivers for fishing, and whatsoever commodity England wanteth.

The trouble was that America was thousands of miles further away than Ireland, and agriculture there would have to be started from scratch. In the interval between arrival and the first successful harvest, there would be daunting supply problems. There were also, as it turned out, graver threats to prospective settlers than even the dreaded Papist 'woodkerryes' of Ulster.

As had been true of the development of Britain's trade with India, colonization was a form of 'public–private partnership': the crown set out the rules with royal charters, but it was up to private individuals to take the risk – and put up the money. Those risks turned out to be considerable. The first settlement at Roanoke survived barely a year; by June 1586 it had been abandoned after trouble with the local 'Indians'.* The second expedition to Roanoke in 1587 was led by John White, who left his wife and children there when he returned to England for supplies. When he returned in 1590 they and all the other settlers had vanished. The Virginia Company established in April 1606 was therefore not a concern for the risk-averse.

---

* It is important to bear in mind that at this time the North American coast was primarily of interest as a source of strategic support for Britain's ambitions in the Caribbean, otherwise known as the 'West Indies'. Hence the familiar yet incongruous term 'Indians' for natives of North America.

Little now remains of Jamestown, Virginia, the Company's first American outpost. Although it can legitimately be called the first successful British colony in America, it too nearly suffered the fate of its ill-starred predecessor at Roanoke. Malaria, yellow fever and plague meant that by the end of their first year there, only thirty-eight men were left of the original force of more than a hundred. For almost ten years Jamestown teetered on the brink of extinction. What saved the colony was the tenacious leadership of a now rather overlooked pioneer.

John Smith's greatest misfortune was to be called John Smith: given a less forgettable name, we might all have heard of him. An irascible soldier and intrepid navigator who had once been enslaved by the Turks, Smith was convinced that the future of the British Empire lay in American colonization. Although he had arrived in Virginia as a prisoner – having been accused of mutiny in mid-Atlantic – it was he who imposed order and averted a second Roanoke by conciliating the local Indians. Even so, the odds of surviving a year in Jamestown were roughly 50:50, and the winter of 1609, which Smith had to spend fetching supplies from England, was remembered as 'the starving time'. Only fairly desperate men would gamble their lives with odds like these. What Jamestown needed was skilled craftsmen, farmers, artisans. But what it had, as Smith complained, was the dregs of Jacobean society. Something more was needed if the British plantation in America was really to take root.

One important inducement was the Virginia Company's offer to prospective settlers of fifty-acre plots of land at negligible rents in perpetuity. Under the 'headright' system of land allocation, a settler received fifty acres for every dependant he brought with him. But the prospect of free land alone did not suffice to attract the kind of people John Smith was after. Of equal importance was the discovery in 1612 that tobacco could be grown with ease. By 1621 exports of the weed from Virginia had soared to 350,000 lbs a year. Six years later the King himself was driven to lament to the Governor and Council of Virginia 'that this province is wholly built upon smoke'.

Superficially, tobacco was the answer. It needed little investment: just a few tools, a press and a drying shed. Though time-consuming, it called for only simple skills, like the knack of 'topping' a plant between the thumb and forefinger, and was not physically taxing. The fact that tobacco exhausted the soil after seven years' cultivation merely encouraged the westward spread of settlement. Yet precisely the ease of cultivation very nearly proved Virginia's undoing. Between 1619 and 1639, as supply grew exponentially to 1.5 million lbs a year, the price of tobacco collapsed from three shillings to threepence a pound. The monopoly trading companies of Asia would never have tolerated such a slump. But in America, where attracting settlers was the objective, there could be no such monopolies.

In short, the economics of British America were precarious; and by economics alone British America could not have been built. Something more was needed – an additional inducement to cross the Atlantic over and above the profit motive. That something turned out to be religious fundamentalism.

After breaking with Rome under her father, wholeheartedly embracing the Reformation under her half-brother, then repudiating it under her half-sister, England finally settled on a moderately Protestant 'middle way' at the accession of Queen Elizabeth I. For the people who came to be known as Puritans, however, the Anglican Establishment was a fudge. When it became clear that James I intended to uphold the Elizabethan order, despite his Scottish Calvinist upbringing, a group of self-styled 'Pilgrims' from Scrooby in Nottinghamshire decided it was time to leave. They tried Holland, but after ten years they gave it up as too worldly. Then they heard about America, and precisely what put other people off – the fact that it was a wilderness – struck them as ideal. Where better to found a truly godly society than amid 'a vast and empty chaos'?

On 9 November 1620, nearly eight weeks after leaving Southampton, the Pilgrims landed at Cape Cod. As if to give themselves the cleanest possible slate, they missed Virginia by around

200 miles, ending up instead on the chillier northern shores that John Smith had christened 'New England'. It is interesting to speculate what New England might have been like if the Pilgrims had been the only people on the *Mayflower*. After all, they were not just fundamentalists; they were also in a literal sense communists, who intended to own their property and distribute their produce equally. In fact, only around a third of the 149 people aboard were Pilgrims: the majority had responded to the Virginia Company's advertisements, and their motives for crossing the Atlantic were more material than spiritual. Some were in fact fleeing a depression at home in the East Anglian textile industry. Their aim was to make good rather than be godly, and what attracted them to New England was not so much the absence of bishops and other relics of Popery, but the presence, in large quantities, of fish.

The Newfoundland fisheries had long attracted British fishermen far out into the Atlantic. But it was of course much easier to reach them from America. The coastal waters of New England were also full of fish: they were so abundant off Marblehead that 'it seemed one might goe over their backs dri-shod'. The indefatigable John Smith had grasped the importance of this when he first explored the coastline. 'Let not the meanness of the word Fish distaste you,' he later wrote, 'for it will afford as good gold as the mines of Guiana or Tumbatu, with less hazard and charge, and more certainty and facility.' This was a very different reason for crossing the Atlantic: not God but cod. The weather-beaten gravestones at Marblehead on the Massachusetts coast testify to the existence of a British settlement there from as early as 1628. But the town had no church and no preacher until 1684, over sixty years after the Pilgrims founded Plymouth. By this time the fishing industry was well established, exporting hundreds of thousands of barrels of cod every year. The Pilgrims might have come to the New World to escape from Popery. But the 'main end' of the men of Marblehead 'was to catch fish'.

This, then, was the combination that made New England flourish: Puritanism plus the profit motive. It was a combination institutionalized by the Massachusetts Bay Company, founded in

1629, whose Governor John Winthrop cheerfully united in his person Congregationalism and capitalism. By 1640 Massachusetts was booming, thanks not just to fish but also to fur and farming. Already some 20,000 people had settled there, far more than were living by that time around the Chesapeake Bay. The population of Boston trebled in just thirty years.

There was one other crucial ingredient, however: procreation. Unlike European colonists further south, the New Englanders very quickly began to reproduce themselves, quadrupling their numbers between 1650 and 1700. Indeed, theirs was probably the highest birth rate in the world. In Britain, only around three-quarters of people actually married; in the American colonies it was nine out of ten and the age of colonial women at marriage was also significantly lower – hence their fertility was higher. Here was one of the key differences between British America and Latin America. Spanish settlers tended to be solo male *encomanderos*. Only around a quarter of the total of 1.5 million Spanish and Portuguese migrants to pre-independence Latin America were female; the majority of male Iberian migrants therefore took their sexual partners from the (dwindling) indigenous or the (rapidly growing) slave population. The result within a few generations was a substantial mixed-race population of *mestizos* and *mulattos* (Hispanic and African).* British settlers in North America were not only much more numerous; they were encouraged to bring their wives and children with them, thus preserving their culture more or less intact. In North America as in Northern Ireland, therefore, British colonization was a family affair. As a consequence, New England really was a new England, far more than New Spain would ever be a new Spain.

As in Ulster, so in the New World plantations meant planting – not just people but crops. And planting crops meant tilling the land. The question was, whose land was it?

---

* In 1800 only 3.5 million out of 13.5 million people in Latin America were white, of whom 30,000 were Spanish-born *peninsulares*. The other whites were American-born creoles. By 1820 around a quarter of the population of Latin America were of mixed ethnic origin.

The colonists could hardly pretend nobody had been living here before their arrival. In Virginia alone there were between 10,000 and 20,000 Algonquian Indians; Jamestown was in the heart of Powhatan territory. At first, it is true, there seemed to be a chance of peaceful coexistence based on trade and even intermarriage. The Powhatan chief Wahunsonacock was prevailed upon to kneel and be crowned by John Smith 'as vassal to his majesty', King James. The chief's daughter Pocahontas was the first native American to marry an Englishman: John Rolfe, who had pioneered the cultivation of tobacco. But it was an example few were to follow. When Sir Thomas Dale sought to marry Wahunsonacock's youngest daughter 'because being now one people and he desirous for ever to dwell in his [Wahunsonacock's] country he conceived there could not be a truer assistance of peace and friendship than in such a natural bond of united union', his advances were rebuffed. Wahunsonacock by now suspected that here was a design 'to invade my people, and possesse my Country'. He was right.

In his pamphlet 'A Good Speed to Virginia', the Chaplain to the Virginia Company Robert Gray asked: 'By what right or warrant can we enter into the land of these Savages, take away their rightful inheritance from them, and plant ourselves in their place, being unwronged or unprovoked by them?' Richard Hakluyt's answer was that the native Americans were a people 'crying out to us . . . to come and help' them. The seal of the Massachusetts Bay Company (1629) even had an Indian waving a banner which read 'Come over and Help Us'. But the reality was that the British intended to help themselves. As Sir Francis Wyatt, Governor of Virginia, put it: 'Our first worke is expulsion of the Savages to gaine the free range of the countrey for encrease of Cattle, swine &c which will more than restore us, for it is infinitely better to have no heathen among us.' In order to justify the expropriation of indigenous populations, the British colonists came up with a distinctive rationalization, the convenient idea of 'terra nullius', nobody's land. In the words of the great political philosopher John Locke (who was also Secretary to the Lords Proprietors of Carolina), a man only owned land when he had 'mixed his *Labour* with [it] and joyned it to something that is his own'. Put simply, if land was not already being fenced and farmed then it was up for grabs. According to John Winthrop:

... the Natives in New England they enclose noe land neither have any settled habitation nor any tame cattle to improve the land by & soe have noe other but a naturall right to those countries Soe as if wee leave them sufficient for their use wee may lawfully take the rest, there being more than enough for them & us.

The native Americans were tolerated when they were able to fit in to the emerging British economic order. The Hudson's Bay Company in Canada was happy to rely on Cree Indian hunters and trappers to supply its fur traders with beaver pelts and Caribou skins. The Narragansetts were also treated with respect because they produced the wampum beads – made from purple and white whelk shells on the shores of Long Island Sound – which functioned as the earliest North American currency. But where the Indians claimed the ownership of agriculturally valuable land, coexistence was simply ruled out. If the Indians resisted expropriation, then they could and should (in Locke's words) 'be destroyed as a *Lyon* or a *Tyger*, one of those wild Savage Beasts, with whom Men can have no Society or Security'.

As early as 1642 Miantonomo, a chief of the Narragansett tribe of Rhode Island, could see the writing on the wall for his people:

[Y]ou know our fathers had plenty of deer and skins, our plains were full of deer, as also our woods, and of turkies, and our coves full of fish and foul. But these English having gotten our land, they with scythes cut down the grass, and with axes fell the trees; their cows and horses eat the grass, and their hogs spoil our clam banks, and we shall all be starved.

What had already happened in Central America now repeated itself along the North Atlantic seaboard. In 1500, in what was to become British North America, there had been roughly 560,000 American Indians. By 1700 the number had more than halved. This was just the beginning of a drastic decline that was to affect the entire North American continent as the area of white settlement spread westwards. There were probably around 2 million indigenous people in the territory of the modern United States in 1500. By 1700 the number was 750,000. By 1820 there were just 325,000.

Short but bloody wars with the better-armed settlers took their toll. After the Powhatan attacked Jamestown in 1622, the colonists' views hardened. As Sir Edward Coke saw it, the Indians could only be *perpetui enimici*, 'perpetual enemies ... for between them, as with devils, whose subjects they be, and the Christians there is perpetual hostility, and can be no peace.' Massacres were the order of the day: of the Powhatan in 1623 and 1644, of the Pequots in 1637, of the Doegs and Susquehannocks in 1675, of the Wampanoag in 1676–7. But what really did for the native Americans were the infectious diseases the white settlers brought with them from across the sea: smallpox, influenza, diphtheria. Like the rats of the medieval Black Death, the white men were the carriers of the fatal germs.

For the settlers, on the other hand, the devastating impact of smallpox furnished proof that God was on the colonists' side, conveniently killing off the previous tenants of this new world. One of the things the Pilgrims gave thanks for at Plymouth at the end of 1621 was the fact that 90 per cent of the indigenous peoples of New England had died of disease in the decade before their arrival, having first – very considerately – tilled the land and buried stores of corn for the winter. In the words of John Archdale, Governor of Carolina in the 1690s, 'the Hand of God [has been] eminently seen in thinning the *Indians*, to make room for the *English*'.

The near-disappearance of the original proprietors did not mean that land in colonial America belonged to nobody, however. It belonged to the King, and he could then grant these newly acquired parts of the royal demesne to meritorious subjects. As the viability of the American colonies became apparent, this quickly became a new source of patronage for the Stuart monarchs: colonization and cronyism went hand in hand. This had important implications for the social structure of the nascent British America. In 1632, for example, Charles I granted Maryland to the heirs of Lord Baltimore, modelling the charter on the palatine charters granted to the Bishops of Durham in the fourteenth century, and entitling the 'Lords Proprietors' to create titles and grant land on an essentially feudal basis. In giving Carolina to eight of his close associates, Charles II devised an even more explicitly hierarchical social order, with 'land-graves' and 'cassiques' owning estates of, respectively, 48,000 and 24,000 acres, and governing the colony through a purely aristo-cratic Grand Council. New York acquired its name when, following its capture from the Dutch in 1664, Charles gave it to his brother James, Duke of York.

In much the same way, it was to settle a debt of £16,000 to one of his supporters – William Penn, the admiral who had captured Jamaica – that Charles II granted Penn's son ownership of what became Pennsylvania. Overnight, this made William Penn junior the largest individual landowner in British history, with an estate well over the size of Ireland. It also gave him the opportunity to show what the combination of religious fervour and the profit motive could achieve. Like the Pilgrim Fathers, Penn was a member of a radical religious sect: since 1667 he had been a Quaker, and had even been imprisoned in the Tower of London on account of his faith. But unlike the Plymouth colonists, Penn's 'Holy Experi-ment' was to create a 'tolerance settlement' not just for Quakers but for any religious sect (provided it was monotheistic). In Octo-ber 1682 his ship, the *Welcome*, sailed up the Delaware River and, clutching his royal charter, he stepped ashore to found the city of Philadelphia, the Ancient Greek word for 'brotherly love'.

Penn understood that if his colony was to succeed it would have to be profitable. As he put it candidly: 'Though I desire to extend religious freedom yet I want some recompense for my trouble.' To that end, he became a real estate salesman on a grand scale, selling off huge tracts of land at knockdown prices: £100 bought 5,000 acres. Penn was also a visionary town planner, who wanted his capital to be the antithesis of overcrowded, fire-prone London; hence the now familiar American grid system of streets. Above all, he was a marketing man who knew that even the American dream had to be sold. Not content with encouraging English, Welsh and Irish settlers, he promoted emigration from continental Europe by having his prospectuses translated into German and other languages. It worked: between 1689 and 1815 well over a million continental Europeans moved to mainland North America and the British West Indies, mainly Germans and Swiss. The combination of religious tolerance and cheap land was a powerful lure for settler families. This was real freedom: freedom of conscience – and almost free real estate.*

But there was a catch. Not everyone in this new white Empire could be a landowner. There had to be some workers too, particularly where labour-intensive crops like sugar, tobacco and rice were being grown. The question was how to get them across the Atlantic? And here the British Empire discovered the limits of liberty.

Black and White

The scale of seventeenth- and eighteenth-century migration from the British Isles was unmatched by any other European country. From England alone, total net emigration between 1601 and 1701 exceeded 700,000. At its peak in the 1640s and 1650s – not coincidentally the period of the English Civil War – the annual emigration rate was above 0.2 per thousand (around the same rate currently experienced by Venezuela).

As we have seen, the first British emigrants to America had been drawn by the prospect of freedom of conscience and cheap land. But the attractions of emigration were rather different to those with only their labour to sell. For them, it had little to do with liberty. On the contrary, it meant consciously giving up their liberty. Few such migrants crossed the ocean using their own resources. Most travelled under a system of temporary servitude, known as 'indenture', which was designed to alleviate the chronic labour shortage. In return for the price of their voyage out, they would enter a contract

---

* A further inducement to attract entrepreneurial emigrants to America was the founding of Georgia in 1732 as an asylum for debtors.

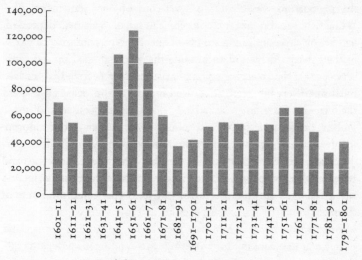

English net emigration, 1601–1801.

pledging their labour for a set number of years, usually four or five. In effect they became slaves, but slaves on fixed-term contracts. This they may not have realized on leaving England. When she arrives as a planter's bride in Virginia, Daniel Defoe's Moll Flanders needs to have it explained to her by her mother (and mother-in-law) that:

the greatest part of the Inhabitants of the Colony came thither in very different Circumstances from England; that, generally speaking, they were of two sorts, either (1) such as were brought over by Masters of Ships to be sold as Servants, such as we call them, my Dear, says she, but they are more properly call'd slaves. Or (2) Such as are Transported from Newgate and other Prisons, after having been found guilty of Felony and other Crimes punishable with Death. When they come here, says she, we make no difference: the Planters buy them, and they work together in the Field till their time is out . . .

Between a half and two-thirds of all Europeans who migrated to North America between 1650 and 1780 did so under contracts of indentured servitude; for English emigrants to the Chesapeake the proportion was closer to seven out of ten. Settlements like Williamsburg, the elegant colonial capital of Virginia, depended heavily on this continuing supply of cheap labour, not only to work in the tobacco fields but to provide the whole range of goods and services that the emerging colonial aristocracy expected. Like slaves, indentured servants were advertised for sale in the local newspaper, the *Virginia Gazette*: 'Just arrived . . . 139 men, women and boys. Smiths, bricklayers, plasterers, shoemakers . . . a glazier, a tailor, a printer, a book binder . . . several seamstresses . . .'

Although the majority of indentured servants were young men between the ages of fifteen and twenty-one, one rather older indentured labourer was the forty-year-old John Harrower, who kept a simple journal of his experiences to give his wife when he could afford to have her join him. For months Harrower had roamed his native country, looking for work to try to support his wife and children, but in vain. His diary entry for Wednesday, 26 January 1774, explains in a nutshell what was really driving British migration by the late eighteenth century: 'This day I being reduced to the last shilling I hade was oblidged to engage to go to Virginia for four years as a schoolmaster for Bedd, Board, washing and five pound during the whole time.' This was anything but a bid for freedom; it was quite simply a last resort. Harrower goes on to describe the horrific conditions below deck when his ship, the *Planter*, encountered a fierce Atlantic storm:

At 8 pm was obliged to batten down both fore and main hatches, and a little after I really think there was the odest shene betwixt decks that ever I heard or seed. There was some sleeping, some spewing, some pishing, some shiting, some farting, some flyting, some damning, some Blasting their leggs and thighs, some their liver, lungs, lights and eyes. And for to make the shene the odder, some curs'd Father Mother, Sister, and Brother.

To underline the full extent of their loss of liberty, the passengers were whipped or clapped in irons if they misbehaved. When Harrower finally landed in Virginia after more than two gruelling months at sea his basic literacy proved an asset. He was taken on as tutor to the children of a local plantation owner. Unfortunately, this was as far as his luck went. In 1777, after just three years away from home, he took ill and died, before he could pay for his wife and children to join him.

Harrower's experience was typical in two respects. As a Scot, he was typical of the second wave of migrants to the American colonies after 1700: the Scots and the Irish accounted for nearly three-quarters of all British settlers in the eighteenth century. It was men from the impoverished fringes of the British Isles who had least to lose and most to gain from selling themselves into servitude. When Johnson and Boswell journeyed through the Highlands and Islands in 1773 they repeatedly saw signs of what the latter disapprovingly called 'this epidemical fury of emigration'. Johnson took a more realistic view.

Mr Arthur Lee mentioned some Scotch who had taken possession of a barren part of America, and wondered why they should choose it. Johnson. 'Why, Sir, all barrenness is comparative. The Scotch would not know it to be barren.' Boswell. 'Come, come, he is flattering the English. You have now been in Scotland, Sir, and say if you did not see meat and drink enough there.' Johnson. 'Why yes, Sir; meat and drink enough to give the inhabitants sufficient strength to run away from home.'

Neither man grasped that what was really 'clearing' men and women from their homes in such numbers was the combination of 'improving' – that is, rack-renting – landlords and a succession of dismal harvests. The Irish were even more likely to be attracted by the prospect of 'happier climes, and less arbitrary government'. Two-fifths of all British emigrants between 1701 and 1780 were Irish, and the migration rate only increased in the succeeding century as the introduction of the potato from America and exponential population growth led the island towards the calamities of the 1840s. This flight from the periphery gave the British Empire its enduringly Celtic tinge.*

---

* By the end of the nineteenth century around three-quarters of the population of Great Britain lived in England, compared with a tenth in Scotland and a tenth in Ireland. But in the Empire the English accounted for barely half of colonists. Scots constituted around 23 per cent of the British-born population in New Zealand, 21

Harrower's premature demise was also far from unusual. Around two in five of the new arrivals died in their first couple of years in Virginia, usually because of malarial or intestinal disorders. Surviving such ailments was the process known euphemistically as 'seasoning'. Those who pulled through were often distinguished by their sickly complexions.

Provided the supply was maintained, indentured labour could work in Virginia, where the climate was bearable and the main crop relatively easy to harvest. But in Britain's Caribbean colonies it simply did not suffice. It is often forgotten that the majority – around 69 per cent – of British emigrants in the seventeenth century went not to America but to the West Indies. That, after all, was where the money was. Trade with the Caribbean dwarfed trade with America: in 1773 the value of British imports from Jamaica was five times greater than those from all the American colonies. Nevis produced three times more British imports than New York between 1714 and 1773, Antigua three times more than New England. Sugar, not tobacco, was the biggest business of the eighteenth-century colonial empire. In 1775 total sugar imports accounted for nearly a fifth of all British imports and were worth more than five times tobacco imports. For most of the eighteenth century, the American colonies were little more than economic subsidiaries of the sugar islands, supplying them with the basic foodstuffs their monoculture could not produce. Given the choice between expanding British territory in America and retaining the French sugar island of Guadeloupe at the end of the Seven Years War, William Pitt favoured the Caribbean option since: 'The state of the existing trade in the conquests in North America, is extremely low; the speculations of their future are precarious, and the prospect, at the very best, very remote.'

The problem was that mortality on these tropical islands was fearful, particularly during the summer 'sickly season'. In Virginia it took a total immigration of 116,000 to produce a settler com-

---

per cent in Canada and 15 per cent in Australia. The Irish constituted 21 per cent of the British-born in Canada and New Zealand, and fully 27 per cent in Australia.

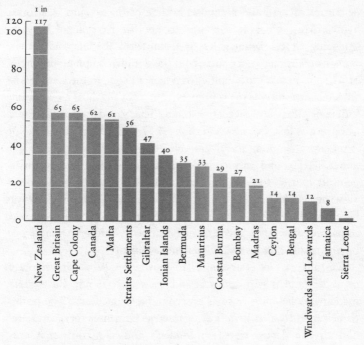

Chances of dying in different parts of the British Empire: mortality among British soldiers *c.* 1817–1838.

munity of 90,000. In Barbados, by contrast, it took immigration of 150,000 to produce a population of 20,000. People soon learned. After 1700 emigration to the Caribbean slumped as people opted for the more temperate climes (and more plentiful land) of America. As early as 1675 the Assembly of Barbados was driven to complain: 'In former tymes Wee were plentifully furnished with Christian servants from England . . . but now Wee can gett few English, having noe lands to give them at the end of their tyme, which formerly was theire main allurement.' There had to be an alternative to indentured labour. There was.

From 1764 until 1779, the parish of St Peter's and St Paul's in Olney, Northamptonshire, was in the care of John Newton, a devout clergyman and composer of one of the world's best-loved hymns. Most of us at one time or another have heard or sung 'Amazing Grace'. What is less well known is the fact that for six years its composer was a successful slave trader, shipping hundreds of Africans across the Atlantic from Sierra Leone to the Caribbean.

'Amazing Grace' is the supreme hymn of Evangelical redemption: 'Amazing Grace how sweet the sound / That saved a wretch like me! / I once was lost, but now am found, / Was blind but now I see.' It is therefore tempting to imagine Newton suddenly seeing the light about slavery and turning away from his wicked profession to dedicate himself to God. But the timing of Newton's conversion is all wrong. In fact, it was after his religious awakening that Newton became the first mate and then the captain of a succession of slave ships, and only much later that he began to question the morality of buying and selling his fellow men and women.

We today are of course repelled by slavery. What we find hard to understand is why someone like Newton was not. But slavery made overwhelming sense as an economic proposition. The profits to be made from cultivating sugar were immense; the Portuguese had already demonstrated in Madeira and São Tomé that only African slaves could stand the work; and the Caribbean planters were willing to pay roughly eight or nine times what a slave cost on the West African coast. Although the business was risky (Newton called it a sort of lottery in which every adventurer hoped to gain a prize), it was lucrative. Annual returns from slaving voyages during the last half century of British slaving averaged between 8 and 10 per cent. Small wonder that slave-trading struck Newton as a 'genteel occupation', suitable even for a born-again Christian.

The numbers involved were huge. We tend to think of the British Empire as a phenomenon of white migration, yet between 1662 and 1807 nearly three and a half million Africans came to the New World as slaves transported in British ships. That was over three times the number of white migrants in the same period. It was also more than a third of all Africans who ever crossed the Atlantic as slaves. At first the British had pretended to be above slavery. When one early merchant was offered slaves in the Gambia, he replied:

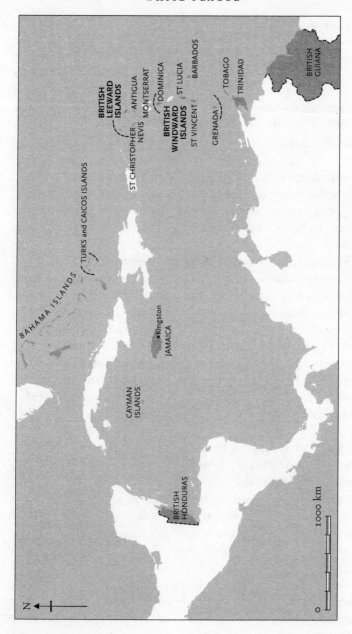

The British Caribbean, 1815

'We are a people who did not deale in any such commodities, neither did wee buy or sell one another, or any that had our owne shape.' But it was not long before slaves from Nigeria and Benin began to be sent to the Barbados sugar plantations. In 1662 the New Royal African Company undertook to supply 3,000 slaves annually to the West Indies, a number which had risen to 5,600 by 1672. After the company's monopoly was done away with in 1698, the number of private slave traders – men like Newton – soared. By 1740 Liverpool was sending thirty-three ships a year on the triangular trip from England to Africa to the Caribbean. This was the same year that James Thomson's song 'Rule Britannia' was sung, with its stirring avowal: 'Britons never, never shall be slaves.' Long since forgotten was the earlier prohibition on buying them.

Newton's involvement with slavery began in late 1745 when, as a young sailor, he entered the service of a trader named Amos Clow who was based on the Benanoes Islands, off Sierra Leone. By a curious inversion he soon found himself being treated as little more than a slave by Clow's African concubine. After more than a year of sickness and neglect, Newton was rescued by a ship called the *Greyhound*; and it was aboard this vessel, during a storm in March 1748, that the young man had his religious awakening. Only after that did he himself become a slave trader, taking command of his first slave ship while he was still only in his twenties.

John Newton's journal for 1750–51, when he was in command of the slave ship *Duke of Argyle*, lays bare the attitudes of those who lived and profited by the trade in human lives. Sailing up and down the coast of Sierra Leone and beyond, Newton spent long weeks bartering goods (including 'the all commanding articles of beer and cyder') for people, haggling over the price and the quality with the local slave traders. He was a choosy buyer, avoiding old 'fallen breasted' women. On 7 January 1751 he exchanged eight slaves for a quantity of timber and ivory, but felt overcharged when he noticed that one of them had 'a very bad mouth'. 'A fine manslave, now there are so many competitors,' he complained, 'is near double the

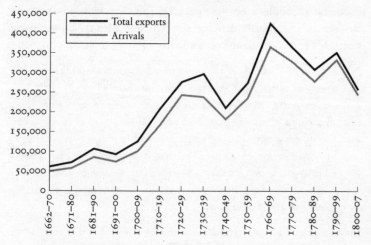

Slave exports from Africa and arrivals in America in British and colonial ships, 1662–1807.

price it was formerly.' Note the word 'it'. He recorded on the same day the death of 'a fine woman slave, No. 11'. But if the Africans were just numbers to Newton, to the Africans Newton seemed a diabolical figure, even a cannibal. Olaudah Equiano was one of the few Africans transported to the British West Indies who left an account of his experience. In it, he testifies to the widespread suspicion that the white (or 'red') people were followers of *Mwene Puto*, the 'Lord of the Dead', seizing slaves in order to eat them. Some of his fellow captives were convinced that the red wine they saw their captors quaffing was made from the blood of Africans and that the cheese on the captain's table was made from their brains. Similar fears clearly actuated the slaves in Newton's hold, who put 'their country fetishes' in one of the ship's water casks, 'which they had the credulity to suppose must inevitably kill all who drank of it'.

By May 1751, when Newton set sail for Antigua, his ship had more Africans aboard than Britons: 174 slaves and less than thirty crew, seven having by now succumbed to disease. This was the time of greatest danger for a slaver, not just because of the risk of an outbreak of cholera or dysentery on the overcrowded ship, but because of the danger that the slaves might mutiny. Newton was rewarded for his vigilance on 26 May:

In the evening, by the favour of Providence, discovered a conspiracy among the men slaves to rise upon us, but a few hours before it was to have been executed. A young man ... who has been the whole voyage out of irons, first on account of a large ulcer, and since for his seemingly good behaviour, gave them a large marline spike down the gratings, but was happily seen by one of the people [crew]. They had it in possession about an hour before I mad [sic] search for it, in which time they made such good dispatch (being an instrument that made no noise) that this morning I've found near 20 of them had broke their irons.

He had a similar experience on a voyage the following year, when a group of eight slaves were found in possession of 'some knives, stones, shot, etc., and a cold chissel'. The offenders were punished with neck yokes and thumbscrews.

Given the conditions aboard slave ships like the *Argyle* – the over-crowding, poor hygiene, lack of exercise and inadequate diet – it is hardly surprising that, on average, one in seven slaves died during the Atlantic crossing.* What is surprising is that a man like Newton, who held religious services for his crew and refused even to talk about business on Sundays, should have been able to do such business with so few qualms. But in a letter to his wife on 26 January 1753 Newton set out a fascinating apologia.

The three greatest blessings of which human nature is capable, are, undoubtedly, religion, liberty, and love. In each of these how highly has God distinguished me! But here are whole nations around me, whose languages are entirely different from each other, yet I believe they all agree in

---

* This was the average mortality rate for the entire period of the British slave trade, 1662–1807. The rate was closer to one in four in the early decades. As Newton's account makes clear, the slaves were kept permanently chained up, lying on ledges barely two and a half feet high 'like books on a shelf'. However, the death rate among the crews of slave ships was even higher – around 17 per cent in the second half of the eighteenth century. Hence the sailor's rhyme, 'Beware and take care / Of the Bight of Benin: / For one that comes out / There are forty go in.'

this, that they have no words among them expressive of these engaging ideas: from whence I infer, that the ideas themselves have no place in their minds. And as there is no medium between light and darkness, these poor creatures are not only strangers to the advantages which I enjoy, but are plunged in all the contrary evils. Instead of the present blessings, and bright future prospects of Christianity, they are deceived and harassed by necromancy, magic, and all the train of superstitions that fear, combined with ignorance, can produce in the human mind. *The only liberty of which they have any notion, is an exemption from being sold* [my emphasis]; and even from this very few are perfectly secure that it shall not, some time or other, be their lot: for it often happens, that a man who sells another on board a ship, is himself bought and sold in the same manner, and perhaps in the same vessel, before the week is ended. As for love, there may be some softer souls among them than I have met with; but for the most part, when I have tried to explain this delightful word, I have seldom been in the least understood.

How could one regard oneself as depriving Africans of liberty, when they had no conception of it beyond 'an exemption from being sold'?

Newton's attitudes were far from exceptional. According to the Jamaican planter Edward Long, Africans were 'devoid of genius, and seem almost incapable of making any progress in civility or science. They have no plan or system of morality among them . . . they have no moral sensations.' They were, he concluded, simply an inferior species. James Boswell, so quick to speak up for liberty in other cases, flatly denied that 'negroes are oppress'd' since 'Africk's sons were always slaves'.

As Newton's journal makes clear, slavery had to be imposed by force from the moment the ships set sail. It continued to be imposed by force when the slaves were unloaded and sold. In Jamaica, one of the markets Newton supplied, white men were outnumbered ten to one by those they had enslaved. In British Guiana the ratio was twenty to one. Without the threat of violence, it is hard to believe that the system could long have been sustained. The instruments of torture devised to discipline the slaves of the Caribbean – like the spiked shackles which made running impossible, or the neck irons on which weights could be hung as punishment – are stark reminders that Jamaica was the front line of eighteenth-century British colonialism.

To be sure, James Grainger's poem 'The Sugar Cane', published in 1764, makes the creole planter's life sound lyrical, if rather trying:

> What soil the Cane affects: what care demands;
> Beneath what signs to plant; what ills await;
> How the hot nectar best to christallize;
> And Africa's sable progeny to treat.

But it was 'Africa's progeny' who suffered for the sake of the British sweet tooth. Not only did they have to sow, tend and harvest the sugar cane; they also had to crush the juice from the cane and immediately boil it in huge vats. The original Spanish word for a sugar plantation was *ingenio* – engine – and producing sugar from cane was as much industry as agriculture. But this was an industry in which not just sugar cane but human beings were the raw materials. By 1750 some 800,000 Africans had been shipped to the British Caribbean, but the death rate was so high and the reproduction rate so low that the slave population was still less than 300,000. One contemporary rule of thumb devised by the Barbados planter Edward Littleton was that a planter with a hundred slaves would need to buy eight or ten a year 'to keep up his stock'. *The Speech of Mr John Talbot Campo-bell* (1736), a pro-slavery pamphlet by a clergyman in Nevis, explicitly acknowledged that 'by the common Computation, about two Fifths of the new-imported Negroes die in the Seasoning'.

Nor should we forget that there was another dimension to the exploitation of Africans in the slave colonies – namely their sexual exploitation. When Edward Long arrived in Jamaica in 1757, he was dismayed to find that his fellow-planters routinely took sexual partners from among their slaves: 'Many are the men, of every rank, quality and degree here, who would much rather riot in these goatish embraces, than share the pure and lawful bliss derived from matrimonial, mutual love.' This practice was known as 'nutmegging', but as Long's diatribe against it suggests, there was growing disapproval of what later became stigmatized as 'miscegenation'.* Significantly, one of the most frequently told stories of the era was that of Inkle and Yarico, which describes an affair between a shipwrecked sailor and a negro virgin:

> Whilst thus in fruitless grief he spent the day,
> A Negro Virgin chanc'd to pass that way;
> He view'd her naked beauties with surprise,
> Her well proportion'd limbs and sprightly eyes!

Having had his fill of nutmegging, however, Inkle loses little time in selling the hapless Yarico into slavery.

Nevertheless, it would be wrong to portray the Africans sold into slavery exclusively as passive victims. For there were many slaves who fought back against their white oppressors. Rebellions were almost as frequent as hurricanes in Jamaica. By one count, there were as many as twenty-eight between the British acquisition of the island and the abolition of slavery. Morever, there was always a part of the black population that was beyond British control: the Maroons.

When William Penn's father captured Jamaica from Spain in 1655, there was already a well-established community of rogue slaves who had escaped from their Spanish masters, living in mountain hideouts. They were known as 'Maroons', a corruption of the Spanish *cimarron* (wild or untamed). Today you can still savour Maroon culture and its culinary gift to the world, jerk pork, at the annual Maroon festival in Accompong. (The town itself takes its name from one of the brothers of the great Maroon leader Captain Cudjoe.) You only need to hear their singing and watch their dancing to see that the Maroons have managed to preserve a substantial part of their ancestral African culture, despite their enforced

---

* In Virginia it was enacted in 1662 that the mulatto children of slave women should themselves be slaves; in 1705 interracial marriage was prohibited.

exile. In one respect only did they bear the imprint of captivity. Although many were originally Akan-speakers from Ghana, Cudjoe insisted that all his followers spoke in English. The reason for this was eminently practical. The Maroons not only wished to avoid being returned to slavery by Jamaica's new British rulers; they also wished to swell their own ranks by liberating newly arrived slaves. (As polygamists, the Maroons were especially keen to free female slaves.) Since the slavers shipped people across the Atlantic from myriads of different tribes, their integration into the Maroon community required the retention of English as a common language.

Led by Cudjoe and inspired by the matriarchal and magical figure of Queen Nanny, the Maroons waged a guerrilla war against the plantation economy. Planters came to dread the distant sound of the *abeng*, the conch shell that signalled the coming of the Maroon raiders. In 1728, for example, George Manning purchased twenty-six slaves for his estate. By the end of the year, almost entirely as the result of Maroon raids, only four remained. Colonel Thomas Brooks was forced by the Maroons to quit his estate in St George altogether. Surviving Jamaican place names like 'the District of Don't Look Behind' testify to the paranoia the Maroons engendered. In desperation, the British called in a force of Miskito Indians from the coast of Honduras to try to counter them. Regular troops were summoned from Gibraltar. Finally, in 1732, the British managed to land a punch with the capture of the Maroons' main settlement, Nanny Town. But the Maroons just melted away into the hills to fight again another day; while the troops from Gibraltar succumbed, predictably, to disease and drink. By the end of 1732, as one Jamaica assemblyman lamented,

The insecurity of our country occasioned by our slaves in Rebellion against us whose insolence is grown so great that we cannot say we are sure of another day and Robbings and Murders so common in our capital Roads, that it is with the utmost hazard we Travel them.

In the end, there was no option but to do a deal. In 1739 a treaty was signed which effectively granted the Maroons autonomy in an area of around 1,500 acres; in return, they agreed not only to stop freeing slaves but also to return runaway slaves to their masters – in return for a reward. It was an early example of the way the British Empire often worked: if the British couldn't beat you, they got you to join them. To be sure, the deal did not put a stop to slave rebellions; on the contrary, it meant that dissatisfied slaves had no option but to rebel, since the escape route to Nanny Town had effectively been closed. There was a spate of slave revolts in the 1760s, at least initially inspired by the Maroons' example. But from now on the Maroons could more or less be relied upon to side with the British against rebel slaves. Indeed, the Maroons themselves became slave owners. It might not be possible to beat them. It was possible to buy them off.

By 1770, then, Britain's Atlantic empire seemed to have found a natural equilibrium. The triangular trade between Britain, West Africa and the Caribbean kept the plantations supplied with labour. The mainland American colonies kept them supplied with victuals. Sugar and tobacco streamed back to Britain, a substantial proportion for re-export to the Continent. And the profits from these New World commodities oiled the wheels of the Empire's Asian commerce. Yet the Maroons were a reminder – troubling to the planters, inspiring to their human chattels – that slaves, upon whose scarred backs the entire imperial edifice seemed to rest, had the capacity to free themselves. Later, in the 1790s, the successful slave revolt on the French colony of St Domingue prompted a crackdown on the Maroons by the then Lieutenant-Governor of Jamaica, Lord Balcarres, which culminated in the expulsion of nearly 600 of the Trelawny town Maroons.* But by the time this happened, the Maroons were the least of the Empire's worries. The slaves of St Domingue had joined forces with disgruntled mulattos and in 1804 established Haiti as an independent republic. But Haiti was not the first New World colony to proclaim its independence. Less than thirty years before, a very different kind of republic had

---

* First to Nova Scotia, then to Sierra Leone.

been proclaimed on the American mainland. And here the challenge to imperial rule took the form not of desperate slaves but of prosperous white colonists.

Civil War

It was the moment when the British ideal of liberty bit back. It was the moment when the British Empire began to tear itself apart. On the village green of Lexington, Massachusetts, British redcoats exchanged fire for the first time with armed American colonists. It was 19 April 1775.

The soldiers had been sent to Concord to confiscate an arms cache belonging to colonial militias whose loyalty the authorities had come to doubt. But the militias were forewarned by Paul Revere, who rode ahead shouting not 'The British are coming!' – they were all still British at this point – but 'The regulars are out!' At Lexington, seventy-seven Minute Men, so-called because they were said to be 'ready in a minute', came out to halt the British advance, forming up on the village green. It is not clear who fired the first shot, but the outcome was never in doubt: the Minute Men were mown down by the well-drilled regulars.

The citizens of Lexington still celebrate the martyrdom of the Minute Men every year with a meticulous re-enactment of the skirmish. It's a good-natured, early-morning celebration of American national identity, a chance to eat muffins and coffee al fresco on a crisp spring morning. But to the British observer – who can hardly be unmoved by the sound of the fifes and drums playing 'Men of Harlech' as the redcoats march on and off the scene – Patriots' Day at Lexington is perplexing. Why did this one-sided encounter not mark the abrupt end of an obscure New England rebellion? The answer is, first, that the colonists' resistance stiffened as the regulars advanced towards Concord; secondly, that the officer in charge of the regulars, the corpulent and indecisive Colonel Francis Smith, all but lost control of his men after himself being hit in the leg. As his force retreated towards Boston, they were decimated by sniper fire. The American War of Independence had begun.

The war is at the very heart of Americans' conception of themselves: the idea of a struggle for liberty against an evil empire is the country's creation myth. But it is the great paradox of the American Revolution – and it strikes you forcefully when you see today's prosperous Lexingtonians trying to relive their forefathers' self-sacrifice – that the ones who revolted against British rule were the best-off of all Britain's colonial subjects. There is good reason to think that, by the 1770s, New Englanders were about the wealthiest people in the world. Per capita income was at least equal to that in the United Kingdom and was more evenly distributed. The New Englanders had bigger farms, bigger families and better education than the Old Englanders back home. And, crucially, they paid far less tax. In 1763 the average Briton paid 26 shillings a year in taxes. The equivalent figure for a Massachusetts taxpayer was just one shilling. To say that being British subjects had been good for these people would be an understatement. And yet it was they, not the indentured labourers of Virginia or the slaves of Jamaica, who first threw off the yoke of imperial authority.

To British eyes, Lexington Green seems the ideal setting not for internecine war but for a game of cricket. It is not a trivial detail of colonial history that Americans once played that most English of games. In 1751, for example, the *New York Gazette and Weekly Post Boy* reported:

Last Monday afternoon (May 1st) a match at cricket was played on our common for a considerable wager between eleven Londoners against eleven New Yorkers. The game was played according to the London method ...

The New Yorkers won by 87 runs. In the light of that result, the question is not an easy one to answer: why did the Americans give up cricket?

Just twenty years before the 'battle' of Lexington, the American settlers had proved their loyalty to the British Empire by turning out in tens of thousands to fight against the French and the Indian allies in the Seven Years War. Indeed, the first shot of that war had been fired by a young colonist named George Washington. In 1760 Benjamin Franklin had written an anonymous pamphlet in which he predicted that rapid population growth in America would

in a century more, make the number of British subjects on that side of the water more numerous than they now are on this;* but I am far from entertaining on that account, any fears of their becoming either useless or dangerous ... and I look on those fears, to be merely imaginary and without any probable foundation.

What went wrong?

Schoolchildren and tourists are still taught the story of the American Revolution primarily in terms of economic burdens. In London, the argument runs, the government wanted some recompense for the cost of expelling the French from North America in the Seven Years War, and of maintaining a 10,000-strong standing army to police the disgruntled Indians beyond the Appalachian mountains, who had tended to side with the French. The upshot was new taxes. On close inspection, however, the real story is one of taxes repealed, not taxes imposed.

In 1765 Parliament passed the Stamp Act, which meant that everything from newspapers to playing cards had to be printed on specially stamped – and hence taxed – paper. The projected revenue was not immense: £110,000, nearly half of it coming from the West Indies. But the tax proved so unpopular that the minister who introduced it, George Grenville, was forced to resign and by March the following year it had been scrapped. From now on, it was accepted, the Empire would tax only external trade, not internal transactions. Two years later, a new Chancellor of the Exchequer, Charles Townshend, tried again, this time with a range of new customs duties. In the hope of sweetening the pill, the duty on one of the most popular articles of colonial consumption, tea, was actually cut from one shilling to threepence per pound. It was no good.

* This was not an unrealistic projection. In 1700 the population of British North America had been around 265,000, by 1750 it was 1.2 million and by 1770 2.3 million – more than the population of Scotland.

Samuel Adams drafted a circular for the Massachusetts Assembly calling for resistance even to these taxes. In January 1770 a new government in Britain, under the famously unprepossessing Lord North,* lifted all the new duties except the one on tea. Still the protests in Boston continued.

Everyone has heard of the 'Boston Tea Party' of 16 December 1773, in which 342 boxes of tea worth £10,000 were tipped from the East India tea ship *Dartmouth* into the murky waters of Boston harbour. But most people assume it was a protest against a hike in the tax on tea. In fact the price of the tea in question was exceptionally low, since the British government had just given the East India Company a rebate of the much higher duty the tea had incurred on entering Britain.† In effect, the tea left Britain duty free and had to pay only the much lower American duty on arriving in Boston. Tea had never been cheaper in New England. The 'Party' was organized not by irate consumers but by Boston's wealthy smugglers, who stood to lose out. Contemporaries were well aware of the absurdity of the ostensible reason for the protest. 'Will not posterity be amazed', wrote one sceptic, 'when they are told that the present distraction took its rise from the parliament's taking off a shilling duty on a pound of tea, and imposing three pence, and call it a more unaccountable phrenzy, and more disgraceful to the annals of America, than that of the witchcraft?'

On close inspection, then, the taxes that caused so much fuss were not just trifling; by 1773 they had all but gone. In any case, these disputes about taxation were trivial compared with the basic economic reality that membership of the British Empire was good –

---

* 'Nothing could be more coarse or clumsy or ungracious than his outside. Two large prominent eyes rolled about to no purpose (for he was utterly short-sighted), a wide mouth, thick lips and inflated visage, gave him the air of a blind trumpeter.' (Horace Walpole)

† Here was the moment when the idiosyncratic institutions of the Asian and American halves of the British Empire fatally clashed. The East India Company had been hard hit by the American colonists' boycott of tea, which was part of the campaign against the Townshend Duties. Struggling with a tea surplus and a burgeoning debt burden, the company simply wanted to unload some of its surplus on the American market.

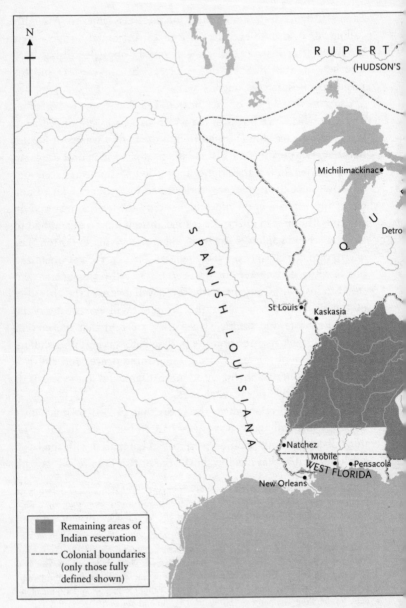

British North America, 1774

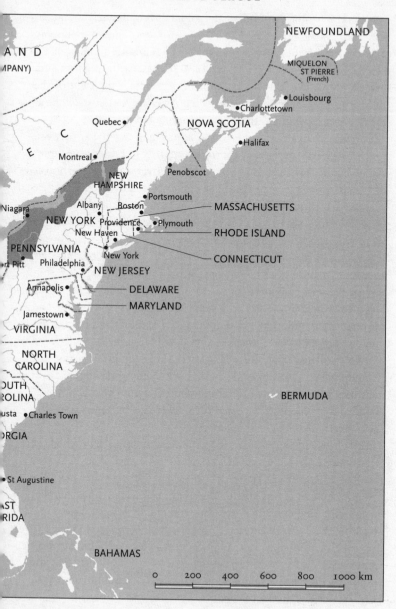

very good – for the American colonial economy. The much-maligned Navigation Acts may have given British ships a monopoly over trade with the colonies, but they also guaranteed a market for North American exports of agricultural staples, cattle, pig iron and, indeed, ships. It was the constitutional principle – the right of the British parliament to levy taxes on the American colonists without their consent – that was the true bone of contention.

For more than a century there had been a tacit tug of war between centre and periphery – between royal authority in London, as represented by the centrally-appointed colonial governors, and the power of the colonists' elected assemblies. It had been a distinctive feature of the early British settlements in America, particularly those in New England, that they had nurtured representative institutions (here was another important difference between North and South America). By comparison, the attempts to plant European-style hereditary aristocracies had comprehensively failed. From 1675 onwards, however, London sought to increase its influence over the colonies, which in their early years had been to all intents and purposes autonomous. Until that time only Virginia had been designated a 'crown colony'. But in 1679 New Hampshire was declared a royal province and five years later Massachusetts became the 'Dominion of New England'. New York came under direct royal authority when its own proprietor became King in 1685, and Rhode Island and Connecticut accepted royal takeovers in rapid succession thereafter.

To be sure, these centralizing tendencies came to a halt when the Stuarts were driven from power in 1688. Indeed, the 'Glorious Revolution' encouraged the colonists to regard their own assemblies as equivalent in status to the Westminster Parliament: a number of colonial assemblies passed laws rehearsing Magna Carta and affirming the rights of those they represented. By 1739 it seemed to one royal official that the colonies were effectively 'Independent Common Wealths', with legislatures that were effectively 'absolute within their respective Dominions' and barely 'accountable for their Laws or Actions' to the crown.

But this proved to be the cue for a fresh wave of centralizing initiatives from London before, during and after the Seven Years War. It is in this constitutional context that the debates over taxation in the 1760s need to be understood. The heavy-handed attempt by Lord North's government to bring the unruly legislators of Massachusetts to heel after the Tea Party by closing the port of Boston and imposing military rule was merely the last of many affronts to colonial legislators. In repealing the Stamp Act in 1766, Parliament had emphatically declared that it 'had, hath and of right ought to have, full power and authority to make laws and statutes of sufficient force and validity to bind the colonies and people of America'. That was what the colonists disputed.

Perhaps there was also an element of colonial chippiness at work. Once, lamented Franklin, there had been 'not only a respect, but an affection, for Great Britain, for its laws, its customs and manners, and even a fondness for its fashions, that greatly increased the commerce. Natives of Britain were always treated with particular regard; to be an Old England-man was, of itself, a character of some respect, and gave a kind of rank among us.' But the colonists were treated in return not as subjects but as 'subjects of subjects'; as a 'republican race, mixed rabble of Scotch, Irish and foreign vagabonds, descendants of convicts, ungrateful rebels etc.' as if they were 'unworthy the name of Englishmen, and fit only to be snubb'd, curb'd, shackled and plundered'. John Adams expressed the same feeling of inferiority more strongly. 'We won't be their Negroes,' he snarled, writing as 'Humphry Ploughjogger' in the *Boston Gazette*. 'I say we are as handsome as old English folks, and so should be as free.'

In this increasingly acrimonious atmosphere, the first Continental Congress was held at Carpenters' Hall in Philadelphia in the autumn of 1774, bringing together the more rebellious elements in the various colonial assemblies. Here, for the first time, resolutions were passed to withhold all taxes from the British government, if necessary by forcible resistance. Yet Samuel Adams's famous slogan 'No taxation without representation' was not a rejection of Britishness, but rather an emphatic *assertion* of Britishness. What the colonists said they were doing was demanding the same liberty enjoyed by their fellow subjects on the other side of the Atlantic. At this stage, they saw themselves as no more than transatlantic Britons who wanted real, local representation, not the 'virtual' representation they were being offered in the distant House of Commons. In other words, they wanted their assemblies to be put on a par with the Westminster Parliament, in what would have been a reformed, quasi-federal Empire. As Lord Mansfield put it in 1775, the colonists 'would stand in relation to Great Britain ... as Scotland stood towards England, previous to the treaty of Union'.

Some far-sighted thinkers in Britain – among them the great economist Adam Smith and the Dean of Gloucester, Josiah Tucker – saw this kind of imperial devolution as the answer. While Smith envisaged an imperial federation, with Westminster merely at the apex of a devolved empire, Tucker proposed a prototype Commonwealth, in which only the sovereignty of the monarch would unite the empire. Moderate colonists like Joseph Galloway also sought a compromise: he proposed the establishment of an American legislative council, its members chosen by the colonial assemblies, but under a president-general appointed by the crown. The government in London ruled out all such solutions. The issue had become quite simply 'the supremacy of Parliament'. Lord North's government was now caught between two equally assertive legislatures, each convinced it was in the right. The most he could offer was that Parliament would put aside (though still reserving) its right of taxation if a colonial assembly were prepared to raise and contribute the required amount to imperial defence, as well as paying for its own civil government. It was not enough. Even the Elder Pitt's plea that the troops be withdrawn from Boston was thrown out by the House of Lords. By this time, in Benjamin Franklin's view, the government's 'Claim of Sovereignty over three Millions of virtuous sensible People in America, seem[ed] the greatest of Absurdities, since they appear'd to have scarce Discretion enough to govern a Herd of Swine'. That was fighting talk.

It took just over a year after the first shots at Lexington for rebellion to turn into outright revolution. On 4 July 1776, in the austere chamber normally used by the Pennsylvania assembly, the Declaration of Independence was adopted by representatives of the thirteen secessionist colonies at the Second Continental Congress. Only two years before, its principal author, the 33-year-old Thomas Jefferson, had still addressed George III in the name of 'your subjects in British America'. Now the transatlantic or 'continental' Britons had become American 'Patriots'. In fact, most of the Declaration is a rather tedious and overstated list of wrongs supposedly inflicted on the colonists by the King, whom they accused of trying to erect a 'Tyranny over these States'. It bears all the hallmarks of a document heavily revised by an outsize committee. It is Jefferson's preamble that people remember today: 'We hold these truths to be self-evident, that all men are created equal, that they are endowed by their Creator with certain inalienable rights, that among these are life, liberty and the pursuit of happiness.'

Nowadays that sounds about as revolutionary as motherhood and apple pie. At the time it was an explosive challenge not just to royal authority but to the traditional values of a hierarchical, Christian society. Before 1776 the debate about the colonies' future had very largely been couched in terms familiar from the British constitutional wrangles of the previous century. With the publication of Thomas Paine's *Common Sense* in 1776, however, an entirely new idea had entered the political debate, and with breathtaking speed carried the day: anti-monarchism, with the strong implication of republicanism. Of course, a republic was nothing new. The Venetians, the Hanseatic Germans, the Swiss and the Dutch all had them; indeed, the British themselves had conducted their own brief experiment with republicanism in the 1650s. But Jefferson's preamble ensured that the American republic would be fashioned in the language of the Enlightenment: in terms of natural rights – above all the right of every individual 'to judge for himself what will secure or endanger his freedom'.

Perhaps the most remarkable thing about the Declaration of Independence was that the representatives of all thirteen colonies were able to sign it. Just over twenty years before, the divisions between them had seemed so wide that Charles Townshend had found it 'impossible to imagine that so many different representatives of so many different provinces, divided in interest and alienated by jealousy and inveterate prejudice, should ever be able to resolve upon a plan of mutual security and reciprocal expense'. Even Benjamin Franklin had admitted that the colonies had

different forms of government, different laws, different interests, and some of them different religious persuasions and different manners. Their jealousy of each other is so great that however necessary an union of the colonies has long been, for their common defence and security against their enemies, and how sensible soever each colony has been of that necessity, yet they have never been able to effect such an union among themselves.

The Declaration was intended to end these divisions. It even coined the name 'United States'. But its consequences were to prove deeply divisive. Jefferson's revolutionary language alienated many more conservative colonists. A surprisingly large number of them turned out to be ready to fight for King and Empire. When Dr James Thatcher resolved to join the Patriots, he found that his friends

afford[ed] me no encouragement, alleging that, as this is a civil war, if I should fall into the hands of the British the gallows will be my fate . . . The Tories assail[ed] me with the following: 'Young man, are you sensible you are about to violate your duty to the best of kings, and run headlong into destruction? Be assured that this rebellion will be of short duration.'

The Hollywood version of the War of Independence is a straightforward fight between heroic Patriots and wicked, Nazi-like Redcoats. The reality was quite different. This was indeed a civil war which divided social classes and even families. And the worst of the violence did not involve regular British troops, but was perpetrated by rebel colonists against their countrymen who remained loyal to the crown.

Take the case of Christ Church in Philadelphia, often thought of as a hotbed of revolution because several of the signatories of the Declaration of Independence worshipped there. In fact, supporters of independence were in the minority of the congregation. Only around a third supported independence; the rest were either against or were neutral. Christ Church, like countless others in colonial America, was a church divided by politics. Nor was it only congregations that were divided; whole families were split asunder by the War of Independence. The Franklin family were regular attenders at Christ Church, so much so that they had their own pew. Benjamin Franklin spent nearly a decade vainly arguing the colonists' case in London before returning to join the Continental Congress and the fight for independence. But his son William, governor of New Jersey, remained loyal to the crown during the war. The two never spoke again.

The pressure on clergymen was particularly acute, since ministers owed their allegiance to the King as head of the Church of England. As Rector of Christ Church, Jacob Duché was torn between loyalty to the Anglican establishment and sympathy for those of his flock who supported the revolution. His own copy of the Book of Common Prayer testifies to the extent of his support for independence. What the Prayer Book originally says is: 'We humbly beseech Thee so to dispose and govern the heart of George thy Servant our king and governor . . .' (meaning George III). But Duché took a pen and struck those words out, replacing them with: 'We humbly beseech Thee so to direct the rulers of these United States . . .' This was without question a revolutionary act. And yet when independence was formally declared, despite the fact that one of the signatories was Duché's own brother-in-law, he got cold feet, returned to the Anglican fold and became a Loyalist. Duché's dilemma illustrates how the American revolution could divide even individuals. Nor was it only Anglicans who rejected rebellion on religious grounds. The Sandemanians of Connecticut remained loyal because they believed unconditionally that a Christian should be a 'loyal Subject, submitting himself in civil Concerns to every Ordinance of Man for the Lord's Sake.'

Overall, something like one in five of the white population of British North America remained loyal to the crown during the war. Indeed, the Loyalist companies often fought far more tenaciously than Britain's hesitant generals. There were even Loyalist songs, like 'The Congress':

> These hardy knaves and stupid fools,
> Some apish and pragmatic mules,
> Some servile acquiescing tools,
> These, these compose the Congress.
>
> Then Jove resolved to send a curse,
> And all the woes of life rehearse
> Not plague, not famine, but much worse
> He cursed us with a Congress.
>
> Then peace forsook this hopeless shore
> Then cannons blazed with horrid roar
> We hear of blood, death, wounds and gore,
> The offspring of the Congress.

In such polemics the two sides routinely labelled one another 'Whigs' and 'Tories'. This really was the second British – or perhaps the first American – Civil War.

One Loyalist who fought in the Carolinas, the bald-headed backwoodsman David Fanning, wrote a gripping account of his wartime experiences. According to one version of Fanning's story, it was after his pack train was pillaged by rebel militia in 1775 that he 'signed in favour of the King', though it seems more probable that the whole area where Fanning lived remained loyal. For six years he was involved in sporadic guerrilla warfare in North Carolina, collecting two bullets in his back and a price on his head in the process. On 12 September 1781 he struck a major blow for the empire when he and his Loyalist followers, supported by a detachment of British regulars, emerged out of a foggy dawn to capture the town of Hillsborough and with it the entire North Carolina General Assembly, the state's rebel governor and numerous officers of the Patriot army. In the wake of this success, the Loyalist ranks in North Carolina swelled to more than 1,200. There were similar Loyalist forces as far afield as New York, East Florida, Savannah, Georgia, and Daufuskie Island in South Carolina.

The possibility clearly existed for closer co-operation between forces like Fanning's irregular militias and the regular redcoat armies. Yet for two reasons this was a war Britain simply could not win. For one thing, the transatlantic civil war quickly became absorbed into the long-running global struggle between Britain and France. Here was Louis XVI's chance to take revenge for the Seven Years War, and he seized it with relish. This time Britain had no continental allies to tie down France – not to mention her ally Spain – in Europe. Under these circumstances, a full-scale campaign in America would have been hazardous in the extreme.

In any case, and just as importantly, many people back home sympathized with the colonists. Samuel Johnson was quite unusual in his splenetic hostility towards them ('I am willing to love all mankind, except an American . . . Sir, they are a race of convicts, and ought to be thankful for any thing we allow them short of hanging'). Indeed, the sheer number of violent arguments he had on the subject, many recorded by his biographer and friend James Boswell, confirms that Johnson was in a minority. Boswell himself had formed 'a clear and settled opinion, that the people of America were well warranted to resist a claim that their fellow-subjects in the mother-country should have the entire command of their fortunes, by taxing them without their own consent'. Many leading Whig politicians took the same view. In Parliament the flamboyant Whig leader Charles James Fox paraded his American sympathies by appearing in the buff and blue colours of Washington's Patriot army. Edmund Burke spoke for many when he declared: 'The use of force alone . . . may subdue for a moment, but it does not remove the necessity of subduing again; and a nation is not governed which is perpetually to be conquered.' In short, London lacked the stomach to impose British rule on white colonists who were determined to resist it. It was one thing to fight native Americans or mutinous slaves, but it was another to fight what amounted to your own people. As Sir Guy Carlton, the British Governor of Quebec said when justifying his lenient treatment of some Patriot prisoners: 'Since we have tried in vain to make them acknowledge us as brothers, let us at least send them away disposed to regard us as first cousins.' The British commander-in-chief William Howe was equally ambivalent about waging civil war; that may explain why he prevaricated when he could have destroyed Washington's army at Long Island.

It is also worth remembering that in economic terms the continental colonies remained of far less importance than those of the Caribbean. They were in fact heavily dependent on trade with Britain and it was not an unreasonable assumption that, regardless of political arrangements, they would remain so for the foreseeable future. With hindsight we know that to lose the United States was to lose a very large slice of the world's economic future. But at the time the short-term costs of reimposing British authority in the thirteen colonies looked considerably larger than the short-term benefits of doing so.

True, the British had some military successes. They won, albeit at high cost, the first major engagement of the war at Bunker's Hill. New York was taken in 1776 and Philadelphia, the rebel capital, in September the following year. The very hall where the Declaration of Independence was signed became a military hospital for wounded and dying Patriots. But the bottom line was that London could provide neither sufficient troops nor good enough generals to turn localized success into full-scale victory. By 1778 the rebels had re-established their control over most of the territory from Pennsylvania to Rhode Island. And when the British sought to switch their operations to the South, where they could count on stronger Loyalist support, localized successes at Savannah and Charleston could not prevent full-scale defeat. Cornwallis was drawn northwards by the rebel generals Horatio Gates and Nathanael Greene until he was forced to shift his headquarters into Virginia. The key moment came in 1781 when Washington, instead of attacking New York (as he had originally planned), moved south against Cornwallis. He did so on the advice of the French commander, comte de Rochambeau. Simultaneously, the French admiral, François de Grasse, defeated the British fleet under Admiral Thomas Graves and blockaded the Chesapeake Bay. Cornwallis was trapped on the Yorktown peninsula between the

James and York rivers. Here was a reversal of the odds at Lexington: it was the British who were now outnumbered – by more than two to one – and outgunned.

Today the Yorktown battlefield looks about as menacing as a golf course. But in October 1781 it was pockmarked by trenches full of armed men and artillery. On 11 October Washington began pounding the British positions with over a hundred mortars and howitzers. Retaining the two defensive positions known as Redoubts 9 and 10 – small forts made of wooden ramparts and sandbags – became crucial if Cornwallis were to hold out until reinforcements arrived. The fiercest hand-to-hand action took place on the night of 14 October when a Patriot force led by the future American Treasury Secretary, Alexander Hamilton, stormed the redoubt to the right with fixed bayonets. It was a heroic and professionally executed assault, proof that the colonists had come a long way as soldiers since the rout at Lexington. But had it not been for the French attacking the other redoubt at the same time, the assault might not have succeeded. Once again, the French contribution was crucial to Patriot success and British defeat. And it was the French navy to his rear that doomed Cornwallis, ruling out the evacuation of his force. On the morning of 17 October he sent a drummer boy to sound the parley. It was, one American soldier noted in his diary, 'the most delightful music to us all'.

Altogether 7,157 British soldiers and sailors surrendered at Yorktown, giving up over 240 artillery pieces and six regimental colours. The story goes that as they marched into captivity their band played 'The World Turned Upside Down'. (Other evidence suggests that the prisoners sought consolation in alcohol when they reached Yorktown itself.) But what exactly had turned the world upside down? Aside from French intervention and incompetent British generalship, at root it was a failure of will in London. When the British army surrendered at Yorktown, Loyalists like David Fanning felt they had been left in the lurch. Joseph Galloway deplored the 'want of wisdom in the plans, and of vigour and exertion in the execution'.

On the other hand, the Loyalists were not sufficiently

disillusioned with British rule to abandon it altogether. Quite the contrary: many of them responded to defeat by emigrating north-wards to the British colonies in Canada, which had all remained loyal. Fanning himself eventually ended up in New Brunswick. In all, around 100,000 Loyalists left the new United States bound for Canada, England or the West Indies. It has sometimes been argued that in gaining Canada in the Seven Years War, Britain had under-mined her position in America. Without the French threat, why should the thirteen colonies stay loyal? Yet the loss of America had the unforeseen effect of securing Canada for the Empire, thanks to the flood of English-speaking Loyalists who, together with new British settlers, would eventually reduce the French Quebecois to a beleaguered minority. The amazing thing is that so many people should have voted with their feet against American independence, choosing loyalty to King and Empire over 'life, liberty and the pur-suit of happiness'.

It was, as we have seen, Thomas Jefferson who coined that famous phrase. But there was a difficulty which the American revolution-aries found rather embarrassing. Did their Declaration that all men were 'created equal' also apply to the 400,000 black slaves they collectively owned – roughly a fifth of the total population of the ex-colonies, and nearly half that of his native Virginia? In his auto-biography, quoted inside his pristine marble memorial on the Mall in Washington DC, Jefferson was quite explicit: 'Nothing is more certainly written in the book of fate than that these people [meaning the slaves] are to be free.' But the autobiography goes on to say – and the sculptors of the memorial unaccountably left this out – that 'the two races' were divided by 'indelible lines of distinction be-tween them'. After all, Jefferson himself was a Virginian landowner with around 200 slaves, only seven of whom he ever freed.

The irony is that having won their independence in the name of liberty, the American colonists went on to perpetuate slavery in the southern states. As Samuel Johnson acidly asked in his anti-American pamphlet *Taxation No Tyranny*: 'How is it that the loudest YELPS for liberty come from the drivers of Negroes?' By contrast, within a few decades of having lost the American colonies, the British abolished first the slave trade and then slavery itself throughout their Empire. Indeed, as early as 1775 the British Governor of Virginia, Lord Dunmore, had offered emancipation to slaves who rallied to the British cause. This was not entirely opportunistic: Lord Mansfield's famous judgement in Somersett's case had pronounced slavery illegal in England three years before. From the point of view of most African-Americans, American independence postponed emancipation by at least a generation. Although slavery was gradually abolished in northern states like Pennsylvania, New York, New Jersey and Rhode Island, it remained firmly entrenched in the South, where most slaves lived.

Nor was independence good news for the native Americans. During the Seven Years War the British government had shown itself anxious to conciliate the Indian tribes, if only to try to lure them away from their alliance with the French. Treaties had been signed which established the Appalachian mountains as the limit of British settlement, leaving the land west of it, including the Ohio Valley, to the Indians. Admittedly, these treaties were not strictly adhered to when peace came, sparking the war known as Pontiac's Uprising in 1763. But the fact remains that the distant imperial authority in London was more inclined to recognize the rights of the native Americans than the land-hungry colonists on the spot.

American independence might have heralded the end of the British Empire. It certainly marked the birth of a new and dynamic force in the world – a revolutionary republic which could now exploit its vast natural resources without having to defer to a distant monarchy. Yet the Empire was far from shattered by this loss, in marked contrast to Spain, which never recovered from the revolt of her South American colonies. Indeed, the loss of the thirteen colonies seemed to spur a whole new phase of British colonial expansion even further afield. True, half a continent had been lost. But on the other side of the world a whole new continent beckoned.

Mars

The British had been attracted to Asia by trade. They had been attracted to America by land. Distance was an obstacle, but one that with fair winds could be overcome. But there was another continent that was attractive to them for diametrically different reasons. Because it was barren. Because it was impossibly remote. Because it was a natural prison.

With its weird red earth and its alien flora and fauna – the eucalyptus trees and kangaroos – Australia was the eighteenth-century equivalent of Mars. This helps explain why the first official response to the discovery of New South Wales by Captain Cook in 1770 was to identify it as the ideal dumping ground for criminals.

Informally, transportation of convicts to the colonies had been going on since the early 1600s, though it did not become a formal part of the penal system until 1717. For the next century and a half, the law stated that minor offenders could be transported for seven years instead of being flogged or branded, while men on commuted capital sentences could be transported for fourteen years. By 1777 no fewer than 40,000 men and women from Britain and Ireland had been transported on this basis to the American colonies, supplementing the supply of indentured labourers (as Moll Flanders's mother explained to her). With the American colonies now lost, somewhere new had to be found to prevent British prisons – not to mention the new prison hulks along the south-east coast – from overflowing with untransportable inmates. There were strategic considerations too. Aware of ancient Spanish claims in the South Pacific and more recent Dutch and French expeditions, some British politicians saw it as imperative that New South Wales be settled, if only to assert British ownership. But getting rid of the convicts was the prime objective.

Northern Ireland had been a day's sailing, North America a few weeks'. But who wanted to start a colony from scratch 16,000 miles away?* Small wonder the early settlement of Australia required compulsion.

On 13 May 1787 a fleet of eleven ships set sail from Portsmouth, crammed with 548 male and 188 female convicts, ranging from a nine-year-old chimney sweep, John Hudson, who had stolen some clothes and a pistol, to an 82-year-old rag-dealer named Dorothy Handland, who had been found guilty of perjury. They arrived at Botany Bay, just beyond what is now Sydney harbour, on 19 January 1788, after more than eight months at sea.

In all, between 1787 and 1853, around 123,000 men and just under 25,000 women were transported on the so-called 'hell ships' to the Antipodes for crimes ranging from forgery to sheep stealing. With them came an unknown number of children, including a substantial number conceived *en route*. Once again, from the very outset the British were intent on reproducing themselves in their new colony. Indeed, sexual licence, fuelled by imported rum, would be one of early Sydney's defining traits.

The settlement of Australia was designed to solve a problem at home – primarily that of crimes against property. In essence, it was an alternative to hanging thieves or building prisons to house them in Britain. But among the convicts there were also political prisoners. Luddites, food rioters, radical weavers, Swing rioters, Tolpuddle Martyrs, Chartists, Quebecois *patriotes* – members of all these groups ended up in Australia. Around a quarter of all those transported were Irish, of whom one in five had been convicted on a political charge. Nor was it only the Irish who ended up there in numbers. Australia had more than its fair share of Scots, though judges in Scotland were more reluctant than their English counterparts to sentence convicted felons to transportation. A surprisingly large number of Fergusons were sent to Australia: ten in all. The sparse records of their crimes and punishments make it clear how

---

* The distance of the first convict fleet's voyage from Portsmouth to Rio de Janiero, from Rio to Cape Town and from Cape Town to Botany Bay was 15,900 miles.

harsh life in the penal colony was. Seven years' forced labour for stealing a couple of hens was a not untypical sentence of the time, handed out to one of my namesakes. Further transgressions once convicts had arrived were corporally punished: discipline in the early penal colony was based on the lash. Those who ran away, naively hoping – as some did – to walk to China, perished in the arid passes of the Blue Mountains.

The great paradox of Australian history is that what started out as a colony populated by people whom Britain had thrown out proved to be so loyal to the British Empire for so long. America had begun as a combination of tobacco plantation and Puritan utopia, a creation of economic and religious liberty, and ended up as a rebel republic. Australia started out as a jail, the very negation of liberty. Yet the more reliable colonists turned out to be not the Pilgrims but the prisoners.

Perhaps the best explanation of the Australian paradox is this. Although the system of transportation made a mockery of the British claim that theirs was an empire of liberty, in practice the effect of the policy was liberating for many of those sent to Australia. This was partly because, at a time when private property was the holiest of holies, British criminal justice routinely convicted people for offences that we today would regard as trivial. Although between half and two-thirds of those transported were 'repeat offenders', nearly all of their crimes were petty thefts. Australia literally started out as a nation of shoplifters.

To begin with, it is true, the convicts were only a little better off than slaves, forced to work for the government or 'assigned' to the growing number of private landowners (among them the officers of the New South Wales Regiment). But once they got their 'tickets of leave' at the end of their stretches, prisoners were free to sell their labour to the highest bidder. Even before then, they were given afternoons off to cultivate their own allotments. As early as 1791, two ex-convicts, Richard Phillimore and James Ruse, were growing enough wheat and maize on their own plots of land in respectively Norfolk Island and Paramatta, to take themselves 'off the store'. In effect, those who survived transportation and served their sentences were given the chance to start a new life – even if it was a new life on Mars.

Yet without inspired leadership, Australia might never have been much more than a vast Devil's Island. In its transformation from dumping ground into reformatory a crucial role was played by the colony's governor between 1809 and 1821, Lachlan Macquarie. A Hebridean-born career army officer who had risen to command a regiment in India, Macquarie was every bit as much of a despot as his naval predecessors. When there was talk of appointing a council to assist him he replied: 'I entertain a fond hope that such an institution will never be extended to this colony.' But, unlike them, Macquarie was an *enlightened* despot. To him, New South Wales was not just a land of punishment, but also a land of redemption. Under his benign rule, he believed, convicts could be transformed into citizens:

The prospect of earning their freedom is the greatest Inducement that Can be held out to the Reformation of the Manners of the Inhabitants . . . [W]hen United with Rectitude and long tried Good Conduct, [it] should lead a man back to that Rank in Society which he had forfeited and do away, as far as the Case will admit, with All Retrospect of former Bad Conduct.

Macquarie took steps to improve conditions on the ships bringing convicts to Australia, drastically reducing the death rate from 1 in 31 to 1 in 122 by following the advice of William Redfern, a transported surgeon who became the governor's family doctor. He softened the colony's system of criminal justice, even allowing convicts with legal experience to represent accused men at trials. But Macquarie's most visible and enduring contribution was to turn Sydney into a model colonial city. Even as *laissez-faire* economics began to set the tone back in London, Macquarie became an unabashed planner. Central to his urban vision were the huge Hyde Park Barracks, the biggest such building in the overseas empire at that time. With their austere symmetrical lines – the work of Francis Howard Greenway, a Gloucestershire architect and transported forger – the Barracks look like the prototype for Jeremy Bentham's

Utilitarian 'panopticon'. Six hundred criminals, with artisan skills, slept there in rows of hammocks, a hundred to a room, easily kept under surveillance through spy-holes. But this was far from a punishment block. It was a centre for the orderly allocation of skilled convict labour, the prisoners who had once been artisans and craftsmen but had fallen on hard times and turned to petty crime. These were the men Macquarie needed for the hundreds of public buildings which he believed would elevate Sydney from convict colony to conurbation, the first of which was a handsome hospital financed from a specially imposed duty on rum.

With the infrastructure of his city largely complete, Macquarie turned his mind to reducing the colony's dependence on imported food. 'Macquarie towns' were established along the fertile banks of the Hawkesbury River up towards the Blue Mountains, rich agricultural land ideally suited to grain and sheep farming. In towns like Windsor, Macquarie sought to realize his vision of colonial redemption by offering thirty-acre land grants to those who had completed their sentences. Richard Fitzgerald had been a London street urchin sentenced to transportation at fifteen, who had quickly established a reputation for 'remarkable activity and regular conduct'. Macquarie made Fitzgerald superintendent of agriculture and stores for the Windsor area. Within just a few years, the former delinquent was a pillar of society, proprietor of the Macquarie Arms pub at one end of town and builder of a solidly imposing local church, St Matthews, at the other.

As more and more convicts did their time or earned remission of their sentences, the character of the colony began to change. With only one in fourteen electing to return to Britain, there were already more free people than convicts in New South Wales by 1828 – and some of the old lags were fast becoming *nouveaux riches*. Samuel Terry was an illiterate Manchester labourer who had been transported for seven years for stealing 400 pairs of stockings. Freed in 1807, he set himself up in Sydney as an innkeeper and moneylender. So successful was Terry in his dual role that by 1820 he had amassed an estate of 19,000 acres, something like a tenth of all the land possessed by all the other freed convicts put together. He became known as the 'Rothschild of Botany Bay'. Mary Reibey, who eventually won immortality on the back of the Australian twenty-dollar note, had been sent to Australia at the age of thirteen for horse theft. She married well and did even better in trade, shipping and real estate. By 1820 she was worth £20,000.

By the end of his term as Governor, Macquarie had made his share of enemies. In London he was regarded as profligate, while there were some in Australia who regarded him as over-lenient. Still, he could quite legitimately claim: 'I found New South Wales a gaol and left it a colony. I found a population of idle prisoners, paupers and paid officials and left a large free community thriving in the prosperity of flocks and the labour of convicts.'

But what had happened to punishment? The success of Macquarie's policies meant that New South Wales was fast becoming a prosperous colony. It also meant that transportation there was no longer a deterrent to crime, but rather a free passage to a new life, with the prospect of a golden handshake in the form of a land grant at the end of one's sentence. The governor of one British prison was astonished when five Irish female prisoners strongly objected to their sentences being reduced to a prison term. They left him in no doubt that they would rather be transported.

That said, not every convict could be redeemed in the way Macquarie envisaged. The question was what was to be done with the hardened reoffenders. The answer was that from the outset there had to be prisons within the prison. Early in his time as Governor, Macquarie had ordered the abandonment of the hellish Norfolk Island, but reoffenders continued to be consigned to Van Diemen's Land, now Tasmania, and Moreton Bay in Queensland. At Port Arthur in Tasmania, the camp commandant Charles O'Hara Booth was effectively given a free hand to take 'the vengeance of the Law to the utmost limits of human endurance'. At Moreton Bay, Patrick Logan routinely hospitalized convicts with the punishment he termed 'flagellatio'. After Norfolk Island was reopened as a prison, new depths of brutality and sadism were plumbed by John Giles Price, who strapped men to old iron bedsteads after they had been whipped, in order to ensure their wounds became infected. Few men in the history of the British Empire have so richly merited the sort of death he suffered at the hands, hammers and crowbars of a group of convicts at Williamstown quarry in 1857.

But if reoffenders were systematically brutalized in such places, it was nothing compared with the way the indigenous or aboriginal people of Australia – of whom there were about 300,000 in 1788 – were treated. Like the American Indians before them, they were the victims of the white plague. The colonists brought with them contamination in the form of infectious diseases to which the Aborigines had no resistance, and cultivation which implied the exclusion of the nomadic tribes from their ancestral hunting grounds. What sugar was to the West Indies and tobacco to Virginia, sheep were to Australia. By 1821 there were already 290,000 sheep in Australia, overrunning the bush where the Aborigines had hunted kangaroo for millennia.

Macquarie, paternalistic as ever, hoped that the Aborigines could be brought from, as he put it, 'their rambling naked state' and transformed into respectable farmers. In 1815 he tried to settle sixteen of them on a small farm on the coast at Middle Head, complete with specially built huts and a boat. After all, he reasoned, if convicts could be turned into model citizens by being given the right kit and a second chance, why not Aborigines? But to Macquarie's despair they quickly lost interest in the well-ordered life he had in mind for them. They lost the boat, ignored the huts and wandered off back into the bush. That kind of indifference – in marked contrast to the belligerent response of the New Zealand Maoris to white colonization – was to seal the Aborigines' fate. The more they rejected 'civilization', the more the land-hungry farmers felt justified in exterminating them. Their 'only superiority above the brute', one visiting naval surgeon declared, 'consisted in their use of the spear, their extreme ferocity and their employment of fire in the cookery of their food.'

In one of the most shocking of all the chapters in the history of the British Empire, the Aborigines in Van Diemen's Land were hunted down, confined and ultimately exterminated: an event which truly merits the now overused term 'genocide'. (Trucanini, the last of them, died in 1876.) All that can be said in mitigation is that, had Australia been an independent republic in the nineteenth century, like the United States, the genocide might have been on a continental scale, rather than just a Tasmanian phenomenon. When the novelist Anthony Trollope visited Australia two years after Trucanini's death he asked a magistrate:

what he would recommend me to do ... if stress of circumstances compelled me to shoot a black man in the bush. Should I go to the nearest police station ... or should I go on rejoicing as though I had ... killed a deadly snake? His advice was clear and explicit: 'No one but a fool would say anything about it.'

Trollope concluded that 'it was their [the Aborigines'] fate to be abolished'. Yet one of the peculiarities of the British Empire was the way that the imperial power at the centre endeavoured to restrain the generally far more ruthless impulses of the colonists on the periphery. Concern in Parliament about mistreatment of indigenous peoples led to the appointment of Aboriginal Protectors in New South Wales and Western Australia in 1838–9. To be sure, these well-meaning efforts could not prevent atrocities like the Myall Creek massacre in 1838, when a group of twelve cattle-ranchers, all but one of them ex-convicts, shot and stabbed twenty-eight unarmed Aborigines to death. A long, low-level war would be waged for decades between farmers and Aborigines as agriculture spread into the outback. But the presence of a restraining authority, no matter how distant, was something that distinguished British colonies from independent settler republics. There was no such restraining influence when the United States waged war against the American Indians.

The case of the Aborigines was a striking example of the way attitudes diverged over distance. The British in London regarded the problem quite differently from the British in Sydney. Here was the very essence of the imperial dilemma. How could an empire that claimed to be founded on liberty justify overruling the wishes of colonists when they clashed with those of a very distant legislature?

That had been the central question in America in the 1770s, and its ultimate answer had been secession. In the 1830s the question was posed again in Canada. But this time the British had a better answer.

Since the American War of Independence, Canada had seemed the most dependable of Britain's colonies, thanks to the influx of defeated Loyalists from the United States. But in 1837 French-speaking Quebecois in Lower Canada and pro-American reformers in Upper Canada revolted. Their main grievance was not unfamiliar: despite being represented in their own House of Assembly, their wishes could be ignored at will by a Legislative Council and Governor who were solely accountable to London. There was genuine alarm in Britain that the rapidly growing United States might seize the opportunity to annex its northern neighbour; its incorporation was, after all, explicitly envisaged in article XI of the American Articles of Confederation. In 1812 the United States had even sent a 12,000-strong army into Canada, though it had been roundly defeated.

The American experiment of going it alone as a republic had been undeniably successful. Would the other white colonies now break away as republics the way the United States had? Would there be a United States of Canada or of Australia? Perhaps the surprising thing is that this did not happen.

Some of the credit for the fact that it did not is due to the unlikely figure of John Lambton, the Earl of Durham, a high-living hangover from the Regency era, who was sent to Canada to head off this fresh colonial revolt. A 'flamboyant despot', in the words of one contemporary, Durham announced his arrival in Quebec by prancing through the streets on a white charger and installing himself at the Château St Louis, dining off gold and silver platters and quaffing vintage champagne. Despite appearances, however, Durham was no lightweight. He had been one of the authors of the 1832 Reform Act, hence his nickname 'Radical Jack'. He also had the wit to be well advised. Charles Buller, his private secretary, had been born in Calcutta, studied history with Thomas Carlyle and had won a reputation as a brilliant barrister before entering the House of

Commons; while Durham's principal adviser, Edward Gibbon Wakefield, had written extensively on land reform in Australia – ironically, while languishing in Newgate prison, where he had been sent for three years for abducting an under-age heiress. He was just one of many thinkers of his generation who were haunted by the spectre, conjured up by the statistician Thomas Malthus, of unsustainable population growth at home. To Wakefield, the colonies were the obvious answer as an overflow for surplus Britons. But to encourage free settlement, as opposed to continued transportation, he was convinced that some kind of accommodation had to be reached with the settlers' inherently British sense of independence.

Durham, Buller and Wakefield spent just six months in Canada before returning to England and presenting their report. Though primarily concerned with the specific problems of Canadian governance, it had a profoundly important subtext relevant to the whole of the British Empire. Indeed, the Durham Report has a good claim to be the book that saved the Empire. For what it did was to acknowledge that the American colonists had been right. They had, after all, been entitled to demand that those who governed the white colonies should be accountable to representative assemblies of the colonists, and not simply to the agents of a distant royal authority. What Durham called for in Canada was exactly what an earlier generation of British ministers had denied the American colonies:

a system of responsible government [such] as would give the people a real control over its own destinies ... The government of the colony should henceforth be carried on in conformity with the views of the majority in the Assembly.

The report also implied that the Americans had been right to adopt a federal structure between their states; that too was to be copied in Canada and later in Australia.

Admittedly, it was not acted upon immediately. Although the government hastened to implement Durham's principal recommendation – that Upper and Lower Canada be united in order to dilute French influence in the former – responsible government was not introduced until 1848, and then only in Nova Scotia. It was not until 1856 that most of the Canadian colonies had been granted it. But by this time the idea had caught on in Australia and New Zealand, which also began moving in the direction of responsible government. By the 1860s the balance of political power in all the white colonies had decisively shifted. From now on, the governors would play more of a decorative role, as representatives of a like-wise increasingly decorative monarch; real power would lie with the colonists' elected representatives.

'Responsible government', then, was a way of reconciling the practice of empire with the principle of liberty. What the Durham Report meant was that the aspirations of Canadians, Australians, New Zealanders and South Africans – which were to be little differ-ent from the aspirations of the Americans in the 1770s – could be and would be answered without the need for wars of independence. From now on, whatever the colonists wanted, they pretty much got. That meant, for example, that when the Australians demanded an end to transportation, London gave in. The last convict ship sailed in 1867.

So there would be no Battle of Lexington in Auckland; no George Washington in Canberra; no declaration of independence in Ottawa. Indeed, it is hard not to feel, when one reads the Durham Report, that its subtext is one of regret. If only the American colonists had been given responsible government when they had first asked for it in the 1770s – if only the British had lived up to their own rhetoric of liberty – there might never have been a War of Independence. Indeed, there might never have been a United States. And millions of British emigrants might have chosen California instead of Canada when they packed their bags to go.*

---

* In fact, and despite government encouragements to migrate to Australia, the US long remained the most popular destination for emigrants from the United Kingdom. Of the 600,000 or so people who left England, Wales and Scotland between 1815 and 1850, 80 per cent went to the United States. Of the staggering 13 million who left the United Kingdom in the sixty years after 1850, the proportion was about the same, with the Irish in particular favouring the 'land of the free' over the Empire. Only as the twentieth century wore on did more and more Britons opt to emigrate to the Empire rather than America. More than 6 million Britons emigrated to the Empire between 1900 and 1963, roughly eight out of ten of all British emigrants.

3

The Mission

*When the contrast between the influence of a Christian and a
Heathen government is considered; when the knowledge of the
wretchedness of the people forces us to reflect on the unspeak-
able blessings to millions that would follow the extension of
British rule, it is not ambition but benevolence that dictates
the desire for the whole country. Where the providence of God
will lead, one state after another will be delivered into his
stewardship.*

Macleod Wylie, *Bengal as a Field of Missions* (1854)

In the eighteenth century the British Empire had been, at best,
amoral. The Hanoverians had grabbed power in Asia, land in
America and slaves in Africa. Native peoples were either taxed,
robbed or wiped out. But paradoxically their cultures were largely
tolerated; in some cases, even studied and admired.

The Victorians had more elevated aspirations. They dreamt not
just of ruling the world, but of redeeming it. It was no longer
enough for them to exploit other races; now the aim became to
improve them. Native peoples themselves would cease to be exploited, but their cultures – superstitious, backward, heathen –
would have to go. In particular, the Victorians aspired to bring
light to what they called the Dark Continent.

Africa was in fact a great deal less primitive than they imagined.
Far from being 'one rude chaos', as an early English traveller
called it, sub-Saharan Africa was home to myriad states and
nations, some of them a good deal more economically advanced

than contemporaneous pre-colonial societies in North America or Australasia. There were substantial towns like Timbuktu (in modern Mali) and Ibadan (in modern Nigeria), gold and copper mines, even a textile industry. However, in three respects it struck the Victorians as benighted. Unlike North Africa, the faiths of sub-Saharan Africa were not monotheistic; except for its northern and southern extremities, it was riddled with malaria, yellow fever and other diseases lethal to Europeans (and their preferred livestock); and, perhaps most importantly, slaves were its principal export – indeed, supplying slaves to European and Arab traders along the coast became the continent's biggest source of revenue. The peculiar path of global economic development led Africans into the business of capturing and selling one another.

Like the non-governmental aid organizations of today, Victorian missionaries believed they knew what was best for Africa. Their goal was not so much colonization as 'civilization': introducing a way of life that was first and foremost Christian, but was also distinctly North European in its reverence for industry and abstinence. The man who came to embody this new ethos of empire was David Livingstone. For Livingstone, commerce and colonization – the original foundations of the Empire – were necessary, but not sufficient. In essence, he and thousands of missionaries like him wanted the Empire to be born again.

This was not a government project, but the work of what we today would call the voluntary sector. But the Victorian aid agencies' good intentions would have unforeseen, and sometimes bloody, consequences.

From Clapham to Freetown

The British have a long tradition of sending aid to Africa. At the time of writing, British servicemen had been stationed in Sierra Leone since May 2000 as peacemakers and peacekeepers. Their mission was, fundamentally, an altruistic one: to help restore stability to a country that had been wracked for years by civil war.* A little less than 200 years ago, a Royal Navy squadron was based in Sierra Leone on a comparably moral mission: to prevent slave ships leaving the African coast for America, and thereby to bring an end to the Atlantic slave trade.

This was an astonishing volte face, especially astonishing to the Africans themselves.† After the British first came to Sierra Leone in 1562 it did not take them long to become slave traders. In the subsequent two and a half centuries, as we have seen, more than three million Africans were shipped into bondage on British ships. But then, towards the end of the eighteenth century, something changed dramatically; it was almost as if a switch was flicked in the British psyche. Suddenly they started shipping slaves back to West Africa and setting them free. Sierra Leone became 'The Province of Freedom'. Its capital was renamed Freetown. The freed slaves walked through a Freedom Arch bearing the inscription – now almost obscured by weeds – 'Freed from slavery by British valour and philanthropy.' Instead of ending up on plantations on the other side of the Atlantic, they were each given a quarter acre of land, a cooking pot, a spade – and their freedom.

The settlements in Freetown were like miniature nations, as they still are today: the Congolese in Congo town, the Fulani in Wilberforce, the Ashanti in Kissy. In the old days the slaves had been brought to the waterfront in chains and locked to iron bars to await shipment across the Atlantic. Now they came to Freetown to lose their chains and begin new lives. What was going on to turn Britain from the world's leading enslaver to the world's leading

* Not only altruistic but remarkably successful. When I visited Freetown in February 2002, three months before free elections were held in the country, one man I met exclaimed, on learning my nationality: 'Thank God for Britain!'

† In the words of King Gezo, who disposed of 9,000 slaves a year, 'The slave trade has been the ruling principle of my people. It is the source of their glory and wealth. Their songs celebrate their victories and the mother lulls the child to sleep with notes of triumph over an enemy reduced to slavery. Can I, by signing . . . a treaty, change the sentiments of a whole people?'

emancipator? The answer lies in a fervent religious revival, the epicentre of which was, of all places, Clapham.

Zachary Macaulay was one of the first governors of Sierra Leone. The son of the minister at Inverary and father of the greatest of Victorian historians, Macaulay had worked for a time as the manager of a sugar plantation in Jamaica. But he quickly found himself unable to reconcile his work with his Christian faith: the daily whippings he witnessed 'sickened' him too much. In search of kindred spirits, he returned to England, where he was quickly taken up by the banker and Member of Parliament Henry Thornton, the principal financial backer of the Sierra Leone Company, which had been set up as a small private colonizing venture with the principal aim of repatriating the small population of former slaves living in London. It was at Thornton's initiative that Macaulay was sent to Sierra Leone in 1793, where his appetite for hard work in a good cause soon secured him the post of Governor. For the next five years, Macaulay immersed himself in the mechanics of the trade he was now resolved to stamp out, dining with the chiefs of African tribes who supplied slaves from the interior and even crossing the Atlantic on a slave ship to witness for himself the sufferings of those on board. By the time he returned to England, Macaulay was not just an expert on the slave trade; he was *the* expert.

There was only one place in London for a man like Macaulay to live, and that was Clapham. There he could be sure of finding like-minded souls. Indeed, it might be said that the moral transformation of the British Empire began in Holy Trinity Church, on the north side of Clapham Common. Macaulay's fellow parishioners, who included Thornton and the dazzling Parliamentary orator William Wilberforce, combined evangelical fervour with hard-nosed political nous. The Clapham Sect, as they came to be known, excelled at mobilizing a new generation of grassroots activists. Armed with Macaulay's first-hand accounts of the slave trade, they resolved to secure its abolition.

It is not easy to explain so profound a change in the ethics of a people. It used to be argued that slavery was abolished simply because it had ceased to be profitable, but all the evidence points the other way: in fact, it was abolished despite the fact that it was still profitable. What we need to understand, then, is a collective change of heart. Like all such great changes, it had small beginnings. There had long been a minority of people within the British Empire opposed to slavery on religious principles. Quakers in Pennsylvania were speaking out against it as early as the 1680s, arguing that it violated the biblical injunction to 'do unto others as you would have others do unto you' (Matthew 7 : 12). In the 1740s and 1750s the so-called Great Awakening in America and the rise of Methodism in Britain spread such scruples into wider Protestant circles. Others were turned against slavery by the teachings of the Enlightenment; both Adam Smith and Adam Ferguson were against the slave trade, Smith because 'the work done by freemen comes cheaper in the end than that performed by slaves'. But it was only in the 1780s that the campaign against slavery gained enough momentum to sway legislators. Slavery was abolished in Pennsylvania in 1780, an example followed with varying degrees of alacrity by a number of other northern states. In 1788 a law was passed in Westminster to regulate conditions on the slave ships; four years later a bill for gradual abolition passed the Commons only to be rejected by the Lords.

The campaign for abolition was one of the first great extra-Parliamentary agitations. Its leadership was remarkably broad. The founders of the Society for the Abolition of the Slave Trade, Granville Sharp and Thomas Clarkson, were Anglicans, but most of their close associates were Quakers. Support for the cause extended beyond Clapham to embrace the Younger Pitt, the ex-slaver John Newton, Edmund Burke, the poet Samuel Taylor Coleridge and the king of the Potteries, Josiah Wedgwood, himself a Unitarian. Men from all these different denominations made common cause against slavery in meetings like the one attended by the young David Livingstone at Exeter Hall.

The most impressive thing about the campaign was the extent of the support that it mobilized. Wedgwood produced thousands of anti-slavery badges, depicting a black figure on a white background and bearing the motto 'Am I not a man and a brother?' They were soon ubiquitous. When 11,000 people in Manchester alone – two-thirds of the male population – signed a petition calling for an end to the trade, it amounted to a call for an ethical foreign policy, a call so widespread that the government did not dare ignore it. In 1807 the slave trade was abolished. From now on convicted slavers faced, by a nice irony, transportation to Britain's penal colony in Australia. Nor were the reformers satisfied with that victory. In 1814 no fewer than 750,000 names were put to petitions calling for the abolition of slavery itself.

This was the birth of a new kind of politics, the politics of the pressure group. Thanks to the work of zealous activists armed only with pens, paper and moral indignation, Britain had turned against slavery. Even more remarkably, the slave trade had been abolished in the face of determined opposition from some powerful vested interests. The West Indian planters had once been influential enough to intimidate Edmund Burke and hire James Boswell. The Liverpool slave traders were not much less formidable. But they were simply swept aside by the Evangelical tide. The only way the Liverpool merchants could survive was to find a new line of business. Appropriately enough, they found a substitute in the importation of West African palm oil for the manufacture of soap. Literally and metaphorically, the ill-gotten gains of the slave trade were to be washed away after abolition.

One victory led to another. For once the slave trade had gone, slavery itself could only wither. Between 1808 and 1830 the total slave population of the British West Indies declined from about 800,000 to 650,000. By 1833 the last resistance had crumbled. Slavery itself was made illegal in British territory; the helots of the Caribbean were emancipated, their owners compensated with the proceeds of a special government loan.

That did not of course put an end to the transatlantic slave trade or slavery in the Americas. It continued not only in the southern United States but also on a far larger scale in Brazil; all told, around 1.9 million more Africans crossed the Atlantic after the British ban, most of them to Latin America. However, the British did their utmost to disrupt this continuing traffic. A British West Africa

wishing you a guid New Year

From Scotland to Saskatchewan: Agnes Brown, *née* Ferguson,
with her family at Glenrock, *c.* 1911–21

Struggles for mastery of the global market: French and Portuguese ships clash off the coast of Brazil, *c.* 1562; Thomas 'Diamond' Pitt, *c.* 1710–20; the Mast House at Blackwall, 1803

Anglo-Indian encounters: 'Robert Clive with his Family and an Indian
Maidservant', by Sir Joshua Reynolds, *c.* 1765–6; Colonel James Todd
travelling by elephant with cavalry and sepoys; Eight Gurkhas,
commissioned by William Fraser, *c.* 1815.

Slavery and liberty in the New World: Slaves below decks, undated water-colour sketch by Lieutenant Francis Meynell; A sugar plantation in the south of Trinidad, *c.* 1850; The Battle of Bunker's Hill, June 1775

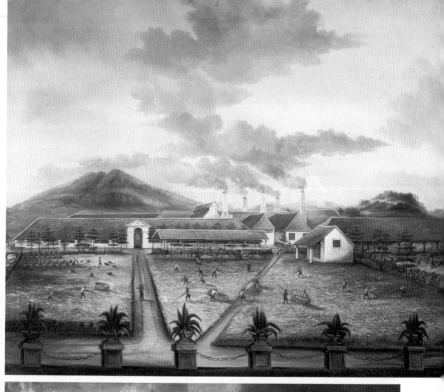

Life on Mars: Flogging of the convict Charles Maher on Norfolk Island,
1823; 'A Government Jail Gang', Sydney, 1830

The Evangelical Ethos: Slaves in chains, Zanzibar;
David Livingstone, c. 1864–5

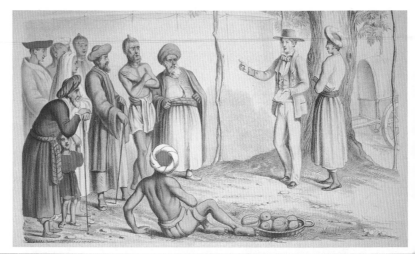

The Religious Origins of the Indian Mutiny: An itinerant preacher in India 'diffuse[s] among the inhabitants ... the light and benign influences of Truth'; 'Relief of Lucknow 1857: Jessie's Dream' by Frederick Goodall.

Squadron was sent to patrol the African coast from Freetown, with bounties offered to naval officers for every slave they intercepted and liberated. With the true zeal of the convert, the British were now determined 'to sweep the African and American seas of the atrocious commerce with which they are now infested'.

The Spanish and Portuguese governments were bullied into accepting prohibitions on the trade, enabling the Royal Navy to proceed against their nationals with impunity; international courts of arbitration were even established. The French rather half-heartedly joined in the patrol, grumbling that the British were interested only in preventing other countries profiting from what they had been foolish enough to prohibit. Only ships flying the flag of the United States defied the British regime. Here was a measure of the strength of the campaign against the slave trade: that it could mobilize not only legislators to ban the trade, but also the Royal Navy to enforce the ban. That the same navy could more or less simultaneously be engaged in opening the ports of China to the Indian opium trade makes clear that the moral impulse for the war against the slave trade did not come from the Admiralty.

The memorial to the Clapham Sect on Holy Trinity Church's east wall salutes Macaulay and his friends who 'rested not until the curse of slavery was swept away from all parts of the British dominions'. But that was only the first stage of a much more ambitious plan. Significantly, the memorial also praises them for labouring 'so abundantly for national righteousness and conversion of the heathen'. That in itself was a new departure. For two hundred years the Empire had engaged in trade, warfare and colonization. It had exported British goods, capital and people. Now, however, it aspired to export British culture. Africans might be backward and superstitious, but to this new generation of British Evangelicals, they also seemed capable of being 'civilized'. As Macaulay put it, the time had come to 'spread over [Africa's] gloomy surface light, liberty and civilization'. Spreading the word of God and thereby saving the souls of the benighted heathen was a new, not-for-profit rationale for expanding British influence. It was to be the defining mission of the century's most successful non-governmental organizations (NGOs).

The missionary societies were the Victorian aid agencies, bringing both spiritual and material assistance to the 'less developed' world. Their origins can be traced back to the Society for the Promotion of the Christian Gospel (1698) and the Society for the Propagation of the Gospel (1701), but these were almost exclusively concerned with the spiritual welfare of British colonists and servicemen posted overseas. Like the anti-slavery movement, the movement to convert indigenous peoples took off in the late eighteenth century. In 1776 the *Evangelical Magazine* devoted an editorial to 'Africa, that much injured country'. It was to 'this benighted and oppressed country' that the magazine's editors were 'desirous of sending the Gospel of Christ . . . that essential blessing which outweighs the evils of the most suffering life'. Sixteen years later William Carey preached a seminal sermon in Nottingham, exhorting his listeners to 'Expect great things from God; Attempt great things for God'; shortly after this, he and some friends formed the first Baptist Society for Propagating the Gospel among the Heathen. This was followed in 1795 by the London Missionary Society, which accepted missionaries from all the non-conformist sects, and in 1799 by the Anglican Church Missionary Society which declared that its aim – indeed, its Christian duty – was 'to propagate the knowledge of the Gospel among the Heathen'. There were also Scottish societies formed in Glasgow and Edinburgh in 1796.

The obvious place to start missionary work in Africa was Free-town. As early as 1804 the Church Missionary Society had begun work there, followed soon after by the Methodists. Both set about converting the Yoruba 'Recaptives' (freed slaves brought to Free-town by the intervention of the Navy). But the intention from the outset was to send missionaries not just to Africa. Anglican missionaries went out to the most remote of British colonies, New Zealand, as early as 1809. On Christmas Day 1814 Samuel Marsden preached from the text 'Behold, I bring you tidings of great joy' to a congregation of uncomprehending Maoris. His survival seems to have attracted others. The Methodists established a mission there in 1823, the Roman Catholics in 1838. By 1839 the Anglicans had eleven mission stations in New Zealand to the Methodists' six. Perhaps the most successful of the early New Zealand missionaries was the Anglican Henry Williams, a fearless ex-sailor who worked there from 1823 until his death in 1867, building the first church (at Paihia) and translating the Bible into Maori. Williams succeeded in winning the respect of the Maoris, not least by intervening to remind them of the Gospel in the middle of a pitched battle. But not every missionary could get away with such challenges to traditional mores. The Revd Carl S. Volkner came to New Zealand in the 1850s, but fell out of favour with the Opotiki Maoris by urging them to desist from bloodshed when war broke out with a rival clan in 1865. One of the Opotiki chiefs hanged him, shot him, decapitated him in his own church, drank his blood and swallowed both his eyes.

Converting the heathen was a dangerous enterprise. To succeed, the missionary movement needed an army of young men – idealistic, altruistic adventurers, willing to go to the ends of the earth to spread the Word. There could not be a greater contrast between the missionaries' motives and those of previous generations of empire-builders, the swashbucklers, the slavers and the settlers.

William Threlfall sailed for South Africa in 1824 at the age of just twenty-three, one of the Methodist Mission's brightest hopes. Even the voyage south came close to killing him when typhus broke out on board his ship, and shortly after going ashore he was taken gravely ill. It gives a flavour of the new idealism of the time that, as he lay on what he feared was his deathbed in Cape Town, he seized hold of a friend's hand and, 'with the most impressive earnestness expressed a wish that he was black, that he might go among the natives of the country without being liable to the suspicion of being influenced by sinister or worldly views'. This time Threlfall recovered. But less than a year later he and a companion were hacked to death by bushmen.

Threlfall and thousands like him were the martyrs of a new evangelical imperialism. Their readiness to sacrifice themselves not for gain but for God was what made the Victorian Empire different from all that had gone before. And behind every missionary – indeed, behind all the Victorian NGOs – were the far more numerous men and women at home who supported and sponsored their work, the type satirized by Dickens in *Bleak House* as Mrs Jellyby, criminally neglectful of her immediate family but passionately dedicated to good causes:

She has devoted herself to an extensive variety of public subjects at various times and is at present (until something else attracts her) devoted to the subject of Africa, with a view to the general cultivation of the coffee berry – AND the natives – and the happy settlement, on the banks of the African rivers, of our superabundant home population ... She was a pretty, very diminutive, plump woman of from forty to fifty, with handsome eyes, though they had a curious habit of seeming to look a long way off. As if ... they could see nothing nearer than Africa!

In many ways, the model mission in Africa was the London Missionary Society's Kuruman establishment in Bechuanaland, nearly 600 miles north-east of Cape Town. Kuruman was regularly cited in LMS literature to show what a well-run mission should be, and you can see why when you go there. It looks like a smart little Scottish village in the heart of Africa, complete with thatched kirk, whitewashed cottages and a red post-box. The essence of the Kuruman project was simple: in turning Africans into Christians, the mission was at the same time civilizing them, changing not just their faith but also their mode of dress, hygiene and housing. The progress made at Kuruman in these respects was enthusiastically reported in the *Missionary Magazine*:

The people are now dressed in British manufactures and make a very respectable appearance in the house of God. The children who formerly went naked and presented a most disgusting appearance are decently clothed ... Instead of a few wretched huts resembling pigsties we now have a regular village, the valley on which it stands which till lately was uncultivated is now laid out in gardens.

In other words, it was not just Christianization that was being attempted here. It was Anglicization.

Then, on 31 July 1841, this ideal mission was struck by a human thunderbolt – a man who was to revolutionize the missionary movement, and to change the relationship between Britain and Africa forever.

Victorian Superman

The son of a tailor turned tea salesman, David Livingstone was born in 1813 in the textile town of Blantyre in Lanarkshire, where he started work in the mill at the age of just ten. He was a prodigious autodidact. Despite a twelve-and-a-half-hour day, six days a week, he buried himself in books, teaching himself Latin and the rudiments of Classical Greek, literally reading as he span. In Livingstone the two great intellectual currents of early nineteenth-century Scotland met: the reverence for science of the Enlightenment, the sense of mission of a revived Calvinism. It was the former that drew him to study medicine; the latter convinced him to put his energies and skills at the disposal of the London Missionary Society. He paid his own way through Anderson's College in Glasgow, then applied to become a missionary in 1838. Two years later, in November 1840, he qualified as Licentiate of the Royal Faculty of Physicians and Surgeons in Glasgow. That same month he was ordained as a minister.

Livingstone's answers to an LMS questionnaire give a revealing insight into the nature of the missionary's vocation:

When first made acquainted with the value of the gospel myself ... the desire that all might enjoy its blessings instantly filled my mind and this next to his own salvation appeared to me ought to be the chief object of every Christian ... [The missionary's] duties chiefly are, I apprehend[,] to endeavour by every means in his power to make known the gospel by preaching, exhortation, conversion, instruction of the young, improving so far as in his power the temporal condition of those among whom he labours by introducing the arts and sciences of civilization and doing everything in his power to commend Christianity to the ears and consciences. He will be exposed to great trials of his faith and patience, from the indifference, distrust and even direct opposition and scorn of those for whose good he is disinterestedly labouring, he may be tempted to despondency from the little apparent fruit to his exertions, and exposed to all the contaminating influences of heathenism . . .

The hardships and dangers of missionary life, so far as I have had the means of ascertaining their nature and extent[,] have been the subjects of serious reflection and in dependence on the promised assistance of the Holy spirit, [I] have no hesitation in saying that I would willingly submit to them considering my constitution capable of enduring any ordinary share of hardship or fatigue.

Livingstone knew quite well what he was letting himself in for. But he also had a strange confidence that he had what it took. And in this he was quite right. After the dark, Satanic mills of Lanarkshire, the world held no terrors for him.

He originally intended to go to China but, when the outbreak of the first Opium War prevented that, persuaded the LMS to send him to South Africa. He seemed the perfect man to carry on the work being done at Kuruman. As both a preacher and a doctor, Livingstone was ideally suited to the task of spreading Christianity and civilization together. Moreover, unlike many a young missionary, he turned out to have an iron constitution that was more than equal to the rigours of African life. He would survive being mauled by a lion and countless attacks of malaria, for which, with characteristic rigour, he devised his own distinctively disagreeable remedy.*

Yet Livingstone was quickly disillusioned by what he found at the Society's model mission. Converting Africans turned out to be painfully slow work, as his early diaries at Kuruman make clear:

The population is sunk into the very lowest state of moral degradation. So much so indeed it must be difficult or rather impossible for Christians

---

* In his own words, 'a violent purgative combined with quinine and the warm bath or ped chivium. I have always observed that as soon as the slightest movement took place in the bowels the perspiration burst forth from the skin and headaches vanished – 3 grains of calomel, 3 of quinine, 10 grains rhubarb, 4 grains of resin jalap mixed with a little spirit is a good combination.' This was the basis of the later 'Livingstone Pill' or 'Zambezi Rouser'.

at home to realize anything like an accurate notion of the grossness which shrouds their minds. No one can conceive the state in which they live. Their ideas are all earthly and it is with great difficulty that they can be brought to detach [them] from sensual objects. . . . All their clothing is soaked in fat, hence mine is soon soiled. And to sit among them from day to day and listen to their roaring music, is enough to give one a disgust to heathenism for ever. If not gorged full of meat and beer they are grumbling, and when their stomachs are satisfied then commences the noise termed singing.

This was the reality behind the *Missionary Magazine*'s pious propaganda. As the mission's founder Robert Moffat admitted, there had been

no conversions, no enquiring after God; no objections raised to exercise our powers in defence. Indifference and stupidity form the wreath on every brow; ignorance – the grossest ignorance – forms the basis of every heart. Things earthly, sensual and devilish, stimulate to motion and mirth, while the great concerns of the soul's redemption appear to them like a ragged garment, in which they see neither loveliness nor worth . . . We preach, we converse, we catechize but without the least apparent success. Only satiate their mendicant spirits by perpetually giving and you are all that is good. But refuse to meet their endless demands, their theme of praise is turned to ridicule and abuse.

Livingstone gradually came to the depressing realization that the Africans showed interest in him not because of his preaching, but because of his medical knowledge – including what they called the 'gun medicine' that enabled him to kill game with his rifle. As he noted dourly of the Bakhtala tribe: 'They wish the residence of white men, not from any desire to know the Gospel, but merely, as some of them in conversation afterwards expressed it, "that by our presence and prayers they may get plenty of rain, beads, guns etc."'

Even when the gospel could be dazzlingly illustrated, using the magic lantern Livingstone carried into every village, the response was disheartening. When Sechele, Chief of the Bakwena, gave him permission to address his people in August 1848, the result came as no surprise:

A good attentive audience but after the service I went to see a sick man and when I returned the chief had retired into a hut to drink beer, and as is the custom about forty men were standing outside and singing to him, or in other words begging beer by that means. A minister who has not seen as much pioneer service as I have done would have been shocked to have seen so little effect produced by an earnest discourse concerning the future Judgement.

It was not until he cured one of Sechele's ailing children that the chief took his message seriously. Only as a healer of the body, it seemed, was it possible to save the African soul.

By now Livingstone had spent seven years as a missionary. Like Moffat, whose daughter Mary he had married in 1845, he had learned the native languages and laboured to translate the Bible into them. But Sechele appeared to be his one and only convert. And just months later, the Chief lapsed, reverting to his tribal custom of polygamy. It was a similar story a few years afterwards, when Livingstone tried to convert members of the Makololo tribe. Another British visitor noted that 'the tribe's favourite pastime' was 'imitating Livingstone reading and singing psalms. This would always be accompanied by howls of derisive laughter.' Not a single Makololo was converted.

Livingstone concluded that doing things by the missionary handbook could never break down what he regarded as 'superstition'. Some better way had to be found to penetrate Africa than simply preaching in the wilderness. The wilderness itself had to be somehow converted – to be made more receptive to British civilization.

But how was he to open up the heart of darkness? To answer that question, Livingstone had to make an unspoken career change. In 1848 he effectively ceased to be a missionary. He became instead an explorer.

Since the foundation of the Royal Geographical Society in 1830 there had been those who had argued that Africa needed to be explored before it could be converted. As early as 1796 Mungo Park had charted the course of the River Niger. Livingstone himself had already dabbled in exploration at Kuruman, but in setting off across the Kalahari desert to find Lake Ngami in 1849 he effectively joined the exploration movement; indeed, his report of the 600–700 mile journey was passed on by the London Missionary Society to the Royal Geographical Society, winning its gold medal and part of its annual Royal Prize for geographical discovery. Whether she liked it or not, his wife now became an explorer too, as did their three children. Livingstone was not unrealistic about the risks involved in taking his entire family into the unknown, but he was unhesitating about the need to run them:

... We have an immense region before us ... It is a venture to take his wife and children into a country where fever, African fever, prevails. But who that believes in Jesus would refuse to make a venture for such a captain? A parent's heart alone can feel as I do when I look at my little ones and ask, Shall I return with this or that one?

It is one of the less easily intelligible characteristics of the early missionaries that they attached more importance to the souls of others than to the lives of their own children. However, a second expedition came so close to killing them all that Livingstone finally decided to send his family home to England. They did not see him again for four and a half years.*

The expeditions to Lake Ngami were the first of a succession of almost superhuman journeys that were to enthral the mid-Victorian imagination. In 1853 Livingstone travelled three hundred miles along the upper reaches of the Zambezi river, then set off from Linyanti in present-day Botswana to Luanda on the coast of Portuguese Angola; in the words of *The Times*, 'one of the greatest geographical explorations of the age'. After recovering his strength, he then retraced his path to Linyanti before embarking on

* Towards the end of his life, Livingstone admitted: 'I have but one regret and that is that I did not feel it my duty to play with my children as much as to teach ... I worked very hard at that and was tired out at night. Now I have none to play with.'

an astonishing march to Quilimane in Mozambique, making him the first European literally to traverse the continent from the Atlantic to the Indian Oceans. Here was the quintessential hero of the age, sprung from humble origins, blazing a trail for British civilization in what was manifestly the least hospitable of all the world's continents. And he was doing it unprompted, voluntarily. Livingstone had become a one-man NGO – the nineteenth century's first *médicin sans frontières*.

To Livingstone, the search for a way to open up Africa to Christianity and civilization was made still more urgent by the discovery that slavery was still thriving. Though the slave trade in the west of the continent had supposedly been suppressed following the British abolition law, slaves continued to be exported from Central and East Africa to Arabia, Persia and India. Perhaps as many as two million Africans fell victim to this eastward traffic in the course of the nineteenth century; hundreds of thousands of them passed through the great slave market on the island of Zanzibar, which linked together the various economies of the Indian Ocean.* To a man of Livingstone's generation, who had no experience of the far larger slave trade the British themselves had once run in West Africa, the spectacle of slave caravans and the devastation and depopulation they left in their wake was profoundly shocking. 'The strangest disease I have seen in this country', he later wrote, 'seems really to be broken-heartedness, and it attacks free men who have been captured and made slaves ... One fine boy of about twelve years ... said he had nothing the matter with him, except pain in his heart.' Livingstone was as indignant about the sufferings of slaves as a previous generation had been indifferent to them.

It is easy to dismiss the Victorian missionaries as cultural chauvinists, unthinkingly dismissive of the African societies they encountered. This charge cannot be levelled at Livingstone. Without the assistance of the indigenous peoples of Central Africa, his

* You can still see the slave cells in Stonetown today: dark, dank and stiflingly hot, they convey as starkly as anything I know the misery inflicted by slavery.

journeys would have been impossible. The Makololo may not have accepted Christianity, but they were eager to work for him; and as he came to know them and the other tribes who helped them, his attitudes gradually changed. The Africans, he wrote, were often 'wiser than their white neighbours'.

To those who portrayed them as murderous, he replied that he had 'never entertained any suspicions of foul play while among pure Negroes and was with one or two exceptions always treated politely, indeed so thoroughly civil were the more central tribes [that] ... a missionary of ordinary prudence and tact would certainly secure respect'. He refused to believe, he would later write, 'in any incapacity of the African in either mind or heart ... In reference to the status of Africans among the nations of the earth, we have seen nothing to justify the notion that they are of a different "breed" or "species" from the most civilized.' It was precisely Livingstone's respect for the Africans he encountered that made the slave trade so repugnant to him; for it was this 'trade of hell' that was destroying their communities before his very eyes.

Up until now Livingstone had only had to contend with what seemed to him primitive superstitions and subsistence economies. Now, however, he was on a collision course with a sophisticated economic system organized from the East African coast by Arab and Portuguese slave traders. Yet in his usual undaunted way, he had soon worked out a scheme that would not only open up Africa to God and civilization, but also dispose of slavery into the bargain. Like so many Victorians, he took it for granted that a free market would be more efficient than an unfree one. In his view, 'the witchery of the slave trade' had distracted attention 'from every other source of wealth' in Africa: 'Coffee, cotton sugar oil iron and even gold were abandoned for the delusive gains of a trade which rarely enriches.' If an easier route could be found by which honest merchants could travel to the interior and establish 'legitimate trade' in these other commodities – buying the products of free African labour rather than taking that labour by force and exporting it – then the slave traders would be put out of business. Free labour would drive out unfree. All Livingstone had to do was to find this route.

In his search for the artery of civilization, Livingstone was indefatigable. Indeed, compared with those who struggled to keep pace with him, he seemed indestructible. Already the first white man to cross the Kalahari Desert, the first white man to see Lake Ngami and the first white man to traverse the continent, in November 1855 he became the first to see what is perhaps the greatest of all the natural wonders of the world. East of Esheke, the smooth flow of the Zambezi is dramatically punctuated by a vast chasm. The locals knew the cascade as Mosioatunya, 'the smoke that thunders'. Livingstone – already aware of the need to attract backing for his work back home – promptly renamed it the Victoria Falls 'as proof of my loyalty'.*

Reading Livingstone's journals, it is impossible not to be struck by his passionate enthusiasm for the African landscape. 'The whole scene was extremely beautiful,' he wrote of the Falls. 'No one can imagine the beauty of the view from anything witnessed in England':

As it broke, wild pieces of water all rushing on in the same direction each gave off several rays of foam exactly as bits of steel when burned in oxygen give off rays of sparks. The snow white sheet seemed like myriads of small comets rushing on in one direction each of which gave off ... from its nucleus streams of foam.

These were 'scenes so lovely they must have been gazed upon by angels in their flight'; they were quite simply 'the most wonderful sight in Africa'. Such sentiments help explain Livingstone's transition from missionary work to exploration. A loner, at times even a misanthrope, he plainly found it more fulfilling to trudge a thousand miles through the African interior for the sake of a sublime view than to preach a thousand sermons for the sake of a single convert. Nevertheless, the sheer beauty of the Victoria Falls only

---

* 'Some other things have taken well in quarters where I did not expect it,' he noted, 'and the whole together may have a smack of the "wisdom of the serpent", though I meant it not so.'

partly explains Livingstone's excitement. For he always insisted that he was travelling with a purpose: to find a way to open up Africa to British commerce and civilization. And in the Zambezi itself he appeared to have found the key to fulfilling his grand design.

Beyond the Falls, Livingstone assumed, the river must be navigable to the sea some 900 miles away. That surely meant that it could be used to bring commerce to the African hinterland, allowing European civilization to flow up river in its wake. As tribal 'superstitions' dissolved under its influence, Christianity would at last take root. And as legitimate commerce spread inland it would undermine the slave trade by creating free employment for Africans. The Zambezi, in short, was – must be – God's intended highway.

And right beside the Victoria Falls was precisely the kind of place where British settlers could establish themselves: the Batoka plateau, a landscape of 'open undulating lawns covered with short herbage such as poets and natives call a pastoral country', but where 'wheat of superior quality and abundant yield' also flourished, along with 'other cereals and excellent roots in great variety'. It was here in the Zambian Highlands that Livingstone believed his countrymen – ideally, poor but hardy Scots like himself – would be able to establish a new British colony. Like so many explorers before and since, he believed he had found the Promised Land. But this was to be a cultural as much as an economic El Dorado. Once settled by white men, the Batoka Plateau would radiate civilizing waves, until the whole continent had been cleansed of superstition and slavery.

Mindful of the need to integrate his new colony into the imperial economy, Livingstone even had a staple crop in mind for Batoka. Cotton would be grown there, reducing the dependence of British textile mills (like the one where he had spent his childhood) on cotton grown by American slaves. It was a bold, messianic vision that linked together not only commerce, civilization and Christianity but also free trade and free labour.

*

In May 1856 Livingstone set off for England on a new mission. This time, however, the people he intended to convert were the British public and government and the good book he was peddling was his own *Missionary Travels and Researches in South Africa*. And this time conversion was instantaneous. He was showered with medals and honours. He was even granted a private audience with the Queen. As for the book, it was an immediate bestseller, selling 28,000 copies in the space of seven months. In *Household Words*, Dickens himself gave it an ecstatic review, candidly confessing that

the effect of it on me has been to lower my opinion of my own character in a most remarkable and most disastrous manner. I used to think I possessed the moral virtues of courage, patience, resolution and self control. Since I have read Doctor Livingstone's volume, I have been driven to the humiliating conclusion that, in forming my own opinion of myself, I have been imposed upon by a false and counterfeit article. Guided by the test of the South African Traveller, I find that my much prized courage, patience resolution and self control turn out to be nothing but plated goods.

What especially impressed Dickens were

the author's unflinching honesty in describing his difficulties and acknowledging his disappointments in the attempt to plant Christianity among the African savages; his sensible independence of all those mischievous sectarian influences which fetter so lamentably the exertions of so many good men; and his fearless recognition of the absolute necessity of associating every legitimate aid which this world's wisdom can give with the work of preaching the Gospel to heathen listeners.

This endorsement, emphasizing as it did the ecumenical breadth of Livingstone's appeal, could not have been better calculated to drum up support for his grand African design. 'None of Doctor Livingstone's many readers', Dickens concluded, 'more cordially wish him success in the noble work to which he has again devoted himself – no one will rejoice more sincerely in hearing of his safe and prosperous progress whenever tidings of him may reach England – than the writer of these few lines.' Even the London Missionary Society, which had been less than happy with Livingstone's desertion of his official missionary duties, had to acknowledge in its 1858 annual report that *Missionary Travels* had 'extended sympathy' for the missionary movement. Faint praise, but praise just the same.

And yet, as the LMS report could not help but add, Livingstone's success had almost at once been overshadowed by 'awful, yet instructive events ... so unexpectedly ... permitted by the providence of God'. For in the very year that the book made its appearance, a storm broke on the other side of the world that would throw the whole strategy of Christianizing the Empire into question.

The Clash of Civilizations

For the missionaries, the interior of Africa was virgin territory. Indigenous cultures struck them as primitive; previous contact with Europeans had been minimal. In India, by contrast, the missionary movement faced an altogether more difficult challenge. Here was a manifestly more sophisticated civilization than Africa's. Polytheistic and monotheistic systems of belief were both deeply entrenched. And Europeans had been living alongside Indians for more than a century and a half without challenging these other faiths.

Until the first decades of the nineteenth century, the British in India had not the slightest notion of trying to Anglicize India, and certainly not to Christianize it. On the contrary, it was the British themselves who often took pleasure in being orientalized. Since the time of Warren Hastings, an overwhelmingly male population of merchants and soldiers had adapted to Indian customs and learned Indian languages; many also took Indian mistresses and wives. Thus, when Captain Robert Smith of the 44th (East Sussex) Regiment travelled around India between 1828 and 1832, he was unsurprised to encounter and admire a beautiful princess from Delhi whose sister was '. . . married although of the royal lineage to the son of an officer of rank in the [East India] Company's service

... She had several children, two of whom I saw and ... they were in outward appearance little mahommedans, wearing turbans etc.' Smith himself found the lady in question's features 'of the highest order of beauty'. Something of an amateur artist, he was fond of sketching Indian women – and not out of purely anthropological interest. As he put it:

The mild expression, so characteristic of this race, the beauty and regularity of the features and the symmetrical form of the head are striking and convey a high idea of the intellectuality of the Asiatic race ... This classical elegance of form is not confined to the head alone, the bust is often of the finest proportions of ancient statuary and when seen through the thin veil of flowing muslin as the graceful Hindu female ascends from her morning ablution in the Ganges is a subject well worth the labour of the poet or artist.*

An Irishman, Smith was already married to a fellow countrywoman before he was posted to India. But men who came out in the East India Company's service as bachelors frequently went further in their admiration of Asian womanhood. In one of his *Home Letters Written from India* (mainly dating from the 1830s) Samuel Snead Brown observed that 'those who have lived with a native woman for any length of time never marry a European ... so amusingly playful, so anxious to oblige and please [are they], that a person after being accustomed to their society shrinks from the idea of encountering the whims or yielding to the fancies of an English-woman'.

This atmosphere of mutual tolerance and even admiration was the way the East India Company liked it, even if it practised religious toleration more out of pragmatism than principle. Although now more like a state than a business, its directors continued to regard trade as their paramount concern; and since by the 1830s and 1840s 40 per cent of the total value of Indian exports took the form of opium, there was not a great deal of room

---

* Smith's only caveat was that he felt the typical Indian woman's lower half was 'badly formed and ill calculated to harmonize with so beautiful a superstructure'. He had clearly given the matter a good deal of thought.

for high-mindedness in the boardroom. The old India hands in Calcutta, Madras and Bombay had no interest whatsoever in challenging traditional Indian culture. On the contrary, they believed that any such challenge would destabilize Anglo-Indian relations; and that would be bad for business. As Thomas Munro, Governor of Madras, put it drily in 1813: 'If civilization is ever to become an article of trade between [Britain and India], I am convinced that this country will gain by the import cargo.' There was no point, in his view, in trying to 'make Anglo-Saxons of the Hindoos':

I have no faith in the modern doctrine of the improvement of the Hindus, or of any other people. When I read, as I sometimes do, of a measure by which a large province had been suddenly improved, or a race of semi-barbarians civilized almost to Quakerism, I throw away the book.

That was why East India Company chaplains were explicitly banned from preaching to the Indians themselves. And that was why the company used its power to restrict the entry of missionaries into India, forcing those who wished to work there to base themselves in the small Danish enclave at Serampore. As Robert Dundas, the President of the Board of Control in India, explained to Lord Minto, the Governor-General, in 1808:

We are very far from being averse to the introduction of Christianity into India . . . but nothing could be more unwise than any imprudent or injudicious attempt to induce it by means which should irritate and alarm their religious prejudices . . . It is desirable that the knowledge of Christianity should be imparted to the native, but the means to be used for that end shall only be such as shall be free from any political danger or alarm . . . Our paramount power imposes upon us the necessity to protect the native inhabitants in the free and undisturbed possession of their religious opinions.

In 1813, however, the company's charter came up for renewal, and the Evangelicals seized their chance to end its control over missionary activity in India. The old orientalism was about to clash head-on with the new evangelicalism.

The men who wanted India open to British missionaries were the same men who had waged the campaign against the slave trade and launched the missionary movement in Africa: William Wilberforce, Zachary Macaulay and the rest of the Clapham Sect, now reinforced by Charles Grant, a former East India Company director who had experienced a religious conversion after a thoroughly misspent youth in India. As an insider, Grant was crucial; he played a role in this campaign analogous to that of Newton, the ex-slaver, and Macaulay, the ex-plantation manager, in the campaigns against slavery. In his *Observations On the state of Society among the Asiatic Subjects of Great Britain*, Grant threw down the gauntlet to Munro and the other advocates of toleration:

Is it not necessary, to conclude that . . . our Asiatic territories . . . were given to us, not merely that we might draw an annual profit from them, but that we might diffuse among their inhabitants, long sunk in darkness, vice and misery, the light and the benign influences of Truth . . .?

The campaign began in the New London Tavern with a meeting of the 'Committee of the Protestant Society', which called for the 'speedy and universal promulgation' of Christianity 'throughout the regions of the East'. In vain did directors of the East India Company protest. By the time Parliament voted, 837 petitions had been sent in from eager Evangelicals all around the country, urging an end to the exclusion of missionaries from India. Altogether nearly half a million people signed them. Twelve of these petitions can still be seen in the House of Lords library, most of them from the south of England. It is a sign of how well oiled the machinery of extra-Parliamentary pressure now was that nearly all use exactly the same preamble:

The inhabitants of the populous regions in India which form an important portion of the British Empire, being involved in the most deplorable state of moral darkness, and under the influence of the most abominable and degrading superstitions, have a pre-eminent claim on the most compassionate feelings and benevolent services of British Christians.

One group of petitioners 'beheld with poignant grief the horrible rites and the degrading immorality which prevail among the

immense population of India, now our fellow subjects and ...
fondly cherished the hope that we can introduce them to the
religious and sound blessings which the inhabitants of Great
Britain enjoy'. This was also a formula, originally adopted at a
Church Missionary Society meeting in Cheapside in April 1813 and
disseminated through Evangelical newspapers like *The Star*.

Here was another carefully co-ordinated public campaign to
challenge the *status quo*; and just as had happened when the issue
was the slave trade, it was Clapham that prevailed over the vested
interests. In 1813 a new East India Act not only opened the door to
missionaries, but also provided for the appointment of a bishop
and three archdeacons for India. At first, these representatives of
the church Establishment were reluctant to antagonize the company
by admitting missionaries. When the missionary George Gogerly
arrived in India in 1819 he was amazed to discover that

missionaries had nothing to expect in the way of encouragement, either
from the Government or the European inhabitants of the place. The morality of the latter was of the most questionable character, and the presence
of the missionary was a check on their conduct which they did not choose
to tolerate; whilst the officers of the Government looked upon them with
suspicion. Both parties did all in their power to make them appear
contemptible in the eyes of the natives; describing them as low-caste people
in their own country and quite unfit to hold conversation with the learned
Brahmins.

But the second Bishop of Calcutta, Reginald Heber, offered the
missionaries more encouragement after his appointment in 1823.
Nine years later there were fifty-eight Church Missionary Society
preachers active in India. The clash of civilizations had begun.

To many of the missionaries, the subcontinent was a battleground in which they, as soldiers of Christ, were struggling against
the forces of darkness. 'Theirs is a cruel religion,' Wilberforce had
bluntly declared. 'All practices of this religion have to be removed.'
Indian reactions only served to harden such attitudes. Just as he
was about to begin a service in his own bungalow, George Gogerly
found himself assailed by two men 'as filthy in their appearance

as it is possible to imagine, with blood-shot eyes and demoniacal look, evidently under the influence of some powerful stimulating drug'.

In loud threatening tones [they] commanded us to be silent. Then, turning to the people they declared that we were the paid agents of the Government, who not only had robbed them of their country, but who were determined by force to put down both Hindooism and Mohammedanism and to establish Christianity throughout the land; that their home would be defiled by the killers of the sacred cow, and eaters of her flesh; that their children would be taught in their schools to revile the holy Brahmins and discontinue the worship of the gods. Pointing to us they then exclaimed, 'These men come to you with honeyed words, but there is poison in their hearts; they intend only to deceive that they may destroy.'

Gogerly was indignant at this interruption, particularly when the crowd set upon him and his colleagues, beat them and chased them through the streets (though he 'rejoic[ed] that we were counted worthy to suffer shame for His name'). But the 'Boiragees' who attacked him were quite right. The missionaries did indeed intend much more than simply to convert Indians to Christianity. Almost as important as the Evangelical project was the idea that India's whole culture needed to be Anglicized.

It was not only the missionaries who took this view. Increasingly influential in mid-nineteenth-century India was the more secular doctrine of Liberalism. Its eighteenth-century precursors, notably Adam Smith, had been hostile to imperialism. But the greatest of the Victorian Liberal thinkers, John Stuart Mill, took a very different view. In 'A Few Words on Non-intervention', Mill asserted that England was 'incomparably the most conscientious of all nations . . . the only one whom mere scruples of conscience . . . would deter' and 'the power which of all in existence best understands liberty'. It was therefore in the best interests of Britain's colonies in Africa and Asia – so he argued in *Considerations on Representative Government* (1861) – that they enjoy the benefits of her uniquely advanced culture:

first, a better government: more complete security of property; moderate taxes; a more permanent . . . tenure of land. Secondly, improvement of the public intelligence; the decay of usages or superstitions which interfere with the effective implementation of industry; and the growth of mental activity, making the people alive to new objects of desire. Thirdly, the introduction of foreign arts . . . and the introduction of foreign capital, which renders the increase of production no longer exclusively dependent on the thrift or providence of the inhabitants themselves, while it places before them a stimulating example.

The crucial phrase here is 'the decay of usages or superstitions which interfere with the effective implementation of industry'. Like Livingstone, Mill saw the cultural transformation of the non-European world as inextricably linked to its economic transformation. These twin currents of the Evangelical desire to convert India to Christianity and the Liberal desire to convert it to capitalism flowed into one another, and over the entire British Empire.

Nowadays, the modern equivalents of the missionary societies campaign earnestly against 'usages' in far-flung countries that they regard as barbaric: child labour or female circumcision. The Victorian non-governmental organizations were not so different. In particular, three traditional Indian customs aroused the ire of British missionaries and modernizers alike. One was female infanticide, which was common in parts of north-western India. Another was thagi (then usually spelt 'thuggee'), the cult of assassin-priests, who were said to strangle unwary travellers on the Indian roads. The third, the one the Victorians most abhorred, was sati (or 'suttee'): the act of self-immolation when a Hindu widow was burned alive on her husband's funeral pyre.*

The British had been aware that certain Indian communities engaged in female infanticide since the late 1780s; the principal reason seems to have been the excessive cost to high-caste families of marrying off their daughters. However, it was not until 1836

---

* The Hindu practice of *anumarana* ('dying after') or *sahamarana* ('dying along with') was incorrectly called 'suttee' by the British. In fact the word *sati* refers to the widow who incinerates herself, and could be translated as 'saint'.

that James Thomason, then the Magistrate of Azamgarh and later Lieutenant-Governor of the North Western Provinces, took the first active steps to stamp it out. In 1839 the Maharaja of Marwar was persuaded to pass a law prohibiting the practice. This was only the beginning of a sustained campaign. A systematic survey in 1854 found that the practice was endemic in Gorakhpur, Ghazipur and Mirzapur. After further research – including detailed analyses of village census data – a new act was passed in 1870, initially applying only to the North Western Provinces but later extended to the Punjab and Oudh.*

The campaign against thagi was pursued with equal zeal, though the extent of the practice was altogether more doubtful. It was a Cornishman named William Sleeman – a soldier turned investigating magistrate – who set out to extirpate what he maintained was a complex and sinister secret society, dedicated to the ritual murder of Indian travellers. According to an influential article on the subject published in the *Madras Literary Gazette* in 1816, the putative Thugs,

. . . skilled in the arts of deception . . . enter into conversation and insinuate themselves, by obsequious attentions, into the confidence of travellers of all descriptions . . . When [they] determine to attack a traveller, they usually propose to him, under the specious plea of mutual safety or for the sake of society, to travel together and on arriving at a convenient place and a fit opportunity presenting one of the gang puts a rope or sash round the neck of the unfortunate persons, while others assist in depriving him of his life.

Modern scholars have suggested that much of this was a figment of the over-heated expatriate imagination, and that what Sleeman was actually dealing with was an increase in common or garden highway robbery owing to the demobilization of hundreds of thousands of native soldiers as the British extended their power into new Indian states. Nevertheless, his dedication to his self-appointed task well illustrates how seriously the British took their mission to modernize Indian culture. By 1838 Sleeman had captured and

* Nowadays spelt 'Awadh', but 'Oudh' to the Victorians.

tried a total of 3,266 Thugs; several hundred more were in prison awaiting trial. In all 1,400 were either hanged or transported for life to the Andaman Islands. One of those he interrogated claimed to have murdered 931 people. Appalled, Sleeman asked him whether he ever felt 'remorse for murdering in cold blood, and after the pretence of friendship, those whom you have beguiled into a false sense of security'. 'Certainly not!' replied the accused. 'Are you yourself not a *shikari* (big-game hunter) and do you not enjoy the thrill of stalking, pitting your cunning against that of an animal, and are you not pleased at seeing it dead at your feet? So with the Thug, who regards the stalking of men as a higher form of sport.' One of the judges who presided over a major trial of alleged Thugs was moved to declare:

In all my experience in the judicial line for upwards of twenty years I have never heard of such atrocities or presided over such trials, such cold-blooded murder, such heart-rending scenes of distress and misery, such base ingratitude, such total abandonment of every principle which binds man to man, which softens the heart and elevates mankind above the brute creation.

If proof of the degeneracy of traditional Indian culture were needed, here it was.

Above all, there was sati. This certainly was no imaginary construct. Between 1813 and 1825 a total of 7,941 women died this way in Bengal alone. Even more shocking than the statistics were the lurid accounts of particular cases. On 27 September 1823, for example, a widow named Radhabyee fled twice from the burning pyre on which her husband's corpse lay. According to the evidence given by one of the two officers who were eye-witnesses, the first time she ran out of the fire she was only burned on the legs. Indeed, she would have survived had she not been forced back on to the pyre by three men, who flung wood on top of her in order to keep her there. When she escaped again and plunged into the river, this time with 'almost every inch of skin on her body burnt', the men followed her and held her under the water in order to drown her. Incidents like this were, of course, exceptional and sati was far from ubiquitous. Indeed, a number of eminent Indian authorities – notably the scholars Mrityunjay Vidyalankar and Rammohun Roy – denounced the practice as inconsistent with Hindu law. Yet many Indians persisted in regarding a widow's self-immolation as the supreme act not just of marital fidelity but of female piety. Although traditionally associated with higher caste Hindus, sati increasingly appealed to lower castes, not least because it neatly solved the problem of which family members should look after an impecunious widow.

For years the British authorities had tolerated sati in the belief that a clampdown would be seen as an unwarranted interference in Indian religious customs. Now and then individual officials, following the example of the founder of Calcutta, Job Charnock,* would intervene where it seemed possible to save a widow; but official policy remained strictly *laissez faire*. Indeed, a regulation of 1812 requiring the presence of an official – to ensure that the widow was not under sixteen, pregnant, the mother of children under the age of three or under the influence of drugs – seemed to condone sati in all other circumstances. Inevitably, it was the Clapham Sect who led the campaign for a ban, and it followed the now familiar pattern: emotive speeches in Parliament, graphic reports in the *Missionary Register* and *Missionary Papers* and a pile of public petitions. In 1829 the recently appointed Governor-General, William Bentinck, responded. Under Regulation XVII, sati was banned.

Of all the Victorian Governors-General, Bentinck was perhaps the most strongly influenced by both the Evangelical and the Liberal movements. Bentinck was a devout modernizer. 'Steam navigation is the great engine of working [India's] moral improvement,' he told Parliament in 1837. 'In proportion as the communication between the two countries shall be facilitated and shortened, so will civilized Europe be approximated, as it were, to these benighted regions; as in no other way can improvement in any large stream be expected to flow in.' An improving landlord in Norfolk, he saw himself as 'chief agent' to a 'great estate', and could hardly wait to drain the marshes

---

* Who married the woman he rescued from her first husband's funeral pyre.

of Bengal – as if the province were one giant fen. Bentinck regarded Indian culture as equally in need of drainage. In the debate which raged between Orientalists and Anglicists over education policy in India, he unhesitatingly sided with the Anglicists, whose object was, in the words of Charles Trevelyan, 'to educate Asiatics in the sciences of the West', not to clutter up good British brains with Sanskrit. Here too was a way the British could contribute to 'the moral and intellectual regeneration of the people of India': by establishing 'our language, our learning, and ultimately our religion in India'. The aim, Trevelyan argued, was to produce Indians 'more English than Hindus, just as the Roman provincials became more Romans than Gauls or Italians'.

Bentinck had made up his mind on the issue of sati even before his appointment in 1827. 'To the Christian and to the Englishman,' he wrote, 'who by tolerating sanctions, and by sanctioning incurs before God the responsibility of this inhuman and impious sacrifice', there could be no excuse for its continuance:

The whole and sole justification is state necessity – that is, the security of the British empire, and even that justification, would be, if at all, still very incomplete, if upon the continuance of the British rule did not entirely depend the future happiness and improvement of the numerous population of this eastern world . . . I do not believe that among all the most anxious advocates of that measure any one of them could feel more deeply than I do, the dreadful responsibility hanging over my happiness in this world and the next, if as the governor-general of India I was to consent to the continuance of this practice for one moment longer, not than our security, but than the real happiness and permanent welfare of the Indian population rendered indispensable.

Only a few old India hands spoke out against the ban. Writing from Sitapur to Bentinck's military secretary, Lt.-Col. William Playfaire offered a dark warning:

Any order of government prohibiting the practise would create a most alarming sensation throughout the native army, they would consider it an interference with their customs and religion amounting to an abandonment of those principles which have hitherto guided government in its conduct towards them. Such a feeling once excited, there is no possibility of predicting what might happen. It might break out in some parts of the army in open rebellion . . .

Such fears were premature, and for the moment could be ignored amid the thousands of congratulatory letters Bentinck received from evangelical Britons and enlightened Indians alike. In any case, other army officers Bentinck consulted supported the prohibition.* But Playfaire's concerns were far from groundless, and they were shared by Horace H. Wilson, one of the most eminent Oriental scholars of the age. A reaction against the imposition of British culture on India was indeed brewing. And Playfaire was all too right about where the trouble would arise.

The rock on which British rule was founded was the Indian Army. Although by 1848 the East India Company was in a position to add territory to the Empire by simply taking over when a ruler died without an heir (the so-called 'doctrine of lapse') it was ultimately the threat of armed force that enabled it to do so. When it had to fight – in Burma in the 1820s, in Sind in 1843, in the Punjab in the 1840s – the Indian Army was rarely beaten. Its only significant nineteenth-century reverses were in Afghanistan, where in 1839 all but one man of an occupying army of 17,000 had been wiped out. Yet eight out of ten of those who served in the Indian Army were sepoys, drawn from the country's traditional warrior castes. British troops – who were in fact very often Irish – were a small minority, albeit often militarily crucial.

---

* Captain Robert Smith, the admirer of Indian feminine beauty encountered above, was adamant that abolishing female infanticide and sati had strengthened not weakened British rule, since 'a very numerous class of the Hindus are not so sensitive on points of their religion now as formerly'. He wanted to see a further ban on the depositing of corpses in the River Ganges. All this would demonstrate 'a determination on the part of the government to relieve [the Hindu population] from the thraldom of a domineering and self interested priesthood; at the same time leaving them the undisturbed practice of their religion when not accompanied by rites at which humanity shudders'.

Unlike their white comrades-in-arms, the sepoys were not drawn from the dregs of society, taking the Queen's shilling as a last resort. Whether they were Hindus, Muslims or Sikhs, the sepoys considered their calling as warriors inseparable from their religious faith. On the eve of battle, Hindu soldiers would make sacrifices or offerings before the idol of Kali, the goddess of destruction, to win her blessing. But Kali was a dangerous, unpredictable deity. According to Hindu legend, when she first came to earth to cleanse it of wrongdoers she ran amok, killing everyone in her path. If the sepoys felt their religion was under threat, they might well follow her example. They had done so once before, at Vellore in the summer of 1806, when new dress regulations abolishing their right to wear caste marks and beards and introducing a new style of turban had precipitated a mutiny. As would be the case in 1857, an apparently trivial point – the fact that the cockade on the new turban appeared to be made of cow or pig hide – masked a much wider dissatisfaction with pay, conditions and politics.* But at root the Vellore mutiny was about religion; its principal victims were in fact native Christians. Sir George Barlow had no hesitation in laying the blame on 'preaching Methodists and wild visionaries' who had been 'disturbing the religious ceremonies of the Natives'.

In that sense, 1857 was a repetition of Vellore, but on a much grander, more terrible scale. As every schoolboy knows, it began with rumours that the new cartridges about to be issued were lubricated with animal fat. As the ends of these had to be bitten off before use, both Hindus and Muslims ran the risk of defilement – the former if the grease was from cows, the latter if it came from pigs. Thus it was that a shot began a conflict before it had even been loaded, much less fired. To many sepoys, it seemed to prove that the British did indeed have a plan to Christianize India – which, as we have seen, many of them did. The fact that the cartridges had nothing whatever to do with that plan was beside the point.

The Indian Mutiny was therefore much more than its name

---

* The mutineers had turned for leadership to the sons of Tipu Sultan, the 'Tiger of Mysore'.

implies. It was a full-blown war. And its causes were more profound than lard-coated cartridges. 'The First War of Independence'
is what the Indian schoolbooks and monuments call it. Yet Indians
fought on both sides and independence was not the issue. It had,
as at Vellore, a political dimension, but the mutineers' aims were
not national in the modern sense. It also had its humdrum causes:
the frustration of Indian soldiers at their lack of promotion
prospects, for example.* Of far greater significance, however, was
their essentially conservative reaction against a succession of British
interferences with Indian culture, which seemed to – and in many
ways actually did – add up to a plot to Christianize India. 'I can
detect the near approach of the storm,' wrote one perceptive and
anxious British officer on the eve of the catastrophe. 'I can hear the
moaning of the hurricane, but I can't say how, when or where it
will break forth . . . I don't think they know themselves what they
will do, or that they have any plan of action except of resistance to
invasion of their religion, and their faith.'

First and foremost, as the scant Indian testimony which has
survived makes clear, this was indeed 'a war in the cause of religion' (the phrase recurs time and again). In Meerut the mutineers
cried: 'Brothers, Hindoos and Mussalmans, haste and join us, we
are going to a religious war':

The kafirs had determined to take away the caste of all Mahomedans
and Hindoos . . . and these infidels should not be allowed to remain in
India, or there would be no difference between Mahomedans and Hindoos,
and whatever they said, we should have to do.

In Delhi the mutineers complained: 'The English tried to make
Christians of us.' Whether they called their rulers the Europeans,

---

* Henry Lawrence's testimony on this point is illuminating: 'The sepoy feels that we
cannot do without him; and yet the highest reward that a sepoy can obtain . . . is
about one hundred pounds a year without a prospect of a brighter career for his son.
Surely this is not inducement to offer to a foreign soldier for special fidelity and long
service.' Was it reasonable to expect 'that the energetic and aspiring among *immense*
military masses should like our . . . arrogation to ourselves . . . of *all* authority and
emolument'?

the Feeringhee, the kafirs, the infidels or the Christians, this was their central grievance.

The first mutineers were men of the 19th Bengal Infantry, stationed at Berhampur, who refused to accept the issue of new cartridges on 26 February. They and the 34th Infantry at Barrackpur – where the first shot of the Mutiny was actually fired – were promptly disbanded. But at Meerut (Mirath) near Delhi the spark was not so easily snuffed out. When eighty-five men in the Bengal Light Cavalry were jailed for refusing the new cartridges, their comrades resolved to free them. Private Joseph Bowater described what happened next, on the fateful evening of Sunday 9 May:

There was a sudden rising . . . a rush to the horses, a swift saddling, a gallop to the gaol . . . a breaking open of the gates, and a setting free, not only of the mutineers who had been court-martialled, but also of more than a thousand cut-throats and scoundrels of every sort. Simultaneously, the native infantry fell upon and massacred their British officers, and butchered the women and children in a way that you cannot describe. Gaolbirds, bazaar riff-raff, and Sepoys – all the disaffected natives in Meerut – blood-mad, set about their work with diabolical cruelty, and, to crown their task, they fired every building they came across.

The revolt spread with astonishing rapidity across the north-west: to Delhi, Benares, Allahabad and Cawnpore. Once they had resolved to defy their white officers, the mutineers seemed to run amok, killing every European they could find, often aided and abetted by local urban mobs.

On 1 June 1857 Mrs Emma Ewart, the wife of a British officer, was huddled inside the besieged Cawnpore barracks with the rest of the white community. She described her fears in a letter to a friend in Bombay: 'Such nights of anxiety, I would have never believed possible. Another fortnight we expect will decide our fate and whatever it may be, I trust we shall be able to bear it.' Six weeks later, with help only a day away, she and more than 200 British women and children were dead, either killed during the siege or hacked to death in the Bibighar or House of the Ladies – after they had been promised safe passage when the garrison surrendered. Among the dead were Mrs Ewart's friends, Miss Isabella White and Mrs George Lindsay, along with the latter's three daughters, Caroline, Fanny and Alice. They and the other women of Cawnpore would provide the British account of the Mutiny with its tragic heroines.

Its heroes were the men of Lucknow. There the British garrison, beseiged at the British Residency, held out defiantly in what was to become the Mutiny's most celebrated episode. The Resident himself was one of the first to die and is buried close to where he fell, under the classically understated epitaph:

Here Lies Henry Lawrence, Who Tried To Do His Duty.

The ruined, bullet-riddled Residency itself became a memorial in its own right. The Union Jack that flew here during the siege was not subsequently lowered until Independence in 1947, echoing Tennyson's tremulous poem on the subject: 'And ever aloft on the palace roof the old banner of England blew.' The siege was certainly one of those rare events genuinely worthy of Tennysonian high diction. Even the senior boys at the nearby La Martinière School joined in the defence, earning the school a unique military decoration (a distinction the entirely Indian pupils today have not forgotten). Under relentless sniper fire and menaced by mines from below, those inside the Residency held out unassisted for nearly three months, and remained under siege even after a relief force broke through in late September and evacuated the women and children. In fact, it was not until 21 March 1858, nine months after the siege had begun, that Lucknow was recaptured by British forces. By that time nearly two-thirds of the British community who had been trapped in the Residency were dead.

Yet two things need to be remembered about Lucknow. First, it was the capital of a province, Oudh, which the British had annexed only a year before; in that sense, the besiegers were simply trying to liberate their own country. Indeed, the annexation may be regarded as one of the political causes of the Mutiny, since a very large number of sepoys – as many as 75,000 within the Bengal army –

hailed from Oudh and were plainly alienated by the deposition of their Nawab and the dissolution of his army.* In the words of Mainodin Hassan Khan, one of the few mutineers who lived to write an account of the experience: 'It [was] pressed upon the Sepoys that they must rebel to reseat the ancient kings on their thrones, and drive the trespassers away. The welfare of the soldier caste required this; the honour of their chiefs was at stake.' Secondly, about half of the 7,000 people who sought refuge in the Residency were loyal Indian soldiers and camp followers. Despite what was later written, the Mutiny was not a simple struggle between black and white.

Even in Delhi the battle lines were blurred. Here was the historic capital of the Mughal Empire, surely the crucial battleground if the mutineers genuinely dreamt of ousting the British from all of India. And indeed many of the Muslim mutineers did look for leadership to the Bahadur Shah Zafar, last of the Mughals, now merely the King of Delhi – much to his consternation. There still survives a five-point proclamation issued in his name appealing to a broad range of Indian social groups – zamindars (the local landowners-cum-tax collectors on whom both Mughal and British rule was based), merchants, public employees, artisans and priests – to unite against British rule. It is perhaps the nearest thing produced during the Mutiny to a manifesto for national independence. True, its fifth paragraph acknowledges that 'at present a war is raging against the English on account of religion' and calls on 'pundits and fakirs . . . to present themselves to me, and take their share in the holy war'. But the rest of the manifesto is wholly secular in its tone. The British are accused of imposing excessive tax assessments on the zamindars, excluding Indian merchants from trade, displacing the products of Indian artisans with British imports and monopolizing 'all the posts of dignity and emolument' in both the civil and armed services. Yet the memorial to the soldiers killed fighting on the British side, which still stands on a hill overlooking Delhi, shows how little this last

---

* It was characteristic of the Evangelical era that Wajid Ali was deposed on the grounds that he was excessively debauched.

appeal was heeded. The inscription shows that a third of the casualties among officers and fully 82 per cent of the casualties among the other ranks were classified as 'native'. When Delhi fell to 'British' forces, those forces were mostly Indian.

The British at home nevertheless insisted on regarding the Mutiny as a revolt of black against white. Nor was it simply the idea that Indians were killing Britons. It was the fact that supposedly loyal sepoys were killing – and, it was rumoured, raping – white women. Eyewitnesses supplied plentiful hints of such atrocities. As Private Bowater put it in his memoir:

Regardless of sex, in spite of their appeals to mercy, deaf to the piteous cries of the little ones, the mutineers had done their monsters' work. Massacre itself would have been terrible enough; but they had not been satisfied with that, for to murder they had added outrage and nameless mutilation . . . I beheld all that was left of the wife of an adjutant, who, before she was shot and cut to pieces, had had her clothes set on fire by men who were no longer human.

Lurid atrocity stories proliferated. In Delhi, it was claimed, forty-eight British women had been paraded through the streets, publicly ravished and then put to death. A captain's wife had been boiled alive in *ghee* (liquefied butter). Such tall tales confirmed in the minds of credulous people at home that the Mutiny was a struggle between good and evil, white and black, Christian and heathen. And if the calamity was to be construed as a manifestation of divine wrath, then that only went to show that the conversion of India had commenced too late for God's liking.

The year 1857 was the Evangelical movement's *annus horribilis*. They had offered India Christian civilization, and the offer had been not merely declined but violently spurned. Now the Victorians revealed the other, harsher face of their missionary zeal. In churches all over the country, the theme of the Sunday sermon switched from redemption to revenge. Queen Victoria – whose previous indifference to the Empire was transformed by the Mutiny into a passionate interest – called the nation to a day of repentance and prayer: 'A Day of Humiliation', no less. In the Crystal Palace, that monument to Victorian self-confidence, a vast congregation of 25,000 heard the incandescent Baptist preacher Charles Spurgeon issue what amounted to a call for holy war:

My friends, what crimes they have committed! . . . The Indian government never ought to have tolerated the religion of the Hindoos at all. If my religion consisted of bestiality, infanticide and murder, I should have no right to it unless I was prepared to be hanged. The religion of the Hindoos is no more than a mass of the rankest filth that imagination ever conceived. The Gods they worship are not entitled to the least atom of respect. Their worship necessitates everything that is evil and morality must put it down. The sword must be taken out of its sheath, to cut off our fellow subjects by their thousands.

Those words would be taken literally when the sections of the Indian army that remained loyal, the Gurkhas and Sikhs in particular, were deployed. In Cawnpore Brigadier-General Neill forced captured mutineers to lick the blood of their white victims before executing them. At Peshawar forty were strapped to the barrels of cannons and blown apart, the old Mughal punishment for mutiny. In Delhi, where the fighting was especially fierce, British troops gave no quarter. The fall of the city in September was an orgy of slaughter and plunder. Mainodin Hassan Khan described how 'the English burst like a pent-up river through the city . . . No one's life was safe. All able-bodied men who were seen were taken for rebels and shot.' In a moment of singular imperial ruthlessness, the King of Delhi's three sons were arrested, stripped and shot dead by William Hodson – the son of a clergyman. He explained his conduct to his brother, also a clergyman:

I appealed to the crowd, saying that these were the butchers who had murdered and brutally used helpless women and children, and that the government had now sent their punishment: seizing a carbine from one of my men I deliberately shot them one after the other . . . the bodies were taken into the city, and thrown out on to the Chiboutra [midden] . . . I intended to have them hung, but when it came to a question of 'They' or 'Us', I had no time for deliberation.

It was, as Zachary Macaulay's son observed, a fearful paroxysm to behold – the vengefulness of the Evangelicals: 'The account of that dreadful military execution at Peshawar . . . was read with delight by people who three weeks ago were against all capital punishment.' *The Times* had demanded that 'every tree and gable-end in the place should have its burden in the shape of a mutineer's carcass'. And indeed the route of the British retaliation could be followed by the scores of corpses they left hanging from trees along the line of their march. In the words of Lieutenant Kendal Coghill: 'We burnt every village and hanged all the villagers who had treated our fugitives badly until every tree was covered with scoundrels hanging from every branch.' At the height of the reprisals, one huge banyan tree – which still stands in Cawnpore – was festooned with 150 corpses. The fruits of the Mutiny were bitter indeed.

No one can be sure how many people died in this orgy of vengeance. What we can be sure of is that sanctimony bred a peculiar cruelty. In the wake of the relief of Lucknow, a young boy approached the gate to the city, supporting a tottering old man,

and throwing himself at the feet of an officer, asked for protection. That officer . . . drew his revolver, and snapped it at the wretched supplicant's head . . . Again he pulled the trigger – again the cap missed; again he pulled, and once more the weapon refused its task. The fourth time – thrice he had time to relent – the gallant officer succeeded, and the boy's life blood flowed at his feet.

To read this story is to be reminded of the way SS officers behaved towards Jews during the Second World War. Yet there is one difference. The British soldiers who witnessed this murder loudly condemned the officer's action, at first crying 'shame' and giving vent to 'indignation and outcries' when the gun went off. It was seldom, if ever, that German soldiers in a similar situation openly criticized a superior.

The project to modernize and Christianize India had gone disastrously wrong; so wrong that it had ended up by barbarizing the British. Those who actually had to run India had been proved right:

interfering with native customs had meant nothing but trouble. Yet the Evangelicals refused to accept this. In their eyes, the Mutiny had happened because Christianization had not progressed fast enough. As early as November 1857, one missionary in Benares wrote that he felt 'as if a blessing were descending on us in answer to the fervent prayers of our brethren in England':

Instead of giving way to despondency, well does it become us to brace ourselves anew for our Master's work, in the full assurance that our labour will not be in vain. Satan will again be defeated. He doubtless intended, by this rebellion, to drive the Gospel from India; but he has only prepared the way, as often before in the history of the Church, for its wider diffusion.

The leaders of the London Missionary Society echoed this view in their 1858 report:

By the deeds of perfidy and blood which have characterized the Sepoy rebellion, the delusion and false security long indulged by multitudes both in Britain and in India, have been for ever destroyed and idolatry, in alliance with the principles and spirit of Mahomet, has exhibited its true character, a character only to be understood to be dreaded and abhorred ... The labours of the Christian Missionary, which were heretofore treated with derision and contempt are now commended as the best and only preservative of property liberty and life.

The Society resolved to send an additional twenty missionaries to India within the next two years, earmarking £5,000 for their 'passage and outfit' and a further £6,000 for their maintenance. By 2 August 1858 the special fund set up for this purpose had already attracted donations totalling £12,000.

In short: it was onward, Christian soldiers.

In Livingstone's Footsteps

On 4 December 1857, just as Cawnpore was being reclaimed from the Indian mutineers, David Livingstone gave a rousing lecture in Cambridge University's Senate House. The man who had set out to

Christianize Africa made it clear that he also saw the Indian Mutiny as the result of too little missionary work, not too much:

I consider we made a great mistake when we carried commerce into India, in being ashamed of our Christianity . . . Those two pioneers of civilization – Christianity and commerce – should ever be inseparable; and Englishmen should be warned by the fruits of neglecting that principle as exemplified in the management of Indian affairs.

Here, however, Livingstone overreached himself. Neither his advice nor the fulminations of the missionary societies were heeded in the reconstruction of British rule in India that followed the Mutiny. On 1 November 1858 Queen Victoria issued a proclamation that explicitly renounced 'the right and the desire to impose Our convictions on any of Our subjects'. India was henceforth to be ruled not by the East India Company – it was to be wound up – but by the crown, represented by a Viceroy. And the new government of India would never again lend its support to the Evangelical project of Christianization. On the contrary, the aim of British policy in India would henceforth be to govern with, rather than against, the grain of indigenous tradition. The attempt to transform Indian culture might have been 'well inspired' and its 'principles right'; but, as the British official Charles Raikes put it, the Mutiny had exposed 'the fatal error of attempting to force the policy of Europe on the people of Asia'. From now on 'political security' would be paramount: India would be administered as an unchanging and unchangeable society, and the missionary organizations would be tolerated by the government of India only if they accepted that basic premise. By the 1880s most British officials had reverted to the habit of their predecessors of the 1820s in regarding missionaries as, at best, absurd, at worst, subversive.

Africa was another matter, however; and the future of Africa was the crux of Livingstone's Cambridge lecture. Here, he argued, the British could avoid the mistakes they had made in India precisely because the commercial development of Africa could *coincide* with its religious conversion. His aim was 'to open a path' to the highlands of the Batoka Plateau and neighbouring Barotseland so that 'civilization, commerce and Christianity might find their way there'; from this bridgehead all Africa would be 'opened ... for commerce and the Gospel':

By encouraging the native propensity for trade, the advantages that might be derived in a commercial point of view are incalculable; nor should we lose sight of the inestimable blessings it is in our power to bestow upon the unenlightened African by giving him the light of Christianity ... By trading with Africa, also, we should at length be independent of slave labour, and thus discountenance practices so obnoxious to every Englishman.

As he concluded in a peroration carefully crafted to stir the youthful ardour of his audience:

The sort of men who are wanted for missionaries are such as I see before me. I beg to direct your attention to Africa; – I know that in a few years I shall be cut off in that country, which is now open, do not let it be shut again! I go back to Africa to try to make an open path for commerce and Christianity; do you carry out the work which I have begun. I LEAVE IT WITH YOU!

In the mood of national crisis engendered by events in India, Livingstone's call to get things right in Africa met with a euphoric reception. Those persuaded by his vision of a Christian Africa rushed to join a new organization, the Universities Mission to Central Africa. Among them was a young pastor from Oxford called Henry de Wint Burrup. Two days before he set off for Africa, Burrup married. It was to be a tragically short-lived union.

In February 1861 Henry Burrup's wife returned home without him. Her husband, together with his newly appointed bishop, Charles Frederick Mackenzie, had perished in a Malawian swamp – Burrup of dysentery, Mackenzie of fever. Nor were they the only victims. The London Missionary Society sent the Revd Holloway Helmore with an assistant named Roger Price to Barotseland, along with their wives and five children. After just two months, only Price and two of the children were left alive. Central and East Africa are scattered with dozens of missionary graves – men, women and children who heeded Livingstone's call and paid for it with their lives. The problem was simple enough. Despite Livingstone's tourist-brochure promises about the 'healthy highlands of Central Africa', the Batoka plateau turned out to be infested with malarial mosquitoes. So was the other site Livingstone had suggested as a possible missionary centre, the Zomba Plateau in what is now Malawi. The local tribes also proved unexpectedly hostile. These places were quite simply uninhabitable by Europeans.

More serious still, there turned out to be a fundamental flaw in Livingstone's geography. Following the Zambezi on foot from Victoria Falls towards the Indian Ocean, he had bypassed a fifty-mile section, believing it to be more of the same wide river. He could not have been more wrong.

In the aftermath of his Cambridge lectures, with his prestige at its zenith, Livingstone had secured – for the first time – government backing for his endeavours. With a government grant of £5,000 and the diplomatic title of Consul, he was able to embark on an expedition up the Zambezi, the principal aim of which was to demonstrate its navigability and suitability for commercial traffic. By now Livingstone's ambitions knew no bounds. Confidentially, he informed the Duke of Argyll and the Cambridge Professor of Geography Adam Sidgwick that the expedition had a further objective:

I take a practical mining geologist from the School of Mines to tell us of the Mineral Resources of the country [Richard Thornton], then an economic botanist [Dr John Kirk] to give a full report on the vegetable productions – fibrous, gummy and medicinal substances together with the dye stuffs – everything which may be useful in commerce. An artist [Thomas Baines] to give the scenery, a naval officer [Commander Norman Bedingfeld] to tell of the capacity of the river communications and a moral agent to lay the foundation for knowing that aim fully [probably a reference to Livingstone's brother Charles, a Congregational minister in the United States]. All this machinery has for its ostensible object the development of African trade and the promotion of civilization but what I have to tell to none but such as you in whom I have full confidence is that I hope it may result in an English colony in the healthy highlands of Central Africa.

With these high hopes, Livingstone arrived at the mouth of the Zambezi on 14 May 1858.

Reality did not take long to intrude. It soon became apparent that the river was much too shallow for the steamer the expedition had been lent by the Colonial Office. The expedition was decanted into a much smaller paddle steamer, but it too constantly grounded on sandbanks. It took until November for them to reach Kebrabasa, by which time sickness and dissension were rife in their ranks. And here they found the most fatal of all the flaws in Livingstone's plan. At Kebrabasa – the place his earlier expedition had bypassed on foot – the Zambezi flows into a narrow, stone-walled channel which transforms it into a raging, impassable torrent; at one point it plunges over a thirty-foot waterfall which no boat could possibly negotiate. In a word, the Zambezi was and is not navigable. And with that, the project to penetrate Africa with commerce, civilization and Christianity was sunk.

Livingstone flailed around, feverishly trying to salvage the situation. He stubbornly insisted that 'a steamer of light draught would pass the rapids without difficulty when the river is in full flood'. He struck up the River Shire, only to encounter more rapids and threatening natives. He struggled on past Lake Shire to Lake Nyasa. By now, however, the expedition was disintegrating: Bedingfeld was forced to resign, Thornton dismissed (though he refused to go), Baines sacked on a bogus charge of pilfering the stores, the engineer, George Rae, sent back to England to get a new boat. In March 1862 came news of the deaths of Bishop Mackenzie and Henry Burrup. A month later Mary Livingstone, who had by now joined her husband, herself succumbed to hepatitis, her constitution weakened by chronic alcoholism. By now Livingstone was in a state of severe mental turmoil, quarrelling bitterly with the few people still with him. Kirk, whose loyalty to Livingstone somehow never wavered, was at one point left behind when he set off to collect specimens on Mount Morumbala and had to run after the expedition's replacement boat, the portable steamer *Lady Nyassa*, yelling desperately for it to stop. 'That will teach you to be twenty minutes late,' was Livingstone's sole comment as Kirk clambered aboard.

Kirk concluded sadly that 'Dr L.' was 'what is termed "cracked"'.

Back in Britain, opinion now turned against Livingstone. On receiving letters from him proposing that a colony could be established in the Shire Highlands, the Prime Minister, Lord Palmerston, retorted bluntly that he was 'very unwilling to embark on new schemes of British possessions'. Livingstone 'must not be allowed to tempt us to form colonies only to be reached by forcing steamers up cataracts'. On 2 July 1863 the expedition was formally recalled. *The Times* led the public backlash with a bitter editorial:

We were promised cotton, sugar and indigo, commodities which savages never produced, and of course we got none. We were promised trade and there is no trade. We were promised converts and not one has been made. We were promised that the climate was salubrious, and some of the best missionaries with their wives and children have died in the malarious swamps of the Zambezi.

At Kuruman Livingstone had failed as a missionary. Now, it seemed, he had failed as an explorer.

Yet this Victorian man of iron simply did not know how to give up. Despite the fiasco of the Zambezi expedition, he still could see a way to snatch a victory from the wreckage. It was just a matter of getting back to the roots of the Evangelical movement: anti-slavery. While languishing by Lake Nyasa, the Zambezi expedition had encountered a number of slave convoys. Once again, Livingstone was galvanized into action by the sight of human suffering. Having sailed the *Lady Nyassa* 2,500 miles across the Indian Ocean to Bombay – in itself an amazing feat, given that the forty-foot vessel was a shallow-bottomed river steamer – Livingstone returned to London and prepared to rejoin the battle against the 'trade of hell'. On 19 March 1866 he set off from Zanzibar with a new expedition and an old purpose: to stamp out slavery once and for all.

The remaining years of Livingstone's life were spent in strange, almost mystical wanderings around Central Africa. At times he seemed to be conducting research on the slave trade; at times obsessively seeking the true source of the Nile, the Holy Grail of Victorian exploration; at times just trudging through the jungle for its own sake. On 15 July 1871 he witnessed a horrific massacre at a town called Nyangwe, where Arab slave traders pulled out their guns after an argument over the price of a chicken and indiscriminately shot more than 400 people. The experience only deepened Livingstone's aversion to the slavers; yet in practice he was forced to rely on them for supplies and porters when his own sources failed. Nor was his search for the source of the Nile any more successful. Like his new Jerusalem on the Zambezi, it too eluded him: the ancient 'fountains' he dreamt of locating, which he believed both Ptolemy and Herodotus had described, turned out to be treacherous swamps that drained into the Congo.

David Livingstone's grave – which looks rather incongruous in the Gothic grandeur of Westminster Abbey – bears a simple inscription in his own words: 'All I can add in my solitude, is, may heaven's rich blessing come down on every one ... who will help to heal this open sore of the world.' The words were a carefully crafted injunction to the next generation. The 'open sore' was, of course, the slave trade, which Livingstone had become convinced was the source of all Central Africa's troubles.

He had died, at Ilala by the shores of Lake Bangweolo, in the small hours of 1 May 1873, a disappointed man; the slave trade seemed, ultimately, to be ineradicable. Yet just over a month later the open sore of slavery did begin to heal. On 5 June that same year the Sultan of Zanzibar signed a treaty with Britain pledging to abolish the East African slave trade.* The old slave market was sold to the Universities Mission to Central Africa who erected above the old slave cells a rather splendid cathedral – a fitting monument to Livingstone's posthumous success as an abolitionist. Symbolically, the altar was built on the exact spot where the slaves had once been flogged.

Nor did Livingstone's triumph from beyond the grave end there. In the shadow of the Batoka Plateau, hard by the Victoria Falls, lies

---

* As usual it took naval force to secure his signature, in the form of a threatened blockade of the island.

the Zambian town of Livingstone, named after the good doctor himself.* For decades after his visit no Christian could come here and hope to survive because of malaria and native hostility. Yet between 1886 and 1895 the number of Protestant missions in Africa trebled. Today Livingstone, with a population of just 90,000, has no fewer than 150 churches, making it surely one of the most intensively evangelized places on earth. And this is only one small town in a continent where millions of people today embrace Christianity. Africa is in fact a more Christian continent than Europe. There are now, for example, more Anglicans in Nigeria than in England.

How did a project that had seemed a total washout in Livingstone's lifetime yield such astonishing long-term results? Why was it possible in the end to achieve in vast areas of Africa what had failed so badly in India? Part of the explanation obviously lies in the development of effective quinine-based prophylactics against malaria. That made being a missionary a far less suicidal vocation than in the early 1800s; by the end of the century there were as many as 12,000 British missionaries 'in the field', representing no fewer than 360 different societies and other bodies.

But the other half of the answer lies in one of the most famous meetings in the history of the British Empire.

Henry Morton Stanley – born John Rowland, the illegitimate son of a Welsh housemaid – was an ambitious, unscrupulous and trigger-happy American journalist. Apart from an iron constitution and equally ferrous will, he had almost nothing in common with David Livingstone. A turncoat and a deserter during the American Civil War, Stanley had established his reputation as an ace reporter by bribing a telegraph clerk to send his copy ahead of his rivals during the Anglo-Abyssinian War.† When the editor of the *New York Herald* commissioned him to find Livingstone, who had not been heard of for months since embarking on yet

---

* Though I was assured by the chief of nearby Mukuni that the name derives from the notion that the chief of Mukuni is a 'living stone'.

† See Chapter 4.

another expedition up the Rovuma river towards Lake Tanganyika, Stanley scented the biggest scoop of his career.

After a ten-month hunt, interrupted when he became embroiled in a minor war between Arabs and Africans, Stanley finally found Livingstone at Ujiji on the northern shore of Lake Tanganyika on 3 November 1871. His account of the encounter makes it clear that he was almost overwhelmed by his moment of glory:

[W]hat would I not have given for a bit of friendly wilderness, where unseen, I might vent my joy in some mad freak, such as idiotically biting my hand, turning a somersault or slashing at trees in order to allay those exciting feelings that were well-nigh uncontrollable. My heart beats fast, but I must not let my face betray my emotions, lest it shall detract from the dignity of a white man appearing under such extraordinary circumstances.

So I did that which I thought was most dignified. I pushed back the crowds, and, passing from the rear, walked down a living avenue of people, until I came in front of the semicircle of Arabs, in front of which stood the white man with his grey beard. As I advanced slowly towards him I noticed he was pale, looked wearied, had a grey beard, wore a bluish cap with a faded gold band round it, had on a red-sleeved waistcoat and a pair of grey tweed trousers. I would have run to him, only I was a coward in the presence of such a mob – would have embraced him, only, he being an Englishman, I did not know how he would receive me; so I did what cowardice and false pride suggested was the best thing – walked deliberately up to him, took off my hat, and said: 'Dr Livingstone, I presume.'

It took an American to take British understatement to its historic zenith.

When Stanley's story broke, it dominated the front pages of the English-speaking world. Yet this was more than just a scoop. It was also a symbolic meeting between two generations: the Evangelical generation that had dreamt of a moral transfiguration of Africa and a new, hard-nosed generation with more worldly priorities. Cynical though he was, aware though he quickly became of the cantankerous old man's faults, Stanley was touched and inspired by the meeting. Indeed, he came to regard himself as Livingstone's successor, as if their meeting at Ujiji had somehow anointed him. 'If

God willed it,' he later wrote, he would be 'the next martyr to geographical science, or if my life is spared . . . [would] clear up . . . the secrets of the Great River [Nile] throughout its course.' At the time of Livingstone's funeral (at which he was among the eight pall-bearers), Stanley wrote in his diary: 'May I be selected to succeed him in opening up Africa to the Shining light of Christianity.' But he added a significant rider: 'My methods, however, will not be Livingstone's. Each man has his own way. His, I think, had its defects, though the old man, personally has been almost Christ-like for goodness, patience . . . and self-sacrifice.'

Goodness, patience and self-sacrifice were not to be the qualities Henry Stanley brought to Africa. When he led an expedition up the River Congo, he went equipped with Winchester rifles and elephant guns, which he did not hesitate to use on unco-operative natives. Even the sight of spears being shaken at his boat made him reach for his repeating gun: 'Six shots and four deaths', he recorded with grim satisfaction after one such encounter, 'were sufficient to quiet the mocking.' By 1878 Stanley was working on behalf of King Leopold II of the Belgians to create a private colony for his International African Association in the Congo. By an irony that would have appalled Livingstone, the Belgian Congo would soon become notorious for its murderous system of slave labour.

Livingstone had believed in the power of the Gospel; Stanley believed only in brute force. Livingstone had been appalled by slavery; Stanley would connive at its restoration. Above all, Livingstone had been indifferent to political frontiers; Stanley wanted to see Africa carved up. And so it was. In the time between Livingstone's death in 1873 and Stanley's death in 1904 around a third of Africa would be annexed to the British Empire; virtually all the rest would be taken over by a handful of other European powers. And it is only against this background of political domination that the conversion of sub-Saharan Africa to Christianity can be understood.

Commerce, Civilization and Christianity were to be conferred on Africa, just as Livingstone had intended. But they would arrive in conjunction with a fourth 'C': Conquest.

4

Heaven's Breed

A man should, whatever happens, keep to his own caste, race and breed. Let the White go to the White and the Black to the Black.

Kipling

The Victoria Memorial in the centre of Calcutta was intended by the British to be their answer to the Taj Mahal, a timeless expression of imperial grandeur that would awe those over whom they ruled. Today, however, the statue of Queen Victoria, gazing wearily out over the Maidan, looks more like a symbol of the transient nature of British rule. Splendid though it looks, the memorial is a solitary white island in the sea of Bengalis who inhabit every available corner of this miasmic metropolis. The astounding thing is that for the better part of two centuries not just Bengal but the whole of India was ruled by just a few thousand Britons. As someone remarked, the government of India was 'a gigantic machine for managing the entire public business of one-fifth of the inhabitants of the earth without their leave and without their help'.

The British were also able to use India to control an entire hemisphere, stretching from Malta all the way to Hong Kong. It was the foundation on which the entire mid-Victorian Empire stood.

Yet behind the marble façade, the Raj was the conundrum at the very heart of the British Empire. How on earth did 900 British civil servants and 70,000 British soldiers manage to govern upwards of 250 million Indians?

How did the Victorians do it?

The Annihilation of Distance

At the apex of the Victorian Empire was the Queen herself: industrious, opinionated, as passionate in private as she was impassive in public, indefatigably procreative and spectacularly long-lived. Like a latter-day Plantagenet, she was remarkably peripatetic. She disliked Buckingham Palace, preferred Windsor and had a soft spot for remote and rainy Balmoral. Her favourite residence, however, was probably Osborne, on the Isle of Wight. It had been acquired and remodelled at the instigation of her adored husband (and cousin) Albert and it was one of the few places where the couple could enjoy a measure of that privacy – and intimacy – which they were usually denied. It was, she declared, 'so snug & nice to have a place of *one's own*, – quiet & retired . . . It is impossible to imagine a prettier spot, we have a charming beach quite to ourselves – we can walk anywhere without being followed or mobbed.'

Osborne House itself is built in the Renaissance style, a typical piece of nineteenth-century architectural historicism. It is both literally and metaphorically thousands of miles from the global Empire over which Victoria reigned. In other ways, however, it was far from backward looking. The garish allegorical fresco above the main staircase looks at first sight like yet more Italianate pastiche. But closer inspection reveals 'Britannia' receiving the crown of the sea from Neptune, attended by 'Industry', 'Commerce' and 'Navigation'. As those three figures on her right suggest, the royal couple understood full well the connection between Britain's economic power and her global mastery.

Since the late eighteenth century, Britain had been pulling ahead of her rivals as a pioneer of new technology. British engineers were in the vanguard of a revolution – the Industrial Revolution – that harnessed the power of steam and the strength of iron to transform the world economy and the international balance of power. Nothing illustrated this better than the view from Osborne House, which looks straight across the Solent. Reassuringly visible on the other side is Britain's principal naval base at Portsmouth, then the largest in the world, and an imposing manifestation of British sea power. Fog permitting, the Queen could watch the comings and goings of her navy as she and her husband promenaded through Osborne's elegantly landscaped gardens. By 1860 she would have been able to pick out with ease the supreme expression of mid-Victorian might: HMS *Warrior*. Steam-driven, 'iron clad' in five inches of armour plate and fitted with the latest breech-loading, shell-firing guns, *Warrior* was the world's most powerful battle-ship, so powerful that no foreign vessel ever dared to exchange fire with her. And she was just one of around 240 ships, crewed by 40,000 sailors – making the Royal Navy the biggest in the world by far. And thanks to the unrivalled productivity of her shipyards, Britain owned roughly a third of the world's merchant tonnage. At no other time in history has one power so completely dominated the world's oceans as Britain did in the mid-nineteenth century. Queen Victoria had good cause to feel secure by the seaside.

If the British wished to abolish the slave trade, they simply sent the navy. By 1840 no fewer than 425 slave ships had been inter-cepted by the Royal Navy off the West African coast and escorted to Sierra Leone, where nearly all of them were condemned. A total of thirty warships were engaged in this international policing oper-ation. If the British wished the Brazilians to follow their example by abolishing the slave trade, they simply sent a gunboat. That was what Lord Palmerston did in 1848; by September 1850 Brazil had passed a law abolishing the trade. If the British wished to force the Chinese to open their ports to British trade – not least to exports of Indian opium – they could once again send the navy. The Opium Wars of 1841 and 1856 were, of course, about much more than opium. The *Illustrated London News* portrayed the 1841 war as a crusade to introduce the benefits of free trade to yet another benighted Oriental despotism; while the Treaty of Nanking, which ended the conflict, made no explicit reference to opium. Likewise, the Second Opium War – sometimes known as the Arrow War, after the ship that was the *casus belli* – was fought partly to uphold British prestige as an end in itself; just as the ports of Greece had been blockaded in 1850 because a Gibraltar-born Jew claimed that his rights as a British subject had been infringed by the Greek authorities. Yet it is very hard to believe the Opium Wars would have been fought if exports of opium, prohibited by the Chinese authorities after 1821, had not been so crucial to the finances of British rule in India.* The only real benefit of acquiring Hong Kong as a result of the war of 1841 was that it provided firms like Jardine Matheson with a base for their opium-smuggling operation. It is indeed one of the richer ironies of the Victorian value-system that the same navy that was deployed to abolish the slave trade was also active in expanding the narcotics trade.

What these events – the war against slavery and the wars for opium – had in common was that British naval mastery made them possible. At first, it is true, the Admiralty had been appalled by the advent of steam, believing it would 'strike a fatal blow at the naval supremacy of the Empire'. But quickly it became apparent that the new technology had to be adopted, if only to keep up with the French. (The French warship *La Gloire*, launched in 1858, had been one of the principal reasons for building HMS *Warrior*.) Far from weakening the Empire, steam power tended to knit it together. In the days of sail it had taken between four and six weeks to cross the Atlantic; steam reduced that to two weeks in the mid-1830s and just ten days in the 1880s. Between the 1850s and the 1890s, the journey time from England to Cape Town was cut from forty-two to nineteen days. Steamships got bigger as well as faster: in the same period, average gross tonnage roughly doubled.†

Nor was that the only way the Empire became more tightly knit.

---

* It is a remarkable fact that throughout the first half of the nineteenth century the amount the East India Company earned from its monopoly on the export of opium was roughly equal to the amount it had to remit to London to pay the interest on its huge debt (see chart on p. 167). The opium trade was also crucial to the Indian balance of payments.

† Not only did it therefore take much less time to cross the oceans from metropolis to empire; it also cost a great deal less. The cost of shipping a bushel of wheat from New York to Liverpool was halved between 1830 and 1880 and halved again between 1880 and 1914. In 1830 transport costs for bar iron had been not much less than total production costs; by 1910 they were less than a fifth.

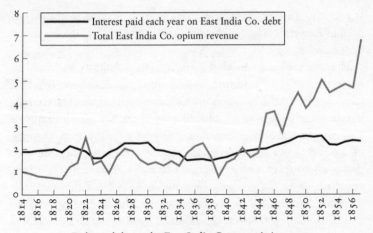

Debt and dope: the East India Company's interest
payments and opium revenue, 1814–1857 (£ million)

In the early years of her reign – until the Indian Mutiny, in fact – Victoria had taken relatively little interest in foreign affairs outside Europe. But the Mutiny awoke her with a jolt to her imperial responsibilities, and as her reign wore on they took up more and more of her attention. In December 1879 she recorded 'a long talk with Ld Beaconsfield, after tea, about India and Affghanistan [*sic*] and the necessity for our becoming Masters of the country and holding it . . .' In July 1880 she was 'urg[ing] strongly on the Govt, to do all in their power to uphold the safety and honour of the Empire'. 'To protect the poor natives and to advance civilization,' she told Lord Derby in 1884, was to her mind 'the mission of Great Britain'. 'It is I think important', she declared airily in 1898, 'that the world at large should not have the impression that we will not let any one but ourselves have anything . . .' In one of the more obscure corners of Osborne House is a clue to why the Queen felt in closer touch with her Empire as she grew older. It was not considered worthy of preservation when the house was given to the nation in 1902, but downstairs in the Household Wing was the Queen's telegraph office. By the 1870s messages from India could reach here in a matter of hours; and the Queen read them attentively. This perfectly illustrates what happened to the world during Victoria's reign. It shrank – and it did so largely because of British technology.

The telegraph was another invention the Admiralty had tried to ignore. Its original inventor, Francis Ronalds, had been rebuffed when he offered the Navy his brainchild in 1816. It was not the military but the private sector that developed the nineteenth century's information highway, initially piggy-backing on the infrastructure of the early railways. By the late 1840s it was clear that the telegraph would revolutionize overland communications; by the 1850s construction in India was sufficiently advanced for the telegraph to play a decisive part in suppressing the Mutiny.* However, the crucial development from the point of view of imperial rule was the construction of durable undersea cables. Significantly, it was an imperial product – a rubber-like substance from Malaya called gutta-percha – that solved the problem, allowing the first cross-Channel cable to be laid in 1851 and the first transatlantic cable to follow fifteen years later. When the Anglo-American Telegraph Company's cable finally reached the American coast on 27 July 1866, having been successfully unrolled and dropped along the ocean floor by Isambard Kingdom Brunel's mighty *Great Eastern*, it was plainly the dawn of a new era. That the cable ran from Ireland to Newfoundland made it clear which power was most likely to dominate the age of the telegraph. That the telegraph link from India to Europe had already been constructed by the government of India several years earlier made it clear that the rulers of that power (for all their *laissez-faire* principles) were resolved that it should do so.† By 1880 there were altogether 97,568 miles of cable across the world's oceans, linking Britain to India, Canada, Australia, Africa and Australia. Now a message could be relayed from Bombay to London at the cost of four shillings a word with the reason-

---

* One mutineer, on his way to execution, identified the telegraph as 'the accursed string that strangles me'.

† Although the British domestic network was nationalized, most of the overseas network was constructed and operated by private enterprise.

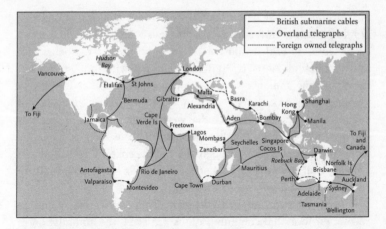

The global telegraph network *c.* 1913: the imperial information highway

able expectation that it would be seen the next day.* In the words of Charles Bright, one of the apostles of the new technology, the telegraph was 'the world's system of electrical nerves'.

The telegraph cable and the steamship route were two of three metal networks that simultaneously shrank the world and made control of it easier. The third was the railway. Here too the British tacitly acknowledged the limitations of the free market. The British railway network had been constructed after 1826 with only minimal state intervention. But the railways the British built throughout their Empire, though they too were constructed by private sector companies, depended on generous government subsidies which effectively guaranteed that they would pay dividends. The first line in India, linking Bombay to Thane twenty-one miles away, was formally opened in 1853; within less than fifty years, track covering more than 24,000 miles had been laid. In the space of a generation, the '*te-rain*' transformed Indian economic and social life: for the first time, thanks to the standard third-class fare of seven annas,

---

* Messages for the Foreign or Colonial Offices had to cross London from the Eastern Telegraph Company's offices in the City; then they had to go through the same registration process as conventional written dispatches.

long-distance travel became a possibility for millions of Indians, 'joining friends and uniting the anxious'. Some contemporaries predicted a cultural revolution arising from this, in the belief that 'thirty miles an hour is fatal to the slow deities of paganism'. Certainly, the Indian railways created a huge market for British locomotive manufacturers, since most of the tens of thousands of engines put into service in India were made in Britain. Yet this network was from its very inception strategic as well as economic in purpose. It was not through the munificence of British share-holders that the main Lucknow railway station was built to resemble a grandiose Gothic fortress.

As one eminent imperial commentator put it, the Victorian revolution in global communications achieved 'the annihilation of distance'. But it also made possible long-distance annihilation. In time of war, distance simply had to be overcome – for the simple reason that Britain's principal source of military power now lay on the other side of the world.

As had long been the case, the standing army in Britain itself was relatively small. In Europe it was the Royal Navy that did the work of defence: more than a third of the country's huge fleet was permanently stationed in home waters or the Mediterranean. It was in India that the British kept the bulk of their offensive military capability. In this respect, little had been changed by the Mutiny. True, the number of native troops was reduced after 1857 and the number of British troops increased by roughly a third. But there were limits to the number of men the British could afford to station in India. A Royal Commission reported in 1863 that the mortality rate for other ranks (enlisted men) in India between 1800 and 1856 was 69 per thousand, compared with a rate for the equivalent age group in British civilian life of around 10 per thousand. Troops in India also had a much higher incidence of sickness. With quintes-sentially Victorian precision, the Commission calculated that, out of an army of 70,000 British soldiers, 4,830 would die each year and 5,880 hospital beds would be occupied by those incapacitated by illness. Since it cost £100 to recruit a soldier and maintain him in India, Britain was thereby losing more than £1 million a year.

Given that a similar force might have cost around £200,000 stationed in Europe, the extra £800,000 had to be regarded as a kind of tropical service premium. This was a very circumlocutory way of saying that no more British troops should be sent to sicken and die in India. Consequently, the sepoy had to stay if the Indian Army was to maintain its strength.

The upshot was that by 1881 the Indian Army numbered 69,647 British troops and 125,000 Native, compared with British and Irish forces at home of 65,809 and 25,353 respectively. As a proportion of the total manpower of all British garrisons in the Empire, the Indian Army therefore accounted for well over half (62 per cent). In Lord Salisbury's acid description, India was 'an English barrack in the Oriental Seas from which we may draw any number of troops without paying for them'. And draw he and his fellow Prime Ministers regularly did. During the half century before 1914 Indian troops served in more than a dozen imperial campaigns, from China to Uganda. The Liberal politician W. E. Forster complained in 1878 that the government was relying 'not upon the patriotism and spirit of our own people' but on getting 'Gurkhas and Sikhs and Mussulmen to fight for us'. There was even a music-hall parody on the subject:

> We don't want to fight,
> But, by Jingo, if we do,
> We won't go to the front ourselves,
> We'll send the mild Hindoo.

Like nearly every component of the mid-Victorian Empire, the Indian Army too depended on technology: not just the technology that produced its rifles but also the technology that produced its maps. We should never forget that as important as the telegraph in the technology of domination was the theodolite.

As early as the 1770s, the East India Company had grasped the strategic importance of cartography, for in the Anglo-Indian wars of the late eighteenth and early nineteenth century, the army with the more accurate maps had a crucial advantage. The British Isles themselves had been mapped – for precisely the same reason – by

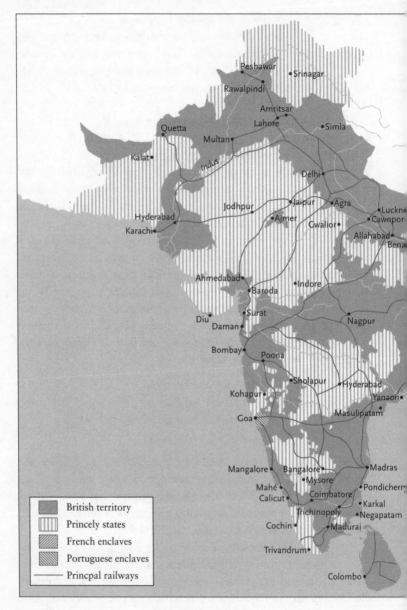

British India, 1931

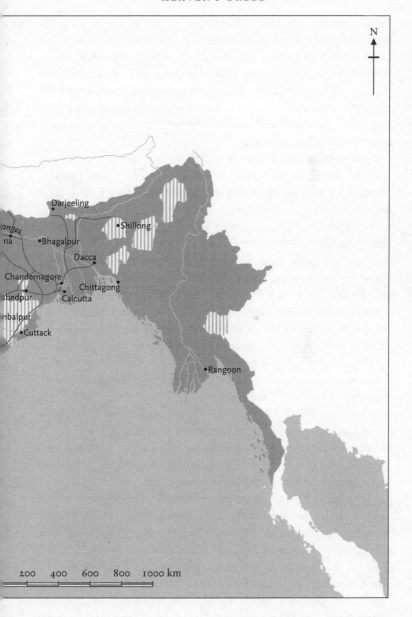

the pioneering Ordnance Survey. In 1800 the Great Trigono-metrical Survey of India had been established under the leadership of intrepid map-makers like William Lambton and, from 1818, George Everest. Working at night to protect their theodolite readings from the distorting heat of the sun, they set out to create the first definitive *Atlas of India* – a vast compendium of geographical, geological and ecological information immaculately set out on a scale of four miles to an inch.

Knowledge is power, and knowing where things are is the most basic knowledge a government requires. But as the Great Trigono-metrical Survey pushed in to the Himalayas – where Everest gave his name to the world's highest mountain – the intelligence being gathered took on a new significance. Where, after all, did British India actually end? It is easy to forget that, at its full extent, it was substantially larger than India today, encompassing present-day Pakistan, Bangladesh and Burma, not to mention southern Persia and Nepal. For a time, it seemed that Afghanistan too would be absorbed into the Raj; some even dreamt of annexing Tibet. On the other side of India's mountainous northern marches, however, lay another European empire with similar aspirations. In the nineteenth century, Russia's empire grew just as rapidly over land as Britain's did over sea – southwards into the Caucasus, through Circassia, Georgia, Erivan and Azerbaijan; eastwards from the Caspian Sea along the Silk Road through Bokhara, Samarkand and Tashkent as far as Khokand and Andijan in the Pamir Mountains. There, barely twenty miles apart, the lion and the bear (as *Punch* cartoons invariably depicted them) glared belligerently at one another across one of the most inhospitable terrains in the world.

From 1879, the date of the second British attempt to invade and control Afghanistan, until the third attempt in 1919, Britain and Russia conducted the world's first Cold War along the North-West Frontier. But the spies in this Cold War were surveyors, for whoever mapped the frontier first stood a good chance of controlling it. The Great Survey of India thus became inextricably bound up with espionage: what one of the early British frontiersmen called the 'Great Game'. At times it really did seem like a game. British agents ventured into the uncharted territory beyond Kashmir and the Khyber Pass disguised as Buddhist monks, measuring the distances between places with the aid of worry-beads – one bead for every hundred paces – and concealing the maps they surreptitiously drew in their prayer wheels.* But this was a deadly game played in a no man's land where the only rule was the merciless Pakhtun or 'Pathan' code of honour: hospitality to the stranger, but a cut throat and an interminable vendetta against all his kin if he transgressed.

The British could never drop their guard on the North-West Frontier. Yet this was not the furthest extremity of British India. Thanks to the Victorians' mastery of technology, the Raj could extend its reach right across the Indian Ocean.

In 1866 the Empire found itself confronted by a distant hostage crisis that tested its system of communications to the limit. A group of British subjects had been imprisoned by the Emperor Theodore (Tewodros) of Abyssinia, who felt the British were showing his regime – the only Christian monarchy in Africa – insufficient respect. Theodore had written to seek British recognition. When the Colonial Office failed to reply, he arrested every European he could get his hands on and marched them to his remote mountain fortress at Magdala. A diplomatic mission was sent, but they too were incarcerated.

It was a truth almost but not quite universally acknowledged: no one treated subjects of Queen Victoria like that and got away with it. But to extricate a group of hostages from darkest Ethiopia was no small undertaking, since it called for the dispatch of what today would be called a rapid reaction force. The remarkable thing was that the force in question was not itself British. Abyssinia was about to feel the full military might of British India.

Without the burgeoning global network of telegraphs and steam engines, the British response would have been impossible. The decision to send an invasion force to free the hostages was taken by the

---

* Among the heroes of this romantic game were 'pandits' like Kishen Singh and Sarat Chandra Das, the original of 'Hurry Chunder Mokerjee' in Kipling's *Kim*.

Prime Minister, Lord Derby, after consultation with the Cabinet and sovereign. When the Queen's written appeal of April 1867 for the release of the prisoners went unanswered, the government saw no alternative but to liberate them 'by force'. Naturally, a decision like this had implications for all the great departments of state: the Foreign Office, the War Office, the Admiralty and the Treasury – all had to be consulted. But to be carried out, the invasion order had to cross the world from the Secretary of State for India in London to the Governor of the Bombay Presidency ten thousand miles away, because that was where the necessary troops were. Once such an order would have taken months to arrive. Now it could be sent by telegraph.

The man charged with planning the expedition was Lieutenant-General Sir Robert Napier, a stern disciplinarian of the old school, but also a military engineer of genius. For public consumption, 'Break thou the Chains' was the rousing command he received from the Queen, and Napier afterwards adopted *Tu Vincula Frange* as his motto. But privately Napier approached his task with the gloomy realism of the professional soldier. It was to be hoped, he wrote to the Duke of Cambridge on 25 July 1867,

that the captives may be released by the Diplomatists at any cost of money, for the expedition would be very expensive and troublesome; and if not a hostile shot is fired, the casualties from the climate and accident will amount to ten times the number of the captives. Still if these poor people are murdered, or detained, I suppose we must do something.

As he had probably expected, it fell to him – and therefore to the Indian Army – to do it. On 13 August Napier produced his estimate of the forces required: 'four regiments of Native Cavalry, one squadron of British cavalry, ten regiments of Native Infantry . . . four batteries of Field and Horse Artillery; one mountain train; a battery of six mortars 5½ inch . . . if possible two of them to be 8-inch and a coolie corps, 3,000 strong, for loads and working parties.' Two days later he was offered command of the expedition. By November, Parliament – recalled early by Disraeli, who hoped to reap some electoral benefit from the affair – had voted the neces-

sary funds. Thereafter, as the Secretary of State, Sir Stafford Northcote, informed the Viceroy, 'all further proceedings connected with
the organization and equipment of reinforcements, when called for
by Sir Robert Napier, should rest with the Government of India'.
Northcote also reminded the Viceroy that the 'Native portion' of
Napier's force would continue to be 'maintained' – in other words,
paid for – as usual, by the Government of India.

Within a few months, the invasion force set sail from Bombay to
Massowah on the Red Sea coast. On board the flotilla were 13,000
British and Indian soldiers, 26,000 camp followers and a huge mass
of livestock: 13,000 mules and ponies, an equal number of sheep,
7,000 camels, 7,000 bullocks and 1,000 donkeys – not to mention
44 elephants. Napier even brought a prefabricated harbour, complete with lighthouses and a railway system. It was a huge logistical
feat, perfectly combining Indian muscle with British technology.

The Abyssinian Emperor had taken it for granted that no invad-
ing force would be able to cross the 400 parched and mountainous
miles between the coast and Magdala. He had not reckoned with
Napier. Slowly but inexorably, he marched his men to their destination, leaving the carcasses of thousands of dehydrated beasts in
their wake. They reached the foot of the fortress after three long
months, and, in a mood of relief that the footslogging was over, prepared for the final assault. As a violent thunderstorm broke above
them, and with the band playing 'Garry Owen', the West Riding
and Black Watch regiments led the charge uphill. In just two hours
of fierce fighting Napier's force killed more than 700 of Theodore's
men and wounded 1,200 more. The Emperor himself committed
suicide rather than be captured. Only twenty British soldiers were
wounded; not one was killed. As one member of the expedition
gleefully recalled: 'There was a fluttering of silk regimental Colours,
the waving of helmets, and the roaring of triumphant cheers. The
sounds of victory rang down the hill and travelled along the plateau
for a distance of two miles . . . and the hills re-echoed "God Save
the Queen".'

Napier's victory was the archetypal mid-Victorian surgical strike:
what was known at the time as a 'butcher and bolt' operation. Vast

superiority in logistics, firepower and discipline had overthrown an emperor with the minimum of British casualties. The victor returned in triumph, bearing with him not only the freed hostages but also such spoils of war as he and his men had been able to find – notably 1,000 ancient Abyssinian Christian manuscripts and the Emperor's necklace, for the delectation of Disraeli. His delighted sovereign had no hesitation in conferring a peerage on Napier, not to mention the inevitable equestrian statue, which now stands stiffly erect in the gardens of the old Viceregal residency at Barrackpore.

The fact that Indian troops could be deployed as far afield as Ethiopia with such success spoke volumes about how India had changed since the 1857 Mutiny. Just ten years before Napier's expedition, British rule in India had been shaken to its foundations by the Mutiny. But the British were determined to learn from that bitter experience. In the Mutiny's aftermath, there was a transformation in the way they ruled India. The East India Company was finally wound up, ending the anomaly whereby a corporation had governed a subcontinent. Admittedly, some of the changes were merely a matter of labelling. The old Governor-General became the new Viceroy, and there were only minor changes to the structure of the six-member Cabinet which advised him. In theory, ultimate authority now rested with the Secretary of State for India in London, advised by his India Council (a combination of the old Court of Directors and Board of Control). But the assumption was that 'the government of India must be, on the whole, carried out in India itself'. And in her proclamation of November 1858 the Queen gave her Indian subjects two assurances about how this government would be conducted. The first we know already: there would be no further meddling with traditional Indian religious culture, an implicit recognition of one of the principal causes of the Mutiny. But the proclamation also referred to 'the principle that perfect equality was to exist, so far as all appointments were concerned, between Europeans and Natives'. This would subsequently prove to be an important hostage to fortune.

Of course, this still left India a despotism, without a shred of representation of the Queen's millions of Indian subjects. As one later Viceroy put it, India was 'really governed by confidential correspondence between the Secretary of State and the Viceroy'. Moreover, the conciliatory assurances in the proclamation were accompanied by practical measures on the ground which were altogether more confrontational. What happened in Lucknow reveals just how radically British rule was being reconstructed at the grassroots. Even as the dust settled after the Mutiny, it was clear to at least one man, a brigadier in the Bengal Engineers, that only the most profound changes could prevent a repetition of the events of 1857. As he observed in his 'Memorandum on the Military Occupation of the City of Lucknow', 'The city of Lucknow, from its vast extent, and from the absence of any very prominent features of the ground on which it stands, must always remain difficult to control except by a large body of troops.' The engineer's name was Robert Napier, the same man who would later lead the British to victory at Magdala, and his solution to the Lucknow problem was devised in much the same methodical spirit:

That difficulty may be greatly diminished by establishing a sufficient number of military posts . . . and by opening broad streets through the city . . . so that troops may move rapidly in any direction . . . All suburbs and cover . . . which would interrupt the free movement of troops . . . must be swept away . . . With regard to the [new] streets . . . they are absolutely necessary . . . Hardship will no doubt be inflicted upon individuals whose property may be destroyed, but the community generally will benefit, and may be made to compensate the individual sufferers.

First, therefore, the population was expelled from the city; then the demolitions began. By the time Napier had finished, he had knocked down around two-fifths of the old town and added insult to injury by converting the principal mosque into a temporary barracks. And it was all paid for by the inhabitants, who were not allowed to return until they had settled their tax bills.

As in every major Indian city, the main garrison was now placed outside the built-up area, in a 'cantonment' from which their soldiers could emerge at a moment's notice to quell any challenge to British rule. Within the cantonment, each officer was housed in his own bungalow which had a garden – varying in size according to his rank – servants' quarters and a carriage house. The British troops had their brick barracks in close proximity, while the native troops lived further away in thatched huts that they were expected to build for themselves. Even the new Lucknow railway station was designed with the preservation of order in mind, for the building itself was structured like a fortress and its long platforms were purpose-built for disembarking reinforcements, should they be needed. Outside it, Napier's broad boulevards ensured that British troops would have a clear field of fire. It is often said that Victorian Britain did nothing to match Haussmann's rebuilding of Paris for Napoleon III. At Lucknow they came close.

Napier's re-engineering of Lucknow illustrates a basic and inescapable fact about the British Raj in India. Its foundation was military force. The army here was not just an imperial strategic reserve. It was also the guarantor of the internal stability of its Asian arsenal.

Yet British India was not ruled solely by the mailed fist. As well as martinets like Napier, it also had its mandarins: the civilian administration that actually governed India, dispensing justice and grappling with an infinity of local crises, ranging from petty disputes about broken bridges to full-blown famines. Though it was a thankless and sometimes hellish job, the elite who did it gloried in their nickname: 'the heaven born'.

The View from the Hills

Every year, towards the end of March, the Indian plains become intolerably hot and stay that way right through the monsoon rains until late September:

Every door and window was shut, for the outside air was that of an oven. The atmosphere within was only 104°, as the thermometer bore witness, and heavy with the foul smell of badly-trimmed kerosene lamps; and this stench, combined with that of native tobacco, baked brick, and dried earth, sends the heart of many a strong man down to his boots, for it is the smell of the Great Indian Empire when she turns herself for six months into a house of torment.

Before the advent of air conditioning, India in the summer was indeed 'a house of torment' for Europeans, a torment scarcely relieved by the ineffectual fanning of the punkah wallahs. As they sweated and swore, the British yearned to escape from the enervating heat of the plains. How could they govern a subcontinent without succumbing every year to heat exhaustion? The solution was found in the foothills of the Himalayas, where the midsummer weather offered a passable imitation of the climate back in 'the old country'.

There were several lofty refuges for chronically sunburned Britons – Darjeeling to the east, Ootacamund in the south – but one particular hill station was in a league of its own. If you take the train that runs northwards from Delhi and winds its way up into the mountains of what is now Himachal Pradesh, you follow the path taken by generations of British soldiers and administrators, not to mention their wives and sweethearts. Some of them went there on leave, to promenade, party and pair off. But most went because for seven months every year it was the seat of the government of India itself.

Simla is just over 7,000 feet above sea level and more than 1,000 miles from Calcutta. Until the railway from Kalka was built in 1903, the only way to get up there was to ride or be carried in a *dooly* or a *dandy*. When the rivers flooded, elephants were required. To the modern visitor, Simla seems even more remote than that suggests. With its breathtaking mountain views, its towering pines and its exquisitely chilled air – not to mention the occasional rain cloud – it looks more like the Highlands than the Himalayas. There is even a Gothic kirk and a Gaiety Theatre. It comes as no surprise that it was a Scotsman who founded it, one Charles Pratt Kennedy, who built himself the first hilltop house there in 1822. To the Victorians, taught by Romanticism to idealize the Caledonian mountains, Simla seemed a paradise: the mountain air, one early visitor enthused, 'seemed to have instilled ether in my veins, for I felt as I could have bounded headlong into the deepest glens, or spring nimbly up their abrupt sides with a daring ease ...' The men who ruled in India soon picked up the scent of this rejuvenating air. Lord Amherst visited Simla as Governor-General as early as 1827, and in 1864 it became the Viceroy's official summer residence. From then on, the Viceregal Lodge atop Observatory Hill became the summer seat of power.

Perched on its mountaintop, Simla was a strange, little hybrid world – part Highlands, part Himalayas; part powerhouse, part playground.* It was a world no one understood better than Rudyard Kipling. Born in Bombay in 1865, Kipling had spent more of the first five years of his life with his Indian *ayah* than with his parents, had spoken Hindustani before he spoke English and had loathed England when he was sent there to be educated at the age of five. He returned eleven years later to take up a post as assistant editor of the Lahore-based *Civil and Military Gazette*, which he soon enlivened with a stream of jaunty verses and stories depicting Anglo-Indian life with (in his own phrase) 'no half-tints'. As a keen cub reporter, Kipling loved to wander in search of good copy through the bazaars of Lahore ('that wonderful, dirty, mysterious ant hill') bantering and bargaining with Hindu shopkeepers and Muslim horse-traders. This was the real India, and he found its assault on his senses intoxicating: '[The] heat and smells of oil and spices, and puffs of temple incense, and sweat, and darkness, and dirt and lust and cruelty, and, above all, things wonderful and fascinating innumerable.' At night, he even took to visiting opium dens. A prim man who yearned to be risqué, Kipling thought the drug 'an excellent thing in itself'.

---

* Below the commanding heights of the Viceregal Lodge and the Commander-in-Chief's residence, the Peterhof, the slopes soon became rather cluttered with mock-Tudor holiday homes. Lutyens said of Simla: 'If one was told that the monkeys had built it all one could only say [would be]: "What wonderful monkeys – they must be shot in case they do it again." '

By contrast, Kipling was ambivalent about Simla. Like everyone who came there, he relished the 'champagne air' of the mountains and delighted in the 'grass-downs swelling like a woman's breasts ... the wind across the grass, and the rain among the deodars say[ing] "Hush-hush-hush"'. He found the social life a diverting whirl of 'garden-parties, and tennis-parties, and picnics, and luncheons at Annandale, and rifle-matches, and dinners and balls; besides rides and walks.' At times, life at Simla seemed 'the only existence in this desolate land worth the living'. Half seriously, Kipling acknowledged in his own 'Tale of Two Cities' (Calcutta and Simla):

> That the Merchant risks the perils of the Plain
>> For gain.
> Nor can Rulers rule a house that men grow rich in,
>> From its kitchen.

He could understand perfectly well why

> ... the Rulers in that City by the Sea
>> Turned to flee –
> Fled, with each returning spring-tide from its ills
>> To the Hills.

Besides the pleasant weather, there was the fun of flirting with other men's wives consigned to the hills for the good of their health by trusting husbands sweating it out down in the plains.

Still, Kipling could not help wondering if it was entirely wise that the Viceroy and his advisers should choose to spend half the year 'on the wrong side of an irresponsible river', as cut off from those they governed as if they were 'separated by a month's sea voyage'. Fond though he was of Simla's grass widows, Kipling's sympathies were always with his countrymen who stuck it out down in the plains: Kim, the orphan son of a British soldier, 'going native' along the Great Trunk Road; the stoical squaddie Corporal Terence Mulvaney, speaking his strange patois, half Irish, half Hindustani; and, above all, the District Officers of the Indian Civil Service, sweltering in their sun-baked outposts. They might, as he once put it, be 'cynical, seedy and dry'. They might, like poor Jack Barrett, be betrayed by their wicked wives up in the hills.* But the 'Civilians' were the men who held the Raj together.

Perhaps the most baffling statistic of all about British India was the size of the Indian Civil Service. Between 1858 and 1947 there were seldom more than 1,000 members of the covenanted Civil Service,† compared with a total population which, by the end of British rule, exceeded 400 million. As Kipling remarked, 'One of the few advantages that India has over England is a great Knowability . . . At the end of twenty [years, a man] knows, or knows something about, every Englishman in the Empire.' Was this, then, the most efficient bureaucracy in history? Was a single British civil servant really able to run the lives of up to three million Indians, spread over 17,000 square miles, as some District Officers were supposed to do? Only, Kipling concluded, if the masters worked themselves like slaves:

Year by year England sends out fresh drafts for the first fighting-line, which is officially called the Indian Civil Service. These die, or kill themselves by overwork, or are worried to death or broken in health and hope in order

* 'Jack Barrett went to Quetta
  Because they told him to.
He left his wife at Simla
  On three-fourths his monthly screw:
. . .
  'Jack Barrett went to Quetta,
And there gave up the ghost,
  Attempting two men's duty
In that very healthy post;
  And Mrs. Barrett mourned for him
Five lively months at most.'

† The covenanted Civil Service was known as such because its members entered a covenant with the Secretary of State of India. For most of the nineteenth century it had around 900 members. Only in the twentieth century did the number of ICS officers rise significantly above a thousand. In 1939 there were 1,384. Nor was this skeletal staffing unique to India. The entire administrative elite of the African colonial service – spread over a dozen colonies with a population of around 43 million – numbered just over 1,200. The Malayan civil service had 220 administrators for 3.2 million people, which by Indian standards was chronic overmanning.

that the land may be protected from death and sickness, famine and war, and may eventually become capable of standing alone. It will never stand alone, but the idea is a pretty one and men are willing to die for it, and yearly the work of pushing and coaxing and scolding and petting the country into good living goes forward. If an advance be made all credit is given to the native while the Englishmen stand back and wipe their foreheads. If a failure occurs the Englishmen step forward and take the blame.

'Until steam replaces manual power in the working of the Empire,' wrote Kipling in 'The Education of Otis Yeere', there would always be 'men who are used up, expended, in the mere mechanical routine'. Such men were 'simply the rank and file – the food for fever – sharing with the ryot [peasant] and the plough-bullock the honour of being the plinth on which the State rests'. Otis Yeere was the archetypal 'sunken-eyed man who, by official irony, was said to be "in charge" of [a] seething, whining, weakly hive, impotent to help itself, but strong in its power to cripple, thwart, and annoy'.

As Kipling describes it, the ICS hardly sounds an attractive career option. Yet competition for places was fierce, so fierce that selection had to be based on perhaps the toughest exams in history. Consider some of the questions the candidates were set back in 1859. By modern standards, it is true, the History paper is something of a crammer's delight. Here are two not untypical questions:

14. Enumerate the chief Colonies of England, and state how and when she acquired each of them.

15. Name the successive Governors-General of British India as far as 1830, giving the dates of their Governments, and a brief summary of the main Indian transactions under each.

By comparison, the Logic and Mental Philosophy paper is more demanding – and more elegantly phrased:

3. What Experimental Methods are applicable to the determination of the true antecedent in phenomena where there may be a Plurality of Causes.

5. Classify Fallacies.

But it is the Mental and Moral Philosophy paper which is the most challenging, and revealing, part of the ICS exam:

1. Describe the various circumstances of situations which give birth to the pleasurable sentiment of Power.

If ever there was a trick question, that is it (presumably any candidate who acknowledged that Power *did* induce a pleasurable sentiment would be failed). Nor is the next question much easier:

2. Specify, as far as you are able, the particular duties coming under the general head of Justice.

Finally, just to separate the cream of Balliol* from the rest, comes this:

7. State the arguments for and against Utility, considered as (1) the actual, and (2) the proper, basis of morals.

Things had certainly changed since the days of Thomas Pitt and Warren Hastings. Then, jobs in the East India Company had been bought and sold as part of an elaborate system of aristocratic patronage. Even after the creation of Haileybury College as a school for future Indian civil servants in 1805 and the introduction of the first qualifying exam in 1827, the company's directors still regarded ICS places as being in their gift. Only in 1853 was patronage replaced by meritocracy. The Government of India Act of that year did away with Haileybury's effective monopoly on ICS posts and introduced instead the principle of open competition by examination. The Victorians wanted India to be ruled by the ultimate academic elite: impartial, incorruptible, omniscient.

The idea was to attract university achievers into imperial administration directly after they had completed their first degree, ideally at Oxford or Cambridge, and then put them through one or two years of training in law, languages, Indian history and riding. In practice, the ICS tended not to attract the Oxbridge *crème de la*

* Especially under the Empire-minded mastership of Benjamin Jowett, Balliol became the college of choice for would-be proconsuls. Between 1874 and 1914 no fewer than 27 per cent of Balliol graduates were employed in the Empire.

crème – the Scholars, Double Firsts and University Prize winners. The men who opted for the rigours of the subcontinent tended to be those whose prospects at home were modest: bright young sons of provincial professionals who were willing to cram for the sake of a prestigious job overseas – men like Devon-born Evan Machonochie. His great-uncle and elder brother had both been Indian civil servants and it had been their letters home which had convinced him that 'Eastward lay the path to happiness'. In 1887, after two years of cramming, he passed the ICS entrance exam and set off for Bengal after another couple of years at Oxford mugging up and passing further exams in Indian history, law and languages. Nor was that the end of the selection process, since his first few months in India were spent preparing for yet more exams. After a preliminary test in Hindustani, Machonochie was formally gazetted as a Third-Class Magistrate. To his embarrassment, he managed to 'bungle' his first departmental exams in Gujarati, Indian Law, Treasury Procedure and Revenue Accounts (because his head was 'full of much more interesting matters, my first horses, my fox terrier pup [and] the right range at which to down a quail'); but he scraped through at the second attempt.

Machonochie found the life of a magistrate (now Second-Class) and then a District Collector surprisingly enjoyable:

The early mornings were spent, in the absence of any special work, in exercising the horses, tent-pegging and the like, in the garden or with a camera. The day's work occupied the middle hours from eleven to five, and, after that a game of tennis and a chat in the collector's veranda carried us on to dinner time … Imagine then, the young Assistant setting forth on horseback on a crisp November morning, after a good monsoon … he has few cares, his heart is light and it must be a dull soul that does not respond to the vision. On the way there will be villages to inspect, perhaps, if time permits, a quiet shoot … Many a clue as to what the villager is thinking is gained over a chat between beats or while watching one's float by a quiet pool …

But the life of an expatriate mandarin had another side to it. There was the tedium of hearing appeals against tax assessments, when 'on a hot-weather afternoon, after a long morning round (in the camps) and a hearty breakfast, the effort to keep awake while recording evidence or listening to the reading of vernacular papers amounted almost to physical pain . . .' Then there was the loneliness of being the only white man for hundreds of miles:

When I first started out none of my office staff, but few of the Mamlatdars, and no one else in the Talukas, spoke English, and I rarely met another District Officer. For seven months I scarcely spoke English and was thrown very much on my own resources.

Worst of all was the responsibility of governing literally millions of people, particularly during crises like the plague that swept Bombay in 1896 or the famine of 1900. As Machonochie later recalled, 'that time marked the end of happy irresponsible days. In the years that followed, they were rarely free from the haunting anxiety attendant on pestilence and famine.'* Finally, in 1897, came respite: a posting to Simla as Under-Secretary in the Department of Revenue and Agriculture. It was there that he was able to appreciate that 'you were not merely an individual of no importance . . . but part of a great machine to whose efficiency you were in honour bound to contribute'.

Machonochie had no doubt about the importance of the lone District Officer in the eyes of the people in his care. 'To the raiyat [peasant] the visit of a "saheb" or a casual meeting with one has some of the qualities of excitement . . . It will be talked of for days over the village fire and remembered for years. The white man will be sized up shrewd and frankly. So take heed unto your manners and your habits!'

---

* It is fashionable to allege that the British authorities did nothing to relieve the drought-induced famines of the period. But this is not so. In 1874 H. M. Kisch, an ICS magistrate of the Second Class, was sent to organize famine relief in an area of Behar covering 198 square miles and a population of around 100,000. 'Since I came here,' he wrote home proudly, 'I have erected 15 government grain store-houses, and opened about 22 relief works, I give employment to about 15,000 men and women per day, and am feeding gratuitously about 3,000 more. I have full authority to do what I choose, and I do it.' The calamity of 1877 was due to a failure to adopt the same methods.

Yet between the lines of his memoir, a crucial, though tacit, reality can be discerned. Everything he and the other District Officers did was dependent on another, much larger tier of bureaucracy below them. This was the uncovenanted civil service, composed of Indians, and it was they who took responsibility for the day-to-day administration of each District's local *talukas* and *tahsils*. There were 4,000 Indians in the uncovenanted service by 1868, and below them was a veritable army of lesser public employees: the telegraph clerks and ticket collectors, many of whom were Eurasians or Indians. In 1867 there were around 13,000 public sector jobs paying 75 or more rupees per month, of which around half were held by Indians. Without this auxiliary force of civil servants who were native born, the 'heaven born' would have been impotent. This was the unspoken truth about British India; and that was why, as Machonochie himself put it, it did not really feel like 'a conquered country'. Only the Indian rulers had been supplanted or subjugated by the British; most Indians carried on much as before – indeed, for an important class of them British rule was an opportunity for self-advancement.

The key to the emergence of a pro-British Indian elite was education. Though the British themselves were at first dubious about offering natives Western education, many Indians – particularly high-caste Bengalis – were quick to discern the benefits of speaking the language and understanding the culture of their new masters. As early as 1817 a Hindu College had been founded in Calcutta by prosperous Bengalis eager for Western education; offering European history, literature and natural sciences, it was the first of many such institutions. As we have seen, the proponents of modernizing as well as evangelizing India seized on the idea of giving Indians access to Western education. In 1835 the great Whig historian and Indian administrator Thomas Babington Macaulay – son of the abolitionist Zachary – spelt out explicitly what could be achieved this way in his famous Minute on Education:

It is impossible for us, with our limited means, to attempt to educate the body of the people. We must at present do our best to form a class who may be interpreters between us and the millions whom we govern; a class of persons, Indian in blood and colour, but English in taste, in opinions, in morals, and in intellect.

By 1838 there were forty English-based seminaries under the control of the General Committee of Public Instruction. By the 1870s, Macaulay's vision had been in large measure realized. Six thousand Indian students had enrolled in higher education and no less than 200,000 in Anglophone secondary 'schools of the higher order'. Calcutta had acquired a substantial English-language publishing industry, capable of turning out more than a thousand works of literature and science a year.

Among the beneficiaries of the expansion of Anglicized education was an ambitious young Bengali named Janakinath Bose. Educated in Calcutta, Bose was called to the Bar in the town of Cuttack in 1885 and went on to serve as Chairman of the Cuttack municipality. In 1905 he became Government Pleader and Chief Prosecutor, and seven years later crowned his career by being appointed to the Bengal Legislative Council. Bose's success as a lawyer enabled him to buy a spacious mansion in the fashionable district of Calcutta. It also won him from the British the title of Rai Bahadur, the Indian equivalent of a knighthood. And he was not alone: two of his three brothers entered government service, one of them in the Imperial Secretariat at Simla.

This new elite even penetrated the ranks of the covenanted ICS itself. In 1863 Satyendernath Tagore became the first Indian to pass the exam – which was always open to applicants regardless of skin colour, just as Queen Victoria had promised – and in 1871 another three natives were admitted to the ranks of the 'heaven born'.

Bose and his ilk were the people on whom the Empire really depended in India. Without their ability to turn the orders of the ICS into reality, British rule in India simply would not have worked. Indeed, the truth was that government throughout the Empire was only really possible with the collaboration of key sections of the

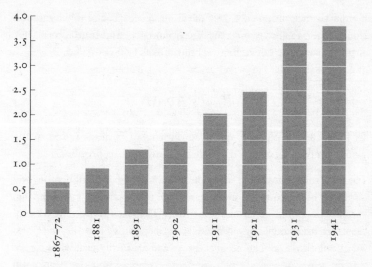

Under British rule the percentage of the Indian population in primary and secondary education rose steadily, though it remained low by European standards. In 1911 the percentage of European populations in school lay between 8 and 18 per cent.

governed. That was comparatively easy to secure in places like Canada, Australia and New Zealand, where the native populations had been reduced to insignificant minorities. The key problem was how to retain the loyalty of both settlers and indigenous elites where it was the white community that was in the minority, as in India where the British population amounted to at most a mere 0.05 per cent of the total.*

Under Indian conditions, administrators sent out from London saw no alternative but to co-opt an elite of natives. But this was precisely what the British who were actually resident in India ruled out. The men on the spot preferred to keep the natives down: to

* There were only 31,000 British in India in 1805 (of whom 22,000 were in the army, 2,000 in civil government and 7,000 in the private sector). In 1881 the British in India numbered 89,778 in total. By 1931 there were 168,000 in all: 60,000 in the army and police, 4,000 in civil government and 60,000 employed in the private sector.

coerce them if necessary, but never to co-opt them. This was the great imperial dilemma of the Victorian era – and on its horns not just India but the entire British Empire was to be impaled.

Races Apart

In June 1865 a placard appeared on a wharf gate at Lucea in the Jamaican parish of Hanover bearing a mysterious prophecy:

I heard a voice speaking to me in the year 1864, saying, 'Tell the sons and daughters of Africa that a great deliverance will take place for them from the hand of oppression', for, said the voice, 'They are oppressed by Government, by magistrates, by proprietors, by merchants', and the voice also said, 'Tell them to call a solemn assembly and to sanctify themselves for the day of deliverance which will surely take place; but if the people will not harken I will bring the sword into the land to chastise them for their disobedience and for the iniquities which they have committed.' . . . The calamity which I see coming upon the land will be so grievous and so distressing that many will desire to die. But great will be the deliverance of the sons and daughters of Africa, if they humble themselves in sackcloth and ashes, like the children of Ninevah before the Lord our God; but if we pray truly from our hearts, and humble ourselves, we have no need to fear; if not the enemy will be cruel for there will be Gog and Magog to battle. Believe me.

The placard was signed simply 'A Son of Africa'.

Jamaica had once been the centre of the most extreme form of colonial coercion: slavery. But its abolition had not much improved the lot of the average black Jamaican. The ex-slaves had been given wretchedly small allotments to farm for themselves. A period of drought had pushed up food prices. Meanwhile, without the subsidy provided by unfree labour, the old plantation economy stagnated. Sugar prices were falling and the development of coffee as a cash crop was only a partial substitute. Where once men had been literally worked to death, now they were idle as unemployment soared. Yet power – political and above all legal – remained concentrated in the hands of the white minority, who dominated the island's Assembly and its magistracy. A tiny few Jamaican blacks acquired enough property and education to form an embryonic middle class, but they were viewed with intense suspicion by the ruling 'plantocracy'. Only in their churches were the majority of black Jamaicans able to express themselves freely.

It was against this background that a religious revival swept across the island in the 1860s, a revival that blended Baptism with the African religion Myal to produce a heady millenarian mixture. The sense of an approaching 'great deliverance', so vividly anticipated in the Lucea placard, was only heightened by the publication of a letter by Edward Underhill, the secretary of the Baptist Missionary Society, which called for an inquiry into Jamaica's plight. Rumours circulated that Queen Victoria had meant the ex-slaves to be given land as well as their freedom, instead of having to rent it from their former masters. Meetings were held to debate the contents of Underhill's letter. A classic revolution of rising expectations was in the making.

It began in the town of Morant Bay in the parish of St Thomas in the East on Saturday 7 October 1865, the date set for the appeal of one Lewis Miller against a minor charge of trespass brought by a neighbouring planter. Miller was the cousin of Paul Bogle, the owner of a small farm at Stony Gut and an active member of the local black Baptist church, who had been galvanized into direct political action by the Underhill letter. Previously Bogle had favoured the creation of alternative black 'courts'; now he had formed his own armed militia. At the head of around 150 men he marched to the courthouse where his cousin's case was to be heard. The ensuing skirmishes with the police outside the court gave the authorities good reason to arrest Bogle and his men, but the police were seen off with death threats when they sought to carry out this order at Stony Gut the following Tuesday. The next day, several hundred people sympathetic to Bogle marched into Morant Bay 'with a blowing of shells or horns, and a beating of drums' and confronted the volunteer militia who had been sent to protect a meeting of the parish vestry. In the ensuing violence, the crowd stabbed or beat to death eighteen people, among them members of the vestry; seven of their own number were killed by the militia. In the following days, two planters were murdered as violence spread through the parish and beyond. On 17 October Bogle sent a circular letter to his neighbours which was nothing less than a call to arms:

Everyone of you must leave your house, takes your guns, who don't have guns take your cutlisses down at once ... Blow your shells, roal your drums, house to house, take out every man ... war is at us, my black skin, war is at hand from to-day to to-morrow.

As those words suggest, this was now an overtly racial conflict. One white woman claimed she heard the rebels singing a bloodcurdling song:

> Buckras' [whites'] blood we want,
> Buckras' blood we'll have.
> Buckras' blood we are going for,
> Till there's no more to have.

A planter received a death threat signed by 'Thomas Killmany, and intend to kill many more'.

There had been revolts against white rule in Jamaica before. The last one, in 1831, had been suppressed ferociously. To the newly appointed Governor-in-Chief, Edward Eyre, a man baked hard in the Australian outback,* there could only be one response. In his view, the only causes of black poverty were 'the idleness, improvidence, and vice of the people'. On 13 October he declared martial law throughout the county of Surrey and sent in regular troops. In the course of a month of unbridled retribution, around 200 people were executed, another 200 flogged and 1,000 houses

---

* The third son of a Whipsnade curate, Eyre had been the first white man to walk across the Australian desert from Adelaide to Moorundie. Ironically, in the light of subsequent events at Morant Bay, his reward for this feat of exploration and endurance was to be made Magistrate and Protector of the Aborigines in the area. Today a lake, a peninsula and the motorway between Adelaide and Perth are all named after him.

razed. The tactics Eyre sanctioned were strongly reminiscent of those adopted to suppress the Indian Mutiny just eight years before. To say the least, there was scant regard for due legal process; indeed, the soldiers – many of whom were in fact black themselves, as it was the 1st West India Regiment which was deployed, with the Maroons in support – were effectively licensed to run amok. A number of prisoners were simply shot without trial. One invalid youth was shot dead in front of his mother. A woman was raped in her own home. There were countless floggings.

Besides Bogle himself, among those executed was George William Gordon. A landowner, a former magistrate and a member of the island's elected assembly, Gordon was a pillar of the black community and an unlikely revolutionary; the only surviving photograph of him shows the bespectacled, bewhiskered incarnation of respectability. He had almost certainly played no part in the uprising. He was in fact nowhere near Morant Bay when it broke out, though the parish of St Thomas in the East was his constituency and he had recently been expelled from the vestry there. But as a 'half-caste' – the son of a planter and slave girl – who had publicly championed the cause of the former slaves, Gordon had been marked down by Eyre as a troublemaker; indeed, it had been Eyre who had dismissed him from the magistracy three years before. Now, to ensure that he was finally disposed of, Eyre had him arrested and removed from Kingston to the area where martial law was in force. After a hurried trial, he was convicted – partly on the basis of highly dubious written depositions – of inciting the rebellion. On 23 October he was hanged.

The Morant Bay rising had been emphatically and ruthlessly crushed; but the white planters who applauded Eyre's handling of the crisis were in for a shock – as was Eyre himself. Having initially been praised by the Colonial Secretary for his 'spirit, energy and judgment', he was stunned to hear that a Royal Commission had been set up to inquire into his conduct and that he himself had been temporarily replaced as Governor. This reaction against his brutal tactics originated among the membership of the British and Foreign Anti-Slavery Society, who still kept the old flame of abolitionism burning and saw Eyre's use of martial law as a reversion to the days of slavery. In far-flung Africa, even David Livingstone heard of the affair and fulminated:

England is in the rear. Frightened in early years by their mothers with 'Bogie Blackman' they were terrified out of their wits by a riot, and the sensation writers, who act the part of the 'dreadful boys' who frighten the aunts, yelled out that emancipation was a mistake. 'The Jamaica negroes were as savage as when they left Africa.' They might have put it much stronger by saying, as the rabble ... that collects at every execution at Newgate.

But the campaign against Eyre soon spread beyond what one of his defenders called 'the old ladies of Clapham' to embrace some of the great liberal intellectuals of the Victorian era, including Charles Darwin and John Stuart Mill. Not content with his dismissal as Governor, the committee they formed mounted four separate legal actions against him, beginning with a charge of accessory to murder. However, the deposed Governor also had influential supporters: among them Thomas Carlyle, John Ruskin, Charles Dickens and the poet laureate Alfred Lord Tennyson. None of the legal actions was successful, and Eyre was able to retire to Devon on a government pension, which he collected until his death, aged eighty-six, in 1901.

Nevertheless, from the moment Eyre left Jamaica, the old regime of rule by the planter class was over. From now on, the island would be governed directly from London through the Governor; a Legislative Council dominated by his appointees would replace the old Assembly. Here was a step back to the old days before 'responsible government' had devolved political power to British colonists; but it was a step taken in a progressive rather than a reactionary spirit, designed to circumscribe the power of the plantocracy and protect the rights of black Jamaicans.* This was to become a fundamental feature of the later British Empire. In Whitehall and Westminster,

---

* No one considered for a moment that this might best be achieved by allowing them to be properly represented in the Assembly and magistracy.

Liberal ideas were in the ascendant, and that meant the rule of law had to take precedence, regardless of skin colour. If that did not seem to be happening, then the will of colonial assemblies would simply have to be overridden. Yet British colonists – the men and women on the spot – increasingly saw themselves as not just legally but biologically superior to other races. As far as they were concerned, the people who attacked Eyre were ingenuous *bien pensants* who had no experience or understanding of colonial conditions. Sooner or later, these two visions – the liberalism of the centre and the racism of the periphery – were bound to collide again.

By the 1860s race was becoming an issue in all of the British colonies, in India as much as in Jamaica; and no one took the issue more seriously than the Anglo-Indian business community.* Jamaica was an economy in decline. Victorian India, by contrast, was booming. Immense sums of British capital were being invested in a range of new industries: cotton and jute spinning, coal mining and steel production. Nowhere was that more obvious than in Cawnpore, on the banks of the River Ganges: once the site of some of the most bitter fighting of the Indian Mutiny, transformed within a few years into the 'Manchester of the East', a thriving industrial centre. This transformation was due in large measure to hard-faced men like Hugh Maxwell. His family – originally from Aberdeenshire – had settled in the district in 1806, where they had pioneered the cultivation of indigo and raw cotton. After 1857 it was Maxwell and men of his stamp who brought the industrial revolution to India by importing British spinning and weaving machinery and building textile mills on the British pattern. In the age before steam power, India had led the world in manual spinning, weaving and dyeing. The British had first raised tariffs against their products; then demanded free trade when their alternative industrial mode of production had been perfected. Now they were intent on rebuilding

* The term Anglo-Indian is sometimes used, confusingly, to denote people of mixed British and Indian parentage. I have preferred to follow the Victorian practice of using 'Anglo-Indian' to refer to British long-term residents in India and 'Eurasian' to refer to the issue of ethnically mixed unions.

India as a manufacturing economy using British technology and cheap Indian labour.

Our image of British India tends to be that of the official classes, the soldiers and civil servants described so vividly by Kipling, E. M. Forster and Paul Scott. As a result it is easy to forget how few of them there actually were. In fact they were outnumbered several times by businessmen, planters and professionals. And there was a profound difference in attitude between those in government employ and the business community. Men like Hugh Maxwell felt threatened by the growth of an educated Indian elite, not least because it implied that they themselves might be dispensable. After all, why should not a properly educated Indian be every bit as good at running a textile factory as a member of the Maxwell family?

When people feel threatened by another ethnic group, their reaction is usually to disparage it, in order to affirm their own superiority. This was the way the Anglo-Indians behaved after 1857. Even before the Mutiny, there had been a creeping segregation of the white and native populations, a kind of informal apartheid that divided towns like Cawnpore in two: the white town behind the 'Civil Lines' and 'Blacktown' on the other side. Between the two ran what Kipling called 'the Borderline, where the last drop of White blood ends and the full tide of Black sets in'. While the most progressive liberals in London looked forward to a distant future of Indian participation in government, the Anglo-Indians increasingly used the language of the American South to disparage the native 'niggers'. And they expected the law to uphold their superiority.

This expectation was to be shattered in 1880 when the newly formed Gladstone government appointed George Frederick Samuel Robinson, Earl de Grey and Marquess of Ripon, as Viceroy. Even Queen Victoria was 'greatly astounded' to hear of the appointment of this notably progressive figure, who also happened to be a convert to Catholicism (a black mark in her eyes). She wrote to warn the Prime Minister that she 'thought it a very doubtful appointment, as, though a very good man, he was weak'. It did not take Ripon long to vindicate her doubts. No sooner had he arrived in

Calcutta than he began to meddle in matters old India hands like Hugh Maxwell took very seriously indeed.

Between 1872 and 1883 there was a crucial difference between the powers of British district magistrates and session judges in the Indian countryside – the *Mofussil* – and their native-born counterparts.* Although both were members of the covenanted civil service, the Indians were not entitled to conduct trials of white defendants in criminal cases. In the eyes of the new Viceroy, this was an indefensible anomaly; so he requested a bill to do away with it. The task fell to the Law Member of his Council, Courtenay Peregrine Ilbert. As earnest a Liberal as his chief, Ilbert was in many ways the antithesis of Hugh Maxwell. Maxwell's family had been born and bred in India for generations; Ilbert had only just arrived there, a rather timid little lawyer who had seen little of the world beyond his rooms in Balliol and his chambers in Chancery. Nevertheless, he and Ripon had no hesitation in putting principle before experience. Under the legislation Ilbert drafted, suitably qualified Indians would be allowed to try defendants regardless of the colour of their skin. Justice would henceforth be colour-blind, like the blindfolded statue representing her in the gardens of the Calcutta High Court.

In practice, the change affected the position of no more than twenty Indian magistrates. To the Anglo-Indian community, however, what Ilbert proposed was an insupportable assault on their privileged status. Indeed, the reaction to the Ilbert Bill was so violent that some called it a 'White Mutiny'. On 28 February 1883, within just a few weeks of the Bill's publication, and after a preliminary bombardment of irate letters to the press, a crowd of several thousand gathered inside Calcutta's imposing neo-classical Town Hall to hear a series of inflammatory speeches directed against the educated Indian civil servant, the despised 'Bengali Babu'. The charge was led by the imposing J.J.J. 'King' Keswick, a senior partner in the tea and trading firm Jardine Skinner & Co. 'Do you think', Keswick asked his audience, 'that native judges will, by three or four years' residence in England, become so Europeanized in nature and

---

* This was not the case in the cities of Bombay, Calcutta and Madras.

character, that they will be able to judge as well in false charges against Europeans as if they themselves were bred and born? Can the Ethiopian change his skin, or the leopard his spots?' Educating the Indians had done no good:

The education which the Government has given them . . . they use chiefly to taunt it in a discontented spirit . . . And these men . . . now cry out for power to sit in judgment on, and condemn the lion-hearted race whose bravery and whose blood have made their country what it is, and raised them to what they are[!]

To Keswick, training Indians to be judges was simply pointless, since an Indian was incapable by both birth and upbringing of judging a European. 'Under these circumstances,' he concluded to rousing cheers, 'is it any wonder that we should protest – if we should say that these men are not fit to rule over us, that they cannot judge us, that we will not be judged by them?' It was a peroration only outdone in its crudeness by the evening's second main speaker, James Branson:

Truly and verily the jackass kicketh at the lion. (*Thunders of applause.*) Show him as you value your liberties; show him that the lion is not dead; he sleepeth, and in God's name, let him dread the awakening. (*Cheers, and shouts from all sides.*)

Across the street, in Government House, Ripon was taken aback by this audibly hostile reaction to the Ilbert Bill. 'I quite admit', he confessed to the Colonial Secretary Lord Kimberley, 'that I had no idea that any large number of Englishmen in India were animated by such sentiments.'

I deserve such blame as may be attached to me for not having found out in a residence of 2¹/₂ years in India the true feeling of the average Anglo-Indian toward the natives among whom he lives. I know them now, and the knowledge gives me a feeling akin to despair as to the future of this country.

Ripon nevertheless resolved to press on, in the belief 'that as we have taken the question up, we had better go through with it, and get it settled out of the way of our successors'. As far as he could see, the question was clear-cut: was India to be ruled 'for the benefit of the Indian people of all races, classes, and creeds', or 'in the sole interest of a small body of Europeans'?

Is it England's duty to try to elevate the Indian people, to raise them socially, to train them politically, to promote their progress in material prosperity, in education, and in morality; or is it to be the be-all and the end-all of her rule to maintain a precarious power over what Mr Branson calls 'a subject race with a profound hatred of their subjugators'?

Ripon was right, of course. The opposition of the Calcutta business community was based not just on visceral racial prejudice but on narrow self-interest: put simply, men like Keswick and Branson were used to having the law their own way in the Mofussil, where their firms' jute, silk, indigo and tea plantations were located. But now that their opposition to the Ilbert Bill was out in the open, the Viceroy needed to think about practicalities as well as principles. Unfortunately, he let precedent dictate his tactics. Having dropped his bombshell on the white community, Ripon left Calcutta almost immediately. Summer was approaching, after all, and nothing could alter the Viceroy's sacrosanct routine. It was time for him to take the annual trip to Simla, so off to Simla he went. This retreat to the hills was never an option to the businessmen in the Calcutta counting houses; business went on as usual down in the plains, whatever the temperature. The spectacle of Ripon swanning off to Simla was not calculated to mollify the likes of 'King' Keswick.

Also heading for the hills – for Chapslee, his elegant Simla residence – was the author of the controversial bill himself. Ilbert's strategy was to sit out the summer and hope the fuss would go away. 'As to the kind and amount of feeling which the Bill was likely to excite,' he wrote anxiously to his Oxford mentor Benjamin Jowett, 'I had no knowledge of my own . . . and . . . certainly did not anticipate such a storm.' 'I am intensely sorry', he told another friend, 'that the measure should have disclosed and intensified racial animosities.' From the Board of Trade, his friend Sir Thomas Farrer wrote to reassure Ilbert that Liberal opinion was on his side:

The struggle between lust of dominion, pride of race [and] mercantile avarice . . . on the one hand and true self-regard, humanity, justice to inferiors, sympathy (Sermon on the Mountism – what an abominable word) on the other, goes on like the fight between the angel and the devil . . . for the soul of man.

As that suggests, the Ilbert Bill was polarizing opinion not just in India but in England as well. To Liberals like Farrer, this was a moral struggle. The enlightened devotees of the Sermon on the Mount were, however, less numerous in Calcutta than they were in Clapham. Indeed, the deepening crisis over the Ilbert Bill was about to illustrate perfectly the perils of ruling a continent *from* a mount.

Across the country, in the searing heat of the Indian summer, the agitation spread. Committees were formed and money was raised as non-official Anglo-India mobilized. Kipling weighed in, accusing Ripon of 'sketch[ing] a swart utopia, nourishing the Babu's pride / On the fairy-tales of justice – with a leaning to his side.' This, he complained, was the Viceroy's policy: 'turmoil and babble and ceaseless strife'. From Cawnpore, Hugh Maxwell too joined in the chorus of dissent. It had been, he declared dourly, 'unwise' of the government 'to provoke so much race animosity'. Why could Ripon and Ilbert not see 'how unfit the native mind is to appreciate and sympathize with European ideas of administering the government of a country and people'?

This 'White Mutiny' was intimately connected with memories of the original Indian Mutiny, just twenty-five years before. Then every white woman in Cawnpore had been killed – and, as we have seen, a legend soon sprang up of rape as well as murder, as if every Indian man only awaited the opportunity to ravish the nearest memsahib. In a strangely similar vein, a recurrent theme of the anti-Ilbert campaign was the threat posed by Indian magistrates to English women. In the words of an anonymous letter to the *Englishman*: 'One's wife may be walked off for an imaginary offence and . . . what would more please our fellow subjects – than to bully and disgrace a wretched European woman? . . . The higher her husband's station and the greater respectability, the greater the delight of her torturer.' Writing in the same vein to the *Madras Mail*, a correspondent demanded to know: 'Are our wives to be torn from our homes on false pretenses [to] be tried by men who do not respect women, and do not understand us, and in many cases hate us? . . . Fancy, I ask you Britishers, her being taken before a half-clad native, to be tried and perhaps convicted . . .' Such language laid bare one of the odder complexes of the Victorian Empire: its sexual insecurity. It is no coincidence that the plots of the Raj's best-known novels – Forster's *A Passage to India* and Scott's *The Jewel in the Crown* – begin with an alleged sexual assault by an Indian man against an English woman, followed by a trial presided over by an Indian judge. Such cases did in fact occur. As the anti-Ilbert campaign reached its climax, an Englishwoman named Hume accused her sweeper of raping her and, though the allegation turned out later to be false (they had in fact been lovers), in the febrile atmosphere of the time it seemed somehow to prove the point.

The question is why the threat of Indian judges trying Englishwomen was so often linked to the danger of sexual contact between Indian men and British women. After all, there was no shortage of such contact in the other direction, between British men and Indian women; until 1888 there had even been legalized brothels for British soldiers. Yet somehow the Ilbert Bill seemed to threaten to break down the walls not just of the cantonment but of the bungalow bedroom too. Ninety thousand white people who claimed to rule 350 million brown ones saw equality before the law as the high road to inter-racial rape.*

*

* One possible source of sexual anxiety was the awareness that the supposedly clear line between 'White and Black' was in reality quite blurred. After two centuries of contact with Europeans, there was a substantial mixed race population, usually referred to as 'Eurasians', who were often employed in low-level public sector jobs (particularly on the railways and telegraphs). Revulsion against 'miscegenation' was an important feature of the later Victorian period: Kipling devotes at least two short stories to the 'fact' that the hue of a woman's fingernails was the best guide to the purity of her breeding (a darkness to the semicircles along the base of the nail spelling ostracism). One Indian-born soldier who won notoriety after the First World War heard his mother exclaim when his father lit his cigarette from a Burmese girl's

When Ripon finally returned to Calcutta from Simla in December, it was to a mixed – or rather a racially divided – reception. As he crossed the bridge from the railway station the streets were packed with applauding Indians, cheering their 'friend and saviour'. But at Government House he was hissed, booed and jeered by a crowd of his own countrymen, one of whom was moved to call him a 'damned old bugger'. At public dinners, only officials were prepared to drink the Viceroy's health. There were even rumours of a plot to kidnap him and pack him off back to England. An effigy of the hapless Ilbert was publicly burned.

As weak as his Queen had predicted he would be – and not helped by an ill-timed visit by her son, the Duke of Connaught, who dismissed Ripon as 'the greatest fool in Asia' – the Viceroy gave way. The Ilbert Bill was emasculated, giving white defendants in any criminal case that might be heard by an Indian magistrate the right to ask for a jury, not fewer than half of whose members must be English or American. That may sound as arcane a compromise as could be imagined. Yet it was a climb-down, and one that was pregnant with peril for the future of the Raj. To educated Indian magistrates and their friends, the contempt with which they were regarded by the majority of Anglo-Indians was now out in the open. As one of Ilbert's colleagues observed uneasily, the tone of the press campaign against the bill had been recklessly intemperate. The letters had 'teemed with wild invective and insulting domineering attacks against the Native, on whom every railway guard or indigo planter's foreman pretends to trample, as a master upon serfs, with impunity'. The 'political veil which the Government has always thrown over the delicate relations between the two races' had been 'rudely rent in twain' by a 'mob shaking their fists in the face of the whole Native population'. And now, just as he feared, the really important consequence of the Ilbert Bill became apparent: not the 'White Mutiny', but the reaction that this provoked among Indians.

---

cheroot: 'That sort of looseness is what has peopled Simla with thirty thousand Eurasians!' The fact that the majority of such liaisons were between white men and Indian women did not stop people fantasizing about inter-racial sex with the genders reversed.

Quite unintentionally, Ripon had brought into being a genuine Indian national consciousness. As the *Indian Mirror* put it:

For the first time in modern history, Hindus, Mohammedans, Sikhs, Rajputs, Bengalis, Madrasis, Bombayites, Punjabis, and Purbiahs have united to join a constitutional combination. Whole races and classes, who never before took any interest in the affairs of their country, are taking it now with a zeal and an earnestness which more than atone for their former apathy.

Just two years after the White Mutiny, the first meeting of the Indian National Congress was held. Though initially intended by its British founder to channel and thereby defuse Indian disaffection, Congress would quickly become the crucible of modern Indian nationalism.* From the outset, it was attended by stalwarts of the educated class who served the British Raj, men like Janakinath Bose and an Allahabad lawyer named Motilal Nehru.

The latter's son Jawaharlal would be the first Prime Minister of an independent India. Bose's son Subhas Chandra would lead an army against the British in the Second World War. It is not too much to see the White Mutiny as the fount and origin of their families' alienation from British rule.

India was the strategic core of the British Empire. If the British alienated the Anglicized elite that foundation would begin to crumble. But could another section of Indian society be found to prop up the British Raj? Somewhat improbably, the alternative to Asian apartheid was sought by some in the English class system.

Tory-entalism

For many British officials in India, toiling for years on end in a far-flung land, the thought of 'home' – not simulated in Simla,

---

* Congress was founded by Allan Octavian Hume, a Liberal ICS man who had been sickened by the anti-Ilbert campaign.

but the real thing, to which a man might one day retire – provided consolation in the heat of the plains. As the Victorian era drew to a close, however, the expatriates' memories of home became increasingly at odds with the reality. Theirs was a nostalgic, romantic vision of an unchanging rural England, of squires and parsons, thatched cottages and forelock-tugging villagers. It was an essentially Tory vision of a traditional, hierarchical society, ruled by landed aristocrats in a spirit of benign paternalism. The fact that Britain was now an industrial giant – where as early as 1870 most people lived in towns with more than 10,000 inhabitants – was somehow forgotten.

A similar process happened in the other direction, however, as people in Britain imagined India. 'What should they know of England, who only England know?' Kipling once asked, a reproach to his countrymen who ruled a global Empire without setting foot outside the British Isles. He might have put the question to Queen Victoria herself. She was delighted when Parliament bestowed on her the title of Empress of India (at her own suggestion) in 1877. But she never actually went near the place. What Victoria preferred was for India to come to her. By the 1880s her favourite servant was an Indian named Abdul Karim, also known as the 'Munshi', or teacher. He came with her to Osborne in 1887, the personification of the India the Queen liked to imagine: courteous, deferential, obedient, faithful. Not long after that, the Queen-Empress added a new wing to Osborne House, the centrepiece of which was the spectacular Durbar Room. The work was overseen by Lockwood Kipling, Rudyard's father, and was clearly inspired by the ornately carved interiors of Mughal palaces: indeed, parts of it look like a white version of Delhi's Red Fort. The Durbar Room offers another distinctly backward-looking vision, giving no hint of the new India of railways, coalmines and cotton mills the British were bringing into being. In this, it was typical of the way the British liked to see India in the 1890s. It was a fantasy.

Then, in 1898, the Marquess of Salisbury's Conservative government appointed a Viceroy whose whole career in India was an attempt to turn that fantasy into a reality.

To many of his contemporaries, George Nathaniel Curzon was a most insufferable person. Born into an aristocratic Derbyshire family who liked to trace their line back to the Norman Conquest, he had risen like an arrow through Eton, Oxford, the House of Commons and the India Office. In truth, there was nothing effortless about his famous superiority.* Entrusted as a child to a deranged governess, he was periodically forced to parade through the village wearing a large conical cap bearing the words 'liar', 'sneak' and 'coward'. ('I suppose', he later mused, 'no children well-born and well-placed ever cried so much or so justly.') At school Curzon was 'bent on being first in what I undertook and . . . I meant to do it in my way and not theirs'. At Oxford – 'that brief interval which must intervene between Eton and the Cabinet,' as someone joked – he was no less driven. Denied a First by the examiners, he determined to 'show them they had made a mistake', proceeding to win the Lothian Prize, the Arnold Prize and a Fellowship of All Souls in swift succession. Margot Asquith could not help being impressed by his 'enamelled self-assurance'. Others were less gentle in their mockery. A cartoon of him addressing Parliament at the Dispatch Box was entitled 'A Divinity addressing Black Beetles'.

When Curzon was appointed Viceroy he was not yet forty. It was a job for which he felt himself predestined. After all, was not the Viceroy's magnificent Calcutta residence an exact replica of his family's country seat at Kedleston? The Viceroyalty, he openly avowed, was 'the dream of my childhood, the fulfilled ambition of my manhood, and my highest conception of duty to the State'. In particular, Curzon felt himself called to restore British rule in India, which Liberals like Ripon had been undermining. The Liberals believed all men should have equal rights, regardless of skin colour; the Anglo-Indians, as we have seen, preferred a kind of apartheid, so that a tiny white minority could lord it over the mass of 'blacks'. But to a Tory aristocrat like Curzon, Indian society could never be as simple as these two opposing visions implied. Raised to see

* He was most concisely satirized in verse: 'My name is George Nathaniel Curzon, / I am a most superior person, / My cheek is pink, my hair is sleek, / I dine at Blenheim once a week.'

himself as very close to the pinnacle of a pyramid of status extending downwards from the monarch, Curzon thirsted above all after hierarchy. He and those like him sought to replicate in the Empire what they admired about Britain's feudal past. An earlier generation of British rulers in India had immersed themselves in Indian culture to become true Orientalists. Curzon was what you might call a 'Tory-entalist'.

The outlines of a feudal India were not far to seek. The so-called 'princely states' accounted for about a third of the area of India. There, traditional Maharajas remained nominally in charge, though always under the beady eye of a British Private Secretary (a role performed in other Oriental Empires under the title of 'Grand Vizier'). Even in the areas directly ruled by the British, most rural districts were dominated by aristocratic Indian landowners. In Curzon's eyes, it was these people who were the natural leaders of India. As he himself put it in a speech to Calcutta University's Convocation in 1905:

I have always been a devoted believer in the continued existence of the native states in India, and an ardent well-wisher of the native princes. But I believe in them not as relics, but as rulers, not as puppets but as living factors in the administration. I want them to share the responsibilities as well as the glories of British rule.

The kind of people Curzon had in mind were men like the Maharaja of Mysore, who acquired a new Private Secretary in 1902 in the person of Evan Machonochie. The Maharaja was, in theory at least, the heir to the throne of Tipu Sultan, once the most dangerous of the East India Company's foes. Those days, however, had long gone. This Maharaja had been educated by a senior ICS man, Sir Stuart Fraser; and it was thought, as Machonochie recalled, 'that a private secretary drawn from the same service and equipped with the requisite experience would be able to relieve His Highness of drudgery, show him something of our methods of disposing of work and, while suppressing his own personality, exercise some influence in the direction desired'. Machonochie's account of his seven years at the Mysore court neatly exemplifies the puppet-like role such princes were expected to play:

> His Highness ... on young shoulders carried a head of extraordinary maturity, which was, however, no bar to a boyish and wholehearted enjoyment of manly sports ... He [also] had the taste and knowledge to appreciate western music as well as his own ...
>
> We [meanwhile] got to work, cleared out the slums, straightened and widened the roads, put in a surface drainage system leading into the main sewers that discharged into septic tanks, provided new quarters for the displaced population, and tidied up generally.

The playboy Maharaja – wealthy, Westernized and weakened to the point of political impotence – was to become a familiar figure throughout India.

In return for running their kingdoms for them and granting them a generous allowance, the British expected only one thing: supine loyalty. Generally they got it. When Curzon paid a viceregal visit to Nashipur he was presented with a specially composed poem to mark the occasion:

> Welcome to Thee, Oh Viceroy, Mighty Ruler of India,
> Lo! Thousand eyes are eagerly waiting Thee to behold!
> Over flowed are our hearts with joy transcendent,
> Sanctified are we and our desires fulfilled;
> And Nashipur is hallowed with the touch of Thy Feet.
>
> Glorious and mighty is England's rule in India.
> Blessed are the people that have a Ruler so benevolent.
> Constant has been Thy aim to promote Thy subjects' welfare;
> Loving and protecting them like a kind hearted father;
> Oh! Where shall we get a Noble Ruler like Thee!

Where indeed?

In fact, Curzon's preoccupation with hierarchy was nothing new. As Viceroy, Disraeli's fellow romantic Lord Lytton had been even more extravagant in his hopes of the Indian 'feudal nobility', on the principle that 'the further East you go, the greater becomes the importance of a bit of bunting'. Lytton had even tried to create a new section of the Indian Civil Service specifically earmarked for the sons of this Oriental aristocracy. The aim, as one Punjab official said in 1860, was to 'attach to the state by timely concessions ... a body scattered throughout the country considerable by its property and rank'. Nor was Tory-entalism confined to India. In Tanganyika Sir Donald Cameron strove to reinforce the links from 'the peasant ... up to his Headman, the Headman to the Sub-Chief, the Sub-Chief to the Chief, and the Chief to the District Officer'. In West Africa Lord Kimberley thought it better to 'have nothing to do with the "educated natives" as a body. I would treat with the hereditary chiefs only'. Lady Hamilton, the wife of the Governor of Fiji, even regarded the Fijian chiefs as her social equals (unlike her children's English nanny). 'All Orientals think extra highly of a Lord,' insisted George Lloyd, before taking up his duties as the newly ennobled High Commissioner in Egypt. The whole purpose of the Empire, argued Frederick Lugard, the architect of Britain's West African empire, was 'to maintain traditional rulerships as a fortress of societal security in a changing world ... The really important category was status.' Lugard invented an entire theory of 'indirect rule' – the antithesis of the direct rule that had been imposed on the Jamaican planters in 1865 – according to which British rule could be maintained at minimal cost by delegating all local power to existing elites, retaining only the essentials of central authority (in particular the purse strings) in British hands.

Complementary to the restoration, preservation or (where necessary) invention of traditional hierarchies was the elaboration of the Empire's own administrative hierarchy. Protocol in India was strictly governed by the 'warrant of precedence', which in 1881 consisted of no fewer than seventy-seven separate ranks. Throughout the Empire, officials thirsted after membership of the Most Distinguished Order of St Michael and St George, whether as CMG ('Call Me God'), KCMG ('Kindly Call Me God') and, reserved for the very top tier of governors, GCMG ('God Calls Me God'). There was, declared Lord Curzon, 'an insatiable appetite [among] the British-speaking community all the world over for titles and precedence'.

There was also, he was sure, an appetite for grand architecture. Under Curzon, the Taj Mahal and Fatehpur Sikri were restored and the Victoria Memorial was built in Calcutta. Significantly, the place in India Curzon most disliked was the place the Victorians themselves had built from scratch: Simla. It was, he complained, 'nothing more than a middle class suburb on a hilltop', where he had to lunch with 'a set of youths interested only in polo and dancing'. The Viceroy's Lodge struck the Curzons as odiously vulgar. ('I keep trying not to be disappointed,' confessed Lady Curzon. 'A Minneapolis millionaire would revel in it.') The company at dinner made them feel that they were dining 'every day in the housekeeper's room with the butler and the lady's maid'. It got so bad that they took to camping in a field near the Simla golf course. The sad truth was that the British in India were just too unbearably common.

The zenith of Curzon's Tory-entalism was the Delhi Durbar of 1903, a spectacular display of pomp and ceremony which he personally staged to mark the accession of Edward VII. The Durbar – or 'Curzonation', as it was dubbed – was the perfect expression of the Viceroy's pseudo-feudal view of India. Its highlight was a richly symbolic elephant procession in which the Indian princes played a prominent role. It was, as one observer said,

a magnificent sight, and all description must fail to give an adequate idea of its character, its brilliancy of colour and its ever-changing features, the variety of howdahs and trappings and the gorgeousness of the dress adorning the persons of the Chiefs who followed in the wake of the Viceroy . . . A murmur of admiration, breaking into short-lived cheers, rose from the crowd.

There they all were, from the Begum of Bhopal to the Maharaja of Kapurtala, swaying atop their elephants behind the Grand Panjandrum himself. One journalist covering the Durbar 'carried away the impression of black-bearded Kings who swayed to and fro with each movement of their gigantic steeds . . . The sight was not credible of our nineteenth century [sic].' Amid this extravaganza, there came a message for the absent King-Emperor, which so neatly expressed the Viceroy's own view that it can only have been penned by Curzon:

His Empire is strong ... because it regards the liberties and respects the dignities and rights of all his feudatories and subjects. The keynote of the British policy in India has been to conserve all the best features in the fabric of native society. By that policy we have attained the wonderful measure of success: in it we recognise an assured instrument of further triumphs in the future.

There was, however, a fatal flaw in all this.* The Durbar was splendid theatre, no doubt; but it was a façade of power, not the real thing. After the Indian army, the true foundation of British power was not the Maharajas on their elephants but the elite of Anglicized lawyers and civil servants Macaulay had called into being. Yet these were the very people Curzon regarded as a threat. Indeed, he pointedly shunned the so-called 'Bengali Babus'. When asked why so few natives were promoted in the covenanted Civil Service under him, he replied dismissively: 'The highly placed native is apt to be unequal to [the task], does not attract the respect of his subordinates, European or even Native, and is rather inclined to abdicate, or to run away.'

Just two years after the Durbar, Curzon launched a premeditated attack on the 'Babus'. He announced – ostensibly for the sake of administrative efficiency – that their homeland, Bengal, would be divided in two. As the capital of both Bengal and India, Calcutta was the power-base of the Indian National Congress, which had by now ceased to be (if it ever was) a mere safety-valve for native disgruntlement. Curzon knew full well that his plan for partition would incense the emergent nationalist movement. The capital was, as he himself put it, 'the centre from which the Congress party is manipulated ... Any measure in consequence that would divide

---

* And it was not just the fact that (as Machonochie observed) many of the Indian princes privately resented the 'schoolmasterly' way Curzon was inclined to treat them. Curzon even managed to upset them at the moment of their apotheosis at the Durbar by failing to return their visits.

the Bengali-speaking population ... or that would weaken the influence of the lawyer class, who have the entire organization in their hands, is intensely and hotly resented by them.' So unpopular was the proposal that it unleashed the worst political violence against British rule since the Mutiny.

The nationalists began by organizing, for the first time, a boycott of British goods, invoking the ideal of *swadeshi*, Indian economic self-sufficiency. This was the strategy endorsed by moderates like the writer Rabindranath Tagore.* There were also widespread strikes and demonstrations. But some protesters went further. Throughout Bengal, there was a rash of violent attacks on British administrators, including several attempts on the life of the Governor of Bengal himself. At first the authorities assumed the violence was the work of poor, uneducated Indians. But on 30 April 1908, when two British women were killed by a bomb meant for the Mazafferpur District Judge, J. D. Kingsford, police raids uncovered the more disturbing truth: this was an altogether different threat from that posed by the mutinous sepoys of 1857. They had been simple soldiers, defending their traditional religious culture against British interference. This, by contrast, was modern terrorism: extreme nationalism plus nitroglycerine. And the ringleaders were anything but poor coolies. One of the terrorist organizations, known as the Anushilan Samiti, was led by Pramathanath Mitra P. Mitra, a Calcutta High Court barrister. When the Special Branch swooped on five eminently respectable Calcutta addresses, they found them stuffed with bomb-making equipment. Twenty-six young men – not the suspected coolies, but members of Bengal's Brahmin elite – were arrested.

Those who subsequently stood trial at Alipore could hardly have had more respectable backgrounds. One of the defendants, Aurobindo Ghose, was in fact a former head boy at St Paul's School in London and scholar at King's College, Cambridge. He even turned

---

* It was a grave blow to the self-esteem of the British literary elite when Tagore was awarded the Nobel prize for Literature in 1913. George Bernard Shaw sneered at 'Stupendranath Begorr' – a cheap dig that illustrates how widespread the aversion to educated Bengalis had become.

out to be an exact contemporary of one of the magistrates who tried him; indeed, Ghose had beaten him at Greek in the ICS exam and had failed to secure an ICS place only because he missed the riding test. As one of the other British lawyers involved in the case noted, it was

a matter for regret that a man of Arabindo's [sic] mental calibre should have been ejected from the Civil Service on the ground he could not, or would not, ride a horse ... Had room been found for him in the Educational Service for India I believe he would have gone far not merely in personal advancement but in welding more firmly the links which bind his countrymen to ours.

But it was too late for regrets now. The British had set out to create Indians in their own image. Now, by alienating this Anglicized elite, they had produced a Frankenstein's monster. Aurobindo Ghose personified the nationalism that would soon manifest itself throughout the Empire precisely because he was the product of the ultimate English education.

Yet the Alipore case was revealingly different from the Morant Bay trials of just over forty years before. Instead of the summary justice meted out then, this trial lasted nearly seven months, and in the end Aurobindo Ghose was acquitted. Even the death sentence passed on the group's ringleader – his brother Barendra Kumar Ghose – was later commuted, despite the fact that he admitted during the trial to having authorized the assassination of the chief prosecutor. The final humiliating climbdown came in 1911, when the decision to partition Bengal was itself revoked. That would have to wait – ironically, until Indian independence. This show of weakness was not calculated to put a stop to terrorism. It did not.

Meanwhile, however, the British had devised a better way of chastising Bengal's unruly capital. They decided to move the seat of government to Delhi, the erstwhile capital of the Mughal emperors. Once, before the advent of the bothersome Babu, Calcutta had been the natural base for an Empire based on the profit motive. Delhi would be a headquarters altogether more suitable to the Tory-ental era; and New Delhi would be the supreme expression of that era's ineffable snobbery.

It was Curzon's misfortune that he did not survive in office long enough to see the great canvas city he had constructed for the Durbar turned into a real city of glowing pink stone. The architects of New Delhi, Herbert Baker and Edwin Lutyens, had no doubt that their objective was to build a symbol of British power that would match the achievements of the Mughals. This, they understood at once, was to be the ineradicable legacy of the Tory-ental Empire: as Lutyens himself confessed, simply being in India made him feel 'very Tory and pre-Tory feudal' (he even married Lord Lytton's daughter). Baker at once recognized 'the political standpoint in a political capital'; the aim, he thought, was to 'give them Indian sentiment where it does not conflict with grand principles, as the Government should do'. What the two men created was and is an astounding achievement: the British Empire's one architectural masterpiece. New Delhi is grandiose, certainly. The Viceroy's Palace alone covered four and a half acres, and had to be staffed by 6,000 servants and 400 gardeners, fifty of whom were solely employed to chase birds away. But it is undeniably beautiful. It would take a very hard-hearted anti-imperialist not to be moved by the sight of the changing of the guard at what is now the President's Palace, as the great towers and domes glow in the hazy rays of dawn. Nevertheless, the political message of New Delhi is clear; so clear that it does not have to be inferred from the symbolism of the architecture. For Baker and Lutyens crowned their creation with an inscription on the walls of the Secretariat that must be the most condescending in the entire history of the Empire:

> LIBERTY DOES NOT DESCEND TO A
> PEOPLE. A PEOPLE MUST RAISE THEMSELVES TO
> LIBERTY. IT IS A BLESSING THAT MUST BE
> EARNED BEFORE IT CAN BE ENJOYED.

Not Curzon's words, to be sure – but in their patronizing tone, distinctly Curzonesque.

The supreme irony was that this architectural extravagance was paid for by none other than the Indian taxpayer. Clearly, before they earned their liberty the Indians would have to go on paying for the privilege of being ruled by the British.

Was it a privilege worth paying for? The British took it for granted that it was. But even Curzon himself once admitted that British rule 'may be good for us; but it is neither equally, nor altogether, good for them'. Indian nationalists agreed whole-heartedly, complaining that the wealth of India was being drained into the pockets of foreigners. In fact, we now know that this drain – the colonial burden as measured by the trade surplus of the colony – amounted to little more than 1 per cent of Indian net domestic product a year between 1868 and 1930. That was a lot less than the Dutch 'drained' from their East Indies empire, which amounted to between 7 and 10 per cent of Indonesian net domestic product in the same period.

And on the other side of the balance sheet were the immense British investments in Indian infrastructure, irrigation and industry. By the 1880s the British had invested £270 million in India, not much less than one-fifth of their entire investment overseas. By 1914 the figure had reached £400 million. The British increased the area of irrigated land by a factor of eight, so that by the end of the Raj a quarter of all land was irrigated, compared with just 5 per cent of it under the Mughals. They created an Indian coal industry from scratch which by 1914 produced nearly 16 million tons a year. They increased the number of jute spindles by a factor of ten. There were also marked improvements in public health, which increased Indian average life expectancy by eleven years.* It was the British who introduced quinine as an anti-malarial prophylactic, carried out public programmes of vaccination against smallpox – often in the face of local resistance – and laboured to improve the urban water supplies that were so often the bearers of cholera and

* From 21 years to 32. However, in the same period (between 1820 and 1950), British life expectancy increased from 40 to 69 years.

other diseases. And, although it is simply impossible to quantify, it is hard to believe that there were not some advantages in being governed by as incorruptible a bureaucracy as the Indian Civil Service. After independence, that idiosyncratic Anglophile Chaudhuri was sacked from All India Radio for dedicating his *Autobiography of an Unknown Indian* to 'the memory of the British Empire in India . . . because all that was good and living within us was made, shaped and quickened by the same British Empire'. That was wilful overstatement. But it had a grain of truth, which was of course why it so outraged Chaudhuri's nationalist critics.

True, the average Indian had not got much richer under British rule. Between 1757 and 1947 British per capita gross domestic product increased in real terms by 347 per cent, Indian by a mere 14 per cent. A substantial share of the profits which accrued as the Indian economy industrialized went to British managing agencies, banks or shareholders; this despite the fact that there was no shortage of capable Indian investors and entrepreneurs. The free trade imposed on India in the nineteenth century exposed indigenous manufacturers to lethal European competition at a time when the independent United States of America sheltered its infant industries behind high tariff walls. In 1896 Indian mills supplied just 8 per cent of Indian cloth consumption.* It should also be remembered that Indian indentured labourers supplied much of the cheap labour on which the later British imperial economy depended. Between the 1820s and the 1920s, close to 1.6 million Indians left India to work in a variety of Caribbean, African, Indian Ocean and Pacific colonies, ranging from the rubber plantations of Malaya to the sugar mills of Fiji. The conditions in which they travelled and worked were often little better than those that had been inflicted on African slaves in the century before. Nor could the best efforts of civil servants like Machonochie avert terrible famines in 1876–8 and 1899–1900. Indeed, in the former the British predilection for

* That changed in the inter-war years however. By 1945 Indian mills supplied three-quarters of domestic consumption.

laissez-faire economics actually made matters worse.* But would Indians have been better off under the Mughals? Or, for that matter, under the Dutch – or the Russians?

It might seem self-evident that they would have been better off under Indian rulers. That was certainly true from the point of view of the ruling elites the British had overthrown and whose share of national income, something like 5 per cent, they then appropriated for their own consumption. But for the majority of Indians it was far less clear that their lot would improve under independence. Under British rule, the village economy's share of total after-tax income actually rose from 45 per cent to 54 per cent. Since that sector represented around three-quarters of the entire population, there can therefore be little doubt that British rule reduced inequality in India. And even if the British did not greatly increase Indian incomes, things might conceivably have been worse under a restored Mughal regime had the Mutiny succeeded. China did not prosper under Chinese rulers.

The reality, then, was that Indian nationalism was fuelled not by the impoverishment of the many but by the rejection of the privileged few. In the age of Macaulay, the British had called into being an English-speaking, English-educated elite of Indians, a class of civil service auxiliaries on whom their system of administration had come to depend. In time, these people naturally aspired to have some share in the government of the country, just as Macaulay had predicted.† But in the age of Curzon, they were spurned in favour of decorative but largely defunct Maharajas.

The result was that by the Empress-Queen's twilight years, British rule in India was like one of those palaces Curzon so adored. It

---

* It is, however, quite unjustifiable to compare British reliance on the free market in the famine of 1877 with the Nazi policy of genocide against the Jews. The Viceroy, Lord Lytton, was certainly wrong to imagine that market forces would suffice to feed the starving after the catastrophic drought of 1876. But his *intention* was not murderous. Hitler's was.

† 'To have found a great people sunk in the lowest depths of slavery and superstition, to have ruled them as to have made them desirous and capable of all the privileges of citizens, would indeed be a title to glory all our own.'

looked simply splendid on the outside. But downstairs the servants were busy turning the floorboards into firewood.

> Far-called our navies melt away;
>> On dune and headland sinks the fire:
> Lo, all our pomp of yesterday
>> Is one with Nineveh and Tyre!
> Judge of the Nations, spare us yet,
> Lest we forget – lest we forget!

Kipling wrote his doleful 'Recessional' in 1897, sending a shiver of apprehension down the spines of his countrymen as they celebrated Queen Victoria's Diamond Jubilee. Sure enough, like the proud citadels of Nineveh and Tyre, most of Curzon's works have not endured. As Viceroy he had striven with all his self-assured zeal to make the British government of India more efficient. He believed passionately that without India Britain would drop from being 'the greatest power in the world' to being 'third rate'. But it was British rule he wanted to modernize, not India. Like its ancient monuments, he wanted to slap a preservation order on the Indian princes; to fill the listed buildings with a reliable aristocracy of 'listed' people. It was never a realistic undertaking.

Curzon himself would go on to be Lord Privy Seal in 1915 and Foreign Secretary in 1919. Yet he never attained the highest office he so desired. He was passed over for the Tory leadership after a confidential memorandum dismissed him as 'representing that section of privileged conservatism' which no longer had a place 'in this democratic age'. That may also suffice as an epitaph for the entire Tory-entalist project.

The MP Arthur Lee once encountered Lord Curzon in Madame Tussaud's, 'gazing with concentrated attention, but a trace of disappointment at his own effigy in wax'. How much more disappointed he would have been to see the statues of the Queen-Empress and sundry imperial proconsuls that stand today in the neglected back yard of Lucknow Zoo, where they were dumped after Indian independence. There can be few more vivid emblems of the transience of imperial achievement than the immense marble Victoria that dominates this shabby little spot. Simply transporting such a vast lump of carved stone from London to Lucknow had been a remarkable feat, only possible with the cranes, steamships and trains that were the true engines of Victorian power. Yet today the idea that this lugubrious-looking old lady once ruled India seems almost preposterous. Removed from her plinth in whichever public place she once occupied, the great white Queen-Empress has forfeited her totemic power.*

Then again, by the turn of the century it could be argued – *pace* Curzon – that India had ceased to be the indispensable jewel it had been back in the 1860s, the be all and end all of British imperial power. Elsewhere in the world, a new generation of imperialists was coming of age, men who believed that if the Empire was to survive – if it was to adapt to the challenges of a new century – it would have to expand in new directions.

In their view, the Empire had to drop the pomp and return to its pre-Victorian roots: to penetrate new markets, to settle new colonies and – if necessary – to wage new wars.

* Even so, the fact that someone has bashed off her nose still seems strangely sacrilegious.

5

Maxim Force

There are two oriflammes; which shall we plant on the far-thest islands – the one that floats in a heavenly fire, or that hangs heavy with foul tissue of terrestrial gold? There is indeed a course of beneficent glory open to us, such as never was yet offered to any poor group of mortal souls. But it must be – it is with us, now, 'Reign or Die' . . . And this is what [England] must either do, or perish: she must found colonies as fast and as far as she is able, formed of her most energetic and worthiest men; – seizing every piece of fruitful waste ground she can set her foot on.

John Ruskin, inaugural lecture as
Slade Professor at Oxford, 1870

[T]ake Constitution Jesuits if obtainable and insert English Empire for Roman Catholic Religion.

Cecil Rhodes, outlining the original concept of the Rhodes
Scholarships to Lord Rothschild, 1888

You cannot have omelettes without breaking eggs; you cannot destroy the practices of barbarism, of slavery, of superstition . . . without the use of force.

Joseph Chamberlain

In the space of just a few years, as the nineteenth century gave way to the twentieth, British attitudes towards their Empire flipped over from arrogance to anxiety. The last years of Queen Victoria were a time of imperial hubris: there simply seemed no limit to what could be achieved by British firepower and finance. As both policeman and banker to the world, the British Empire attained a geographical extent unrivalled in history. Even its nearest competitors, France and Russia, were dwarfed by the Britannic Titan – the first true superpower. Yet even before the Queen-Empress expired in her bedroom at Osborne House in 1901, nemesis struck. Africa, which had seemed to be British by right, dealt the Empire an unexpected and painful blow. While some responded by retreating into a defiant jingoism, others were assailed by doubts. Even the most gilt-edged generals and proconsuls exhibited symptoms of what is best described as decadence. And Britain's most ambitious imperial rival was not slow to scent the opportunity such doubts presented.

Cape to Cairo

In the mid-nineteenth century, apart from a few coastal outposts, Africa was the last blank sheet in the imperial atlas of the world. North of the Cape, British possessions were confined to West Africa: Sierra Leone, Gambia, the Gold Coast and Lagos, most of them left-overs from the battles for and then against slavery. Within twenty short years after 1880, however, ten thousand African tribal kingdoms were transformed into just forty states, of which thirty-six were under direct European control. Never in human history had there been such drastic redrawing of the map of a continent. By 1914, apart from Abyssinia and Liberia (the latter an American quasi-colony), the entire continent was under some form of European rule. Roughly a third of it was British. This was what came to be known as 'the Scramble for Africa' – though the Scramble *of* Africa might be nearer the mark.

The key to the Empire's phenomenal expansion in the late Victorian period was the combination of financial power and fire-power. It was a combination supremely personified by Cecil Rhodes. The son of a clergyman in Bishop's Stortford, Rhodes had emigrated to South Africa at the age of seventeen because – so he later said – he 'could no longer stand cold mutton'. He was at once business genius and imperial visionary; a robber baron, but also a mystic. Unlike the other 'Rand Lords', not least his partner Barney Barnato, it was not enough for Rhodes to make a fortune from the vast De Beers diamond mines at Kimberley. He aspired to be more than a money maker. He dreamt of becoming an empire builder.

Though his public image was that of a lone colossus bestriding Africa, Rhodes could not have won his near-monopoly over South African diamond production without the assistance of his friends in the City of London; in particular, the Rothschild bank, at that time the biggest concentration of financial capital in the world. When Rhodes had arrived at the Kimberley diamond fields there had been more than a hundred small companies working the four major 'pipes', flooding the market with diamonds and driving one another out of business. In 1882 a Rothschild agent visited Kimberley and recommended large-scale amalgamation; within four years the number of companies was down to three. A year later, the bank financed the merger of Rhodes's De Beers Company with the Compagnie Française, followed by the final crucial fusion with the bigger Kimberley Central Company. Now there was just one company: De Beers. It is usually assumed that Rhodes owned De Beers, but this was not the case. Nathaniel de Rothschild was a bigger shareholder than Rhodes himself; indeed, by 1899 the Rothschilds' stake was twice that of Rhodes. In 1888 Rhodes wrote to Lord Rothschild:* 'I know with you behind me I can do all I have said. If however you think differently I have nothing to say.' So when Rhodes needed financial backing for a new African scheme in October 1888 he had no hesitation about where to turn.

The proposition Rhodes wanted Rothschild to consider was the concession he had just secured from the Matabele chief, Lobengula, to develop the 'simply endless' gold fields that Rhodes believed existed beyond the Limpopo River. The terms of his letter to Rothschild make it clear that his intentions towards Lobengula were

---

* Nathaniel Rothschild was elevated to the peerage in 1885, the first Jew to enter the House of Lords.

anything but friendly. The Matabele king, he wrote, was 'the only block to Central Africa, as, once we have his territory, the rest is easy, as the rest is simply a village system with a separate headman, all independent of each other ... The key is Matabele Land, with its gold, the reports as to which are not based solely on hearsay ... Fancy, this Gold Field which was purchasable, at about £150,000 two years ago, is now selling for over ten millions.' Rothschild responded positively. When Rhodes joined forces with the existing Bechuanaland Company to create a new Central Search Association for Matabeleland, the banker was a major shareholder, and increased his involvement when this became the United Concessions Company in 1890. He was also among the founding shareholders when Rhodes established the British South Africa Company in 1889; indeed, he acted as the company's unpaid financial adviser.

The De Beers Company had fought its battles in the boardrooms of Kimberley. The British South Africa Company, by contrast, fought real battles. When Lobengula realized he had been hoodwinked into signing over much more than mere mineral rights, he resolved to take Rhodes on. Determined to dispose of Lobengula once and for all, Rhodes responded by sending an invasion force – the Chartered Company's Volunteers – numbering 700 men. The Matabele had, by African standards, a powerful and well-organized army; Lobengula's *impis* numbered in the region of 3,000. But Rhodes's men brought with them a devastating secret weapon. Operated by a crew of four, the 0.45 inch Maxim gun could fire 500 rounds a minute, fifty times faster than the fastest rifle available. A force equipped with just five of these lethal weapons could literally sweep a battlefield clear.

The Battle of Shangani River in 1893 was among the earliest uses of the Maxim in battle. One eyewitness recorded what happened:

The Matabele never got nearer than 100 yards led by the Nubuzu regiment, the king's body guard who came on yelling like fiends and rushing on to certain death, for the Maxims far exceeded all expectations and mowed them down literally like grass. I never saw anything like these Maxim guns, nor dreamed that such things could be: for the belts of cartridges were run through them as fast as a man could load and fire. Every man in the laager owes his life under Providence to the Maxim gun. The natives told the king that they did not fear us or our rifles, but they could not kill the beast that went pooh! pooh! by which they mean the Maxim.

To the Matabele it seemed that 'the white man came . . . with . . . guns that spat bullets as the heavens sometimes spit hail, and who were the naked Matabele to stand up against these guns?' Around 1,500 Matabele warriors were wiped out. Just four of the 700 invaders died. *The Times* reported smugly that the Matabele 'put our victory down to witchcraft, allowing that the Maxim was a pure work of an evil spirit. They have named it "S'cockacocka", owing to the peculiar noise it makes when in action.'

Lest anyone should be in any doubt as to who had masterminded the operation, the conquered territory was renamed Rhodesia. Behind Rhodes, however, lay the financial might of Rothschild. Significantly, a member of the French branch of the family noted with satisfaction the connection between the news of 'a sharp engagement having taken place with the Matabeles' and 'a little spurt in the shares' of Rhodes's British South Africa Company. The Rothschilds' sole worry – and it was amply justified – was that Rhodes was channelling money from the profitable De Beers Company into the altogether speculative British South Africa Company. When the maverick Conservative politician Lord Randolph Churchill returned from a visit to South Africa in 1891 declaring that 'no more unwise or unsafe speculation exists than the investment of money in [mining] exploration syndicates' and accusing Rhodes of being 'a sham . . . [who] could not raise £51,000 in the City to open a mine', Rothschild was incensed. There were few graver crimes in the eyes of a *fin de siècle* financier than to talk down an investment.

The official Matabeleland campaign souvenir, published on the fortieth anniversary of this one-sided little conflict, opens with Rhodes's 'tribute' to the men who had conquered the Matabele 'savages'. The highlight, however, is a grotesque hymn dedicated to the conqueror's favourite weapon. The hymn actually started life as a Liberal satire on the expedition, but Rhodes's men brazenly adopted it as their anthem:

> Onward Chartered Soldiers, on to heathen lands,
> Prayer books in your pockets, rifles in your hands.
> Take the glorious tidings where trade can be done,
> Spread the peaceful gospel – with a Maxim gun.
>
> Tell the wretched natives, sinful are their hearts,
> Turn their heathen temples into spirit marts.
> And if to your teaching they will not succumb,
> Give them another sermon with the Maxim gun.
>
> . . .
>
> When the Ten Commandments they quite understand,
> You their Chief must hocus, and annex their land;
> And if they misguided call you to account,
> Give them another sermon – with a Maxim from the Mount.

The Maxim gun was in fact an American invention. But its inventor, Hiram Maxim, always had his eye firmly on the British market. As soon as he had a working prototype ready in his underground workshop in Hatton Garden, London, he began issuing invitations to the great and the good to give the weapon a trial. Among those who accepted were the Duke of Cambridge, then Commander-in-Chief, the Prince of Wales, the Duke of Edinburgh, the Duke of Devonshire, the Duke of Sutherland and the Duke of Kent. The Duke of Cambridge responded with that alacrity so characteristic of his class. He was, he declared, 'greatly impressed with the value of machine guns'; indeed, he felt 'confident they will, ere long, be used generally in all armies'. However, he did 'not think it advisable to buy any just yet', adding: 'When we require them we can purchase the most recent patterns, and their manipulation can be learnt by intelligent men in a few hours.' Others were quicker to appreciate the huge potential of Maxim's invention. When the Maxim Gun Company was established in November 1884 Lord Rothschild was on its board. In 1888 his bank financed the £1.9

million merger of the Maxim Company with the Nordenfelt Guns and Ammunition Company.

So close was Rhodes's relationship with the Rothschilds that he even entrusted the execution of his will to Lord Rothschild, specifying that his estate should be used to fund an imperialist equivalent of the Jesuit order – the original intention of the Rhodes Scholarships. This would be 'a society of the elect for the good of the Empire'. 'In considering question suggested take Constitution Jesuits if obtainable,' Rhodes scribbled, 'and insert English Empire for Roman Catholic Religion.' Rothschild in turn assured Rhodes: '[O]ur first and foremost wish in connection with South African matters is that you should remain at the head of affairs in that Colony and that you should be able to carry out that great Imperial policy which has been the dream of your life.'

The creation of his own personal country and his own imperialist holy order were indeed merely components of a much bigger Rhodesian 'Imperial policy'. On a huge table-sized map of Africa (which can still be seen in Kimberley today) Rhodes drew a pencil line stretching from Cape Town to Cairo. This was to be the ultimate imperial railway. From the Cape it would run northwards like some huge metal spine through Bechuanaland, from Bechuanaland through Rhodesia, from Rhodesia through Nyasaland, then on past the Great Lakes to Khartoum and finally up the Nile to its final destination in Egypt.

By this means, Rhodes envisaged bringing the whole African continent under British domination. His justification was simple: 'We are the first race in the world, and the more of the world we inhabit, the better it is for the human race.' There were literally no limits to Rhodes's ambitions. He could talk with total seriousness of 'the ultimate recovery of the United States of America as an integral part of the British Empire'.

At one level, wars like the one waged by Rhodes against the Matabele were private battles planned in private clubs like the Kimberley Club, that stuffy bastion of capitalist conviviality of which Rhodes himself was among the founders. Matabeleland had become part of the Empire at no cost to the British taxpayer since the entire campaign had been fought by mercenaries employed by Rhodes and paid for by the shareholders in the British South African and De Beers companies. If it turned out that Matabeleland had no gold, then they would be the losers. In effect, the process of colonization had been privatized, a return to the early days of empire when monopoly trading companies had pioneered British rule from Canada to Calcutta. Rhodes was indeed consciously learning from history. British rule in India had begun with the East India Company; now British rule in Africa would be founded on his business interests. In one letter to Rothschild he even referred to De Beers as 'another East India Company'.

Nor was he alone in thinking this way. George Goldie, the son of a family of Manx smugglers who spent his youth as a dissolute soldier of fortune, also dreamt as a boy of 'colouring the map red'; his grand design was to annex every square mile from the Niger to the Nile. In 1875 he had gone to West Africa to try to salvage a small merchant house belonging to his sister-in-law's family. By 1879 he had merged it with a number of other palm oil companies to form the National African Company. But Goldie quickly became convinced that 'it was hopeless to try to do business where they could not impose real law and order'. In 1883 he proposed that the National African Company take over the whole of the lower and middle Niger region on the basis of a royal charter. Three years later he got what he wanted: a charter was granted to a revived Royal Niger Company. Again, it was the seventeenth-century model of sub-contracted colonization, with shareholders rather than taxpayers bearing the risk. Goldie prided himself on seeing 'that the shareholders, with whose money the company was built up, were fairly treated':

The phrase was that 'the pioneer was always ruined' and I said that in this case the pioneer should not be ruined, and he was not. I had gone into the street, and induced people to give me a million to begin with. I was bound to see that they got a fair return on their money. If I had not done so, I should have been committing a breach of trust. My work was an international struggle to obtain British possession of that territory, and I may remind you that the work was brought to a successful conclusion before the Niger Charter came to an end. I think that you will agree with me that I was absolutely bound to protect the shareholders' interests in the first place . . .

The government was only too happy to proceed on this basis. As Goldie put it in 1892, Britain had 'adopted the policy of advance by commercial enterprise . . . The sanction of Parliament was not to be expected for the employment of imperial resources' to further his ambitions.

For Goldie as for Rhodes, what was good for his company was self-evidently good for the British Empire. And like his South African counterpart, Goldie saw the Maxim gun as the key to the expansion of both. By the end of the 1880s he had conquered several of the Fulani emirates and launched wars against the settlements of Bida and Ilorin. Though he had little more than 500 men at his disposal, the Maxims enabled them to defeat armies thirty times as large. It was a similar story in East Africa, where Frederick Lugard had established British primacy in Buganda while in the employ of the Imperial British East Africa Company.* So impressed was Goldie by Lugard's performance that he hired him to work for his Niger Company. When Northern Nigeria was made a British protectorate in 1900, Lugard was appointed its first High Commissioner; twelve years later he became Governor-General of a united Nigeria. That transformation from trading monopoly to protectorate was typical of the way the Scramble for Africa proceeded. The politicians let the businessmen make the running, but sooner rather than later they stepped in to create some kind of formal colonial government. Although the new African companies resembled the East India Company in their original design, they governed Africa for far shorter periods than their Indian precursor had governed India. On the other hand, even when British rule became 'official' it remained skeletal in its structure. In his book

---

* Lugard was the son of two missionaries who had joined the Indian Army after failing the Indian Civil Service exam. He had gone to Africa after catching his wife in bed with another man, which caused him to lose his faith in God (not to mention his wife).

The Dual Mandate in British Tropical Africa (1922), Lugard would later define indirect rule as the 'systematic use of the customary institutions of the people as agencies of local rule'. This was a rather elaborate way of saying that Africa would be ruled the way the princely states of India were ruled: with existing African rulers as puppets and a minimal British presence.

That, however, was only half the story of the Scramble for Africa. For while Rhodes was working northwards from the Cape, and while Goldie was working eastwards from the Niger, British politicians were working southwards, from Cairo. And they were doing so in large measure because they feared that if they did not, someone else would.

It was the French who made the running in North Africa, chipping away far more readily at the edges of the Ottoman Empire than the British. Their first bid for supremacy in Egypt had been made by Napoleon, only to be sunk decisively by the Royal Navy at the Battle of Aboukir in 1798. But the French did not wait long after Napoleon's fall to resume their activities in the region. As early as 1830 a French army had invaded Algeria; within seven years the French controlled most of the country. They had also been quick to give their backing to Mehmet Ali, the modernizing Egyptian leader who sought to flout, if not to overthrow, the Ottoman Sultan's authority. Above all, it was French investors who took the lead in the economic development of Turkey and Egypt. The man who designed and built the Suez Canal was a Frenchman, Ferdinand de Lesseps, and the greater part of the capital invested in that vast and strategically portentous undertaking – opened in November 1869 – was French. Time and again, however, the British were able to insist that the future of the Ottoman Empire was a matter to be decided between the five great powers: not just Britain and France, but also Russia, Austria and Prussia.

Indeed, it is impossible to understand the Scramble for Africa without seeing that it had its antecedents in the perennial struggle between the great powers to maintain – or overthrow – the balance of power between them in Europe and the Near East. In 1829–30 they had reached a consensus about the future of Greece and Belgium. In the wake of the Crimean War (1854–6), they reached a more fragile consensus about the future of Turkey's remaining European possessions, in particular the Black Sea Straits. What happened over Africa in the 1880s was in many ways simply the continuation of European diplomacy in other places – with the important qualification that neither Austria nor Russia had ambitions south of the Mediterranean. Thus, at the Congress of Berlin in 1878, the offer to France of Tunis was a mere sub-clause of the much more complex agreements reached about the future of the Balkans.

When it became clear in 1874 that the governments of both Egypt and Turkey were bankrupt, it seemed at first that matters would be settled by the usual great-power confabulation. However, first Disraeli and then his arch-rival Gladstone could not resist the temptation to take unilateral action to give Britain the edge in the region. When the Khedive of Egypt offered to sell his shares in the Suez Canal Company for £4 million, Disraeli seized the opportunity, turning to his friends the Rothschilds – who else? – for the colossal cash advance necessary to close the deal. True, ownership of 44 per cent of the Canal Company's original shares did not give Britain control over the canal itself, especially as the shares had no voting rights until 1895 and had only ten votes thereafter. On the other hand, the Khedive's pledge to pay 5 per cent of the value of the shares every year in lieu of dividends gave the British government a new and direct interest in Egyptian finances. Disraeli was in fact wrong to suggest that the Canal Company was in a position to close the canal to the growing volume of British shipping now using it. On the other hand, there was no guarantee that the law binding the Company to keep the canal open would always be respected. As Disraeli rightly said, the ownership of the shares gave Britain an additional 'leverage'. It also turned out to be an exceptionally good investment of public money.*

---

* By January 1876 the share price had risen from £22 10s 4d to £34 12s 6d, a 50 per cent increase. The market value of the government's stake was £24 million in 1898,

French hard feelings were in some measure assuaged by the subsequent reorganization of Egyptian finances, which (at the suggestion of the French government), established a multinational commission on which England, France and Italy were equally represented. In 1876 an international Bank for the Egyptian Public Debt (*Caisse de la dette publique*) was established and two years later, at its suggestion, Egypt acquired an international government with an Englishman as Finance Minister and a Frenchman as Minister of Public Works. Simultaneously, the English and French Rothschilds agreed to float an £8.5 million loan. The *Journal de Débats* went so far as to describe this cosy arrangement as 'almost equivalent to the conclusion of an alliance between France and England'. One British statesman summed up the rationale of the compromise: 'You may renounce – or monopolize – or share. Renouncing would have been to place the French across our road to India. Monopolizing would have been very near the risk of war. So we resolved to share.' But this policy of sharing was not to last. In 1879 the Khedive dismissed the international government. The powers responded by deposing him in favour of his supine son Tewfiq. But when Tewfiq was overthrown by the Egyptian military, led by the anti-European Arabi Pasha, it quickly became apparent that a move was afoot to free Egypt from foreign economic dominance altogether. Alexandria was fortified and a dam built across the Canal. A full-scale default on the country's external debt became a serious possibility. The very lives of the 37,000 Europeans resident in Egypt seemed under threat.

As leader of the Opposition, Gladstone had objected violently to Disraeli's foreign policy in the Near East. He had instinctively disliked the purchase of the Suez Canal shares; he also accused Disraeli of turning a blind eye to Turkish atrocities against Christian communities in Bulgaria. Yet now that he was in power, Gladstone

---

£40 million on the eve of the First World War and £93 million by 1935 (around £528 a share). Between 1875 and 1895, the government received its £200,000 a year from Cairo; thereafter it was paid proper dividends, which rose from £690,000 in 1895 to £880,000 in 1901.

executed one of the great U-turns of Victorian foreign policy. True, his instincts were to stick to the system of Anglo-French dual control in Egypt. But the crisis coincided with one of those domestic political *bouleversements* so common in the history of the Third Republic. While the French quarrelled among themselves, the risk of an Egyptian default loomed larger. There were now full-scale anti-European riots in Alexandria. Egged on by his more hawkish Cabinet colleagues, and assured by the Rothschilds that the French would not object, Gladstone agreed on 31 July 1882 to 'put down Arabi'. British ships had already shelled the Alexandrian forts, and on 13 September General Sir Garnet Wolseley's invasion force – which consisted of three squadrons of Household Cavalry, two guns and about 1,000 infantry – surprised and destroyed Arabi's much larger army in the space of just half an hour at Tel-el-Kebir. The next day they occupied Cairo; Arabi was taken prisoner and packed off to Ceylon. In the words of Lord Rothschild, it was now 'clear that England must secure the future predominance' in Egypt. That predominance would never be formalized into outright colonization. No sooner had they occupied Egypt, than the British began reassuring the other powers that their presence there was only a temporary expedient: a reassurance repeated no fewer than sixty-six times between 1882 and 1922. Formally, Egypt continued to be an independent entity. In practice, however, it was run as a 'veiled Protectorate' by Britain, with the Khedive yet another princely puppet and real power in the hands of the British Agent and Consul-General.

The occupation of Egypt opened a new chapter in imperial history. Indeed, in many ways, it was the real trigger for the African Scramble. From the point of view of the other European powers – and French acquiescence did not last long – it was now clearly imperative to act, and act fast, before the British took over the entire continent. The British, for their part, were willing to share the spoils, provided they retained control of the strategic hubs at the Cape and Cairo. The biggest game of Monopoly in history was about to begin. Africa was the board.

*

Such carve-ups were nothing new in the history of imperialism, as we have seen. Until now, however, the future of Africa had been of concern only to Britain, France and – as the first European power to establish colonies there – Portugal. Now, however, there were three new players at the table: the kingdom of Belgium (founded in 1831), the kingdom of Italy (founded in 1861) and the German Empire (founded in 1871). The Belgian King, Leopold II, had set up his International Association in 1876, sponsoring exploration of the Congo with a view to its conquest and economic exploitation. The Italians fantasized about a new Roman Empire extending across the Mediterranean, identifying Tripoli (modern Libya) as their first target of acquisition; later they invaded Abyssinia, lost ignominiously at Adowa in 1896 and had to rest content with part of Somalia. The Germans played a more subtle game – at first.

The German Chancellor, Otto von Bismarck, was one of the few authentic geniuses among nineteenth-century statesmen. When Bismarck said that his map of Africa was the map of Europe,* he meant that he saw Africa as an opportunity to sow dissension between Britain and France – and to lure German voters away from his liberal and socialist opponents at home. In April 1884 Bismarck announced a protectorate over the bay of Angra Pequena, in what is today Namibia. He then extended German claims to include the entire territory between the northern border of the British Cape Colony and the southern border of Portuguese Angola, adding for good measure Cameroon and Togo further up the West African coast and, finally, Tanganyika on the other side of the continent. Having thereby established Germany's credibility as an African player, Bismarck then called a major international conference on Africa, which met in Berlin between 15 November 1884 and 26 February 1885.† Ostensibly, the Berlin Conference was intended to

---

* What Bismarck said to the explorer Eugen Wolff was this: 'Your map of Africa is all very fine, but my map of Africa lies in Europe. Here is Russia and here' – pointing to the left – 'is France, and we are in the middle; that is my map of Africa.'

† The countries represented were Austria-Hungary, Belgium, Denmark, France, Germany, Great Britain, Italy, the Netherlands, Portugal, Russia, Spain, Sweden, Turkey and the United States. Significantly, not a single African representative was

ensure free trade in Africa and particularly freedom of navigation on the Congo and Niger Rivers. Those are the issues that take up most of the clauses of the conference's final 'General Act'. It also paid lip service to the emancipatory ideals of the Livingstonian era, binding all the signatories

to watch over the preservation of the native tribes, and to care for the improvement of the conditions of their moral and material well-being and to help in suppressing slavery, and especially the Slave Trade. They shall, without distinction of creed or nation, protect and favour all religious, scientific, or charitable institutions and undertakings created and organized for the above ends, or which aim at instructing the natives and bringing home to them the blessings of civilization. Christian missionaries, scientists, and explorers, with their followers, property, and collections, shall likewise be the objects of especial protection. Freedom of conscience and religious toleration are expressly guaranteed to the natives, no less than to subjects and to foreigners.

But the real purpose of the conference was (as its opening agenda made clear) to 'define the conditions under which future territorial annexations in Africa might be recognized'. The crux of the business was Article 34, which stated:

Any power which henceforth takes possession of a tract of land on the coasts of the African Continent outside of its present possessions, or which, being hitherto without such possessions, shall acquire them and assume a protectorate . . . shall accompany either act with a notification thereof, addressed to the other Signatory Powers of the present Act, in order to enable them to protest against the same if there exists any grounds for their doing so.

By way of refinement, Article 35 vaguely asserted the signatories' 'obligation to ensure the establishment of authority in the regions occupied by them on the coasts of the African Continent sufficient to protect existing rights'. The 'existing rights' of native rulers and

---

present, despite the fact that at this stage less than a fifth of the continent was under European rule.

their peoples were patently not what the act's authors had in mind.

Here was a true thieves' compact: a charter for the partition of Africa into 'spheres of influence' based on nothing more legitimate than their 'effective occupation'. And the division of the spoils began at once. It was during the conference that the German claim to Cameroon was recognized; so too was Leopold II's sovereignty over the Congo. Yet the significance of the Conference went deeper than that. In addition to slicing up a continent like a cake, it brilliantly achieved Bismarck's core objective of playing Britain and France off against one another. In the subsequent decade, the two powers clashed repeatedly, over Egypt, over Nigeria, over Uganda, over the Sudan. For British policymakers, French explorers like Mizon and Marchand were among the great nuisances of the 1890s, necessitating bizarre showdowns like the Fashoda incident of 1898, a surreal contretemps in the nowhere-land of the Sudan. Indeed, the British were doubly duped by the German Chancellor; for their initial reaction to his triumph at Berlin was to give him everything he wanted (or seemed to want) in Africa, and more.

Soon after the conclusion of the Berlin Conference, the British Consul in Zanzibar was sent a telegram from the Foreign Office in London. It announced that the German Emperor had declared a protectorate over the territory bounded by Lakes Victoria, Tanganyika and Nyasa, which had been claimed the previous year by the explorer Carl Peters's German Colonization Society. The telegram bluntly instructed the Consul to 'cooperate with Germany in everything'. He was to 'act with great caution'; he should 'not permit any communications of a hostile tone to be addressed to German Agents or Representatives by [the] Zanzibar authorities'. The British Consul in Zanzibar was John Kirk, the botanist on David Livingstone's ill-fated Zambezi expedition who, after Livingstone's death, had pledged to continue his work to end the East African slave trade. The order to co-operate with the Germans astounded him. For years he had laboured to win the confidence of the ruler of Zanzibar, Sultan Bargash, on the basis of a straightforward bargain that if the Sultan stamped out the slave trade, Kirk would help extend his East African domain and enrich him through legitimate commerce. The Sultan had indeed banned slave trading in Zanzibar in 1873 and, in return, Kirk had done as he had promised. By 1885 the Sultan's empire on the mainland stretched for a thousand miles along the East African coast and as far inland as the Great Lakes. Now the Sultan was simply to be dropped by a British government anxious to appease Bismarck.

Kirk had no alternative but to obey his orders from London. 'I advised the Sultan', he replied dutifully, 'to withdraw his opposition to the German protectorate, & admit their claims.' But he made no effort to conceal his dismay. 'My position has throughout been delicate and difficult and at one time I hardly expected to be able to induce the Sultan to yield without thereby losing further influence over him.' As he wrote angrily to a friend in England:

To my mind there cannot be a doubt that Germany means to absorb the whole of Zanzibar, & if so why does she not say so? I see . . . an ominous reference to an agreement of which I know nothing between England and Germany that we are not to run counter to German schemes in this region. Surely when this was agreed to, German schemes were defined, & if so, why was I not told – ? Are these schemes Govt. schemes, or private German schemes? . . . Reference is made to my instructions, but no instructions have reached me till quite lately with regard to Germany & the German policy. I have been left to follow my old & approved line of action . . . summed up in the Treaty Declarat[io]n which . . . I got from the Sultan that he should not cede any of his rights or territory or give the Protectorate of his Kingdom or any part of it to any person without consent of England . . . I never had orders to make way for Germany, but I soon saw how the situation stood & I acted cautiously & I hope discreetly . . . But why did the Conference powers not jointly invite H[is] H[ighness] [the Sultan to Berlin] . . .? They ostentatiously ignored him when they assembled & so far as I have heard never told him what they had done.

Kirk felt he was now being asked 'to compromise through no known fault of mine a good name for past services'. If he exerted pressure on the Sultan to accede to the German demands, as London clearly expected him to, the Sultan would 'simply drop' him, '& I will have the blame for what I have no power to prevent'.

I am loathe to kick the last prop away so long as we have a chance of redeeming even to a small extent lost ground or saving even a part that may be useful some day in the many changes that will take place here before dominion is finally settled, for this German colonization scheme is a farce & cannot last. Either the country will be worse than ever or Germany will have to expend blood & money and make this what we have made India, an Empire. It will pay her to do so, but there is no sign that she contemplates this as yet. So we bid fair to lose the fairly good Protectorate & freedom we have under the Sultan in exchange for a long period of confusion when all my work will be undone.

Yet the very idea that the Sultan should have been invited to the Berlin Conference marked Kirk out as one of yesterday's men. Imperial Monopoly was a game played according to the amoral rules of *Realpolitik*, and the British Prime Minister Lord Salisbury was as ready to play by those rules as Bismarck. The Sultan, by contrast, was an African ruler. There could be no place round the board for him.

Bulky, scruffy, reactionary and crafty, Salisbury was almost entirely cynical about imperialism. His definition of the value of empire was simple: 'victories [divided] by taxation'. 'The Buffalo' had no patience whatever with the 'superficial philanthropy' and 'roguery' of the 'fanatics' who advocated expansion in Africa for its own sake. Like Bismarck, colonies only interested Salisbury as properties on the board of great power politics. He was openly dismissive of Rhodes's vision of extending British power across the length of the African continent. As he told his fellow peers in July 1890, he found it

a very curious idea ... that there is some special advantage in having a stretch of territory extending all the way from Cape Town to the sources of the Nile. Now, this stretch of territory North of Lake Tanganyika could only [be] a very narrow one ... I cannot imagine any trade going in that direction ... It is over an impracticable country, and leading only into the Portuguese possessions, into which, as far as I know, during the last 300 years there has been no very eager or impetuous torrent of trade. I think that the constant study of maps is apt to disturb men's reasoning powers

... But if you look beyond the merely commercial considerations to those which are of a strategic character, I can imagine no more uncomfortable position than the possession of a narrow strip of territory in the very heart of Africa, three months' distance from the coast, which should be separating the forces of a powerful empire like Germany and ... another European Power. Without any advantages of position we should have had all the dangers inseparable from its defence.

In other words, it was only worth acquiring new territory if it strengthened Britain's economic and strategic position. It might look well on a map, but the missing link that would have completed Rhodes's 'red route' from the Cape to Cairo did not pass that test. As for those who resided in Africa, their fate did not concern Salisbury in the slightest. 'If our ancestors had cared for the rights of other people,' he had reminded his Cabinet colleagues in 1878, 'the British Empire would not have been made.' Sultan Bargash was soon to discover the implications of that precept.

In August 1885 Bismarck sent four warships to Zanzibar and demanded the Sultan hand over his empire to Germany. By the time they left a month later, the territories had been divided up neatly between Germany and Britain, leaving the Sultan with just a coastal strip. Nor was the Sultan the only loser in this. John Kirk's work in Africa was at an end, for the Germans demanded and got his resignation. Not that the Germans cared two pfennigs for Zanzibar. Just a few years later, in July 1890, Bismarck's successor recognized a British protectorate over it in exchange for the island of Heligoland, off Germany's North Sea coast. This truly was Monopoly on a global scale.

Across Africa the story repeated itself: chiefs hoodwinked, tribes dispossessed, inheritances signed away with a thumbprint or a shaky cross and any resistance mown down by the Maxim gun. One by one the nations of Africa were subjugated – the Zulus, the Matabele, the Mashonas, the kingdoms of Niger, the Islamic principality of Kano, the Dinkas and the Masai, the Sudanese Muslims, Benin and Bechuana. By the beginning of the new century, the carve-up was complete. The British had all but realized Rhodes's vision of unbroken possession from the Cape to Cairo: their African empire stretched northwards from the Cape Colony through Natal, Bechuanaland (Botswana), Southern Rhodesia (now Zimbabwe), Northern Rhodesia (Zambia), and Nyasaland (Malawi); and southwards from Egypt, through the Sudan, Uganda and East Africa (Kenya). German East Africa was the only missing link in Rhodes's intended chain; in addition, as we have seen, the Germans had South West Africa (Namibia), Cameroon and Togo. True, Britain had also acquired the Gambia, Sierra Leone, the Gold Coast (Ghana) and Nigeria in West Africa, as well as the north of Somaliland (Somalia). But the West African colonies were islands in a French sea. From Tunis and Algeria in the north, downwards through Mauritania, Senegal, French Sudan, Guinea, the Ivory Coast, Upper Volta, Dahomey, Niger, Chad, the French Congo and Gabon, the greater part of West Africa was in French hands; their only eastern possession was the island of Madagascar. Besides Mozambique and Angola, Portugal retained an enclave in Guinea. Italy acquired Libya, Eritrea and most of Somaliland. Belgium – or to be precise the Belgian King – owned the vast central territory of Congo. And Spain had Rio de Oro (now southern Morocco). Africa was now almost entirely in European hands, and the lion's share belonged to Britain.

Greater Britain

In 1897, the year of her Diamond Jubilee, Queen Victoria reigned supreme at the apex of the most extensive empire in world history. The figures are astonishing. In 1860 the territorial extent of the British Empire had been some 9.5 million square miles; by 1909 the total had risen to 12.7 million. The British Empire now covered around 25 per cent of the world's land surface – making it three times the size of the French and ten times the size of the German – and controlled roughly the same proportion of the world's population: some 444 million people in all lived under some form of British rule. Not only had Britain led the Scramble for Africa. She

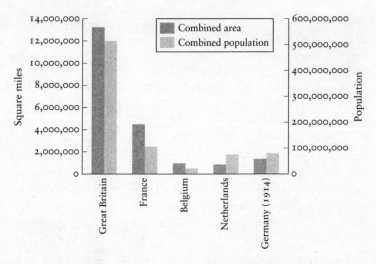

The European empires: area and population *c.* 1939

had been in the forefront of another Scramble in the Far East, gobbling up the north of Borneo, Malaya, and a chunk of New Guinea, to say nothing of a string of islands in the Pacific: Fiji (1874), the Cook Islands (1880), the New Hebrides (1887), the Phoenix Islands (1889), the Gilbert and Ellice Islands (1892) and the Solomons (1893).* According to the *St James's Gazette*, the Queen-Empress held sway over 'one continent, a hundred peninsulas, five hundred promontories, a thousand lakes, two thousand rivers, ten thousand islands'. A postage stamp was produced showing a map of the world and bearing the legend: 'We hold a vaster Empire than has ever been.' Maps showing its territory coloured an eye-catching red hung in schools all over the country. Small wonder the British began to assume that they had the God-given right to rule the world. It was, as the journalist J. L. Garvin put it in 1905, 'an extent and magnificence of dominion beyond the natural'.

The extent of Britain's Empire could be seen not only in the world's atlases and censuses. Britain was also the world's banker,

---

* The New Hebrides were governed jointly with France.

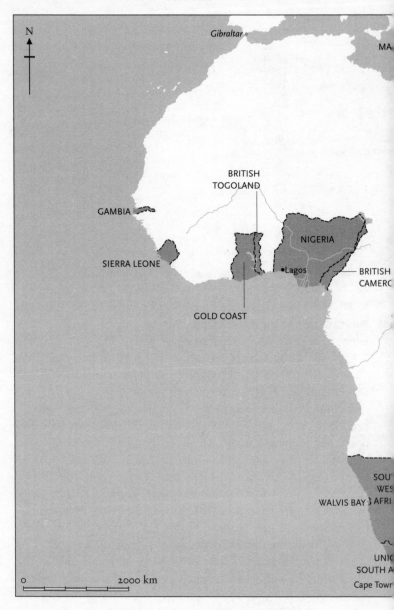

British Africa and the Middle East, *c.* 1939

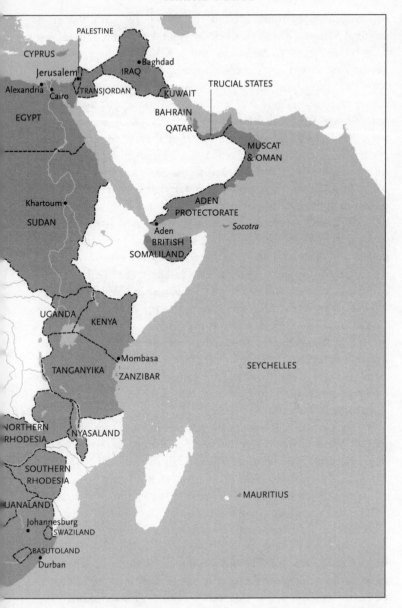

investing immense sums around the world. By 1914 the gross nominal value of Britain's stock of capital invested abroad was £3.8 billion, between two-fifths and a half of all foreign-owned assets. That was more than double French overseas investment and more than three times the German figure. No other major economy before or since has held such a large proportion of its assets overseas. Between 1870 and 1913 capital flows averaged around 4.5 per cent of gross domestic product, rising above 7 per cent at their cyclical peaks in 1872, 1890 and 1913. More British capital raised on the stock market was invested in the Americas than in Britain itself. In addition, these flows were far more geographically dispersed than those of other European economies. Only around 6 per cent of British overseas investments were in western Europe. Around 45 per cent were in the United States and the white settler colonies. A fifth were in Latin America, 16 per cent in Asia and 13 per cent in Africa. True, only £1.8 billion was actually invested in British colonies, and nearly all of this was invested in the older colonies; hardly anything was invested in the new African acquisitions of the Scramble. But the importance of the Empire was increasing. On average it attracted around 38 per cent of portfolio investment between 1865 and 1914, but by the 1890s the share had risen to 44 per cent. Likewise, the Empire's share of total British exports was on the increase, rising from between a quarter and a third to almost two-fifths in 1902.

In any case, not all of the British Empire was formally under British rule; the maps actually underestimated the extent of the imperial reach. The immense amounts of capital sunk into Latin America, for example, gave Britain so much leverage – especially in Argentina and Brazil – that it seems quite legitimate to speak of 'informal imperialism' in these countries. It might of course be objected that British investors had no business investing in Buenos Aires and Rio when they should have been modernizing the industries of the British Isles themselves. But the anticipated returns on overseas investment were generally higher than those from domestic manufacturing. In any case, this was not a zero-sum game. New foreign investment soon became self-financing, since earnings from

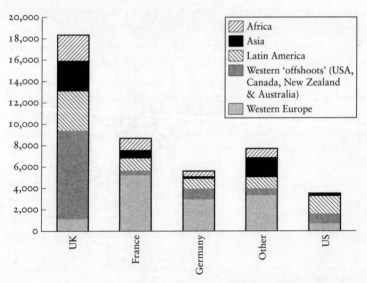

Total foreign investment in 1914: whence it came,
where it went ($ million)

existing overseas assets consistently exceeded the value of new
capital out-flows: between 1870 and 1913 total overseas earnings
amounted to 5.3 per cent of GDP a year. Nor is there any com-
pelling evidence that British industry was hampered by a shortage
of capital before 1914.

It was not only through investment that the British extended
their informal Empire. Commercial negotiations also pushed large
sectors of the world economy to accept free trade; witness the trade
treaties with Latin American countries, Turkey, Morocco, Siam,
Japan and the South Sea islands. By the late nineteenth century,
around 60 per cent of British trade was with extra-European
partners. Free trade with the developing world suited Britain. With
her huge earnings from overseas investment, not forgetting other
'invisibles' like insurance and shipping, she could afford to import
vastly more than she exported. In any case, the terms of trade – the
relationship between export and import prices – moved by around
10 per cent in Britain's favour between 1870 and 1914.

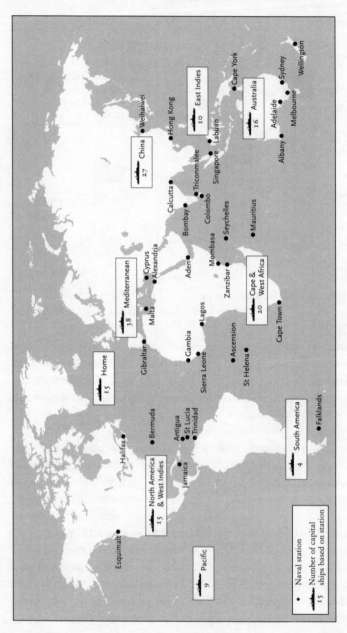

British Imperial naval stations *c.* 1898

Britain also set the standard for the international monetary system. In 1868 only Britain and a number of her economic dependencies – Portugal, Egypt, Canada, Chile and Australia – were on the gold standard (which fixed the value of a country's paper money in terms of gold and obliged its central bank to convert notes into gold on demand). France and the other members of the Latin Monetary Union, as well as Russia, Persia and some Latin American states were on the bimetallic (gold and silver) system, while most of the rest of the world was on the silver standard. By 1908, however, only China, Persia and a handful of Central American countries were still on silver. The gold standard had become, in effect, the global monetary system. In all but name, it was a sterling standard.

Perhaps the most remarkable thing about all this was how cheap it was to defend. In 1898 there were 99,000 regular soldiers stationed in Britain, 75,000 in India and 41,000 elsewhere in the Empire. The navy required another 100,000 men, and the Indian native army was 148,000 strong. There were barracks and naval coaling stations, thirty-three of them in all, dotted all over the world. Yet the total defence budget for that year was just over £40 million: a mere 2.5 per cent of net national product. That is not much higher than the relative burden of Britain's defence budget today, and far less than the equivalent percentage spent on the military during the Cold War. Nor did the burden rise significantly when Britain boldly modernized her entire fleet by building the first Dreadnought, a ship so advanced – with its 12-inch guns and its revolutionary turbines – that it rendered all existing battleships obsolete the moment it was launched. Between 1906 and 1913, Britain was able to build twenty-seven of these floating fortresses at a cost of £49 million, less than the annual interest charge on the national debt. This was world domination on the cheap.

The British, however, knew too much ancient history to be complacent about their hegemonic position. Even at the zenith of their power they thought, or were reminded by Kipling, of the fate of Nineveh and Tyre. Already, there were many who looked forward uneasily to the decline and fall of their own empire, like all the empires before it. Matthew Arnold had already pictured Britain as 'The weary Titan, with deaf / Ears, and labour-dimm'd eyes ... Staggering on to her goal; / Bearing on shoulders immense, / Atlantean, the load, / Well-nigh not to be borne / Of the too vast orb of her fate.' But could the Titan somehow be revived? Could the inevitable waning of her power be arrested and reversed before she staggered and fell? One man thought that it could.

John Robert Seeley was the son of an Evangelical publisher in whose office the Church Missionary Society had held its meetings. A moderately successful classical scholar, Seeley had made his name in 1865 with *Ecce Homo*, which told the story of Christ's life with a scrupulous inattention to the supernatural. Four years later he was elected to the Chair of Modern History at Cambridge, where he devoted his time to modern diplomatic history and a biography of the nineteenth-century Prussian reformer Stein. Then in 1883, rather to everyone's surprise, Seeley produced a best-seller, *The Expansion of England*. In the space of just two years it sold more than 80,000 copies, and remained in print until 1956.

Seeley's *Expansion* purports to be a history of the British Empire from 1688 to 1815. It is still remembered today for its memorable characterization of the unplanned nature of the eighteenth-century Empire: 'We seem ... to have conquered and peopled half the world in a fit of absence of mind.' But it was the book's contemporary political message that captured the public imagination. Seeley acknowledged the vast extent of Britain's Empire, but he foresaw imminent decline if Britain persisted in its absent-minded attitude to imperialism:

If the United States and Russia hold together for another half century, they will at the end of that time completely dwarf such old European states as France and Germany and depress them into a second class. They will do the same to England, if at the end of that time England still thinks of herself as simply a European State.

Seeley insisted that it was time to move beyond the haphazard, improvised Empire of the past. Britain should take advantage of two inescapable facts: first, that British subjects in the colonies would soon outnumber those at home; secondly, that the technology of the telegraph and steamship made it possible to unite them as never before. Only by knitting together this 'Greater Britain' could the Empire hope to compete with the superpowers of the future.

Seeley himself was no empire-builder. He had never ventured beyond Europe; indeed the idea for the book had come to him while on holiday in Switzerland. Plagued by insomnia and a nagging wife, he was a byword in Cambridge for donnish pomposity, 'an almost excessive gravity of deportment' as one contemporary put it. But his call for a strengthening of the bonds between Britain and the white, English-speaking colonies was music to the ears of a new generation of imperialists. Such ideas were in the air. In 1886, after a visit to Australia, the historian J. A. Froude published *Oceana, or England and her Colonies*. Four years later the disgraced Liberal politician Sir Charles Dilke – whose career had been ruined by an ugly divorce case – brought out *Problems of Greater Britain*. 'Greater Britain' was perhaps the most succinct expression of what all these writers had in mind. As Dilke put it, the aim was for 'Canada and Australia [to] be to us as Kent and Cornwall'. When such notions found a champion in high places, the result was a profound shift in government policy towards the Empire.

Joseph Chamberlain was Britain's first authentically, self-consciously imperialist politician. Originally a Birmingham manufacturer who had made a fortune from manufacturing wooden screws, Chamberlain had risen through the ranks of the Liberal Party via the National Education League and local government, only to quarrel with Gladstone over the question of Irish Home Rule and gravitate – as a 'Liberal Unionist' – towards the Conservatives. The Tories never really understood him. What was one supposed to make of a man who played lawn tennis wearing 'a closely buttoned black frock coat and top hat'? But they had few better weapons against the Liberals, particularly as Chamberlain's Liberal Unionism soon evolved into Liberal Imperialism. Chamberlain read Seeley's *Expansion of England* avidly; indeed, he later claimed it was the reason for sending his son Austen to Cambridge. When he heard Froude was visiting Cape Town, he wrote: 'Tell them in my name that they will find the Radical Party more sternly Imperial than the most bigoted Tory.'

In August 1887, to test the flamboyant defector out, Salisbury invited Chamberlain to cross the Atlantic and attempt to broker an agreement between the United States and Canada, who were bickering over fishing rights in the Gulf of St Lawrence. The trip opened Chamberlain's eyes. In per capita terms, he discovered, Canadians consumed five times more British exports than Americans; yet there were many influential Canadians who openly contemplated a commercial union with the US. Even before he reached Canada, Chamberlain fired off a broadside against this idea. 'Commercial union with the United States', he declared, 'means free trade between America and the Dominion,* and a protective tariff against the mother country. If Canada desires that, Canada can have it; but Canada can only have it knowing perfectly well that [it] means political separation from Great Britain.' Speaking in Toronto, Chamberlain sought to counter Canadian drift with an impassioned appeal to 'The greatness and importance of the distinction reserved for the Anglo-Saxon race, that proud, persistent, self-asserting and resolute stock which no change of climate or condition can alter . . .'

The question, Chamberlain asked, was whether 'the interest of true democracy' lay in 'the disintegration of the Empire' or in 'the uniting together of kindred races with similar objects'. The key, he suggested, lay in 'the working out of the great problem of federal government' – something that Canadians had achieved in their own country, but which ought now to be done for the Empire as a whole. If imperial federation was a dream, he concluded, it was nevertheless 'a grand idea. It is one to stimulate

---

* In 1867 Canada, Nova Scotia and New Brunswick were united to form 'One Dominion under the Name of Canada', to which the other Canadian provinces gradually acceded. From 1907 the status of Dominion was extended to all the self-governing colonies of white settlement.

the patriotism and statesmanship of every man who loves his country; and whether it be destined or not to perfect realization, at least let us . . . do all in our power to promote it.' On his return home, he fervently proclaimed his new faith in 'the ties between the different branches of the Anglo-Saxon race which form the British Empire'.

Chamberlain had yearned for some time to be a 'Colonial Minister'. In June 1895 he surprised Salisbury by turning down both the Home Office and the Exchequer in favour of the Colonial Office. As Colonial Secretary he repeatedly affirmed his 'belief' in 'the wider patriotism . . . which encloses the whole of Greater Britain'. Only if the Empire stood still would it be surpassed; imperial federation was the way forward, even if that did imply compromises on the part of both metropolis and colonies. 'The British Empire', Chamberlain declared in 1902, 'is based upon a community of sacrifice. Whenever that is lost sight of, then, indeed, I think we may expect to sink into oblivion like the empires of the past, which . . . after having exhibited to the world evidences of their power and strength, died away regretted by none, and leaving behind them a record of selfishness only.'

Chamberlain was by no means the only politician of the time to embrace the ideal of Greater Britain. Almost as dedicated a believer was Alfred Milner, whose *Kindergarten* of young devotees in South Africa – later reconstituted in London as the 'Round Table' – would come close to realizing Rhodes's dream of an imperial Jesuit order. 'If I am also an imperialist,' Milner declared, 'it is because the destiny of the English race, owing to its insular position and its long supremacy at sea, has been to strike fresh roots in distant parts of the world. My patriotism knows no geographical but only racial limits. I am an imperialist and not a Little Englander because I am a British race Patriot. It is not the soil of England . . . which is essential to arouse my patriotism, but the speech, the traditions, the spiritual heritage, the principles, the aspirations, of the British race . . .' This kind of rhetoric was infectious – especially, it should be added, to social outsiders like Chamberlain and Milner who did not always find it easy to share the government benches with complacent scions of the aristocracy.*

Of course, all this presupposed a readiness on the part of the Dominions to redefine their relationship with the metropolis – a relationship which most of them, on reflection, preferred to leave on the rather vague, devolved basis that had grown out of the Durham Report. The white colonies were not short of enthusiasm for the idea of Greater Britain. Indeed, they were quicker than the British at home to adopt the Earl of Meath's suggestion of an annual 'Empire Day' on the Queen's birthday (24 May), which became an official public holiday in Canada in 1901, in Australia in 1905, in New Zealand and South Africa in 1910, but only belatedly, in 1916, in the mother country. But there was a difference between symbolism and the reduction of autonomy implied by the idea of imperial federation. Crucially, as things stood, the Canadians were entitled to – and from 1879 did – impose protectionist tariffs on British goods, an example soon followed by Australia and New Zealand; it was highly unlikely that this would be the case in a federal Empire. Another glaring hole in the federalist argument was India, whose role in a predominantly white Greater Britain was far from clear.† But the biggest hole of all was Ireland.

Ireland, the first of all the colonies of settlement, was the last to be granted what the other white colonies by the 1880s took for granted, 'responsible government'. There were three reasons for this. The first was that the majority of Irishmen, though impeccably

* Radical nationalism often attracted its strongest adherents from the periphery of the European empires; in this the Greater Britain movement had something in common with the contemporary Pan German League. Milner himself was brought up in Germany, while his most loyal acolyte, Leo Amery, was born in India of (though he kept it quiet) Hungarian Jewish parentage. Another relative outsider, the Scottish novelist John Buchan, formed part of their circle. The idea of Greater Britain is nowhere more appealingly expressed than in his novels.

† India baffled Chamberlain. It seemed to him, he wrote in 1897, 'to be between the Devil and the deep sea – on the one hand most serious danger of attack from outside & internal disturbance unless full preparations are made – & on the other the prospect of most serious financial embarrassment.' A man who liked foreign cities the more they resembled Birmingham was unlikely to be captivated by Calcutta.

fair-skinned, were Catholics and, in the eyes of many Englishmen, as racially inferior as if they had been the colour of coal. The second was that a minority – particularly the descendants of those who had settled on the island in the seventeenth century – preferred the arrangement established by the Act of Union of 1800, whereby Ireland was governed from Westminster as an integral part of the United Kingdom. The third and ultimately decisive reason, however, was that men like Chamberlain persuaded themselves that to allow Ireland to have its own parliament – as it had before 1800, and as the other white colonies already had – would somehow undermine the integrity of the Empire as a whole. This, above all other reasons, was why Gladstone's attempts to grant Ireland Home Rule failed.

There were of course radical Irish nationalists who would never have been satisfied with the very modest devolution of power Gladstone envisaged in his two Home Rule bills of 1885 and 1893. The Fenian Brotherhood had attempted an uprising in 1867; though it failed, they were still able to mount a mainland bombing campaign in its aftermath. In 1882 a Fenian splinter group known as the Invincibles assassinated Lord Frederick Cavendish, the Secretary of State for Ireland, and Thomas Henry Burke, his Under-Secretary, in Phoenix Park. That Irishmen should resort to such violence against British rule was not surprising. Direct rule from Westminster had without question exacerbated the disastrous famine of the mid-1840s, in which more than a million people had died of dearth and disease. It may have been *phytophthora infestans* that ruined the potatoes; but it was the dogmatic *laissez-faire* policies of Ireland's British rulers that turned harvest failure into outright famine. Yet the men of violence were always a small minority. The majority of Home Rulers – men like the founder of the Home Government Association, Isaac Butt – aspired to nothing more extreme than the degree of devolution then enjoyed by Canadians and Australians.* He and the movement's most charismatic leader, Charles Stewart

---

* Gladstone himself made the analogy explicit: 'Canada did not get Home Rule because she was loyal and friendly, but she has become loyal and friendly because she has got Home Rule.' This was quite right, but the Liberal Unionists were deaf to reason.

Parnell, were not merely Anglicized in their speech and culture; they were also good Protestants. Had Parnell not been destroyed by the scandal of his affair with Kitty O'Shea, he would have made a perfectly good colonial premier: as defensive of Ireland's interests as Canadian premiers were of theirs, no doubt, but hardly an ice-breaker for 'Rome Rule'.*

The defeat of both Home Rule bills signalled a return on the part of both Liberal Unionists and the Conservatives to the blinkered politics of the 1770s, when their counterparts in Parliament had obstinately refused devolution to the American colonists. The question their position begged was plain. How could Greater Britain possibly be made a reality if Ireland, the first of all the colonies of settlement, could not even be trusted with its own parliament? This was the contradiction between Unionism and the new 'constructive' imperialism to which Chamberlain and his associates seemed blind. True, Chamberlain toyed with the idea of giving the British Isles an American-style federal constitution, allowing Ireland, Scotland and Wales their own separate legislatures and leaving imperial affairs to Westminster; but it is hard to believe he took such schemes seriously. Indeed, given Chamberlain's relative ignorance of Ireland, it is tempting to think that his desire to 'sit on' Home Rule was principally actuated by Gladstone's adoption of it. The core belief of the Unionists became, in the words of the Tory maverick Lord Randolph Churchill, that Home Rule would 'plunge the knife into the heart of the British Empire'. In truth, it was the postponement of Home Rule until 1914 that plunged a knife into the heart of Ireland, since by that time Unionist opposition in Ulster had hardened to the point of armed resistance.

Still, none of this diminished the appeal of 'Greater Britain' within Great Britain itself. It was partly a matter of targeting voters' narrow economic self-interest. To Chamberlain, the former industrialist, Empire meant above all export markets and jobs. In this he had in some measure been anticipated by Salisbury, who had asked

* Paradoxically, however, there were few bastions of Unionist sentiment more staunch than Canada. As early as 1870 Ontario had 900 Orange Lodges, pledged to 'resist all attempts to . . . dismember the British Empire'.

an audience at Limehouse in 1889 to 'conceive what London would be without the empire ... a collection of multitudes, without employment, without industrial life, sinking down into misery and decay'. But Chamberlain took such economic rationalization much further. As he told the Birmingham Chamber of Commerce in 1896:

The Foreign Office and the Colonial Office are chiefly engaged in finding new markets and in defending old ones. The War Office and Admiralty are mostly occupied in preparations for the defence of these markets, and for the protection of our commerce ... Therefore, it is not too much to say that commerce is the greatest of all political interests, and that Government deserves most the popular approval which does the most to increase our trade and to settle it on a firm foundation.

It was self-evident to Chamberlain that 'a great part of our population is dependent ... upon the interchange of commodities with our colonial fellow-subjects'. Ergo, they must all be imperialists.

Was the Empire really economically beneficial to the mass of British voters? It is not immediately obvious that it was. The benefits of overseas investment were not enjoyed by the majority of people, whose savings (if they had any) were generally invested in British government bonds through savings banks and other financial intermediaries. At the same time, the costs of imperial defence, though not excessively high, were borne primarily by British taxpayers, not by taxpayers in the colonies of white settlement. Indeed, it is arguable that the principal beneficiaries of the Empire at this time were those British subjects who emigrated to the Dominions – of whom, as we have seen, there were a great many. Around two and a half million British nationals emigrated to the Empire between 1900 and 1914, three-quarters of them to Canada, Australia and New Zealand. In most cases, emigration substantially increased their incomes and reduced their tax burdens.

Yet imperialism did not have to pay to be popular. For many people it was sufficient that it was *exciting*.

In all, there were seventy-two separate British military campaigns in the course of Queen Victoria's reign – more than one for every year of the so-called *pax britannica*. Unlike the wars of the twentieth century, these conflicts involved relatively few people. On average, the British armed forces during Victoria's reign amounted to 0.8 per cent of the population; and servicemen were disproportionately drawn from the Celtic periphery or the urban underclass. Yet those who lived far from the imperial front line, never hearing a shot fired in anger save at wildfowl, had an insatiable appetite for tales of military derring-do. As a source of entertainment – of sheer psychological gratification – the Empire's importance can never be exaggerated.

No medium was safe. From the pen of G. A. Henty – a product of Westminster, Gonville and Caius, Crimea and Magdala – poured forth countless novels with titles like *By Sheer Pluck* and *For Name or Fame*. Primarily a hack writer of historical fiction, Henty's most overtly imperialist works were those inspired by relatively recent military campaigns: *With Clive In India* (1884), *With Buller in Natal* (1901) and *With Kitchener in the Soudan* (1903). These were hugely popular: in all, total sales of Henty's novels were put at 25 million by the 1950s. Almost as voluminous was the torrent of verse inspired by Empire. From the talents of Tennyson to the triteness of Alfred Austin and W. E. Henley, this was the age of 'high diction': an era when every second man was a poetaster looking for something to rhyme with 'Victoria' other than 'Gloria'.

The iconography of Empire was no less ubiquitous, from the romanticized battle scenes rendered on canvas by Lady Butler and exhibited in grandiose new museums, to the imperial kitsch that advertised everyday articles of consumption. The manufacturers of Pears' Soap were especially fond of the imperial leitmotif:

The first step towards lightening

The White Man's Burden

is through teaching the virtues of cleanliness.

Pears' Soap

is a potent factor in brightening the dark corners of the earth
as civilization advances while amongst the cultures of all nations
it holds the highest place – it is the ideal toilet soap.

This admirable product was also, so the public were assured, 'the formula of British conquest'; its arrival in the tropics had marked 'the birth of civilization'. Others took up the theme. Parkinson's Sugar Coated Pills were 'A Great British Possession'. The route taken by Lord Roberts from Kimberley to Bloemfontein during the Boer War supposedly spelt out 'Bovril'. 'We Are Going to Use "Chlorinol" [bleach]', ran one pre-1914 campaign, 'And Be Like De White Nigger.'

The Empire furnished material for the music hall too, often seen as the most important institution for promoting Victorian popular 'jingoism'. Indeed, the word itself was coined by the lyricist G. W. Hunt, whose song 'By Jingo' was performed during the Eastern Crisis of 1877–8 by the music hall artiste G. H. Macdermott. There were countless variations on the theme of the heroic 'Tommy', one exemplary stanza of which will probably suffice:

> And whether he's on India's coral strand,
> Or pouring out his blood in the Soudan,
> To keep our flag a flying, he's doing and a dying,
> Every inch of him a soldier and a man.

The link between this kind of entertainment and that offered by the great imperial exhibitions of the period was close. What had once been intended as international and educational (the prototype was Prince Albert's Great Exhibition of 1851) were becoming by the 1880s more imperial and entertaining. In particular, the impresario Imre Kiralfy's extravaganzas – 'Empire of India' (1895), 'Greater Britain' (1899) and 'The Imperial International' (1909) – were designed to make money by offering the public the thrill of the exotic: Zulu warriors in the flesh were an especial hit of his 1899 exhibition. This was the Empire as circus.

But it was above all through the popular press that the Empire reached a mass audience at home. Probably no one understood better how to satisfy the public appetite for ripping yarns than Alfred Harmsworth, later (from 1905) Lord Northcliffe. A Dubliner by birth, Harmsworth learned his craft on the pioneering *Illustrated London News* and made his fortune by importing the style of the illustrated magazine into the newspaper market. Pictures, banner headlines, free gifts and serialized stories made first the *Evening News* and then the *Daily Mail* and *Daily Mirror* irresistibly attractive to a new class of reader: lower middle class, female as well as male. Northcliffe was also quick to discover the price elasticity of newspaper demand, cutting the price of *The Times* after he acquired it in 1908. But it was his choice of content above all that made the Northcliffe titles sell. It was no coincidence that the *Mail* first sold more than a million copies in 1899, during the Boer War. As one of his editors replied when asked what sells a newspaper,

The first answer is 'war'. War not only creates a supply of news but a demand for it. So deep rooted is the fascination in a war and all things appertaining to it that ... a paper has only to be able to put up on its placard 'A Great Battle' for its sales to go up.

Another Northcliffe employee regarded 'the depth and volume of public interest in Imperial questions' as 'one of the greatest forces, almost untapped, at the disposal of the Press'. 'If Kipling be called the Voice of Empire in English Literature,' he added, 'we [the *Daily Mail*] may fairly claim to [be] the Voice of Empire in London journalism.' Northcliffe's own recipe was simple: 'The British people relish a good hero and a good hate.'

From their earliest days, the Northcliffe papers leaned to the political Right; but it was possible to promote the Empire from the Left as well. William Thomas Stead, who inherited the *Pall Mall Gazette* from Gladstone's ardent votary John Morley and then founded the *Review of Reviews*, described himself as an 'imperialist plus the ten commandments and common sense'. Stead was a man of many passions. The Hague Peace Conference of 1899 won his backing, as did the idea of a common European currency and the fight against the 'white slave trade' (Victorian for prostitution), but his guiding assumption was that 'The Progress of the World' depended on the conduct of the British Empire. In the eyes of men like Stead, the Empire was something that transcended party politics.

It also transcended age; for among the most devoted readers of imperialist literature were schoolboys, generations of whom were raised on the *Boys' Own Paper*, founded in 1879 by the Religious Tract Society. Along with its sister title the *Girls' Own Paper*, the *BOP* reached a circulation of more than half a million by offering its young readers a steady stream of ripping yarns set on exotic colonial frontiers. For some however, these magazines were not sufficiently overt in their purpose: hence the appearance of *Boys of the Empire* in October 1900, which sought to indoctrinate its young readers more systematically with articles like 'How to be Strong', 'Empire Heroes' and 'Where the Lion's Cubs are Trained: Australia and her Schools'. The last of these can be considered fairly representative in its tone and central assumptions:

The native problem has never been acute in ... Australia ... The Aborigines have been driven back and are quickly dying out ... Australian schools are not half black and half white; nor can the term 'chess board' be flung at any of the dining halls of an Australian school, as has been the case in at least one college of the ancient universities of Oxford and Cambridge.

The same edition of the magazine featured a competition run by the Boys' Empire League* which promised:

A Free Start on a Farm out West ... to the TWO boys each year who shall gain the highest marks in an Examination.

The Prizes include FREE KIT, FREE PASSAGE and FREE LOCATION with a selected farmer in North-West Canada.

The heroic archetypes of this popular imperialism – and many of its consumers – were not themselves men of the people; rather, they were members of an elite educated at Britain's exclusive public schools. At most, these schools could accommodate around 20,000 pupils in a given year – little more than 1 per cent of boys aged between fifteen and nineteen in 1901. Yet boys outside the public school system seem to have had little difficulty in identifying with their fictional adventures. This may well have been because, as

---

* Motto: 'Many Countries, but One Empire.' The League had 7,000 members in 1900.

countless authors of pot-boilers made clear, what made public school products capable of heroism on the Empire's behalf was not what they learned in the classroom, but what they learned on the games field.

Viewed from this angle, the British Empire of the 1890s resembled nothing more than an enormous sports complex. Hunting continued to be the favourite recreation of the upper classes, but it was now waged as a war of annihilation against game, with bags growing exponentially from the Scottish moors to the Indian jungles.* To give a single example, the total bag of the Viceroy (Lord Minto) and his party during 1906 included 3,999 sandgrouse, 2,827 wildfowl, 50 bears, 14 pigs, 2 tigers, 1 panther and 1 hyena. Hunting was also commercialized, evolving in some colonies into a form of armed tourism. Attracting wealthy tourists to East Africa seemed to Lord Delamere the only way to make money from the famously unprofitable Mombasa–Uganda railway.

It was team games, however, that did most to make a reality of the ideal of Greater Britain. Soccer, the gentleman's game played by hooligans, was of course the country's most successful recreational export. But 'football' was always a promiscuous sport, appealing to everyone from the politically suspect working class to the even more suspect Germans; to everyone, in fact, except the Americans.† If any sport truly summed up the new spirit of 'Greater Britain' it was rugby, the hooligans' game played by gentlemen. An intensely physical team sport, rugby was swiftly adopted right across the white Empire, from Cape Town to Canberra. As early as 1905 the

* Curzon regarded tiger shooting as the greatest of all the perks of being Viceroy, and took a particularly egregious pleasure in being photographed bestriding his victims. As he described it breathlessly to his father: 'You can hear your heart beat as he comes, unseen, with the leaves crackling under his feet, and suddenly emerges, sometimes at a walk, sometimes at full gallop, sometimes with an angry roar.'

† The modern game known to Americans as 'football' in fact evolved from the same common British ancestor as both soccer and rugby. For a time it seemed likely that the American colleges would adopt the English Football Association's rules, but in the 1870s they agreed on a hybrid game and by the 1880s had adopted rules (forward passes, tackling off the ball) quite distinct from and incompatible with those of either soccer or rugby.

New Zealand All Blacks toured the Empire for the first time, beating all the home sides except Wales (who vanquished them by a single try). They would probably have gone on to beat all the other white colonies but for the ban imposed by South Africa on the fielding of Maori players.

Yet it was cricket – with its subtle, protracted rhythms, its team spirit in fielding and its solo heroics at the crease – that transcended such racial divisions, spreading not just to the colonies of white settlement but throughout the Indian subcontinent and the British Caribbean. Cricket had been played within the Empire since the early eighteenth century, but it was in the late nineteenth century that it became institutionalized as the quintessential imperial game. In 1873–4 the Titan of English cricket, W. G. Grace, led a mixed team of amateurs and professionals to Australia, easily winning their fifteen three-day matches. But when a professional XI returned to play what is usually seen as the first international Test match at Melbourne in March 1877, the Australians won by 45 runs. Worse was to follow when the Australians came to the Oval in 1882, winning the victory that inspired the celebrated obituary notice in the *Sporting Times*, 'In Affectionate Remembrance of English cricket which died at the Oval on 29th August, 1882, deeply lamented by a large circle of sorrowing friends and acquaintances. R.I.P. N.B. – The body will be cremated and the ashes taken to Australia.'

For years to come, the English habit of losing to colonial teams would help knit Greater Britain together. Institutions like the Imperial Cricket Conference, which first met in 1909 to harmonize the rules of the game, were as crucial to the formation of a sense of collective imperial identity as anything Seeley wrote or Chamberlain said.

Perhaps the archetypal product of playing-field imperialism was Robert Stephenson Smyth Baden-Powell – 'Stephe' to his friends. Baden-Powell progressed inexorably from sporting success at Charterhouse, where he was captain of the First (soccer) XI, to an army career in India, Afghanistan and Africa. It was he, as we shall see, who explicitly likened the most famous siege of the era to a cricket match. And it was he who would ultimately codify the late imperial ethos in the precepts of the Boy Scout movement he founded, another highly successful recreational export which aimed to generalize the team spirit of the games field into an entire way of life:

We are all Britons, and it is our duty each to play in his place and help his neighbours. Then we shall remain strong and united and then there will be no fear of the whole building – namely, our great Empire, – falling down because of rotten bricks in the wall . . . 'Country first, self second,' should be your motto.

What that meant in practice is clear from the roll of honour at Baden-Powell's own school. The walls of the main cloister at Charterhouse are studded with war memorials to half-forgotten campaigns, from Afghanistan to Omdurman, listing the names of hundreds of young Carthusians who 'played up, played up and played the game'* and paid for doing so with their lives.

And what of the other side in this great imperial game? If the British were, as Chamberlain and Milner believed, the master race, with a God-given right to rule the world, it seemed to follow logically that those they fought against were their natural-born inferiors. Was this not the conclusion drawn by Science itself – increasingly regarded as the ultimate authority in such matters?

In 1863 Dr James Hunt had dismayed his audience at a meeting in Newcastle of the British Association for the Advancement of Science by asserting that the 'Negro' was a separate species of human being, half way between the ape and 'European man'. In Hunt's view the 'Negro' became 'more humanized when in his natural subordination to the European', but he regretfully concluded that 'European civilization [was] not suited to the Negro's requirements or character'. According to one eyewitness, the African traveller Winwood Reade, Hunt's lecture went down

---

* The refrain of Henry Newbolt's 'Vitaï Lampada' (1897), the classic depiction of school cricket as a form of military apprenticeship. Newbolt was a product of Clifton.

badly, eliciting hisses from some members of the audience. Yet within a generation such views had become the conventional wisdom. Influenced by, but distorting beyond recognition, the work of Darwin, nineteenth-century pseudo-scientists divided humanity into 'races' on the basis of external physical features, ranking them according to inherited differences not just in physique but also in character. Anglo-Saxons were self-evidently at the top, Africans at the bottom. The work of George Combe, author of *A System of Phrenology* (1825), was typical in two respects – the derogatory way in which it portrayed racial differences and the fraudulent way in which it sought to explain them:

When we regard the different quarters of the globe [wrote Combe], we are struck with the extreme dissimilarity in the attainments of the varieties of men who inhabit them . . . The history of Africa, so far as Africa can be said to have a history . . . exhibit[s] one unbroken scene of moral and intellectual desolation . . . 'The negro, easily excitable, is in the highest degree suscept-ible to all the passions . . . To the negro, remove only pain and hunger, and it is naturally a state of enjoyment. As soon as his toils are suspended for a moment, he sings, he seizes a fiddle, he dances.'

The explanation for this backwardness, according to Combe, was the peculiar shape of 'the skull of the negro': 'The organs of Vener-ation, Wonder and Hope . . . are considerable in size. The greatest deficiencies lie in Conscientiousness, Cautiousness, Ideality and Reflection.' Such ideas were influential. The idea of an ineradic-able 'race instinct' became a staple of late nineteenth- and early twentieth-century writing – as in Cornelia Sorabji's tale of the educated Indian lady doctor who willingly (and fatally) submits to the ordeal by fire during a pagan rite; or the account by Lady Mary Anne Barker of how her Zulu nanny reverted to savagery when she returned home to her village; or W. Somerset Maugham's 'The Pool', in which a hapless Aberdonian businessman tries in vain to Westernize his half-Samoan bride.

Phrenology was only one of a number of bogus disciplines tend-ing to legitimize the assumptions about racial difference that had long been current among white colonists. Even more insidious, because intellectually more rigorous, was the scientific snake-oil known as 'eugenics'. It was the mathematician Francis Galton who, in his book *Hereditary Genius* (1869), pioneered the ideas that a 'man's natural abilities are derived by inheritance'; that 'out of two varieties of any race of animal who are equally endowed in other respects, the most intelligent variety is sure to prevail in the battle of life'; and that on a sixteen-point scale of racial intelligence, a 'Negro' is two grades below an Englishman.* Galton sought to validate his theories by using composite photography to distinguish criminal and other degenerate types. However, a more systematic development was undertaken by Karl Pearson, another Cambridge-trained mathematician, who in 1911 became the first Galton Professor of Eugenics at University College London. A brilliant mathematician, Pearson became convinced that his statistical techniques (which he called 'biometry') could be used to demonstrate the danger posed to the Empire by racial degeneration. The problem was that improved welfare provision and health care at home were interfering with the natural selection process, allowing genetically inferior individuals to survive – and 'propagate their unfitness'. 'The right to live does not connote the right of each man to reproduce his kind,' he argued in *Darwinism, Medical Progress and Parentage* (1912). 'As we lessen the stringency of natural selection, and more and more of the weaklings and the unfit survive, we must increase the standard, mental and physical, of parentage.'

There was, however, one alternative to state intervention in reproductive choices: war. For Pearson, as for many other Social Darwinists, life was struggle, and war was more than just a game – it was a form of natural selection. As he put it, 'National progress depends on racial fitness and the supreme test of this fitness was war. When wars cease mankind will no longer progress for there will be nothing to check the fertility of inferior stock.'

Needless to say, this made pacifism a particularly wicked creed. But fortunately, with an ever-expanding empire, there was

---

* A Lowland Scot was fractionally superior to an Englishman. Ancient Athenians came top.

no shortage of jolly little wars to be waged against racially inferior opponents. It was gratifying to think that in massacring them with their Maxim guns, the British were contributing to the progress of mankind.

One final oddity needs to be noted. If Social Darwinists worried that the racially inferior underclass was reproducing itself too rapidly, they said rather less about the procreative efforts of those men who were deemed to be at the top of the evolutionary scale. In the absence of survivors from ancient Athens, the pick of the human species was self-evidently to be found in the British officer class, which combined excellence of pedigree with regular exposure to the martial form of natural selection. The fiction of the period is crowded with the type: Leo Vincey in Henry Rider Haggard's *She*, handsome, brave and not excessively bright, who 'at twenty-one might have stood for a statue of the youthful Apollo'; or Lord John Roxton in Arthur Conan Doyle's *The Lost World*, with his 'strange, twinkling, reckless eyes – eyes of a cold light blue, the colour of a glacier lake', to say nothing of

the strongly-curved nose, the hollow, worn cheeks, the dark, ruddy hair, thin at the top, the crisp, virile moustaches, the small, aggressive tuft upon his projecting chin . . . [He] was the essence of the English country gentleman, the keen, alert, open-air lover of dogs and of horses. His skin was of a rich flower-pot red from sun and wind. His eyebrows were tufted and overhanging, which gave those naturally cold eyes an almost ferocious aspect, an impression which was increased by his strong and furrowed brow. In figure he was spare, but very strongly built – indeed, he had often proved that there were few men in England capable of such sustained exertions.

Men like this certainly did exist. Yet a remarkably high proportion of them made only the most half-hearted, if any, contribution to the reproduction of the race they exemplified – for the simple reason that they were homosexuals.

A distinction must be drawn carefully here between men whose upbringing and life in almost exclusively male institutions inclined them towards a culture of homoeroticism and condemned them to have difficulties with girls; and those who were practising pederasts. In the former category probably belonged Rhodes, Baden-Powell and Kitchener (of whom more below). In the latter category certainly belonged Hector Macdonald.

Like Rhodes's relationship with his private secretary Neville Pickering, Baden-Powell's intense attachment to Kenneth 'The Boy' McLaren (a fellow officer in the 13th Hussars) was almost certainly not physically consummated. The same doubtless also goes for Kitchener's friendship with his aide Oswald Fitzgerald, his constant companion for nine years. Each of these men, so masculine in public, could be extraordinarily effeminate in private. Kitchener, for example, shared with his sister Millie a love of fine fabrics, flower arrangements and fine porcelain, and would take time off during campaigns in the desert to correspond with her about interior decoration. But this, in conjunction with a shred of malicious saloon-bar gossip, hardly suffices to label him 'gay'. All three exhibited far clearer symptoms of well-nigh superhuman repression – a phenomenon seemingly incomprehensible to the early twenty-first century mind, but an indispensable element of Victorian over-achievement. Kitchener's nanny, doubtless no great Freudian, spotted it early in her charge: 'I am afraid Herbert will suffer a great deal from repression,' she remarked after he concealed an injury from his mother. Ned Cecil also hit the mark when he observed that Kitchener 'loathed any form of moral or mental undressing'.

Macdonald was a quite different case. The son of a Ross-shire crofter, he was unusual in that he rose all the way through the ranks, having begun his career as a private in the Gordon Highlanders and ending it a major-general with a knighthood. Distinguished from the outset by his often reckless bravery, Macdonald's private life was reckless in a different way. Though he married and fathered a child, he did so secretly and saw his wife no more than four times after their wedding; when overseas, however, he was notoriously prone to homosexual adventures and was finally caught *in flagrante* with four boys in a Ceylonese railway compartment. As late Victorian Britain grew ever more prudish – and laws against sodomy were ever more stringently enforced – the

Empire offered homosexuals like 'Fighting Mac' boundless erotic opportunities. Kenneth Searight was another; before leaving England at the age of twenty-six he had known only three sexual partners, but once in India he found a very wide scope, detailing his numerous sexual exploits there in verse.

Overkill

What happened in the Sudan on 2 September 1898 was the zenith of late Victorian imperialism, the apogee of the generation that regarded world domination as a racial prerogative. The Battle of Omdurman pitted an army of desert tribesmen against the full military might of the biggest empire in world history – for, unlike the earlier and privately funded wars waged in southern and western Africa, this was official. In a single battle, at least 10,000 enemies of the Empire were annihilated, despite a huge numerical advantage on their side. As in Newbolt's 'Vitaï Lampada', the sand of the desert was 'sodden red'. Omdurman was the acme of imperial overkill.

Once again, the British were drawn to extend their imperial reach by a combination of strategic and economic calculation. The advance into the Sudan was partly a reaction to the ambitions of other imperial powers, in particular the French, who had their eyes on the upper waters of the Nile. It also appealed to the City bankers like the Rothschilds, who by now had substantial investments in neighbouring Egypt. But this was not the way the British public saw it. For the readers of the *Pall Mall Gazette*, which took up the subject with gusto, the subjugation of the Sudan was a matter of revenge, pure and simple.

Since the early 1880s the Sudan had been the scene of a full-blown religious revolution. A charismatic holy man claiming to be the Mahdi (the 'Expected Guide', last in succession of the twelve great imams) had mustered a vast army of dervishes, their heads shaven, their bodies clad in the simple *jibbeh*, all ready to fight for his strict Wahabbist brand of Islam. Drawing his support from the desert tribes, the Mahdi openly challenged the power of British-occupied Egypt. In 1883 his forces even had the temerity to wipe out, to the last man, a 10,000-strong Egyptian army led by Colonel William Hicks, a retired British officer. After an indignant press campaign led by W. T. Stead, it was decided to send General Charles George Gordon, who had spent six years in Khartoum as the Egyptian Khedive's Governor of 'Equatoria' during the 1870s. Although a decorated veteran of the Crimean War and the commander of the Chinese army that had crushed the Taiping rebellion in 1863–4, Gordon was always regarded by the British political establishment as half mad, and with some reason.* Ascetic to the point of being masochistic, devout to the point of being fanatical, Gordon saw himself as God's instrument, as he explained to his beloved sister:

To each is allotted a distinct work, to each a destined goal; to some the seat at the right-hand or left of the Saviour . . . It is difficult for the flesh to accept 'Ye are dead, ye have naught to do with the world.' How difficult for any one to be circumcised from the world, to be as indifferent to its pleasures, its sorrows, and its comforts as a corpse is! That is to know the resurrection.

'I died long ago,' he told her on another occasion; 'I am prepared to follow the unrolling of the scroll.' Charged with evacuating the Egyptian troops stationed in Khartoum, he set off alone, resolved to do the very opposite and hold the city. He arrived on 18 February 1884, by now determined to 'smash up the Mahdi', only to be surrounded, besieged and – nearly a year after his arrival – hacked to pieces.

While marooned in Khartoum, Gordon had confided to his diary his growing suspicion that the government in London had left him

* He was offered, accepted but then resigned after just three days the Private Secretaryship to Lord Ripon, on the latter's appointment as Viceroy of India. The sticking point was a letter he was asked to write in response to an address to the Viceroy, to the effect that the Viceroy had read it with interest. 'You know perfectly,' he declared, 'that Lord Ripon has never read it, and I can't say that sort of thing.' He also had an obsessive aversion to dinner parties, which would have been a serious handicap in a Viceroy's Private Secretary.

in the lurch. He imagined the Foreign Secretary, Lord Granville, complaining as the siege dragged on:

Why, HE *said distinctly* he could *only* hold out *six months*, and that was in March (counts the months). August! Why he ought to have given in! What is to be done? They'll be howling for an expedition ... It is no laughing matter; *that abominable Mahdi*! Why on earth does he not guard his roads better? *What* IS to be done? ... What that Mahdi is about I cannot make out. Why does he not put all his guns on the river and stop the route? Eh what? 'We will have to go to Khartoum!' Why, it will cost millions, what a wretched business!

Even more reviled was the British Agent and Consul-General in Egypt, Sir Evelyn Baring, who had opposed Gordon's mission from the very outset. There was a grain of realism in Gordon's paranoia. Gladstone, still uneasy at having ordered the occupation of Egypt, had no intention of being drawn into the occupation of Sudan. He repeatedly evaded suggestions that Gordon should be rescued and authorized the despatch of Sir Garnet Wolseley's relief expedition only after months of prevarication. It arrived three days too late. By now the readers of the *Pall Mall Gazette* had come to share Gordon's suspicions. When the news of his death reached London there was an outcry. The Queen herself wrote to Gordon's sister:

To think of your dear, noble, heroic Brother, who served his Country and his Queen so truly, so heroically, with a self-sacrifice so edifying to the World, not having been rescued. That the promises of support were not fulfilled – which I so frequently and constantly pressed on those who asked him to go – is to me grief inexpressible! Indeed, it has made me ill ... Would you express to your other sisters and your elder Brother my true sympathy, and what I do so keenly feel, the stain left upon England for your dear Brother's cruel, though heroic, fate!

Gladstone was reviled – no longer the 'Grand Old Man', now 'Gordon's Only Murderer'. Yet it was thirteen long years before Gordon could be avenged.

The Anglo-Egyptian army that invaded the Sudan in 1898 was led by General Herbert Horatio Kitchener. Behind a patina of Prussian military ruthlessness, as we have seen, Kitchener was a complex, in some ways even effeminate character. He was not without a sense of humour: cursed with poor eyesight all his life, he was such a poor shot that he named his gundogs Bang, Miss and Damn. But as a young and self-consciously Christian soldier, he had been powerfully attracted to Gordon's asceticism when the two men had met briefly in Egypt. The thought of avenging Gordon brought out the hard man in Kitchener. Having been a junior officer in Wolseley's earlier invasion force, the man who was now Sirdar (Commander-in-Chief) of the Egyptian army knew the terrain well. As he led his expeditionary force southwards into the desert wastes, he had only one thought: to repay his debt to Gordon with compound interest, or rather to make Gordon's killers pay it. The Mahdi himself might by now be dead; but the sins of the father would be visited on his heir, the Khalifa.

It was at Omdurman on the banks of the Nile that the two civilizations clashed: on one side, a horde of desert-dwelling Islamic fundamentalists; on the other, the well-drilled Christian soldiers of Greater Britain, with their Egyptian and Sudanese auxiliaries. Even the way the two sides lined up expressed the difference between them. The dervishes, who numbered about 52,000, were spread out across the plain beneath their bright black, green and white flags, forming a line five miles long. Kitchener's men – there were just 20,000 – stood shoulder to shoulder in their familiar squares, backs to the Nile. Watching from the British lines was the 23-year-old Winston Churchill, an Old Harrovian army officer who was supposed to be in India, but had wangled his way into Kitchener's expedition as a war correspondent for the *Morning Post*, a position now regarded as equivalent in status to a cavalry captaincy. As dawn broke, he had his first sight of the enemy:

I suddenly realized that all the masses were in motion and advancing swiftly. Their Emirs galloped about and before their ranks. Scouts and patrols scattered themselves all over the front. Then they began to cheer. They were still a mile away from the hill, and were concealed from the Sirdar's army by the folds of the ground. The noise of the shouting was heard, albeit faintly, by the troops down by the river. But to us, watching on the hill, a tremendous roar came up in waves of intense sound, like the tumult of the rising wind and sea before a storm . . . One rock, one mound of sand after another was submerged by that human flood. It was time to go.

The courage of the dervishes profoundly impressed Churchill. It was based on a burning religious zeal: the shouting he heard was the chant of '*La llaha illa llah wa Muhammad rasul Allah*' – 'There is one God and Muhammad is the Messenger of God'. Nor was the battle entirely without risk for their opponents. Indeed, there was a moment late in the day when only prompt action by Hector Macdonald – in defiance of the Sirdar's orders – averted much heavier British casualties. Ultimately, however, the dervishes stood no chance against what Churchill called, with more than a hint of irony, 'that mechanical scattering of death which the polite nations of the earth have brought to such monstrous perfection'. The British had Maxim guns, Martini–Henry rifles, heliographs and, moored in the river behind the British force, gunboats. The dervishes had, it is true, a few Maxims of their own; but mostly they relied on antiquated muskets, spears and swords. Churchill vividly described the inevitable outcome:

The Maxim guns exhausted all the water in their jackets, and several had to be refreshed from the water-bottles of the Cameron Highlanders before they could go on with their deadly work. The empty cartridge-cases, tinkling to the ground, formed small but growing heaps beside each man. And all the time out on the plain on the other side bullets were shearing through flesh, smashing and splintering bone; blood spouted from terrible wounds; valiant men were struggling on through a hell of whistling metal, exploding shells, and spurting dust – suffering, despairing, dying . . . The charging Dervishes sank down in tangled heaps. The masses in the rear paused, irresolute.

It was all over in the space of five hours.

By one estimate, the dervish army suffered close to 95 per cent casualties; at the very least a fifth of their number were killed outright. By contrast, there were fewer than four hundred casualties on the Anglo-Egyptian side, and only forty-eight British soldiers lost their lives. Surveying the field afterwards, Kitchener laconically remarked that the enemy had been given 'a good dusting'. Nor did this satisfy him, for he proceeded to order the destruction of the Mahdi's tomb and, in Churchill's words, 'carried off the Mahdi's head in a kerosene-can as a trophy'. He then shed mawkish tears as the assembled military bands performed what amounted to an open-air concert, the programme of which ran the whole compressed gamut of Victorian emotion:

God Save the Queen

The Khedival anthem

The Dead March from *Saul*

Handel's March from *Scipio* ('Toll for the Brave') (all performed by the band of Grenadier Guards)

Coronach Lament (performed by the pipe band of the Cameron and Seaforth Highlanders)

Abide with Me (performed by the band of the 11th Sudanese)

Privately, Churchill deplored not only the desecration of the Mahdi's remains but also 'the inhuman slaughter of the wounded' (for this too he held Kitchener responsible). He was profoundly shocked by the way British firepower had transformed the vibrant dervish warriors into mere 'dirty bits of newspaper' strewn over the plain. Yet for public consumption he dutifully pronounced Omdurman 'the most signal triumph ever gained by the arms of science over barbarians'. Fifty years later, after annihilating the Japanese fleet air arm at the Mariana Islands, the Americans would call this kind of thing a 'turkey shoot'.

The lesson of Omdurman seemed to be the old and unambiguous one that no one challenged British power with impunity. There was, however, another lesson that could be drawn. Watching the battle intently that day was Major von Tiedemann, the German military attaché, who duly noted the devastating impact of the British Maxim guns, which one observer reckoned accounted for around three-quarters of the dervish casualties. To Tiedemann, the real lesson was obvious: the only way to beat the British was to match their firepower.

The Germans had not been slow to appeciate the war-winning potential of the Maxim. Wilhelm II had witnessed a demonstration of the gun as early as 1888 and had commented simply: 'That is the gun – there is no other.' In 1892, through the agency of Lord Rothschild, a licence was granted to the Berlin machine tool and arms manufacturer Ludwig Loewe to produce Maxim guns for the German market. In the immediate aftermath of the Battle of Omdurman the decision was taken to give each Jäger battalion in the German army a four-gun Maxim battery. By 1908 the Maxim was standard issue for every German infantry regiment.

By the end of 1898 there was only one tribe in Southern Africa that still defied the might of the British Empire. They had already trekked hundreds of miles northwards to escape from British influence at the Cape; they had already fought the British once to retain their independence, inflicting a heavy defeat on them at Majuba Hill in 1881. This was Africa's only white tribe: the Boers – farmers descended from the early Dutch settlers of the Cape.

To Rhodes, Chamberlain and Milner, the Boers' independent-mindedness was intolerable. As usual, British calculations were both strategic and economic. Despite the growing importance of the Suez Canal for British trade with Asia, the Cape remained a military base of 'immense importance for England' (Chamberlain) for the simple reason that the Canal might be vulnerable to closure in a major European war. It remained, in the Colonial Secretary's view, 'the cornerstone of the whole British colonial system'. At the same time, it was hardly without significance that one of the Boer republics had turned out to be sitting on the biggest gold seams in the world. By 1900 the Rand was producing a quarter of the world's gold supply and had absorbed more than £114 million of mainly British capital. Having been an impoverished backwater, the Transvaal suddenly seemed set to become the economic centre of gravity in southern Africa. But the Boers saw no reason why they should share power with the tens of thousands of British immigrants, the *Uitlanders*, who had swarmed into their country to pan for gold. Nor did they approve of the (somewhat) more liberal way the British treated the black population of Cape Colony. In the eyes of their president Paul Kruger, the Boers' strictly Calvinist way of life was simply incompatible with British rule. The problem for the British was that this African tribe was unlike all the others – though the difference turned out to lie less in the fact that they were white than in the fact that they were well armed.

It can hardly be denied that Chamberlain and Milner provoked the Boer War, believing that the Boers could be bullied quickly into giving up their independence. Their demand that the *Uitlanders* be given the vote in the Transvaal after five years' residence – 'Home Rule for the Rand', in Chamberlain's hypocritical phrase – was merely a pretext. The real thrust of British policy was revealed by the pains taken to prevent the Boers securing a rail link to the sea via the Portuguese-controlled Delagoa Bay, which would have freed them and the gold mines from dependence on the British railway running to the Cape. At all costs, even at the cost of war, the Boers had to lose their independence.

Chamberlain was confident of victory: did he not already have offers of military assistance from Victoria, New South Wales, Queensland, Canada, West Africa and the Malay States?* As the Irish MP John Dillon caustically remarked, it was 'the British Empire against 30,000 farmers'. But the Boers had been given ample time to prepare for war. Ever since 1895, when Rhodes's crony Dr Leander Starr Jameson had led his abortive 'raid' into the Transvaal, it had been obvious that a showdown was imminent. Two years later, the appointment of Milner as High Commissioner for South Africa had sent another unambiguous signal: his stated view was that there could be no room in South Africa for 'two absolutely conflicting social and political systems'. The Boers duly stocked up with the latest armaments: Maxim guns, of course, but also as much of the Essen company Krupp's latest artillery as they could afford,

---

* By the end of the war, Canada, Australia and New Zealand did indeed supply 30,000 troops.

as well as caseloads of the latest Mauser rifles, accurate over 2,000 yards. Their way of life had made them crack shots; now they were well armed too. And of course they knew the terrain far better than the British *rooinekke* (Afrikaans for 'rednecks', on account of the typical Tommy's sunburnt skin). By Christmas 1899 the Boers had struck deep into British territory. This time, it seemed, the turkeys were shooting back. And nothing demonstrated the accuracy of their shooting better than what happened at Spion Kop.

General Sir Redvers Buller – soon to be nicknamed 'Sir Reverse' – had been sent to relieve the 12,000 British troops besieged by the Boers at Ladysmith, in the British province of Natal. In turn, Buller gave Lieutenant-General Sir Charles Warren the job of breaking through the Boer defences around the hill known as Spion Kop. On 24 January 1900 Warren ordered a mixed force of Lancasters and *Uitlanders* to scale the hill's steep, rocky face under cover of night and fog. They encountered only a single enemy picket, who fled; the Boers, it seemed, had surrendered the hill without a fight. In the thick dawn mist, the British hacked out a perfunctory trench, confident that they had won an easy victory. But Warren had misread the lie of the land. The British position was completely exposed to Boer artillery and rifle fire from the surrounding hills; indeed, they had not even reached the highest point of Spion Kop itself. As the mist cleared, the slaughter began. This time the British were on the receiving end.

Once again the battle was witnessed by Churchill in his capacity as war correspondent. The contrast between this débâcle and the scenes he had witnessed at Omdurman just seventeen months earlier could hardly have been more stark. With Boer shells raining down 'at the rate of seven or eight a minute', he could only stare in horror as the 'thick and continual stream of wounded flowed rearwards. A village of ambulance waggons [*sic*] grew up at the foot of the mountain. The dead and injured, smashed and broken by shells, littered the summit till it was a bloody reeking shambles.' 'The scenes at Spion Kop,' he confessed in a letter to a friend, 'were among the strangest and most terrible I have ever witnessed.' And Churchill was not in the eye of the storm of steel. One survivor described seeing his comrades incinerated, blown in half and decapitated; he himself lost his left leg. For newspaper readers at home, who were spared such grisly details, the news was still scarcely credible. Greater Britain was being beaten hollow – by 30,000 Dutch farmers.*

Mafeking

What Vietnam was to the United States, the Boer War very nearly was to the British Empire, in two respects: its huge cost in both lives and money – 45,000 men dead† and a quarter of a billion pounds spent – and the divisions it opened up back home. Of course, the British had suffered reverses in Africa before, not only against the Boers but also against the Zulu *impis* at Isandhlwana in 1879. This, however, was on an altogether larger scale. And at the end of it all it was far from clear that the British had achieved their original objective. The challenge for the jingoists of the press was to make something that looked so like a defeat feel like another imperial victory.

Mafikeng – as it is now spelt – is a rather dusty, scruffy little town; you can almost smell the Kalahari desert to the north-west. It was even less to look at a hundred years ago: just a railway station, a hospital, a Masonic hall, a gaol, a library, a courthouse, a few blocks of houses and a branch of the Standard Bank – in short, the usual dowdy imperial outpost. The only building with more than one storey was the distinctly un-British Convent of the Sacred Heart. Today it hardly seems worth fighting over. But in 1899 Mafeking mattered. It was a border town, practically the last in Cape Colony before the Transvaal. It was from there that the Jameson Raid had been launched. And even before the war began,

---

* 30,000 was an underestimate. According to the Boers' figures, 54,667 men took up arms, but by 1903 the British were claiming a total of 72,975.

† It should be noted that around two-thirds of British mortality was due to typhoid, dysentery and other diseases, not enemy action.

it was there that a regiment of irregulars were stationed, with the idea of mounting another, bigger raid into Boer territory. It never happened. Instead, the troops found themselves under siege. Fears began to grow that, if Mafeking fell, the many Boers living in the Cape might throw in their lot with their cousins in the Transvaal and Orange Free State.

The siege of Mafeking was portrayed back in Britain as the war's most glorious episode, the moment when the spirit of the public school playing fields finally prevailed. Indeed, the British press treated the siege as a kind of big imperial game, a seven-month Test match between England and the Transvaal. As luck would have it, on this occasion the English managed to field the ideal captain: the old Carthusian 'Stephe' Baden-Powell, now the colonel in command of the First Bechuanaland Regiment. To Baden-Powell, the siege was indeed the ultimate cricket fixture. He even said as much in a characteristically light-hearted letter to one of the Boer commanders: '. . . Just now we are having our innings and have so far scored 200 days, not out, against the bowling of Cronje, Snijman, Botha . . . and we are having a very enjoyable game.' Here was the hero that the war – or at least the war correspondents – so desperately needed, a man who instinctively knew how to 'play the game'. It was not so much Baden-Powell's stiff upper-lip that impressed those around him as his indefatigable boyishness, his 'pluck' (a favourite B.-P. word). Every Sunday he organized real cricket matches followed by dancing. George Tighe, a civilian who joined the Mafeking Town Guard, never doubted that Baden-Powell was 'thoroughly able to beat the Boers at their own "slim" game'. A talented mimic, he did comic turns on stage to boost morale. Humorous stamps were issued for 'the independent republic of Mafeking' with Baden-Powell's head on them in place of the Queen's. Not even the *Boy's Own Paper* could have made that up.

For 217 days Mafeking held out against a Boer force that was substantially larger and had lethally superior artillery. The defending force had two muzzle loading 7-pounders and an ancient cannon which fired a projectile 'exactly like a cricket ball' (what else?), against Cronje's nine field guns and a 94-pounder Creusot

Long Tom, nicknamed in true schoolboy fashion 'Old Creechy'. Reports from newspaper correspondents inside the town, particularly Lady Sarah Wilson's for the *Daily Mail*, kept readers in a state of agonized suspense. Would B.-P. hold out? Would the Boer fast bowlers prove too much even for him? When at last Mafeking was relieved on 17 May 1900 there were scenes of hysterical jubilation ('mafficking') in the streets of London – as if, in the words of the anti-imperialist Wilfrid Scawen Blunt, 'they had beaten Napoleon'. Baden-Powell was rewarded with the command of a new force, the South African Constabulary, the uniform of which he enthusiastically set about designing.

But what was the price of holding on to this one-horse town? True, more than 7,000 Boer troops had been diverted into a sideshow in the opening phase of the war, when they might have achieved more elsewhere. But in terms of human life this had been anything but a game of cricket. Nearly half the original defending force of 700 were either killed, wounded or taken prisoner. And what the papers did not report was that the real brunt of the defence of Mafeking was borne by the black population, despite the fact that this was supposed to be a 'white man's war'. Baden-Powell not only drafted more than 700 of them (though he later put the number at less than half that); he also excluded them from the protective trenches and shelters in the white part of town. And he systematically reduced their rations in order to feed the white minority. Civilian casualties of both colours totalled more than 350. But the number of black residents who died of starvation may have been twice that number. As Milner cynically remarked: 'You have only to sacrifice "the nigger" absolutely, and the game is easy.'

The British public had been given their symbolic victory; the poetasters could rush into print:

> What! Wrench the Sceptre from her hand,
>   And bid her bow the knee!
> Not while her Yeomen guard the land,
>   And her ironclads the sea!
>
>   (Austin, *To Arms!*)

The sinews of Victorian power: 'Passing the Cable on Board the *Great Eastern*', 1866; Indian soldiers with elephants, British soldiers with a gun, 1897; Steamships on the Hugli River, 1900

Tory-entalism and Terrorism: Curzon and fellow aristocrats at
Aina-Khana, Maharaja Peshkai's Palace, *c.* 1900; The Delhi Durbar,
1903; Aurobindo Ghose – St Paul's School; King's College,
Cambridge; Alipore Courthouse

Imperial hubris: Scottish troops round the Sphinx at Giza, 1882; Hiram
Maxim with his gun, *c.* 1880; Dervish dead after Omdurman, 1898

Imperial nemesis: Winston Churchill bound for England, 1899; French cartoon lambasting the British concentration camps in South Africa, 1901; Spion Kop, 1900

War of Empires I: France, England, Russia, Japan and Germany get their claws into China, German cartoon, 1900; French postcard of British and Indian Soldiers, Nantes, c. 1916; T. E. Lawrence, 1917

War of Empires II: Sketch of Konyu–Hintok cutting, Thailand,
by Jack Chalker, 1942; Japanese cartoon inciting Indians to throw off
British rule, c. 1942; 'Allied teamwork wins the game', cartoon by
Conrado Massaguer

The Empire sunk: Egyptians mob Colonel Gamal Abdel-Nasser, 29
March 1954; The blockade of Port Said during the Suez Crisis, 19
November 1956

So front the realms, your point abashed;
  So mark them chafe and foam;
And if they challenge, so, by God,
  Strike, England, and strike home!
      (Henley, *For England's Sake*)

But it was a triumph of newsprint only. As Kitchener shrewdly noted, Baden-Powell was 'more outside show than sterling worth'. He could have said the same of Mafeking's relief.

By the summer of 1900, the tide of the war appeared to be turning. The British Army, now under the more effective leadership of the Indian Army veteran Lord Roberts, had relieved Ladysmith and advanced into Boer territory, capturing both Bloemfontein, the capital of the Orange Free State, and Pretoria, capital of the Transvaal. Convinced he was winning the war, Roberts rode in triumph through the streets of Bloemfontein and installed himself in the Residency. In the spacious ballroom on the ground floor, his officers came to dance.

It was supposed to be a dance of victory. Yet despite the loss of their principal towns the Boers stubbornly refused to surrender. Instead, they switched to guerrilla tactics. 'The Boers', complained Kitchener, 'are not like the Soudanese who stood up for a fair fight, they are always running away on their little ponies.' If only they would charge the British Maxims with spears like good sports! In frustration, Roberts therefore adopted a ruthless new strategy designed to hit the Boers where they were most vulnerable.

Sporadic destruction of their farms had been going on for some time, usually on the grounds that particular farmhouses were sheltering snipers or supplying the guerrillas with food and intelligence. But now British troops were authorized to burn down the Boers' homes systematically. In all, around 30,000 were razed. The only question this begged was what to do with their wives and children, whom the Boer guerrillas had left behind when they joined their commandos in the *veld*, and who were now being rendered homeless in their thousands. In theory, the scorched earth tactic would soon force the Boers to surrender, if only to protect their loved ones. But until that happened, those loved ones were the responsibility of the British. Should they be treated as prisoners of war or refugees? Roberts's initial view was that 'to feed people whose relatives are in arms against us will only encourage [the] latter to prolong resistance besides being [a] severe burden on us'. But his idea that they should be compelled 'to join their relatives beyond our lines unless the latter come in to surrender' was not realistic. After some dithering, the generals came up with an answer. They herded the Boers into camps – to be precise, concentration camps.

These were not the first concentration camps in history – Spanish forces had used similar tactics in Cuba in 1896 – but they were the first to earn infamy.* Altogether, 27,927 Boers (the majority of them children) died in the British camps. That was 14.5 per cent of the entire Boer population, and they died mainly as a result of malnourishment and poor sanitation. More adult Boers died this way than from direct military action. A further 14,000 of 115,700 black internees – 81 per cent of them children – died in separate camps.

Meanwhile, at the Bloemfontein Residency, the band played on. Eventually, after several months of the Gay Gordons and Strip the Willow, the ballroom floor began to wear thin. To avoid any mishaps befalling officers' wives, the old floorboards obviously had to be replaced, and so they were. Happily for the accounts of the officers' mess, a use was found for the old ones. They were sold to Boer women to make coffins for their children, at the price of 1s 6d a plank.

The combination of scorched earth and concentration camps certainly undermined the Boers' will to fight. But it was not until Kitchener, who succeeded Roberts in November 1900, had covered

---

* Sir Nevile Henderson, the British ambassador in Berlin in the 1930s, recalled that when he remonstrated with Goering about the brutality of the Nazi concentration camps, the latter took down from his shelves a volume of a German encyclopaedia: 'Opening it at *Konzentrationslager* . . . he read out: "First used by the British in the South African War."'

the country with a deadly web of barbed wire and blockhouses that they were forced to the negotiating table. Even then, the final outcome was anything but unconditional surrender. True, under the Treaty of Vereeniging (31 May 1902), the two Boer republics lost their independence and were absorbed into the Empire. But that meant that the British had to pay for the reconstruction of what they had destroyed. At the same time, the treaty left the question of black and coloured voting rights to be settled after the introduction of self-government, thus disenfranchizing the vast majority of South Africa's inhabitants for three generations. Above all, the peace could do nothing to prevent the Boers from capitalizing on the restricted franchise. In 1910, exactly eight years after the Treaty, the self-governing Union of South Africa was created, with the Boer Commandant-General Louis Botha as its premier and several other war heroes in his Cabinet. Within three years, a Native's Land Act had been passed which effectively confined black South African land ownership to the least fertile tenth of the country.* In effect, the Boers now ruled not only their original states but the British territories of Natal and the Cape as well, and had taken the first step towards imposing apartheid throughout South Africa. Milner had hoped that the future would be '2/5ths Boers and 3/5ths Britishers – Peace, Progress and Fusion'. In the event, not enough British emigrants went to South Africa to achieve that.

In many ways the consequences of the Boer War in Britain were even more profound than in South Africa, for it was revulsion against the war's conduct that decisively shifted British politics to the Left in the 1900s, a shift that was to have incalculable implications for the future of the Empire.

On the outskirts of Bloemfontein stands a sombre and imposing monument to the Boer women and children who died in the concentration camps. Buried there, next to the wartime President of the Orange Free State, are the remains of a Cornish clergyman's daughter named Emily Hobhouse, one of the twentieth century's

---

* The effects of the legislation were bitterly described by Solomon Plaatje in his *Native Life in South Africa* (1916).

first anti-war activists. In 1900 Hobhouse got wind of 'poor [Boer] women who were being driven from pillar to post' and resolved to go to South Africa to assist them. She established a Relief Fund for South African Women and Children 'to feed, clothe, harbour and save women and children – Boer, English and other – who were left destitute and ragged as a result of the destruction of property, the eviction of families or other incidents resulting from . . . military operations'. Shortly after her arrival in Cape Town in December 1900 she secured permission from Milner to visit the concentration camps, though Kitchener tried to confine her access to the camp at Bloemfontein, then home to 1,800 people. The grossly inadequate accommodation and sanitation, with soap regarded by the military authorities as 'an article of luxury', profoundly shocked her. Despite Kitchener's obstructive efforts, she went on to visit other camps at Norvalspont, Aliwal North, Springfontein, Kimberley, Orange River and Mafeking. It was the same story in all of them. And by the time she returned to Bloemfontein conditions had worsened.

In an effort to put a stop to the policy of internment, Hobhouse returned to England but she found the War Office more or less indifferent. Only reluctantly did the government agree to appoint a committee of women under Millicent Fawcett to investigate Hobhouse's claims, and she was pointedly excluded from it. Incensed, she sought to return to South Africa but was not even allowed to go ashore. Now her only weapon was publicity.

Conditions in the camps went from bad to worse during 1901. In October a total of 3,000 inmates died, a mortality rate of more than a third. This was not a deliberately genocidal policy; rather it was the result of disastrous lack of foresight and rank incompetence on the part of the military authorities. Nor was the Fawcett Commission as toothless as Hobhouse had feared; it produced a remarkably hard-hitting report and secured rapid improvements in medical provision in the camps. Although Chamberlain refused to criticize the War Office publicly, he too was shocked by what Hobhouse had revealed and hastened to transfer the camps to the civilian authorities in South Africa. With striking speed, conditions improved: the mortality rate fell from 34 per cent in October

1901 to 7 per cent in February 1902 and just 2 per cent by May.*

Milner at least was contrite. The camps, he admitted, were 'a bad business, the one thing, as far as I am concerned, in which I feel that the abuse so freely heaped upon us for everything we have done and not done is not without some foundation.' But contrition, no matter how sincere, could not undo the damage. Hobhouse's revelations about the camps triggered a bitter public backlash against the government. In Parliament the Liberals seized their chance. Here at last was the perfect opportunity to wade into the coalition of Tories and Chamberlainites that had dominated British politics for nearly two decades. As early as June 1901 Sir Henry Campbell-Bannerman, the party's leader, denounced what he called the 'methods of barbarism' being used against the Boers. Speaking in the Commons, David Lloyd George, the darling of the party's radical wing, declared:

A war of annexation . . . against a proud people must be a war of extermination, and that is unfortunately what it seems we are now committing ourselves to – burning homesteads and turning women and children out of their homes . . . the savagery which must necessarily follow will stain the name of this country.

It did.

Not only was imperialism immoral, argued the critics. According to the Radicals, it was also a rip-off: paid for by British taxpayers, fought for by British soldiers, but benefiting only a tiny elite of fat-cat millionaires, the likes of Rhodes and Rothschild. That was the thrust of J. A. Hobson's profoundly influential *Imperialism: A Study*, published in 1902. 'Every great political act', argued Hobson, 'must receive the sanction and the practical aid of this little group of financial kings':

As speculators or financial dealers they constitute . . . the gravest single factor in the economics of Imperialism . . . Each condition . . . of their profitable business . . . throws them on the side of Imperialism . . . There

---

* Improvements were much slower in coming to the black camps. Significantly, the peak of mortality there – 38 per cent – was in December 1902.

is not a war ... or any other public shock, which is not gainful to these men; they are harpies who suck their gains from every sudden disturbance of public credit ... The wealth of these houses, the scale of their operations, and their cosmopolitan organization make them the prime determinants of economic policy. They have the largest definite stake in the business of Imperialism, and the amplest means of forcing their will upon the policy of nations ... [F]inance is ... the governor of the imperial engine, directing the energy and determining the work.

Henry Noel Brailsford took Hobson's argument further in his *The War of Steel and Gold: A Study of the Armed Peace* (written in 1910, but not published until 1914). 'In the heroic age,' Brailsford wrote, 'Helen's was the face that launched a thousand ships. In our golden age the face wears more often the shrewd features of some Hebrew financier. To defend the interests of Lord Rothschild and his fellow bondholders, Egypt was first occupied, and then practically annexed by Great Britain ... The extremest case of all is, perhaps, our own South African War.' Was it not obvious that the Boer War had been fought to ensure that the gold mines of the Transvaal remained securely in the hands of their capitalist owners? Was not Rhodes merely, in the words of the Radical MP Henry Labouchere, an 'Empire jerry-builder who has always been a mere vulgar promoter masquerading as a patriot, and the figurehead of a gang of astute Hebrew financiers with whom he divides the profits'?

Like those modern conspiracy theories which explain every war in terms of the control of oil reserves, the Radical critique of imperialism was an over-simplification. (Hobson and Brailsford little knew what a liability Rhodes had been during the siege of Kimberley.) And like those other modern theories that attribute sinister power to certain financial institutions, some anti-imperialism conveyed more than a hint of anti-Semitism. Nevertheless, when Brailsford called it 'a perversion of the objects for which the State exists, that the power and prestige, for which all of us pay, should be used to win profits for private adventurers', he was not entirely wide of the mark. 'We are engaged in Imperial trading,' he wrote, 'with the flag as its indispensable asset, but the profits go exclusively into private pockets.' That was substantially true.

Most of the huge flows of money from Britain's vast stock of overseas investments flowed to a tiny elite of, at most, a few hundred thousand people. At the apex of this elite was indeed the Rothschild Bank, whose combined capital in London, Paris and Vienna amounted to a staggering £41 million, making it by far the biggest financial institution in the world. The greater part of the firm's assets was invested in government bonds, a high proportion of which were in colonial economies like Egypt and South Africa. Nor is there any question that the extension of British power into those economies generated a wealth of new business for Rothschilds. Between 1885 and 1893, to give a single example, the London, Paris and Frankfurt houses were jointly responsible for four major Egyptian bond issues worth nearly £50 million. What is even more conspicuous is the closeness of the relationships enjoyed by the Rothschilds with the leading politicians of the day. Disraeli, Randolph Churchill and the Earl of Rosebery were all in various ways connected to them both socially and financially. The case of Rosebery – who served as Foreign Secretary under Gladstone and succeeded him as Prime Minister in 1894 – is particularly striking, since in 1878 he actually married Lord Rothschild's cousin Hannah.

Throughout his political career, Rosebery was in regular communication with male members of the Rothschild family, a correspondence which reveals the intimacy of the connections between money and power in the late Victorian Empire. In November 1878, for example, Ferdinand de Rothschild suggested to Rosebery: 'If you have a few spare thousand pounds (from £9–10) you might invest them in the new . . . Egyptian loan which the House brings out next week.' When he joined the government following the news of Gordon's death at Khartoum, Lord Rothschild wrote to him in revealing terms: '[Y]our clear judgments and patriotic devotion will help the Govt. and save the country. I hope you will take care that large reinforcements are sent up the Nile. The campaign in the

Soudan must be a brilliant success and no mistake.' In the fortnight after he joined the government, Rosebery saw members of the family on at least four occasions, including two dinners. And in August 1885, only two months after Gladstone's resignation had temporarily removed him from office again, Rosebery was allotted £50,000 of the new Egyptian loan issued by the London house. When he became Foreign Secretary, Lord Rothschild's brother Alfred assured him that 'from all sides & even distant climes we hear nothing but great satisfaction at the nomination of the new Minister of Foreign Affairs'.

Though it is hard to find conclusive evidence that the Rothschilds benefited materially from Rosebery's policy when he was in office, there was at least one occasion when he undoubtedly did give them advance warning of an important diplomatic decision. In January 1893 he used Reginald Brett to communicate to New Court the government's intention to reinforce the Egyptian garrison. 'I saw Natty [Lord Rothschild] and Alfred,' reported Brett,

and told them that you were much obliged to them for having given you all the information at their disposal, and therefore wished them to know [of the reinforcement] before reading it in the papers . . . Of course they were delighted and most grateful. Natty wished me to tell you that all the information and any assistance which he can give you is always at your disposal.

Nor was Rosebery the only politician who failed to achieve the complete separation of his private and public interests. One of the principal beneficiaries of the occupation of Egypt was none other than Gladstone himself. In late 1875 – possibly just before his rival Disraeli's purchase of the Suez Canal shares – he had invested £45,000 in the Ottoman Egyptian Tribute loan of 1871 at a price of just 38.* He had added a further £5,000 by 1878, and a year later invested a further £15,000 in the 1854 Ottoman loan, which was also secured on the Egyptian Tribute. By 1882 these bonds accounted for more than a third of his entire portfolio. Even before

---

* Nineteenth-century bond prices were quoted in percentages of their nominal value. These loans were Turkish bonds secured on the 'tribute' paid annually by Egypt to Turkey.

the military occupation of Egypt, these proved a good investment: the price of the 1871 bonds rose from 38 to 57 in the summer of 1882. The British takeover brought the Prime Minister still greater profits: by December 1882 the price of 1871 bonds had risen to 82. In 1891 they touched 97 – a capital gain of more than 130 per cent on his initial investment in 1875 alone. Small wonder Gladstone once described Turkish state bankruptcy as 'the greatest of all *political* crimes'. And was it entirely without significance that the British Agent and Consul-General in Egypt for nearly a quarter of a century after 1883 was a member of the Baring family – second only to the Rothschilds among City dynasties?

Revulsion against the government's methods of fighting the war mingled with mounting anxiety about the soaring cost of the conflict and dark suspicions about who its beneficiaries might be. The result was a political sea change. The government, now led by Salisbury's nephew, the brilliant but fundamentally frivolous Arthur Balfour, was deeply divided over how best to pay for the war. Fatally, as it proved, Chamberlain seized the moment to argue for a restoration of protectionist tariffs. The idea was to turn the Empire into a Customs Union, with common duties on all imports from outside British territory: Chamberlain's catch-phrase for the scheme was 'Imperial Preference'. The policy had even been tried out during the Boer War, when Canada had been exempted from a small and temporary duty on imported wheat and corn. This was yet another bid to turn the theory of Greater Britain into political practice. But to the majority of British voters it looked more like an attempt to restore the old Corn Laws and put up the price of food. The Liberals' campaign against imperialism – now widely regarded as a term of abuse – culminated in January 1906 with one of the biggest election landslides in British history, when they swept into power with a majority of 243. Chamberlain's vision of a people's Empire seemed to have dissolved in the face of the old, insular fundamentals of British domestic politics: cheap bread plus moral indignation.

Yet if the Liberals hoped they would be able to pay voters an anti-imperial peace dividend they were swiftly disappointed, for a new threat to the security of the Empire was now unmistakably looming. It was not a threat from disaffected subjects – though the gathering storm in Ireland for a time loomed much larger – but from a rival empire just across the North Sea. It was a threat not even the peace-loving Liberals could afford to ignore. And, by a singular irony, it was a threat posed by the one people whom both Cecil Rhodes and Joseph Chamberlain (to say nothing of Karl Pearson) had regarded as the English-speaking race's equals. The Germans.

In 1907 the Foreign Office mandarin Eyre Crowe, who had himself been born in Leipzig, drafted a 'Memorandum on the present state of British relations with France and Germany'. Its stark message was that Germany's desire to play 'on the world's stage a much larger and more dominant part than she finds allotted to herself under the present distribution of material power' might lead her 'to diminish the power of any rivals, to enhance her own [power] by extending her dominion, to hinder the co-operation of other states, and ultimately to break up and supplant the British Empire'.

In the 1880s, when France and Russia had still seemed to be Britain's main imperial rivals, British policy had been to conciliate Germany. But by the early 1900s it was Germany that seemed to pose the biggest threat to the Empire. Crowe's case was not difficult to make. Already the German economy had overtaken the British. In 1870 the German population had been 39 million to Britain's 31 million. By 1913 the figures were 65 to 46 million. In 1870 Britain's GDP had been 40 per cent higher than Germany's. By 1913 Germany's was 6 per cent bigger than Britain's, meaning that Germany's average annual growth rate of per capita GDP had been more than half a percentage point higher. In 1880 Britain's share of world manufacturing production was 23 per cent, Germany's 8 per cent. In 1913 the figures were, respectively, 14 and 15 per cent. Meanwhile, as a result of Admiral Tirpitz's plan to build a North Sea battle fleet, beginning with the naval law of 1898, the German navy was fast becoming the Royal Navy's most dangerous rival. In 1880 the ratio of British to German warship tonnage had been seven to one. By 1914 it was less than two to one.* Above all, the German army dwarfed Britain's by 124 divisions to ten, every single infantry regiment armed with MG08 Maxim guns. Even counting the seven British divisions based in India did little to close this huge gap. In terms of manpower, Britain could expect to mobilize 733,500 men in the event of war; the Germans would have 4.5 million.

The Conservatives and Unionists claimed to have answers to the German question: conscription to match the German army man for man and German-style tariffs to help pay for it. But the new Liberal government rejected both on principle. They retained only two of their predecessors' policies: the commitment to match and, if possible, outstrip German naval construction and the policy of *rapprochement* with France.

In 1904 an 'Entente Cordiale' had been reached with the French on a wide range of colonial issues. At long last, the French acknowledged the British dominance of Egypt, while in return the British offered the French a free hand in Morocco. A few trivial British territories in West Africa were conceded in return for the renunciation of vestigial French fishing claims off Newfoundland. Although with hindsight it might have made more sense to seek such an arrangement with Germany – and indeed Chamberlain himself flirted with the idea in 1899† – at the time the Anglo-French Entente made a good deal of sense. True, there seemed to be a number of potential areas for Anglo-German overseas cooperation, not just in East Africa but also in China and the Pacific as well as in Latin America and the Middle East. Financially, there was close cooperation between British and German banks on railway projects ranging from the Yangtse valley in China to the Delagoa Bay in Mozambique. As Churchill later put it, 'We were no enemies to German colonial expansion.' The German Chancellor himself

---

* The German aim, it should be noted, was partly defensive, and far from irrational given Britain's projected use of a naval blockade in the event of a war with Germany.

† At one point he talked grandly of a 'New Triple Alliance between the Teutonic race and the two great branches of the Anglo-Saxon race'.

said in January 1913 that 'colonial questions of the future point to co-operation with England'.

In strategic terms, however, it was still France and her ally Russia that were Britain's principal rivals overseas; and settling old disputes on the periphery was a way of freeing British resources to meet the growing continental challenge from Germany. As the Assistant Under-Secretary at the Foreign Office, Francis Bertie, said in November 1901, the best argument against an Anglo-German alliance was that if one were concluded 'we [should] never be on decent terms with France, our neighbour in Europe and in many parts of the world, or with Russia, whose frontiers are coterminous with ours or nearly so over a large portion of Asia'. That was the reason Britain backed France against Germany over Morocco in 1905 and again in 1911, despite the fact that formally the Germans were in the right.

Nevertheless, the Liberals' Francophilia, which quickly translated what had been a colonial understanding into an implicit military alliance, was profoundly hazardous in isolation. Without adequate military preparations for the eventuality of a European war, the 'continental commitment' to France made by the Foreign Secretary Sir Edward Grey was indefensibly dangerous. It might conceivably deter Germany from going to war, but if it did not, and Britain were obliged to honour Grey's commitments to the French, what exactly would happen then? Britain retained its naval superiority over Germany; in that arms race the Liberals had not shown weakness. After his move to the Admiralty in October 1911, Churchill even upped the ante by aiming to maintain a new '60 per cent standard ... in relation not only to Germany but to the rest of the world'. 'The Triple Alliance is being outbuilt by the Triple Entente,' he crowed to Grey in October 1913. 'Why', he asked bluntly the following month, 'should it be supposed that we should not be able to defeat [Germany]? A study of the comparative fleet strength in the line of battle will be found reassuring.' Superficially it was. On the eve of war, Britain had forty-seven capital ships (battleships and battle cruisers) to Germany's twenty-nine and enjoyed a similar numerical advantage in virtually every other category of vessel.

Moreover, calculations of the total firepower of the rival navies made the differential between them even larger. But Tirpitz had never aspired to build a fleet bigger than Britain's; just one big enough to ensure 'that, even for the adversary with the greatest sea power, a war against it would involve such dangers as to imperil its position in the world'. A navy between two-thirds and three-quarters the size of the British would, Tirpitz had explained to the Kaiser in 1899, suffice to make Britain 'concede to Your Majesty such a measure of maritime influence which will make it possible for Your Majesty to conduct a great overseas policy'. That had very nearly been achieved by 1914.* And by this time the Germans were producing technically superior battleships.

It was also far from clear that naval superiority would affect the outcome of a continental land war; by the time a British blockade had ground down the German economy, the German army might have been in Paris for months. Even the Committee of Imperial Defence recognized that the only meaningful help that could be offered to France in the event of a war would have to come from the army. Yet in the absence of conscription, as we have seen, the British army was dwarfed by the German; and that was the crux of the matter. The politicians might try to argue that a handful of British divisions could make the difference between a German and a French victory, but in London, Paris and Berlin the soldiers knew it was a lie. The Liberals could credibly have either a commitment to defend France *and* conscription, or a policy of neutrality and no conscription. The combination they preferred – the French commitment but no conscription – was to prove fatal. Kitchener acidly remarked in 1914: 'No one can say my colleagues in the Cabinet are not courageous. They have no Army and they declared war against the mightiest military nation in the world.'

In 1905 a book appeared with the intriguing title of *The Decline and Fall of the British Empire*. It purported to be published in Tokyo in 2005 and envisaged a world in which India was under

---

* To be precise, the German battlefleet was by then two-thirds the size of the British.

Russian rule, South Africa under German rule, Egypt under Turkish rule, Canada under American and Australia under Japanese. This was just one of a veritable library of dystopian fictions published in the decades before the First World War. As time passed, and with the encouragement of Lord Northcliffe, whose *Daily Mail* serialized such works on generous terms, more and more authors dwelt on the potential consequences of a German military threat to the Empire.

There was Headon Hill's *The Spies of Wight* (1899); Erskine Childers' *The Riddle of the Sands* (1903), L. James's *The Boy Galloper* (also 1903); E. Phillips Oppenheim's *A Maker of History* (1905); William Le Queux's *The Invasion of 1910*; Walter Wood's *The Enemy in our Midst* (1906); A. J. Dawson's *The Message* (1907); Le Queux's *Spies of the Kaiser* (1909) and Captain Curties's *When England Slept* (also 1909). In every case, the premise was that the Germans had a malevolent plan to invade England or otherwise overthrow the British Empire. The fear spread down even as far as the readership of the *Boys' Own Paper*. In 1909 the Aldeburgh Lodge school magazine rather wittily imagined how children would be taught in 1930, assuming that England by then would have become merely 'a small island off the western coast of Teutonia'. Even Saki (Hector Hugh Munro) tried his hand at the genre with *When William Came: A Story of London under the Hohenzollerns* (1913).

Imperialist hubris – the arrogance of absolute power – had been and gone, to be replaced by acute fear of decline and sudden fall. Rhodes was dead, Chamberlain dying. The scramble for Africa, those halcyon days of Maxims against the Matabele, suddenly seemed a distant memory. It was the scramble for Europe, now fast approaching, that would determine the fate of the Empire. Baden-Powell's response was to found, in imitation of the earlier Boys' Brigade, the Boy Scouts, the most successful of all the period's attempts to mobilize youth behind the Empire. With its quirky mix of colonial kit and Kipling-esque jargon, the Scout movement offered a distilled and sanitized version of frontier life to generations of bored town-dwellers. Though it was undoubtedly good, clean fun – indeed its appeal soon spread it far beyond the boundaries of the Empire – the political purpose of scouting was made quite explicit in Baden-Powell's best-selling *Scouting for Boys* (1908):

There are always members of Parliament who try to make the Army and Navy smaller, so as to save money. They only want to be popular with the voters of England, so that they and the party to which they belong may get into power. These men are called 'politicians'. They do not look to the good of their country. Most of them know and care very little about our Colonies. If they had had their way before, we should by this time have been talking French, and if they were allowed to have their way in the future, we may as well learn German or Japanese, for we shall be conquered by these.

Yet the Scouts were hardly a match for the Prussian General Staff; a point nicely made in P. G. Wodehouse's *The Swoop! or, How Clarence Saved England* (1909), in which a *Daily Mail*-reading Boy Scout finds the news that Britain has been invaded – by the Germans, the Russians, the Swiss, the Chinese, Monaco, Morocco and 'the Mad Mullah' – relegated to a single paragraph between the cricket scores and the late racing results.

The leaders of international financial capitalism – the Rothschilds in London, Paris and Vienna, the Warburgs in Hamburg and Berlin – insisted that the economic future depended on Anglo-German co-operation, not confrontation. The theorists of British mastery were equally adamant that the future of the world lay in the hands of the Anglo-Saxon race. Yet that hyphen between 'Anglo' and 'Saxon' proved wide enough to prevent a stable relationship between Greater Britain and the new Empire between the Rhine and the Oder. Like so many other things after 1900, imperial nemesis turned out to be made in Germany.

6

Empire for Sale

If we are defeated this time, perhaps we will have better luck next time. For me, the present war is most emphatically only the beginning of a long historical development, at whose end will stand the defeat of England's world position . . . [and] the revolution of the coloured races against the colonial imperialism of Europe.

Field Marshal Colmar von der Goltz, 1915

In the end the sneering yellow faces of young men that met me everywhere, the insults hooted after me when I was at a safe distance, got badly on my nerves . . . [It] was perplexing and upsetting. For at that time I had already made up my mind that imperialism was an evil thing and the sooner I chucked up my job and got out of it the better. Theoretically – and secretly, of course – I was all for the Burmese and all against their oppressors, the British. As for the job I was doing, I hated it more bitterly than I can perhaps make clear . . . But I could get nothing into perspective . . . I did not even know that the British Empire is dying, still less did I know that it is a great deal better than the younger empires that are going to supplant it.

George Orwell, 'Shooting an Elephant'

In the last decade of the Victorian era, an obscure public schoolboy made a prophecy about the British Empire's fate in the coming century:

I can see vast changes coming over a now peaceful world; great upheavals, terrible struggles; wars such as one cannot imagine; and I tell you London will be in danger – London will be attacked and I shall be very prominent in the defence of London ... I see further ahead than you do. I see into the future. The country will be subjected somehow to a tremendous invasion ... but I tell you I shall be in command of the defences of London and I shall save London and the Empire from disaster.

Winston Churchill was just seventeen when he spoke those words to a fellow Harrovian, Murland Evans. They were astonishingly prescient. Churchill did save London, and indeed Britain. But, in the end, not even he could save the British Empire.

Within a single lifetime, that Empire – which had not yet reached its furthest extent when Churchill made his prophecy in 1892 – unravelled. By the time Churchill died in 1965, all its most important parts had gone. Why? Traditional accounts of 'decolonization' tend to give the credit (or the blame) to the nationalist movements within the colonies, from Sinn Fein in Ireland to Congress in India. The end of Empire is portrayed as a victory for 'freedom fighters', who took up arms from Dublin to Delhi to rid their peoples of the yoke of colonial rule. This is misleading. Throughout the twentieth century, the principal threats – and the most plausible alternatives – to British rule were not national independence movements, but other empires.

These alternative empires were significantly harsher in their treatment of subject peoples than Britain. Even before the First World War, Belgian rule in the notionally 'independent' Congo had become a byword for the abuse of human rights. The International Association's rubber plantations and railways were built and operated on the basis of slave labour and the profits flowed directly into the pocket of King Leopold II.* Such was the rapacity of his regime that the cost in human life due to murder, starvation, disease and reduced fertility has been estimated at ten million – half the existing population. There was nothing hyperbolic about Joseph Conrad's

---

* The promenade at Ostend and the golf course at nearby Klemskerke are just two of the fruits of Leopold II's regime there.

portrayal of 'the horror' of this in *Heart of Darkness*. It was in fact two Britons who exposed what was going on in the Congo: the British Consul, Roger Casement; and a humble Liverpool clerk named Edmund Morel, who spotted that immense quantities of rubber were being shipped out of Belgium but virtually no imports except guns were going in. Morel's campaign against the Belgian regime was, he said, 'an appeal addressed to four principles: human pity the world over; British honour; British Imperial responsibilities in Africa; [and] international commercial rights *coincident with and inseparable from native economic and personal liberties*'. True, the British Empire had not treated African slaves in Jamaica much better in the eighteenth century. But the correct comparison must be between these other empires and the British Empire as it was in the twentieth century. On that basis, differences were already manifesting themselves even before the First World War, and not only in comparison with Belgian rule.

The German satirical magazine *Simplicissimus* made the point light-heartedly in 1904 with a cartoon contrasting the different colonial powers. In the German colony even the giraffes and croco-diles are taught to goose-step. In the French, relations between the races are intimate to the point of indecency. In the Congo the natives are simply roasted over an open fire and eaten by King Leopold. But British colonies are conspicuously more complex than the rest. There, the native is force-fed whisky by a businessman, squeezed in a press for every last penny by a soldier and compelled to listen to a sermon by a missionary. In reality, the differences were more profound – and deepening. The French did not behave much better than the Belgians in their part of Congo: popula-tion loss was comparably huge. In Algeria, New Caledonia and Indochina too, there was a policy of systematic expropriation of native land which made a mockery of Gallic rhetoric about uni-versal citizenship. German overseas administration was no more liberal. When the Hereros sought to resist the encroachments of German colonists in 1904, Lieutenant-General Lothar von Trotha issued a proclamation which declared that 'every Herero, whether found with or without a rifle, with or without cattle, will be shot'.

Although this 'annihilation order' (*Vernichtungsbefehl*) was later withdrawn, the Herero population was reduced from around 80,000 in 1903 to just 20,000 in 1906. For this Trotha was awarded the *Pour le Mérite*, the highest German military decoration. The Maji Maji rising in East Africa in 1907 was suppressed with equal harshness.

Nor should the comparisons be confined to West European powers. Japanese colonial rule in Korea – a protectorate from 1905 and a colony directly ruled from Tokyo from 1910 – was conspicuously illiberal. When hundreds of thousands took to the streets to demonstrate in support of Yi Kwang-su's Declaration of Independence, the so-called March First Movement, the Japanese authorities responded brutally. Over 6,000 Koreans were killed, 14,000 were injured, and 50,000 were sentenced to imprisonment. We should also remember the quality of Russian rule in Poland, the Ireland of Central Europe; and in the Caucasus, where it extended as far as Batum on the Black Sea and Astara on the Caspian Sea; in the Central Asian provinces of Turkestan and Turkmenia; and in the Far East, where the new Trans-Siberian Railway conveyed the Tsar's writ all the way to Vladivostok and finally into Manchuria. To be sure, there were resemblances between Russian colonization of the steppe and the roughly contemporaneous colonization of the American prairies. But there were differences too. In their European colonies the Russians pursued aggressive policies of 'russification'; coercion of the Poles was increasing at a time when the British were debating Home Rule for Ireland. In Central Asia, resistance to Russian colonization was dealt with uncompromisingly; a revolt by Muslims in Samarkand and Semirechie in 1916 was bloodily suppressed and the rebel death toll may have reached hundreds of thousands.

Yet all this would pale into insignificance alongside the crimes of the Russian, Japanese, German and Italian empires in the 1930s and 1940s. By the time Churchill became Prime Minister in 1940, the most likely alternatives to British rule were Hirohito's Greater East Asia Co-Prosperity Sphere, Hitler's Thousand Year Reich and Mussolini's New Rome. Nor could the threat posed by Stalin's

Soviet Union be discounted, though until after the Second World War most of his energies were devoted to terrorizing his own subjects. It was the staggering cost of fighting these imperial rivals that ultimately ruined the British Empire. In other words, the Empire was dismantled not because it had oppressed subject peoples for centuries, but because it took up arms for just a few years against far more oppressive empires. It did the right thing, regardless of the cost. And that was why the ultimate, if reluctant, heir of Britain's global power was not one of the evil empires of the East, but Britain's most successful former colony.

Weltkrieg

In 1914 Winston Churchill was First Lord of the Admiralty, the minister responsible for the world's biggest navy. The bold and bumptious war correspondent who had made his reputation covering the triumph of Omdurman and the travesties of the Boer War had entered Parliament in 1901 and, after a brief period on the Conservative backbenches, had crossed the House and risen rapidly to the front rank of the Liberal Party.

No one was more keenly aware than Churchill of the threat to Britain's position of world power posed by Germany. No one was more determined to maintain Britain's naval supremacy, regardless of how many new battleships the Germans built. Yet by 1914, as we have seen, he was confident: in his view, 'naval rivalry had . . . ceased to be a cause of friction' with Germany, since 'it was certain we could not be overtaken'. On colonial questions too there seemed room for Anglo-German compromise, even co-operation. As late as 1911 the assumption among British military planners was that, in the event of a European war, any British Expeditionary Force would be deployed in Central Asia; in other words, it was taken for granted that the foe in such a war would be Russia. Then, in the summer of 1914, a crisis in another empire – in the Austro-Hungarian province of Bosnia-Herzegovina – brought the British and German empires quite suddenly into a calamitous collision.

Like many other statesmen of the time, Churchill was tempted to explain the war as a kind of natural disaster:

[The] nations in those days [were] prodigious organizations of forces . . . which, like planetary bodies, could not approach each other in space without . . . profound magnetic reactions. If they got too near the lightnings would begin to flash, and beyond a certain point they might be attracted altogether from the orbits . . . they were [in] and draw each other into due collision.

In reality, the First World War came about because politicians and generals on both sides miscalculated. The Germans believed (not unreasonably) that the Russians were overtaking them militarily, so they risked a pre-emptive strike before the strategic gap grew any wider.* The Austrians failed to see that stamping on Serbia, useful though that might be in their war against Balkan terrorism, would embroil them in a European-wide conflagration. The Russians overestimated their own military capability almost as much as the Germans did; they also stubbornly ignored the evidence that their political system would crack under the strain of another war so soon after the fiasco of defeat by Japan in 1905. Only the French and the Belgians had no real choice. The Germans invaded them. They had to fight.

The British too had the freedom to err. At the time, the government claimed that intervention was a matter of legal obligation because the Germans had flouted the terms of the 1839 Treaty governing Belgian neutrality, which all the great powers had signed. In fact, Belgium was a useful pretext. The Liberals went to war for two reasons: first, because they feared the consequences of a German victory over France, imagining the Kaiser as a new Napoleon, bestriding the Continent and menacing the Channel coast. That

---

* The Germans acted more out of a sense of weakness than strength. The Chief of the Great General Staff, Helmuth von Moltke, told the State Secretary at the Foreign Office Gottlieb von Jagow in May 1914: 'We must wage a preventive war to conquer our opponents as long as we still have a reasonable chance in this struggle.' Note the doleful phrase 'a reasonable chance'. But Moltke was convinced 'that we would never again find a situation as favourable as now, when neither France nor Russia had completed the extension of their army organizations'.

may or may not have been a legitimate fear; but if it was, then the Liberals had not done enough to deter the Germans, and the Conservatives had been right to press for conscription. The second reason for going to war was a matter of domestic politics, not grand strategy. Since their triumph in 1906, the Liberals had seen their electoral support wither away. By 1914 Herbert Asquith's government was on the verge of collapse. Given the failure of their foreign policy to avert a European war, he and his Cabinet colleagues ought indeed to have resigned. But they dreaded the return to Opposition. More, they dreaded the return of the Conservatives to power. They went to war partly to keep the Tories out.

The familiar images of the First World War are of the 'storm of steel' at the Somme and the muddy hell of Passchendaele. Because the war began in Sarajevo and ended at Versailles, we still tend to think of it as primarily a European conflict. Certainly, the core German war aims were 'Euro-centric': the main objective was to defeat Russia, and the German army's immense sweep through Belgium into northern France was merely a means to that end, designed to protect Germany's back by knocking out or at least badly hurting the Tsar's principal ally. On closer inspection, however, the war was a truly global clash of empires, comparable in its geographical range to Britain's eighteenth-century wars against France, which had ended nearly a century before.

It was the Germans who first spoke of the war as '*der Weltkrieg*', the world war; the British preferred the 'European War' or, later, the 'Great War'. Conscious of their own vulnerability in the war on two fronts in Europe, the Germans sought to globalize the conflict – and divert British resources away from Europe – by undermining their rule in India. The true fulcrum of this new imperial war was supposed to be not Flanders but the gateway to India, the Middle East.

John Buchan's wartime thriller *Greenmantle* is an apparently far-fetched yarn about a German plot to subvert the British Empire by stirring up an Islamic holy war. At first glance, the story is one of Buchan's most fanciful:

'There is a dry wind blowing through the East, and the parched grasses await the spark. And that wind is blowing towards the Indian border. Whence comes that wind, think you? ... Have you an explanation, Hannay?'

... 'It looks as if Islam had a bigger hand in the thing than we thought,' I said.

'You are right ... There is a Jehad [sic] preparing. The question is, How?'

'I'm hanged if I know,' I said; 'but I'll bet it won't be done by a pack of stout German officers in pickelhaubes . . .'

'Agreed ... But supposing they had got some tremendous sacred sanction – some holy thing . . . which will madden the remotest Moslem peasant with dreams of Paradise? What then, my friend?'

'Then there will be hell let loose in those parts pretty soon.'

'Hell which may spread. Beyond Persia, remember, lies India.'

As Hannay's comrade Sandy Arbuthnot discovers, 'Germany could gobble up the French and the Russians whenever they cared, but she was aiming at getting all the Middle East in her hands first, so that she could come out conqueror with the practical control of half the world.' It all sounds perfectly absurd; and the later appearance of two ludicrously caricatured German villains, the sadist von Stumm and the *femme fatale* von Einem, only serves to heighten the comic effect. Yet Buchan was basing his plot on genuine intelligence reports, to which he had privileged access.* Subsequent research has confirmed that the Germans did indeed aim to sponsor an Islamic *jihad* against British imperialism.

Turkey was central to the Germans' global strategy, not least because its capital Istanbul – then known as Constantinople – straddles the Bosphorus, the narrow channel that separates the Mediterranean from the Black Sea and Europe from Asia. In the

---

* At the start of the war Buchan was a war correspondent before joining the army. He served on the Headquarters Staff of the British Army in France as temporary Lieutenant-Colonel and when Lloyd George became Prime Minister was appointed Director of Information (1917–18). He was briefly Director of Intelligence, but had informal access to intelligence information throughout the war.

age of naval power this was one of the world's strategic bottle-necks, not least because it was through the Black Sea Straits that much of Russia's trade was conducted. In time of war, a hostile Turkey could menace not only the flow of supplies to Russia but also Britain's imperial lines of communication to India. For these reasons, the Germans had worked hard to secure Turkey as an ally in the years before 1914. Kaiser Wilhelm II had visited Constantinople twice, in 1889 and 1898. Since 1888 the Deutsche Bank had played a leading role in the financing of the so-called Berlin-Baghdad Railway.* The Germans also offered their military expertise. Between 1883 and 1896 the German general Colmar von der Goltz was employed by the Sultan to overhaul the Ottoman army. Another German, Otto Liman von Sanders, was appointed the army's Inspector General in 1913.

On 30 July 1914, even before the Turks had finally committed themselves to fight alongside Germany, the Kaiser was already planning the next move in characteristically intemperate terms:

Our consuls in Turkey, in India, agents . . . must fire the whole Mohammedan world to fierce rebellion against this hated, lying, conscienceless nation of shopkeepers, for if we are to bleed to death, England shall at least lose India.

In November 1914 the Turkish sultan, the spiritual head of all Sunni Muslims, duly responded to German prompting by declaring a holy war on Britain and her allies. Given that just under half of the world's 270 million Muslims were under British, French or Russian rule, this could have been a masterstroke of German strategy. Just as the Germans hoped, the British responded to the

---

* Though there was already a railway connection between Berlin and Constantinople (via Vienna), the Sultan's aim was to extend the line across Anatolia via Ankara to Baghdad. The German bankers only really wanted to build the line to Ankara but in 1899 were forced into going on to Baghdad by the Kaiser. They then sought to make the line profitable by extending it to Basra. There had been considerable British suspicion of the project, but it cannot be regarded as a cause of the war. In fact a deal had been struck on the very eve of the war giving the Germans the right to extend the line to Basra in return for letting the British lead the exploitation of the Mesopotamian oilfields.

Turkish threat by diverting men and materiel away from the Western Front to Mesopotamia (present-day Iraq) and the Dardanelles.

The German General Staff had gone to war without giving much thought to Britain. By comparison with their vast army, the British Expeditionary Force sent to France was indeed, as the Kaiser said, 'contemptibly' small. Henry Wilson, the Director of Military Operations from 1910, candidly admitted that six divisions were 'fifty too few'. However, Germany was fighting not just the British Army but the 'Greater Britain' that ruled over a quarter of the world. The British response to the German declaration of world war was to mobilize her imperial forces on an unprecedented scale.

Symbolically, the first shots fired on land by British troops, on 12 August 1914, were aimed at the German wireless station at Kamina in Togoland. Soon the fighting spread to all Germany's African colonies (Togoland, the Cameroons, South-West Africa and East Africa). Though it is often forgotten, the First World War was as 'total' in Africa as resources permitted it to be. In the absence of extensive railways and reliable beasts of burden, there was only one solution to the problem of logistics: men. Over 2 million Africans served in the First World War, nearly all as carriers of supplies, weapons and wounded, and although they were far from the fields of Flanders, these forgotten auxiliaries had as hellish a time as the most exposed front-line troops in Europe. Not only were they underfed and overworked; once removed from their usual locales they were every bit as susceptible to disease as their white masters. Roughly a fifth of all Africans employed as carriers died, many of them the victims of the dysentery that ravaged all colonial armies in the tropics. In East Africa 3,156 whites in British service died in the line of duty; of these less than a third were victims of enemy action. But if black troops and carriers are included, total losses were over 100,000.

The familiar rationale of white rule in Africa was that it conferred the benefits of civilization. The war made a mockery of that claim. 'Behind us we leave destroyed fields, ransacked magazines and, for the immediate future, starvation,' wrote Ludwig Deppe, a doctor in the German East African Army. 'We are no longer the agents of culture; our track is marked by death, plundering and evacuated villages, just like the progress of our own and enemy armies in the Thirty Years War.'

The key to British world power was supposed to be the Royal Navy. Its performance in the war was disappointing. It proved unable to destroy the German navy in the North Sea; the one full-scale encounter between the surface fleets, at Jutland, was one of military history's great draws. Partly this was because of technical backwardness. Although Churchill had converted the navy from coal to oil before the war began, the British lagged behind the Germans in the accuracy of their gunnery, not least because the Admiralty had refused to adopt the range-adjusting system known as the Argo clock, which compensated for a ship's rolling. The Germans also enjoyed superiority in wireless communications, though they tended to broadcast 'in clear' or in easily crackable codes. The Royal Navy, by contrast, stuck to Nelson-era semaphore signals, impossible for the enemy to read at a distance but not much easier for the intended recipient to decipher.

However, the Navy did succeed in inflicting immense disruption on German sea-borne commerce outside the Baltic. Not only was the German merchant marine ruthlessly mopped up within a matter of months of the war's outbreak; under the Orders in Council of March 1915, even the ships of neutrals suspected of carrying supplies to Germany were liable to be boarded, searched and, if contraband was found, ransacked. Although these tactics caused irritation abroad, the German response of unrestricted submarine warfare caused much more, especially when the British liner *Lusitania* was sunk without warning with more than 100 American passengers on board. Admittedly, for a time in the spring of 1917 it seemed as if unrestricted submarine attacks would fatally impede British imports of food – in the month of April, one in four vessels leaving British ports was sunk. But the rediscovery of the convoy system, familiar to the Admiralty in Nelson's day, swung the sea war back in Britain's favour.

Much more impressive was the British Empire's military capability on land. Fully a third of the troops Britain raised during the First World War were colonial. The most celebrated contributions came from the furthest flung colonies of all. New Zealand sent 100,000 men and women (as nurses) overseas, a tenth of the entire population. At the very outbreak of the war, Andrew Fisher, the Scottish-born leader of the Australian Labour Party, pledged 'our last man and last shilling in defence of the mother country'. The initial rush of volunteers was impressive, though it is significant that a very high proportion of Australian volunteers had been born in Britain (the same was true of Canadian volunteers) and conscription was later rejected in two referenda. J. D. Burns of Melbourne captured the mood of effulgent loyalty that swept through these first-generation immigrants:

> The bugles of England are blowing o'er the sea,
> Calling out across the years, calling now to me.
> They woke me from dreaming, in the dawning of the day,
> The bugles of England: and how could I stay?

Though at first the British commanders were reluctant to rely on colonial troops, they soon came to appreciate their quality. The Australians in particular ranked alongside the Scottish Highland regiments when it came to ferocity in battle: the 'Diggers' were as much feared by the other side as the 'devils in skirts'.

Perhaps the supreme symbol of the imperial war effort was the Imperial Camel Corps, formed in 1916. Although Australians and New Zealanders accounted for around three-quarters of its entire strength, there were also troops from Hong Kong and Singapore, volunteers from the Rhodesian Mounted Police, a South African mining prospector who had fought against the British in the Boer War, a fruit grower from the Canadian Rockies and a pearl fisherman from Queensland.

Yet it would be a mistake to think that the imperial contribution to the war effort came primarily from the white Dominions. At the outbreak of war, the man who would become India's most famous political and spiritual leader told his fellow countrymen: 'We are, above all, British citizens of the Great British Empire. Fighting as the British are at present in a righteous cause for the good and glory of human dignity and civilisation . . . our duty is clear: to do our best to support the British, to fight with our life and property.' Many thousands of Indians shared Gandhi's sentiments. In the autumn of 1914, around a third of British forces in France were from India; by the end of the war more than a million Indians had served overseas, almost as many as came from the four white Dominions put together. 'The fighting is strange,' wrote Signaller Kartar Singh to his brother from the Western Front. 'On the ground, under the ground, in the sky and in the sea, everywhere. This is rightly called the war of kings. It is the work of men of great intelligence.' As that suggests, the Indians were not reluctant conscripts; they were in fact all volunteers, and enthusiastic volunteers at that. As Kartar Singh explained:

We shall never get another chance to exalt the name of race, country, ancestors, parents, village and brothers, and to prove our loyalty to the government . . . There will never be such a fierce fight . . . Food and clothing, all is of the best; there is no shortage. Motors convey the rations right up to the trenches . . . We go singing as we march and care nothing that we are going to die.

It was not just public schoolboys raised on Horace and Moore who believed '*dulce et decorum est pro patria mori*'. True, there were three mutinies by Muslim soldiers in Iraq who refused to fight their co-religionists (further evidence that the plot of *Greenmantle* had substance to it). But these were the exception to a rule of loyalty and conspicuous valour.*

Only when they were ill treated did colonial troops question the legitimacy of the demands the Empire made on them. The men of the British West Indies Regiment, for example, resented the fact that they were used primarily for the hazardous but inglorious task of ammunition carrying. Plainly, little respect was paid to them by British officers; as a Trinidadian sergeant complained in 1918: 'We

---

* One of the most successful actions at the Somme was the Secunderabad Brigade's attack at Morlancourt.

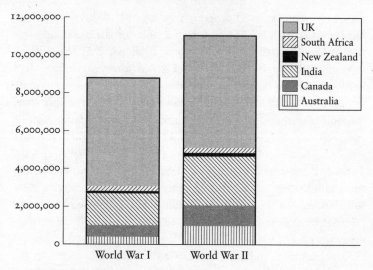

Total men mobilized by the British Empire in the two World Wars

are treated neither as Christians nor British Citizens, but as West Indian "Niggers", without anybody to be interested in or look after us. Instead of being drawn closer to Church and Empire we are driven away from it.' Yet not dissimilar grumbles could have been heard in nearly every part of the British Expeditionary Force* – a thoroughly multinational enterprise which, unlike its Habsburg and Russian counterparts, somehow endured despite profound ethnic divisions and frequently lamentable leadership.

The Australians and New Zealanders are often said (especially by their descendants) to have provided the best fighting men on the British side during the First World War. It was at Gallipoli that they were first put to the test.

There were always two Gallipoli campaigns: a naval operation to break through the Turkish defences in the Dardanelles, and a military operation to land troops on the Gallipoli peninsula itself. If

---

* The Australian Frederic Manning's semi-autobiographical novel *Middle Parts of Fortune* captured the equally disgusted mood among ordinary English soldiers at the Somme.

they had been combined properly they might have been successful; but they never were. The man responsible for the naval side was none other than Churchill, who was confident that the Turkish forts along the Straits could be knocked out 'after two or three days hard action'. Not for the last time in his long career, he was looking for an easy way to win a European war. Not for the last time, the 'soft underbelly' of the enemy turned out to be harder than he expected. In fact, the naval attack on the Dardanelles nearly worked. Twice – on 3 November 1914 and 19 February 1915 – the Turkish forts were badly damaged by Allied bombardments. On the second occasion, a force of sailors and marines was successfully landed. But then there was needless delay, followed by disaster on 18 March when three ships were sunk as a result of careless minesweeping.

Kitchener then decided that the job should be taken over by the army. Five weeks later, in an amphibious operation that resembled a dress rehearsal for D-Day in the next world war, 129,000 troops were landed on beaches around the peninsula. The men of the Australian and New Zealand Army Corps – Anzacs for short – were only part of a huge Allied force which included British regulars and untried Territorials, Gurkhas and even French colonial troops from Senegal. The idea was simple: to establish coastal bridgeheads and then march to Constantinople itself, a hundred miles to the north-east. Churchill (always fond of casinos) privately admitted it was the 'biggest coup' he had ever played for. It was a gamble that would ultimately cost over a quarter of a million Allied casualties.

At dawn on 25 April the Australians and New Zealanders waded ashore at the crescent shaped beach on the west side of the peninsula known henceforth as 'Anzac Cove'. Probably because of the strong currents, they were disembarked about a mile too far north. However, the Turks – among them the future president Mustafa Kemal – were quick to get to the scene and soon the disembarking troops came under a lethal hail of rifle fire and shrapnel. Five hundred Anzacs died on the first day alone; two and a half thousand were wounded. Although there is evidence that some of the troops panicked when they first came under fire, the real problem was simply the terrain, for Anzac Cove is surrounded by a natural wall of soft brown stone with only scrub for cover. The men down on the beach made easy targets for the Turkish snipers. As you climb up the hill today, you can still see the lines of the trenches: the Anzacs' hastily hacked out from the sun-baked earth, the Turks' carefully prepared to German specifications.

Among the Australian infantrymen were two brothers, Alex and Sam Weingott from Annandale, a suburb of Sydney, sons of a successful Jewish clothes manufacturer who had fled persecution in Russian Poland to make a new life in the British Empire. Alex, the elder, was killed within a week, but Sam survived the initial onslaught. The journal he kept is by no means a great work of war literature, but it vividly conveys the intensity of the fighting at Anzac Cove: the proximity of the enemy, the lethal effect of shrapnel and the terrifying brevity of life at the front line.

Sunday 25th April
Arrived at the Gallipoli Peninsula at 5 o'clock am when the battleships opened heavy fire on the enemy. Engaged the Turks from 12 o'clock noon Sun. till daybreak Monday. Elbow grazed by shrapnel. Our fellows suffer heavy casualties.

Monday 26th April
. . . Engage the enemy the whole day. Their guns do awful damage. The biggest majority of our chaps seem to be wiped out.

Friday 30th April
. . . Keep up heavy fire during the day. Snipers still keep going and bag a lot of chaps on the beach. An Indian caught one and [it] cut his head off.

Wednesday 5th May
Went into the firing line at 7 o'clock am and came out at 1 o'clock pm. Had a merry time with the enemy and fired close on 250 shots myself. Enemy do heavy damage with shrapnel and I narrowly miss getting hit with the cap of a shell. Heavy shrapnel fire continues during the day. Turks have a good range. Went into the trenches at 2 am. Kept going all the time. Dead bodies outside the trench begin to smell.

Monday 17th May
Enemy keeps up heavy gun fire and the aim is very accurate. Mate of mine shot through the heart whilst asleep . . . Shell explodes in our trench, killing or seriously wounding Captain Hill.

Tuesday 18th May
Turks give us an awful time. Shift tons of earth. Terrible sights. Men along side of me blown to pieces. Over 50 shells fired. Great moral effect on the troops. Many loose [*sic*] their nerves. Trenches blown to pieces. Work all night fixing them up.

Saturday 29th May
Tremendous bombardment by the enemy guns commencing at 3 o'clock am. They fire at point blank doing great damage to our trenches. One shell burst in my face and although unwounded was knocked out for a few minutes. My rifle was twisted beyond recognition. Put off for the rest of the day.

Tuesday 1st June
Artillery kept busy. Engineers blew up a portion of the enemy's trenches . . . Mortars do a great deal of damage during the night. Appointed Lance Corporal in charge of a section and I feel very proud.

Wednesday 2nd June
Overheard Lieut. Lloyd say that I would make a good N.C.O. as I wasn't at all afraid. Enemy's artillery fairly busy.

That was one of Sam Weingott's last diary entries. Three days later he was shot in the stomach. He died on a hospital ship within a few hours of being evacuated.

Despite an attempted breakout in August, the Anzacs simply could not overcome tenacious Turkish defence of the high ground. And it was much the same story wherever the Allied forces attacked. Frontal infantry assaults were simply suicidal if the Navy's gunners could not knock out Turkish machine guns and artillery. The stalemate was soon obviously as complete as on the Western Front – 'ghastly trench warfare' as the luckless British commander-in-chief Sir Ian Hamilton called it – while the problems of supply and sanitation were far worse. Amid bitter recriminations and buck-passing, Churchill pleaded for more time. On 21 May he wrote to Asquith: 'Let me stand or fall by the Dardanelles – but do not take it from my hands.' Asquith replied bluntly: 'You must take it as settled that you are not to remain at the Admiralty.' Fobbed off with the Duchy of Lancaster, Churchill's political career seemed to be at an end. His wife Clementine thought he would 'never get over the Dardanelles'; it seemed for a time he might even 'die of grief'.*

The folk memory of Gallipoli is of brave Diggers led to their deaths by effete and incompetent 'Pom' officers. It is a caricature, though one that has a grain of truth. The real point was that the British Empire had picked on what it thought was a defunct Oriental despotism, and lost. Well schooled by their German allies, the Turks had been quicker to learn the new techniques of trench warfare. And their morale was also excellent, a combination of 'Young Turk' nationalism and Islamic fervour. Hasan Ethem was a soldier in the 57th regiment of Kemal's 19th Division. On 17 April 1915 he wrote to his mother:

My God, all that these heroic soldiers want is to introduce Thy name to the French and English. Please accept this honourable desire of ours and make our bayonets sharper, so that we may destroy our enemy. You have already destroyed a great number of them, so destroy some more. After praying thus, I stood up. No one could be considered luckier and happier than I after that.

If God wills, the enemy will make a landing and we will be taken to the front lines, then the wedding ceremony [the martyr's union with Allah] will take place, won't it?

Like the mutinies by Indian troops in Iraq, the zeal of Turkish troops at Gallipoli suggested that the German strategy of holy war might be working.

Everywhere it was tried, the frontal assault on Turkish power failed. Despite its initial success in taking Basra and advancing up the Tigris towards Baghdad, the Indian Army's invasion of Mesopotamia ended in disaster when General Charles Townshend's

* In fact he was back in government (as Minister of Supply) just two years later.

army of 9,000 men – two-thirds of them Indian – were besieged for five months at Kut el Amara. Despite attempts at relief, Townshend was forced to surrender.* Yet the British were not slow to devise a new Middle Eastern strategy in the wake of these débâcles. It emerged in a form almost as fantastic as the German plan for an Islamic *jihad* against the British Empire. The idea was to incite a revolt against Turkish rule by the desert-dwelling Arab tribes, under the leadership of the Sharif of Mecca, Husayn ibn Ali. The man who came to be most closely identified with this new strategy was an eccentric Oxford historian turned undercover agent – an archaeologist, a linguist, a skilled cartographer and an intuitive guerrilla fighter, but also a masochistic homosexual who yearned for fame, only to spurn it when it came. This was T. E. Lawrence, illegitimate son of an Irish baronet and his nanny; a flamboyant Orientalist who delighted in wearing Arab dress, a man who made no secret (or did he just dream?) of having been raped by Turkish guards when briefly taken prisoner at Dera'a. His affinity with the Arabs was to prove invaluable.

Lawrence's aim was to break the Ottoman Empire from within, by stirring up Arab nationalism into a new and potent force that he believed could trump the German-sponsored holy war. For centuries Turkish rule over the sandy wastes of Arabia had been resented and sporadically challenged by the nomadic tribes of the region. By adopting their language and dress, Lawrence set out to turn their discontent to Britain's advantage. As liaison officer to Husayn's son Faysal from July 1916, he argued strongly against deploying British troops in the Hejaz. The Arabs had to feel they were fighting for their own freedom, Lawrence argued, not for the privilege of being ruled by the British instead of the Turks. His ambition, he wrote, was

that the Arabs should be our first brown dominion, and not our last brown colony. Arabs react against you if you try to drive them, and they are

---

* The subsequent neglect and high mortality of Townshend's force was a scandal that led to the resignation of Austen Chamberlain as Secretary of State for India, though the fault lay with his subordinates' misguided parsimony.

as tenacious as Jews; but you can lead them without force anywhere, if nominally arm-in-arm. The future of Mesopotamia is so immense that if it is cordially ours we can swing the whole Middle East with it.

It worked. With Lawrence's support, the Arabs waged a highly effective guerrilla warfare against Turkish communications along the Hejaz railway from Medina to Aqaba. By the autumn of 1917 they were probing Turkish defences in Syria as General Edmund Allenby's army marched from Sinai towards Jerusalem itself. On 9 December Allenby invited Lawrence to join him as, with becoming humility, he entered the Holy City on foot through the ancient Jaffa Gate ('How could it be otherwise, *where One had walked before*?'). It was a sublime moment. After three long years of military reverses, here at last was a proper victory with all the desired trimmings: cavalry charges, fleeing foes and a dashing young hero in the vanguard. To the romantically inclined, the fact that Jerusalem was in Christian hands recalled the Crusades – even if the story in the officers' mess was that the surrender of the city was initially accepted by a cockney cook, who had got up early to find some eggs for breakfast.*

By the late summer of 1918 it was clear that the Kaiser's strategy of global war had foundered. In the end it was not so much that *Greenmantle* was fiction; it was that the German strategy lacked realism. Like the plan to send 50,000 Turkish troops to mobilize the Kuban Cossacks under an Austrian officer who happened to be the brother of the Metropolitan of Halyc, or the equally mad bid by the ethnographer Leo Frobenius to win over Lij Yasu, the Emperor of Abyssinia, the *Weltkrieg* was simply unworkable. What the Germans needed were men like Lawrence, human chameleons with the ability to penetrate non-European cultures. But to produce such men requires centuries of Oriental engagement. Typical of the amateurism of the Germans overseas was their expedition

---

* He is supposed to have said, on being handed the keys to the city: 'I don't want yer city. I want some heggs for my hofficers!'

to the Emir of Afghanistan, the fifteen members of which travelled via Constantinople equipped with copies of a Victorian world atlas and disguised as a travelling circus. Small wonder the anti-British *jihad* had done no more than temporarily stiffen Turkish resolve; small wonder that Arab nationalism proved to be the more powerful force.

The First World War was a truly global conflagration. But in the end it was decided in Western Europe. The Austrians won the war they had wanted against Serbia. The Germans also won the war they had wanted, against Russia. They also defeated Romania. On the other hand, the British and French succeeded in beating the Ottoman Empire, not to mention Bulgaria. Even the Italians eventually defeated Austria. None of it was decisive. The only way to end the war was in Flanders and France. There the Germans made one last bid for victory in the spring of 1918, but when those offensives petered out defeat was inevitable and the morale of the German army – so resilient up until this point – began at last to wilt. At the same time, the British Expeditionary Force, having spent four bloody years trying to grasp mass warfare on land, finally ascended its learning curve. With the return of mobility to the Western Front, proper co-ordination of infantry, artillery and air power was at last achieved. In May and June 1918 fewer than 3,000 German prisoners had been taken by British forces. In July, August and September, the number shot up to more than 90,000. On 29 September the German High Command, fearful of a rout, demanded an armistice, leaving the dirty work of negotiating surrender to the hitherto impotent German parliamentarians.

Partly for that reason, many Germans failed to understand why they had lost the war. They sought responsibility within Germany, pinning the blame on one another (the incompetent militarists or the November criminals, according to taste). The reality was that German defeat was exogenous, not endogenous: it was the inevitable result of trying to fight a global conflict without being a global power. Considering the vast differential between the resources of the two empires, the only real puzzle is that it took the British Empire so long to win.

At Versailles, where the peace conference was held, there was much talk, inspired by the American President Woodrow Wilson, of a new international order based on self-determination and collective security. However, when all had been drafted and signed, it looked like just another version of the familiar old story: to the victor the spoils. As the historian H. A. L. Fisher put it, the peace treaties draped 'the crudity of conquest' in 'the veil of morality'.

Despite Lawrence's wartime promises to the Arabs, it was agreed to give Iraq, Transjordan and Palestine the status of British 'mandates' – the euphemism for colonies – while the French got Syria and the Lebanon.* The former German colonies of Togoland, Cameroon and East Africa were added to the British possessions in Africa. In addition, South-West Africa went to South Africa, Western Samoa to New Zealand and northern New Guinea, along with the Bismarck Archipelago and the northern Solomons, to Australia. Phosphate-rich Nauru was shared between the two Australasian dominions and Britain. So now even the colonies had colonies. In all, around 1.8 million square miles were added to the Empire and around 13 million new subjects; as the Foreign Secretary Arthur Balfour complacently noted, the map of the world had 'yet more red on it'. The Secretary of State for India, Edwin Montagu, commented dryly that he would like to hear some arguments against Britain's annexing the whole world. A year later, as if to prove the point, the Colonial Secretary Leo Amery laid claim to all of Antarctica.

By allying with the Turks, the Germans had made the Middle East a theatre of the war. The result had been to hand the Middle East to Britain. Already before the war, Aden, Egypt, the

---

* Under the wartime Sykes-Picot agreement, which Lawrence furiously disavowed. He told Faysal he 'intended to stick to them through thick and thin if necessary to fight against the French for the recovery of Syria'.

Sudan, Cyprus, Northern Somaliland, the Trucial States as well as Muscat, Oman, Kuwait and Qatar had been brought directly or indirectly under British influence. Now the mandates had been added without, as one official put it, 'the official pantomime known as "declaring a protectorate" '. Moreover, British influence was growing over the Pahlavi monarchy in Persia, thanks to the majority British shareholding in the Anglo-Persian Oil Company (later British Petroleum). As an Admiralty memorandum of 1922 put it: 'From the strategical point of view the essential thing is that Great Britain should control the territories on which the oil is situated.' Although at this time the Middle East accounted for only 5 per cent of world output, the British were empire-building with the future in mind.

Nor were these territorial prizes considered sufficient. In 1914 Germany had been Britain's principal rival at sea. The war, the armistice and the peace treaty between them annihilated Germany as a marine power. The British grabbed all they could of both the German navy and merchant fleet. Despite the fact that the Germans scuttled the former at Scapa Flow rather than hand it over, the result was an astonishing naval preponderance. Counting only Dreadnoughts and subsequent models, Britain had forty-two capital ships afloat, against the rest of the world's total of forty-four. The United States was second with just sixteen.

It is well known that at Versailles the decision was taken to make Germany liable for the costs not just of war damage but also of wartime pensions and separation allowances; hence the huge scale of the reparations bill subsequently presented. It is less well known – because the British later tried to blame the French – that this was done largely at the insistence of the Australian Prime Minister William M. Hughes, who discerned that his country would gain nothing if a narrow definition of reparations were adopted. A bombastic Welshman who had emigrated to Australia in his early twenties, Hughes brought to the peace-making process all the refinement of the Sydney waterfront, where he had won his political spurs as a trade union organizer. The Kaiser, he declared, might have led Germany, but she followed not only willingly, but eagerly. Upon the shoulders of all classes and all sections lies the guilt. They were drunk with bestial passion, with the hope of world conquest – Junker, merchant, and workman, all hoped to share in the loot. Upon the German nation, then, rests the responsibility for the war, and she must pay the penalty of her crime.

Perhaps the most vivid expression of the triumphalist post-war mood is Sigismund Goetze's grandiose allegorical mural 'Britannia Pacifatrix' commissioned by the Foreign Office and completed in 1921. Britannia stands resplendent in Roman helmet and red robe, flanked to her left by four clean-cut, Adonis-like figures representing the white dominions, and to her right by her somewhat more exotic allies, France, the United States and (once the fount of their strange republican form of government) Greece. At Britannia's feet, the children of the vanquished enemy prostrate themselves, repentant. Scarcely visible beneath the knees of the great white gods is a little black boy carrying a basket of fruit – presumably to represent Africa's contribution to victory.

Yet there was an illusory quality to Britannia's victorious peace. True, the Empire had never been bigger. But nor had the costs of victory, by comparison with which the economic value of these new territories was negligible, if not negative. No combatant power spent as much on the war as Britain, whose total expenditure amounted to just under £10 billion. That was a steep price to pay even for a million square miles, especially as they generally cost more to govern than they yielded in revenue. The cost of running Iraq, to give just one example, amounted in 1921 to £23 million, more than the total UK health budget.

Before 1914, the benefits of Empire had seemed to most people, on balance, to outweigh the costs. After the war the costs suddenly, inescapably, outweighed the benefits.

Doubts

For most of the twentieth century, the twin concrete towers of Wembley Stadium were the supreme architectural symbol of English football, home of the annual Football Association Cup Final. Originally, however, they were built as a symbol of British imperialism.

The British Empire Exhibition was opened by King George V on 23 April 1924. It was intended as a popular celebration of Britain's global achievement, an affirmation that the Empire had more than just a glorious past but a future too, and in particular an economic future. The official guide was quite explicit about the Exhibition's purpose; it was

To find, in the development and utilization of the raw materials of the Empire, new sources of Imperial wealth. To foster inter-Imperial trade and open fresh world markets for Dominion and home products. To make the different races of the British Empire better known to each other, and to demonstrate to the people of Britain the almost illimitable possibilities of the Dominions, Colonies, and Dependencies together.

To mark the occasion, the drab suburban streets were renamed by Rudyard Kipling after imperial heroes like Drake. But the tone of the event was set by the stadium itself. The fact that it was made of concrete and looked hideous was in itself a bold statement of modernity. The opening of the exhibition was also the occasion of the first royal radio broadcast.

By one measure it was a great success. More than 27 million people flocked to the 200-acre site; indeed, the exhibition was so popular that it had to be reopened in 1925. On Empire Day itself, more than 90,000 people crowded into the stadium for a service of thanksgiving – not quite as many as had watched Bolton Wanderers play West Ham United the year before (127,000), but a large turnout nonetheless. Visitors could marvel at an equestrian statue of the Prince of Wales made entirely out of Canadian butter. They could witness the Zulu Wars, which were spectacularly re-enacted inside the stadium. They could ride from pavilion to pavilion aboard the somewhat hopefully named 'Neverstop Train'. Wherever they looked there were tangible examples of the Empire's continuing vitality – above all, its economic vitality.

The irony was that, despite a government subsidy of £2.2. million, the Exhibition made a loss of over £1.5 million, in marked contrast to the profitable pre-1914 exhibitions. Indeed, in this respect, there were those who saw unnerving parallels between the Empire Exhibition and the Empire itself. Perhaps even more worryingly, the exhibition became something of a national joke. In a story for the *Saturday Evening Post*, P. G. Wodehouse sent his most famous creation, Bertie Wooster, to visit Wembley with his friend Biffy. Preoccupied as they were with the latter's difficulties with a girl, both soon tired of the worthy but dull attractions:

By the time we had tottered out of the Gold Coast and were working towards the Palace of Machinery, everything pointed to my shortly executing a quiet sneak in the direction of the rather jolly Planter's Bar in the West Indian section ... I have never been in the West Indies, but I am in a position to state that in certain of the fundamentals of life they are streets ahead of our European civilization. The man behind the counter, as kindly a bloke as I ever wish to meet, seemed to guess our requirements the moment we hove into view. Scarcely had our elbows touched the wood before he was leaping to and fro, bringing down a new bottle with each leap. A planter, apparently, does not consider he has had a drink unless it contains at least seven ingredients, and I'm not saying, mind you, that he isn't right.

The man behind the bar told us the things were called Green Swizzles; and, if ever I marry and have a son, Green Swizzle Wooster is the name that will go down in the register, in memory of the day his father's life was saved at Wembley.

Billy Bunter of the *Magnet* was another visitor, as was Noël Coward ('I've brought you here to see the wonders of the Empire, and all you want to do is go to the Dodgems'). In *Punch,* H. M. Bateman's cartoon asked simply: 'Do you Wemble?'

Before the 1920s the British had been remarkably good at not 'wembling' – at taking their Empire seriously. That in itself was an important source of imperial strength. Many a heroic deed was done simply because it was what a white man in authority was expected to do. As an assistant superintendent in Burma in the 1920s, George Orwell found himself having to shoot a rogue elephant 'solely to avoid looking a fool':

I was not thinking particularly of my own skin, only of the watchful yellow faces behind. For at that moment, with the crowd watching me, I was not afraid in the ordinary sense, as I would have been if I had been alone. A white man mustn't be frightened in front of 'natives'; and so, in general, he isn't frightened. The sole thought in my mind was that if anything went wrong those two thousand Burmans would see me pursued, caught, trampled on and reduced to a grinning corpse like that Indian up the hill. And if that happened it was quite probable that some of them would laugh. That would never do.

Eric Blair, as he was known then, could scarcely have been better prepared for his task. He had been born in Bengal, the son of a civil servant in the Opium Department, and had been educated at Eton. Yet even he now found it hard to play the role of world policeman with a straight face.

Orwell was far from unique. All over the Empire, a generation was quietly cracking. Leonard Woolf, husband of the novelist Virginia Woolf, had joined the Ceylon civil service in 1904 and was sent to govern a thousand square miles up-country. He had resigned even before the war, convinced of 'the absurdity of a people of one civilization and mode of life trying to impose its rule upon an entirely different civilization and mode of life'. The most an imperial administrator could hope to do, he concluded, was to

prevent people from killing one another or robbing one another, or burning down the camp, or getting cholera or plague or smallpox, and if one can manage to get one night's sleep in three, one is fairly satisfied . . . Out there . . . things happen slowly, inexorably by fate, and you – you don't do things, you watch with the three hundred millions.

As a young man, Francis Younghusband had crossed the Gobi Desert, witnessed the Jameson Raid and in 1904 led the first British expedition to the Dalai Lama's court at Lhasa. By 1923, however, he had been converted to the idea of free love and had taken to referring to himself as Svabhava, 'a follower of the Gleam'; four years later, he produced a book entitled *Life in the Stars: An Exposition of the View that on Some Planets of some Stars exist Beings higher than Ourselves, and on one a World-Leader, the Supreme Embodiment of the Eternal Spirit which animates the Whole*. Erskine Childers is remembered today for his scaremongering thriller *The Riddle of the Sands*. Yet this veteran of the Boer War ran guns from Germany to the Irish Volunteers in 1914, acted as secretary to the Irish delegation in the Treaty negotiations of 1921 and finally faced a firing squad for siding with the extreme Republicans in the Irish Civil War.

An especially strange case was that of Harry St John Bridger Philby. The son of a Ceylon coffee planter, Philby was another man with all the makings of a *Boys' Own Paper* imperial hero: a King's Scholar at Westminster, an outstanding First at Trinity, Cambridge, a place in the Indian Civil Service. Philby's feats in the Middle East during and after the First World War were overshadowed only by those of Lawrence. Yet by obsessively backing the claims of Ibn Saud to supremacy in post-Ottoman Arabia, Philby went against the official line in Whitehall, which was to support Lawrence's nominee King Husayn. In 1921 Philby resigned from government service on the point of being dismissed. By 1930 he had converted to Islam and was assiduously serving the interests of Ibn Saud, who had by now ousted Husayn. The culmination of Philby's defection was his successful negotiation of the vital 1933 deal between the Saudis and Standard Oil, which ensured America's later predominance over Britain in the Arab oil fields. His son, the Soviet spy Kim Philby, later recalled that under his father's influence he was 'a godless little anti-imperialist' even before he reached his teens. Loss of faith in Empire often went hand in hand with loss of faith in God.

Even Lawrence himself, the hero of the Desert War, had a

breakdown. Having been turned into a celebrity by the American impresario Lowell Thomas, whose film *With Allenby in Palestine* opened at Covent Garden in August 1919, Lawrence fled the limelight, first to All Souls and then, more obscurely, to an RAF base at Uxbridge, where he adopted the pseudonym Ross. Having been discharged from the air force, he enlisted in the Tank Corps under the name Shaw, in honour of his new and most unlikely mentor, the maverick playwright George Bernard Shaw. To avoid the stir caused by the publication of the abridged *Seven Pillars of Wisdom*, Lawrence rejoined the RAF and was posted to Karachi, before retiring to Dorset. He was killed in a meaningless motorcycle accident in 1935.

If heroes like these had doubts, it was no wonder that those with little experience of the Empire had them too. E. M. Forster had travelled in India only briefly when he accepted the job of private secretary to the Maharaja of Dewas in 1921. The experience inspired *A Passage to India* (1924), perhaps the most influential literary indictment of the British in India, in which priggish young men say things like 'We're not out here for the purpose of behaving pleasantly' and prim young ladies complain about 'always facing the footlights'. Though his knowledge was acquired from mere tourism, Somerset Maugham delighted in the cracks in the façade of mastery, like the episode in 'The Door of Opportunity', in which a single act of cowardice up-country costs a man both his career and his wife. Here was the key question: 'So you realize that . . . you have covered the Government with ridicule . . . [and] made yourself a laughing-stock in the whole colony[?]' Another literary tourist, Evelyn Waugh, did something still more damaging to the British in Africa with his *Black Mischief* (1932): he made fun of them, from the unscrupulous adventurer Basil Seal to the Oxford-educated Emperor Seth. In the *Daily Express* (whose meddling in colonial affairs inspired Waugh's later *Scoop*), J. B. Morton's 'Beachcomber' column featured a cavalcade of even more ludicrous imperial characters: 'Big White Carstairs', the Resident of Jaboola and the M'babwa of M'Gonkawiwi. But perhaps nothing better captured the new and disreputable image of Empire than David

Low's cartoon character Colonel Blimp. The stereotype of a super-annuated colonial colonel – fat, bald, irascible and irrelevant – Blimp personified all that the interwar generation despised about the Empire. Low later summed up his creation's persona in revealing terms:

Blimp was no enthusiast for democracy. He was impatient with the common people and their complaints. His remedy to social unrest was less education, so that people could not read about slumps. An extreme isolationist, disliking foreigners (which included Jews, Irish, Scots, Welsh, and people from the Colonies and Dominions); a man of violence, approving war. He had no use for the League of Nations nor for international efforts to prevent wars. In particular he objected to any economic reorganization of world resources involving changes in the status quo.

Imperceptibly, even the arch-imperialist was mutating into a Little Englander.

The curious thing about this collective attack of doubt was that it was the traditional imperial elite who seemed most susceptible to it. Popular views of the Empire remained positive, thanks not least to the new and soon all-pervasive mass medium of cinema. The Empire – and a large number of cinemas were themselves called 'The Empire' – was natural box office material. It had action; it had exotic locations; with a bit of imagination it could even have heterosexual romance too. It was not surprising that British film-makers produced films on imperial subjects like *The Drum* (1938) and *The Four Feathers* (1939), a film so powerful that even the *New York Times* called it 'an imperialist symphony'. More surprising was the enthusiasm for imperial themes that manifested itself in 1930s Hollywood, which in the space of just four years produced not only the classic *Lives of a Bengal Lancer* (1935) but also *Clive of India* (1935), *The Sun Never Sets*, *Gunga Din* and *Stanley and Livingstone* (all 1939). Yet somehow this was the Empire for low-brows. Just a year later, John Buchan could write gloomily: 'To-day the word [Empire] is sadly tarnished . . . [identified] with uglinesses like corrugated-iron roofs and raw townships, or, worse still, with callous racial arrogance . . . Phrases which held a world of idealism and poetry have been spoilt by their use in bad verse and after-dinner perorations.'

The creeping crisis of confidence in Empire had its roots in the crippling price Britain had paid for its victory over Germany in the First World War. The death toll for the British Isles alone was around three quarters of a million, one in sixteen of all adult males between the ages fifteen and fifty. The economic cost was harder to calculate. Writing in 1919, John Maynard Keynes looked back fondly on 'that extraordinary episode in the economic progress of man . . . which came to an end in August 1914':

For . . . the middle and upper classes . . . life offered, at a low cost and with the least trouble, conveniences, comforts and amenities beyond the compass of the richest and most powerful monarchs of other ages. The inhabitant of London could order by telephone, sipping his morning tea in bed, the various products of the whole earth in such quantity as he might see fit, and reasonably expect their early delivery upon his doorstep; he could at the same moment and by the same means adventure his wealth in the natural resources and new enterprises of any quarter of the world, and share, without exertion or even trouble, in their prospective fruits and advantages . . .

Now, after the fall, it proved extremely difficult to restore the foundations of the pre-war era of globalization. Even before the war, the first steps had been taken to reduce the international freedom of movement of labour, but afterwards the restrictions proliferated and became tighter, all but choking off the flow of new migrants to the US by the 1930s. Pre-war, tariffs had been on the increase around the world, but they had mostly been designed to raise revenue; in the 1920s and 1930s the barriers against free trade were inspired by visions of autarky.

The biggest economic change of all wrought by the war was in the international capital market. Superficially, this returned to normal in the 1920s. The gold standard was generally restored and the wartime controls on capital movements were lifted. Britain resumed her role as the world's banker, though now the United

States was investing almost as much overseas.* But the great machine that had once worked so smoothly now juddered and stalled. One reason for this was the creation of huge new debts as a result of the war: not just the German reparations debt, but also the whole complex of debts the victorious Allies owed one another. Another was the failure of the American and French central banks to abide by the gold standard 'rules of the game' as they hoarded scarce gold in their reserves. The main problem, however, was that economic policy – once predicated on the classical liberal tenets that budgets should be balanced and banknotes convertible into gold – was now subject to the pressures of democratic politics. Investors could no longer be confident that already indebted governments would have the will to cut spending and put up taxes; nor could they be sure that, in the event of a gold outflow, interest rates would be raised to maintain convertibility, regardless of the domestic squeeze that implied.

Britain, the biggest single beneficiary of the first age of globalization, was unlikely to gain much from its end. In the 1920s the old and tested policies no longer seemed to work. Paying for the war had led to a tenfold increase in the national debt. Just paying the interest on that debt consumed close to half of total central government spending by the mid-1920s. The assumption that the budget should nevertheless be balanced – and ideally show a surplus – meant that public finance was dominated by transfers from income tax-payers to bondholders. The decision to return to the gold standard at the now over-valued 1914 exchange rate condemned Britain to more than a decade of deflationary policies. The increased power of the trade unions during and after the war not only intensified industrial strife – most visibly expressed in the General Strike of 1926 – but also meant that wage cuts lagged behind price cuts. Rising real wages led to unemployment: at the nadir of the Depression in January 1932 nearly three million people, close to a quarter of all insured workers, were out of work.

* Total UK foreign capital stocks in 1930 amounted to $18.2 billion; the figure for the US was $14.7 billion.

Yet the significant thing about the Depression in Britain is not that it was so severe but that, compared with its impact in the United States and Germany, it was so mild. This had nothing to do with the Keynesian revolution in economic theory: although Keynes's *General Theory* (1936) made the case for government demand management – in other words, the use of budget deficits to stimulate a depressed economy – it was not put into practice until much later. What brought recovery was a redefinition of the economics of Empire. Britain had gone back onto gold at the old rate partly out of fear that the dominions would switch to the dollar if the pound were devalued. In 1931 it turned out that the pound could be devalued and the dominions would gladly follow. Overnight the sterling bloc became the world's largest system of fixed exchange rates, but a system freed from its gold mooring. There was also a radical change in trade policy. Twice before the British electorate had rejected protectionism at the polls. But what had been unthinkable in good times came to be seen as indispensable in the general crisis. And just as Joseph Chamberlain had hoped, 'imperial preference' – preferential tariffs for colonial products, adopted in 1932 – boosted trade within the Empire. In the 1930s the share of British exports going to the Empire rose from 44 to 48 per cent; the share of her imports coming from there rose from 30 to 39 per cent. Thus it was that even as the political bonds between Britain and the dominions were loosened by the Statute of Westminster (1931), the economic bonds grew tighter.*

The message of the Wembley Exhibition had not been so misleading: there really was still money in the Empire. And it was a

---

* In 1926 the Balfour Report on Imperial Relations had proposed redefining the dominions as 'autonomous communities within the British Empire, equal in status and in no way subordinate to one another in any aspect of their domestic or external affairs . . . [and] united by a common allegiance to the crown', and this wording was adopted in the 1931 Statute of Westminster. The dominions were still barred from passing legislation contrary to Westminster, but now Westminster could only legislate for the dominions at their request and the dominions were free to withdraw if they wished from what was now rechristened the 'British Commonwealth of Nations'. Interestingly, there was little enthusiasm for this decentralization in either Australia or New Zealand, which did not adopt the statute until the 1940s.

message drummed home relentlessly by bodies like the Empire Marketing Board (established by Leo Amery to convey the case for imperial preference subliminally). In 1930 alone there were over two hundred 'Empire Shopping Weeks' in sixty-five different British towns. At the Board's suggestion, the King's chef provided his own carefully devised recipe for an 'Empire Christmas Pudding':

> 1 lb. of sultanas (Australia)
> 1 lb. of currants (Australia)
> 1 lb. of stoned raisins (South Africa)
> 6 ozs. of minced apple (Canada)
> 1 lb. of bread crumbs (United Kingdom)
> 1 lb. of beef suet (New Zealand)
> 6 ozs. of cut candied peel (South Africa)
> 8 ozs. of flour (United Kingdom)
> 1 lb. of demerara sugar (West Indies)
> 4 eggs (Irish Free State)
> $^1/_2$ oz. of ground cinnamon (Ceylon)
> $^1/_2$ oz. of ground cloves (Zanzibar)
> $^1/_2$ oz. of ground nutmegs (Straits Settlements)
> 1 pinch of pudding spice (India)
> 1 tbsp. of brandy (Cyprus)
> 2 tbsps. of rum (Jamaica)
> 1 pint old beer (England)

The composition of this delectable concoction conveyed an unambiguous message. With the Empire, there could be Christmas pudding. Without it, there would be only breadcrumbs, flour and old beer. Or, as Orwell said, an Empire-less Britain would be just a 'cold and unimportant little island where we should all have to work very hard and live mainly on herring and potatoes'.

The irony was that even as the Empire grew more economically important, its defence sank inexorably down the list of political priorities. Under pressure from their voters to honour wartime pledges to build 'homes fit for heroes', not to mention hospitals and high schools, British politicians first neglected and then simply forgot about imperial defence. In the ten years to 1932 the defence budget was cut by more than a third – at a time when Italian and French military spending rose by, respectively, 60 and 55 per cent. At a meeting of the War Cabinet in August 1919 a convenient rule had been adopted:

It should be assumed, for framing revised Estimates, that the British Empire will not be engaged in any great war during the next ten years, and that no Expeditionary Force is required for this purpose . . . The principal function of the Military and Air Forces is to provide garrisons for India, Egypt, the new mandated territory and all territory (other than self-governing) under British control, as well as to provide the necessary support to the civil power at home.

Every year until 1932 'the Ten-year Rule' was renewed, and every year new spending was put off. The rationale was straightforward: as Chancellor of the Exchequer in 1934, Joseph Chamberlain's son Neville* admitted: 'It was impossible for us to contemplate a simultaneous war against Japan and Germany; we simply cannot afford the expenditure involved.' As Chief of the Imperial General Staff, the 'one thought' of General Sir Archibald Montgomery-Massingberd between 1928 and 1940 was 'to postpone a war – not look ahead'.

In 1918 Britain had won the war on the Western Front by a huge feat of military modernization. In the 1920s nearly everything that had been learned was forgotten in the name of economy. The stark reality was that, despite the victory and the territory it had brought, the First World War had left the Empire more vulnerable than ever before. War had acted as a forcing house for a host of new military technologies – the tank, the submarine, the armed aeroplane. To secure its post-war future, the Empire needed to invest in all of these. It did nothing of the kind. The British took pride in the 'red line' of civilian air services linking Gibraltar to Bahrain and on to Karachi, but next to nothing was done to build up the Empire's air defences. At the Hendon Air Pageants in the 1920s a major

*Chamberlain never shared his father's passion for the Empire, perhaps because as a young man he had been forced by his father to run a 20,000 acre sisal estate in the Bahamas. The venture was a total failure.

attraction was the mock bombing of 'native' villages; but this was about the extent of the Royal Air Force's capability. In 1927 General Sir R. G. Egerton argued passionately against replacing horses with armoured vehicles in the cavalry on the intriguing ground that 'the horse has a humanizing effect on men'. Despite Churchill's espousal of tanks and armoured cars (or perhaps because of it) the decision to motorize cavalry regiments was not taken until 1937. To those responsible for equipping the cavalry, it had seemed more important to design a short lance of the type used in India for pig-sticking. When Britain went to war again in 1939 most of her field guns were still the 1905 model, with half the range of their German equivalents.

The politicians got away with it for a time because the principal threats to the stability of the Empire appeared to come from within rather than from without.

At noon on Easter Monday 1916, a thousand or so extreme Irish nationalists led by the poet Patrick Pearse and the socialist James Connolly marched into Dublin and occupied selected public buildings, notably the huge General Post Office, where Pearse proclaimed an independent republic. After three days of fierce but futile fighting in which British artillery inflicted substantial damage on the city centre, the rebels surrendered. This was plainly an act of treason – the rebels had in fact asked for and been sent German guns – and the initial British response was harsh: the leading conspirators were quickly executed. (The dying Connolly had to be propped up in a chair to be shot.) In the aftermath of the war, the government was willing to deploy former soldiers, the notorious Black and Tans, to try to stamp out militant republicanism, now something more like a mass movement behind the banner of Sinn Fein and its military wing, the Irish Republican Army. But as would happen so often in the period, the British lacked the stomach for repression. When the Black and Tans opened fire on the crowd at a Gaelic football match at Croke Park, there was almost as much revulsion in England as in Ireland. By 1921, with British losses approaching 1,400, the will to fight had gone and a peace deal was hastily cobbled together. Ireland had already been partitioned the previous year between the predominantly Protestant north (six counties) and the Catholic south (the remaining twenty-six). Lloyd George's sole achievement now was to keep both parts within the Empire. But for all the fuss about oaths to the Crown and dominion status, the 'Free State' in the south was well on the road to independence as a republic (which it would finally achieve in 1948).

Time and again, in the inter-war period, this was a pattern that would repeat itself. A minor outbreak of dissent, a sharp military response, followed by a collapse of British self-confidence, handwringing, second thoughts, a messy concession, another concession. But Ireland was the test case. In allowing their very first colony to be split in two, the British had sent a signal to the Empire at large.

Though we hear much less about it, India had made a bigger contribution to the imperial war than Australia in terms of both finance and manpower. The names of over 60,000 Indian soldiers killed in foreign fields from Palestine to Passchendaele are inscribed on the vast arch of the India Gate in New Delhi. In return for their sacrifice, and perhaps also to ensure that any German blandishments to the Indians would be ignored, Montagu had pledged in 1917 what he called 'the progressive realization of responsible government' in India. That was one of those phrases that promised much, but left the date of delivery vague – and possibly very remote. To the more radical members of the Indian National Congress, as well as the more extreme terrorist groups in Bengal, the pace of reform was intolerably slow. True, Indians now had at least a measure of representation for themselves. The Central Legislative Assembly in Delhi even looked like a miniature House of Commons, right down to the green leather seating. But this was representation without power. The government's decision to extend the wartime restrictions on political freedom for a further three years (which empowered it to search without a warrant, detain without a charge and try without a jury) seemed to confirm that the promises of responsible government were empty. Indians looked to Ireland and drew the obvious conclusion. It was no good just waiting to be given Home Rule.

The British had plenty of experience of dealing with violent protest in India. But the diminutive Mohandas Karamchand Gandhi – the Mahatma to his followers, a 'seditious fakir' to Churchill – was something new: an English-trained barrister, a decorated veteran of the Boer War,* a man whose favourite poem was Kipling's 'If', and yet, to judge by his skinny frame and loincloth, a traditional holy man. To protest against the extension of wartime controls, Gandhi called on Indians to harness *satyagraha*, which roughly translates as 'soul force'. It was a deliberately religious appeal to make resistance passive, not violent. Nevertheless, the British were suspicious. Gandhi's idea of a *hartal*, a national day of 'self-purification', sounded to them like just a fancy word for a general strike. They resolved to meet 'soul force' with what the Lieutenant-Governor of Punjab, Sir Michael O'Dwyer, called 'fist force'.

In the spring of 1919, despite Gandhi's pleas (though often in his name), Indian resistance went from passive to active. Violence flared when a crowd tried to enforce the *hartal* at Delhi railway station on 30 March. Three men were killed when troops opened fire. The most notorious clash, however, was at Amritsar in the Punjab, where one man attempted to stop what he saw as an incipient rerun of the Indian Mutiny. In Amritsar, as elsewhere, people had responded to Gandhi's call. On 30 March a crowd of 30,000 gathered in a show of 'passive resistance'. On 6 April there was another *hartal*. The situation was still peaceful at this stage, but sufficiently tense for two of the local nationalist leaders to be taken into custody and deported. When news of their arrest spread, violence flared. Shots were fired; banks attacked; the telephone lines cut. On 11 April a Church of England missionary named Manuella Sherwood was knocked off her bicycle and beaten insensible by a mob. At this point the civilians handed over power to the soldiers. That night, Brigadier-General Rex Dyer arrived to take charge.

A short-tempered, pugilistic chain-smoker, Dyer was not noted for the subtlety of his approach to civil unrest. At Staff College he

---

* Gandhi served as a stretcher-bearer at Spion Kop.

had been summed up as 'happiest when crawling over a Burmese stockade with a revolver in his mouth'. By now, however, he was fifty-four and a sick man, in constant pain from war wounds and riding injuries. His mood was thunderous. On his arrival, he received instructions which stated unambiguously: 'No gatherings of persons nor processions of any sort will be allowed. All gatherings will be fired on.' The next day he issued a proclamation formally prohibiting 'all meetings and gatherings'. When, on 13 April, a crowd of 20,000 people thronged the Jallianwalla Bagh in defiance of these orders, he did not hesitate. He took two armoured cars and fifty Gurkha and Baluchi troops to the scene and, as soon as he had deployed them around the crowd, gave the order to open fire. There was no warning and the crowd had no chance to disperse, since the eight-acre meeting ground was surrounded by walls on all four sides and had only one narrow entrance. In ten minutes of sustained shooting, 379 demonstrators were killed, and more than 1,500 wounded. In the aftermath, Dyer ordered public floggings of high-caste suspects. Any Indian entering the street where Manuella Sherwood had been attacked was forced to crawl on his stomach.*

Just as in Ireland, the hard line initially had support. O'Dwyer endorsed Dyer's action. His superior officers quickly found fresh work for him to do in Afghanistan. Some local Sikhs even made him an Honorary Sikh in a ceremony at the Golden Temple, likening him to 'Nikalseyan Sahib' (John Nicholson, the legendary hero of the 1857 Mutiny). At home, the *Morning Post* opened a sympathy fund for Dyer, collecting over £26,000 from donors, among them Rudyard Kipling. Once again, however, the mood changed quickly from self-righteousness to remorse. Dyer's undoing began when two Congress-supporting lawyers succeeded in having him summoned before an inquiry to answer for his actions. His unabashed admission that his intention had been to 'strike terror into the whole of the Punjab' brought the roof down

---

* The episode is alluded to in Forster's *A Passage to India*: 'Why, they ought to crawl from here to the caves on their hands and knees whenever an English-woman's in sight . . . they ought to be ground into the dust . . .'

on his head. In Parliament Montagu angrily asked of those who defended Dyer: 'Are you going to keep your hold upon India by terrorism, racial humiliation, and subordination, and frightfulness ...?' Less predictable was Churchill's denunciation of the massacre as 'monstrous'. It was

without precedent or parallel in the modern history of the British Empire. It is an event of an entirely different order from any of those tragical occurrences which take place when troops are brought into collision with the civil population. It is an extraordinary event, a monstrous event, an event which stands in singular and sinister isolation.

Insisting that firing on unarmed civilians was 'not the British way of doing business', Churchill accused Dyer of undermining rather than saving British rule in India. This was simply 'the most frightful of all spectacles, the strength of civilization without its mercy'. Dyer was hastily invalided out of the army. Although he was never prosecuted, his career was over.

India was Ireland but on a vast scale; and Amritsar was India's Easter Rising, creating nationalist martyrs on one side and a crisis of confidence on the other. In both countries, the nationalists had begun peacefully by asking for Home Rule, for devolution within the Empire. In both cases, it took violence to get the British to agree. And in both cases, the British response to violence was schizophrenic: harsh on the ground but then emollient at the top. If, as Gandhi said, Amritsar had 'shaken the foundation' of the Empire, then the first tremor had emanated from Dublin three years before. Indeed, the Indians had been learning from the Irish experience for some time. When the young Jawaharlal Nehru visited Dublin, he had found Sinn Fein 'a most interesting movement ... Their policy is not to beg for favours, but to wrest them.' When the Hindu visionary Bal Gangadhar Tilak wished to protest against the partition of Bengal, he adopted the Irish tactic of the boycott. Indeed, an Irishwoman was elected to the presidency of Congress in December 1918: Annie Besant, a half-mad theosophist who believed her adopted son to be the 'vehicle of the world teacher' and saw 'Home Rule' as the answer to the Indian Question.

But what was important was not the nationalist tremors themselves; it was the fact that they made the Empire shake. In previous centuries the British had felt no qualms about shooting to kill in defence of the Empire. That had started to change after Morant Bay. By the time of Amritsar, the ruthless determination once exhibited by the likes of Clive, Nicholson and Kitchener seemed to have vanished altogether.

Yet amid all this inter-war anxiety, there was one man who continued to believe in the British Empire. In his eyes, the British were 'an admirably trained people' who had 'worked for three hundred years to assure themselves the domination of the world for two centuries'. They had 'learned the art of being masters, and of holding the reins so lightly withal, that the natives do not notice the curb'. Even his favourite film, *Lives of the Bengal Lancers*, had an imperial subject.

In *Mein Kampf* and in his later dinner table monologues, Adolf Hitler repeatedly expressed his admiration of British imperialism. What Germany had to do, he argued, was to learn from Britain's example. 'The wealth of Great Britain', he declared, 'is the result . . . of the capitalist exploitation of the three hundred and fifty million Indian slaves.' That was precisely what Hitler most admired: the effective oppression of an 'inferior' race. And there was an obvious place where Germany could endeavour to do the same. 'What India was for England,' he explained, 'the territories of Russia will be for us.' If Hitler had a criticism of the British it was merely that they were too self-critical and too lenient towards their subject peoples:

There are Englishmen who reproach themselves with having governed the country badly. Why? Because the Indians show no enthusiasm for their rule. I claim that the English have governed India very well, but their error is to expect enthusiasm from the people they administer.

As he explained to Britain's Foreign Secretary Lord Halifax in 1937, the way to deal with Indian nationalism was simple: 'Shoot Gandhi, and if that does not suffice to reduce them to submission, shoot a dozen leading members of Congress; and if that does not suffice, shoot 200 and so on until order is established.'

Hitler had no doubt that it was rival empires, not native nationalism, which posed the real challenge to British rule. 'England will lose India', he argued in *Mein Kampf*, 'either if her own administrative machinery falls prey to racial decomposition . . . or if she is bested by the sword of a powerful enemy. Indian agitators, however, will never achieve this . . . If the English give India back her liberty, within twenty years India will have lost her liberty again.' He was also disarmingly frank in admitting that his version of imperialism would be a great deal nastier than the British version:

However miserably the inhabitants of India may live under the British they will certainly be no better off if the British go . . . If we took India, the Indians would certainly not be enthusiastic and they'd not be slow to regret the good old days of English rule.

Yet Hitler disavowed any such desire to 'take' India. On the contrary, as he said in *Mein Kampf*, 'I, as a man of Germanic blood, would, in spite of everything, rather see India under English rule than under any other.' He insisted that he had no desire to bring about the destruction of the British Empire, an act which (as he put it in October 1941) 'would not be of any benefit to Germany . . . [but] would benefit only Japan, the United States, and others.' The Empire, he told Mussolini in June 1940, was 'an important factor in world equilibrium'.

It was precisely this Anglophilia that posed perhaps the gravest of all threats to the British Empire: the threat of diabolical temptation. On 28 April 1939, Hitler made a speech in the Reichstag that deserves to be quoted at length:

During the whole of my political activity I have always expounded the idea of a close friendship and collaboration between Germany and England . . . This desire for Anglo-German friendship and co-operation conforms not merely to sentiments which result from the racial origins of our two peoples, but also to my realization of the importance for the whole of mankind of the existence of the British Empire. I have never left room for any doubt of my belief that the existence of this empire is an inestimable factor of value for the whole of human cultural and economic life. By whatever means Great Britain has acquired her colonial territories – and I know that they were those of force and often brutality – nevertheless, I know full well that no other empire has ever come into being in any other way, and that in the final resort it is not so much the methods that are taken into account in history as success, and not the success of the methods as such, but rather the general good which the methods yield. Now there is no doubt that the Anglo-Saxon people have accomplished immeasurable colonizing work in the world. For this work I have a sincere admiration. The thought of destroying this labour appeared and still appears to me, seen from a higher human point of view, as nothing but the effluence of human wanton destructiveness.

Then he came to the point:

However, this sincere respect of mine for this achievement does not mean forgoing the securing of the life of my own people. I regard it as impossible to achieve a lasting friendship between the German and Anglo-Saxon peoples if the other side does not recognize that there are German as well as British interests, that not only is the preservation of the British Empire the meaning and purpose of the lives of Britishers, but also that for Germans the freedom and preservation of the German Reich is their life purpose.

This was the carefully calculated preamble to a final bid to avert war with Britain by doing a deal based on co-existence: the British would be allowed to retain their overseas Empire if they would give Hitler a free hand to carve out a German Empire in Central and Eastern Europe. On 25 June 1940 Hitler telephoned Goebbels to spell out exactly how such a deal would look:

The Führer ... believes that the [British] Empire must be preserved if at all possible. For if it collapses, then we shall not inherit it, but foreign and even hostile powers will take it over. But if England will have it no other way, then she must be beaten to her knees. The Führer, however, would be agreeable to peace on the following basis: England out of Europe, colonies and mandates returned. Reparations for what was stolen from us after the World War . . .

It was an idea Hitler returned to repeatedly. As late as January 1942 he was still convinced that 'the English have two possibilities: either to give up Europe and hold on to the East, or vice versa'.

We know that there were some elements in the War Cabinet who would have been – were – tempted by such a 'peace' based on surrendering the Continent to Nazism. Halifax had himself approached the Italian ambassador on 25 May to offer colonial bribes (perhaps Gibraltar, perhaps Malta) in return for Mussolini's staying out of the war and brokering a peace conference. Chamberlain privately admitted that if he believed 'that we could purchase peace and a lasting settlement by handing over Tanganyika to the Germans', then he 'would not hesitate for a moment'. But Churchill, to his eternal credit, saw through Hitler's blandishments. Three days later, addressing the full Cabinet rather than just the appeasement-minded War Cabinet, Churchill insisted that 'it was idle to think that, if we tried to make peace now, we should get better terms than if we fought it out. The Germans would demand our Fleet – that would be called disarmament – our naval bases, and much else. We should become a slave state . . .' This was quite right. Hitler's offers of peaceful co-existence with the British Empire were wholly insincere. Why else refer to 'England' as a 'hate-inspired antagonist', as he did in his famous meeting with the German service chiefs on 5 November 1937? On that occasion, Hitler had spoken in a very different tone about the British Empire, frankly predicting its imminent dissolution. This was what Hitler really thought of the Empire, that it was 'unsustainable . . . from the point of view of power politics'. German plans for an Atlantic fleet and an African colonial empire tell the same story.

Nevertheless, Churchill was defying not just Hitler; he was in some measure also defying the military odds. Granted, the Royal Navy was still much larger than the German, provided the Germans did not get their hands on the French navy too. Granted, the Royal Air Force had enough of an edge over the Luftwaffe to stand a reasonable chance of winning the Battle of Britain.* But the 225,000 British troops who had been evacuated from Dunkirk (along with 120,000 French) had left behind not only 11,000 dead and 40,000 captured comrades but also nearly all their equipment. By comparison with the Germans' ten Panzer divisions, the British were all but tankless. Above all, with France vanquished and Russia on Hitler's side, Britain now stood alone.

Or did she? The peroration of Churchill's speech to the Commons on 4 June 1940 is best remembered for its sonorous pledges to fight 'on the beaches ... in the fields and in the streets' and so on. But it was the conclusion that really mattered:

... we shall never surrender, and even if, which I do not for a moment believe, this island or a large part of it were subjugated and starving, then our Empire beyond the seas, armed and guarded by the British Fleet, would carry on the struggle, until, in God's good time, the new world, with all its power and might, steps forth to the rescue and liberation of the old.

Europe had been lost. But the Empire remained. And this had been achieved without further parleying with 'That Man'.

From Masters to Slaves

In December 1937 the Chinese city of Nanking fell to imperial forces. With explicit orders to 'kill all captives', the army ran amok. Between 260,000 and 300,000 non-combatants were killed, up to 80,000 Chinese women were raped and, in grotesque scenes of torture, prisoners were hung by their tongues from meat hooks and

* On 9 August, just before the Germans launched their offensive against Britain's air defences, the RAF had 1,032 fighters. The German fighters available for the attack numbered 1,011. Moreover, the RAF had 1,400 pilots, several hundred more than the Luftwaffe. And crucially, Britain out-produced Germany: during the crucial months from June until September 1940, 1,900 new fighters were churned out by British factories, compared with just 775 in Germany. The technical advantage of radar and a superb system of command and control also greatly enhanced British effectiveness. Overall, German losses (including bombers) were nearly double British (1,733 to 915).

fed to ravenous dogs. Imperial troops competed in prisoner-killing competitions; one officer challenged another to see who would be first to dispatch a hundred Chinese PoWs. Some of the victims were stabbed, some bayoneted, some shot, some covered in petrol and burnt to death. The destruction left half the city in ruins. 'Women suffered most,' recalled one veteran of the 114th Division. 'No matter how young or old, they all could not escape the fate of being raped. We sent out coal trucks ... to the city streets and villages to seize a lot of women. And then each of them was allocated to 15 to 20 soldiers for sexual intercourse and abuse.' 'It would [have been] all right if we only raped them,' one of his comrades confessed. 'I shouldn't say all right. But we always stabbed them and killed them. Because dead bodies don't talk.' With good reason, they called it the Rape of Nanking.

This was imperialism at its very worst. But it was Japanese imperialism, not British. The Rape of Nanking reveals precisely what the leading alternative to British rule in Asia stood for. It is easy to portray the war between the British and Japanese Empires as a collision between an old, self-doubting Empire and a new and utterly ruthless Empire – between the setting and the rising sun. But it was also the collision between an Empire that had some conception of human rights and one that regarded alien races as no better than swine. In the words of Lieutenant-Colonel Ryukichi Tanaka, Director of the Japanese Secret Service in Shanghai: 'We can do anything to such creatures.' By the 1930s many people in Britain had got into the habit of rubbishing the Empire. But the rise of the Japanese empire in Asia during that decade showed that the alternatives to British rule were not necessarily more benign. There were degrees of imperialism, and in its brutality towards conquered peoples Japan's empire went beyond anything the British had ever done. And this time the British were among the conquered.

The naval base at Singapore had been built in the 1920s as the linch-pin of Britain's defences in the Far East. In the words of the Chiefs of Staff, 'The security of the United Kingdom and the security of Singapore would be the keystones on which the survival

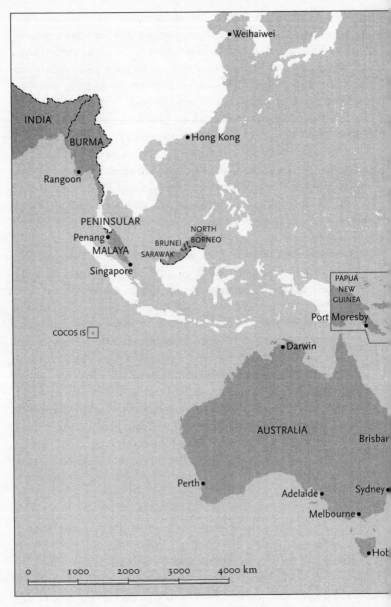

British Southeast Asia and the Pacific, 1920

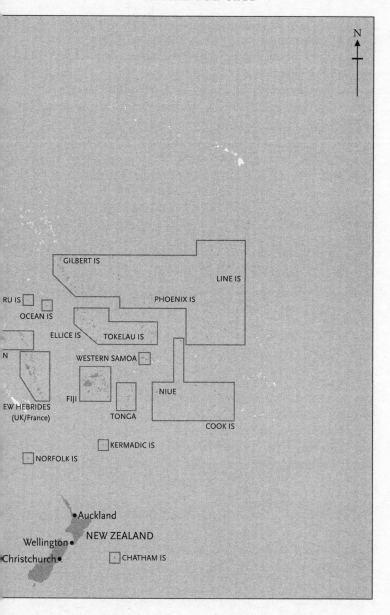

of the British Commonwealth of Nations would depend.'*
Throughout the inter-war period, the declared strategy for defending Singapore in the event of an attack was to send the fleet. But by 1940 the service chiefs had realized that this was no longer an option; and by the end of 1941 even Churchill was attaching a lower priority to defending Singapore than to the triple needs of defending Britain, assisting the Soviet Union and holding on to the Middle East. Even so, not enough was done to protect the base from the threat posed by Japan. On the eve of the invasion there were just 158 first-line aircraft in Malaya where 1,000 were needed; and three and a half divisions of infantry where eight divisions plus two armoured regiments would barely have sufficed. Above all, there had been a woeful failure to build proper fixed defences (minefields, pillboxes and anti-tank obstacles) on the land approaches to Singapore. The result was that, when they attacked, the Japanese found the impregnable citadel was a sitting duck. As shells rained down on the city, the choice was between the horror of a Nanking-style Japanese assault and the humiliation of abject surrender. At 4 p.m. on 15 February 1942, despite Churchill's desperate exhortation to fight 'to the death', the white flag was raised.

Altogether 130,000 imperial troops – British, Australians and Indians – gave themselves up to a force less than half that size. Never in the history of the British Empire had so many given up so much to so few. Only too late did it transpire how worn out the Japanese themselves had been after their gruelling jungle route march. Royal Artillery gunner Jack Chalker was among the prisoners. 'It was hard to believe we were now in Japanese hands,' he later recalled. 'That night, as we wondered what the future held for us, we couldn't help but think of the Rape of Nanking . . . Our prospects were not encouraging.' For Chalker and his comrades, what really rankled was the fact that this was humiliation at Asian hands. As it turned out, Japanese anti-Western rhetoric did not translate into better treatment for the non-white population of

---

* The term 'British Commonwealth of Nations' was first used in the Anglo-Irish Treaty of 1922 to convey the near autonomy of the dominions.

Singapore. The Japanese merely inserted themselves into the privileged position hitherto occupied by the British. If anything, their treatment of the other Asian inhabitants was worse: the Chinese community in particular was subjected to a devastating process of *sook ching* or 'purification by elimination'. However, nothing more clearly expressed the character of the 'new order' in Asia than the way the Japanese treated their British prisoners.

The Japanese high command regarded surrender as dishonour and were contemptuous of enemy soldiers who did lay down their arms. Jack Chalker once asked one of his captors why he was so callous towards PoWs. 'I am a soldier,' he replied simply. 'To be a prisoner of war is unthinkable.' Yet there was more to the ill treatment of British prisoners than (as was sometimes claimed) a mere mistranslation of the Geneva Convention. By 1944 the British authorities had begun to suspect 'an official policy of humiliating white prisoners of war in order to diminish their prestige in native eyes'. They were right. In 1942 Seishiro Itagaki, the Commander-in-Chief of the Japanese Army in Korea, told the Prime Minister Hideki Tojo:

It is our purpose by interning American and British prisoners of war in Korea, to make the Koreans realize positively the true might of our Empire as well as to contribute to the psychological propaganda work for stamping out any ideas of worship of Europe and America which the greater part of Korea still retains at bottom.

The same principle was applied throughout Japanese-occupied Asia.

The British had built railways across their Empire with the labour of Asian 'coolies'. Now, in one of the great symbolic reversals of world history, the Japanese forced 60,000 British and Australian PoWs – as well as Dutch prisoners and conscripted Indian labour – to construct 250 miles of railway through the mountainous jungle on the Thai–Burmese border. Since the mid-eighteenth century, it had been one of the Empire's proudest boasts that 'Britons never, never shall be slaves.' But that is exactly what the PoWs on the railway were. As one British prisoner bitterly observed: 'It must be rather amusing for a Japanese to see the "white lords" trudging the road with basket and pole while they roll by on their lorries!'

Secretly, and at the risk of his own life, Jack Chalker, who had been an art student before the war, drew vivid sketches of the way he and his comrades were treated. Exhausted and on the brink of starvation, they were forced to work even when suffering from malaria, dysentery and, worst of all, the tropical ulcers that could gnaw a man's flesh away to the bone:

Sleep was a shallow, tense business. We could be turned out of our huts at any hour to be paraded for a roll-call, assembled for a working party or to be beaten up; even the desperately ill had to attend regardless of their condition. Such assemblies could last for hours and even a whole day or night . . . on some occasions sick patients died.

Pierre Boulle and David Lean's film made the bridge on the River Kwai famous. But conditions were far worse than the film suggests. And they were worst of all further up the 'Death Railway', near the Burmese border.

The relentless and often sadistic abuse of the prisoners at the Hintok camp was recorded in the meticulous journal kept throughout his captivity by the Australian surgeon and PoW commanding officer, Lieutenant-Colonel Edward Dunlop, nicknamed 'Weary' partly as a pun (Dunlop–Tyre–Tired–Weary) but also because, as a tall man, he had to stoop when speaking to his much shorter captors to save their faces and avoid arousing their usually violent ire:

19th March 1943 . . . tomorrow 600 men are required for the railway . . . light duty and no duty men and all men without boots to go just the same. This is the next thing to murder. Obviously the Ns [Nips] have a great reserve of manpower here and at Singapore and they are showing every intention of just breaking men on this job, with not the faintest consideration for either life or health. This can only be regarded as a cold-blooded, merciless crime against mankind, obviously premeditated . . .

22nd March 1943 I was furious . . . and angrily told Hiroda [the Japanese officer in charge] that I objected strongly to his sending sick men to work . . . I invited him to make good his threat to shoot me (rifles were trained on me). 'You can shoot me, but then my 2 i/c [second-in-command] is as tough a man as me, and after him you will have to shoot them all. Then you will have no workmen. In any case, I have taken steps to one day have you hanged, for you are such a black-hearted bastard!'

In Dunlop's eyes, the railway the Japanese – or rather their captives – were building was 'an astonishing affair' which seemed 'to run without . . . regard for the landscape as though someone had drawn a line on the map . . .' At Konyu the line went directly through a massive rock face 73 metres long and 25 metres high. Working in shifts around the clock, Dunlop's men had to blast, drill and claw their way through. Despite the onset of the monsoon season and a horrific cholera epidemic, they managed to finish the job in just twelve weeks. During the night shift, the light shed by the flickering carbide lamps on the haggard faces of the PoWs earned this cutting the nickname Hellfire Pass. Dunlop's diary makes it clear who the devils in this hell were:

17th May 1943 . . . These days, in which I see men being progressively broken into emaciated, pitiful wrecks, bloated with beriberi, terribly reduced with pellagra, dysentery and malaria, and covered with disgusting sores, a searing hate arises in me whenever I see a Nip. Disgusting, deplorable, hateful troop of men – apes. It is a bitter lesson to all of us not to surrender to these beasts while there is still life in one's body.

Twice he was viciously beaten and tied to a tree to await execution by bayonet, on suspicion of concealing a radio transmitter. Only with seconds to spare was he reprieved. But it was the treatment of one of his men – Sergeant S. R. 'Mickey' Hallam – that seemed to Dunlop to exemplify the gratuitous cruelty of the Japanese:

22nd June 1943 . . . Sgt Hallam (malaria) had checked in with the Nipponese in this camp and had been admitted to hospital . . . [He] was dragged from the hospital very ill with malaria (he had actually fainted on the way to work), then given an indescribable beating by the engineer sergeant and the other Nipponese. This included the following: blows with a fist, hammering over the face and head with wooden clogs, repeatedly throwing over the shoulder heavily on to the ground with a sort of fireman's lift action, then kicking in the stomach and scrotum and ribs etc., thrashing with bamboos frequently over the head, and other routine measures ... This disgusting and brutal affair continued for some hours altogether ... Sgt Hallam was quite collapsed with a temperature of 103.4, face grossly contused – contusions to the neck and chest, multiple abrasions and contusions of limbs ...

Hallam died of his wounds four days later. As Dunlop noted: 'He was slain by those Nipponese sadists more certainly than if they had shot him.'

When Dunlop added up the number of Allied prisoners who had died in the Hintok camp between April 1943 and January 1944 the total came to 676 – one in ten of the Australians, and two out of every three British prisoners. In all around 9,000 British did not survive their time in Japanese hands, roughly a quarter of all those captured. Never had British forces suffered such appalling treatment.

This was the Empire's Passion; its time on the cross. After this, could it ever be resurrected?

With the Empire thus reduced – with its soldiers enslaved by Asian masters – the moment had surely arrived for India's nationalists to rise up and throw off the British yoke. As Subhas Chandra Bose declared, the fall of Singapore seemed to herald 'the end of the British Empire ... and the dawn of a new era in Indian history'.

Yet events in India revealed the weakness of the nationalist movement and the resilience of the Raj. The Viceroy announced India's entry into the war without a word of consultation with the leaders of Congress. The 'Quit India' Campaign launched in 1942 was snuffed out within six weeks by the simple expedients of arresting Gandhi and the campaign's other leaders, censoring the press and reinforcing the police with troops. Congress split, with only a small minority egged on by Bose – a would-be Indian Mussolini –

electing to side with the Japanese.* And even his self-styled Indian National Army proved of little military value. It turned out that the only serious threat to the British in India were the Japanese divisions in Burma; and the Indian Army defeated them roundly at Imphal (March–June 1944). With hindsight, Sir Stafford Cripps's offer of 1942 – full dominion status for India after the war or the option to quit the Empire – was superfluous. As dogmatic a Marxist as only a millionaire can be,† Cripps declared: 'You have only got to look at the pages of British Imperial history to hide your head in shame that you are British.' But Indians only had to look at the way the Japanese conducted themselves in China, Singapore and Thailand to see how much worse the alternative before them was. Gandhi might dismiss Cripps's offer as 'a post-dated cheque on a crashing bank'. But how could anyone seriously claim that driving out the British would improve life, if the effect would be to open the door to the Japanese? (As Fielding jeers in A Passage to India: 'Who do you want instead of the English? The Japanese?')

No one should ever underestimate the role played by the Empire – not just the familiar stalwart fellows from the dominions but the ordinary, loyal Indians, West Indians and Africans too – in defeating the Axis powers. Nearly a million Australians served in the forces; over two and a half million Indians (though only around a tenth of the latter served abroad). Without Canadian pilots, the Battle of Britain might well have been lost. Without Canadian sailors, the Battle of the Atlantic surely would have been. Despite Bose's efforts, most Indian soldiers fought loyally, aside from occasional grumbles about pay differentials (75 rupees a month for a British soldier, 18 for an Indian). Indeed, the mood of *Josh* ('positive spirit') tended to grow as stories about Japanese atrocities filtered down through the ranks. 'I get inspired by a sense of duty,' wrote

---

* In a speech in Tokyo in 1944 Bose explicitly called for an Indian state 'of an authoritarian character'. By this time he was calling himself the *Netaji* (dear leader) and affecting the usual fascist uniform.

† He was the son of Lord Parmoor and the husband of the heiress to the Eno's Fruit Salts fortune.

one sepoy to his family, 'and get excited by the brutal atrocity of the uncivilized Japanese.' The men of the Royal West African Frontier Force had their moment of glory too when a group of Japanese soldiers did the unthinkable and surrendered – fearing, they said, that 'African troops ate the killed in battle, but not prisoners . . . if eaten by Africans, they would not be acceptable to their ancestors in the hereafter'. Even the Irish Free State, the only dominion to adopt the shameful policy of neutrality, produced 43,000 volunteers for the imperial forces. In all, more than five million fighting troops were raised by the Empire, almost as many as by the United Kingdom itself. Considering Britain's desperate plight in 1940, it was an even more laudable show of imperial unity than in the First World War. The Empire Day slogan for 1941 was almost a parody of an earlier Nazi catch phrase: 'One King, One Flag, One Fleet, One Empire', but it had a certain truth to it.

Yet the Empire alone could not have won the Second World War. The key to victory – and the key to the future of the Empire itself – lay, ironically, with the country that had been the first colony to throw off British rule; with a people once dismissed by an earlier Prime Minister of New Zealand* as a 'mongrel race'. And that turned out to mean – as one old Colonial Office hand already sensed – that 'the prize of victory [would] not be the perpetuation, but the honourable interment of the old system'.

In the First World War, American economic and then military support had been important, though not decisive. In the Second World War it was crucial. From the very earliest days Churchill had pinned his hopes on the United States. 'The voice and force of a United States may count for nothing if they are withheld for too long,' he told Roosevelt as early as 15 May 1940. In speeches and radio broadcasts he repeatedly hinted that salvation would come from across the Atlantic. On 27 April 1941, more than seven months before the US entered the war, he memorably quoted the poet Arthur Hugh Clough in a BBC broadcast aimed at American listeners:

* William Ferguson Massey, New Zealand Prime Minister from 1912 to 1925.

And not by eastern windows only,
When daylight comes, comes in the light,
In front, the sun climbs slow, how slowly,
But westward, look, the land is bright.

With his own Anglo-American parentage,* Churchill firmly believed that an alliance of the English-speaking peoples was the key to victory – a victory that would, of course, restore the British Empire to the *status quo ante*. When he heard on the evening of 7 December that the Japanese had attacked the Americans at Pearl Harbor, he could scarcely conceal his excitement. Beforehand, over dinner with two American guests, he had been in deepest gloom, 'with his head in his hands part of the time'. But on hearing the news on the radio, as the American ambassador John G. Winant recalled,

Churchill jumped to his feet and started for the door with the announcement, 'We shall declare war on Japan.'

. . . 'Good God,' I said, 'you can't declare war on a radio announcement.'

He stopped and looked at me half-seriously, half-quizzically, and then said quietly, 'What shall I do?' The question was asked not because he needed me to tell him what to do, but as a courtesy to the representative of the country attacked.

I said, 'I will call up the President by telephone and ask him what the facts are.' And he added, 'And I shall talk with him too.'

Roosevelt's first words to Churchill were: 'We are all in the same boat now.'

Yet from its earliest days, the so-called 'special relationship' between Britain and the United States had its own special ambiguity, at the heart of which lay the Americans' very different conception of empire. To the Americans, reared on the myth of their own fight for freedom from British oppression, formal rule over subject peoples was unpalatable. It also implied those foreign entanglements the Founding Fathers had warned them against. Sooner or later, everyone must learn to be, like the Americans, self-governing

---

* His mother was Brooklyn-born Jennie Jerome, daughter of Leonard Jerome, proprietor of the *New York Times*.

and democratic – at gunpoint if necessary. In 1913 there had been a military coup in Mexico, to the grave displeasure of Woodrow Wilson, who resolved 'to teach the South American Republics to elect good men'. Walter Page, then Washington's man in London, reported a conversation with the British Foreign Secretary Sir Edward Grey, who asked:

'Suppose you have to intervene, what then?'

'Make 'em vote and live by their decisions.'

'But suppose they will not so live?'

'We'll go in and make 'em vote again.'

'And keep this up 200 years?' asked he.

'Yes', said I. 'The United States will be here for two hundred years and it can continue to shoot men for that little space till they learn to vote and to rule themselves.'

Anything, in other words, but take over Mexico – which would have been the British solution.

What such attitudes implied for the future of the British Empire was made blatantly clear in an open letter by the editors of *Life* magazine 'to the People of England', published in October 1942: 'One thing we are sure we are *not* fighting for is to hold the British Empire together. We don't like to put the matter so bluntly, but we don't want you to have any illusions. If your strategists are planning a war to hold the British Empire together they will sooner or later find themselves strategizing all alone.'*

The American president, Franklin Delano Roosevelt, agreed. 'The colonial system means war,' he told his son during the war. 'Exploit the resources of an India, a Burma, a Java; take all the wealth out of those countries, but never put anything back . . . all you're doing is storing up the kind of trouble that leads to war.' A brief stopover in the Gambia on the way to the Casablanca conference confirmed these theoretical suspicions. It was, he declared, a 'hell-hole . . . the most horrible thing I have ever seen in my life':

---

* General Smuts replied in an interview for *Life* the following December that the Commonwealth was 'the widest system of organized human freedom which has ever existed in human history'.

Dirt. Disease. Very high mortality rate. . . . Those people are treated worse than livestock. Their cattle live longer . . . For every dollar that the British . . . have put into the Gambia [he later asserted], they have taken out ten. It's just plain exploitation.

Naively trusting of Stalin, positively sycophantic towards the Chinese nationalist leader Chiang Kai-shek, Roosevelt was deeply suspicious of Churchill's unreconstructed imperialism. As the President saw it: 'The British would take land anywhere in the world, even if it were only a rock or a sand bar.' 'You have four hundred years of acquisitive instinct in your blood,' he told Churchill in 1943, 'and you just don't understand how a country might not want to acquire land somewhere else if they can get it.' What Roosevelt wished to see instead of colonies was a new system of temporary 'trusteeships' for the colonies of all the European powers, paving the way to their independence; these would be subject to some over-arching international authority, which would be given rights of inspection. Such anti-imperialist views were far from being peculiar to the President. In 1942 Sumner Welles, the American Under-Secretary, proclaimed: 'The age of imperialism is ended.' Wendell Wilkie, the Republican presidential candidate in 1940, had used almost the same words.

This, then, was the spirit in which American war aims were formulated; they were in many ways more overtly hostile to the British Empire than anything Hitler had ever said. Article III of the Atlantic Charter of August 1941, which acted as the basis for the Western Allies' war aims, appeared to rule out a continuation of imperial forms after the war, in favour of 'the rights of all peoples to choose the form of government under which they will live'. In 1943 an American draft Declaration on National Independence went even further: as one British official lamented, 'the whole tenor of it is to look forward to the ideal of the dissolution of the British Empire'. Nor did the Americans confine themselves to generalities. On one occasion, Roosevelt pressed Churchill to hand back Hong Kong to China as a gesture of 'goodwill'. He even had the temerity to bring up the question of India, at which Churchill erupted, retorting that an international team of inspection should be sent to the American South. 'We have made declarations on these matters,' Churchill assured the House of Commons: the British government was already committed to 'the progressive evolution of self-governing institutions in the British colonies'. 'Hands off the British Empire' was his pithy slogan in a December 1944 minute: 'It must not be weakened or smirched to please sob-stuff merchants at home or foreigners of any hue.' He had egged the Americans on to join the war. Now he bitterly resented the feeling that the Empire was being 'jockeyed out or edged nearer the abyss'. He simply would not consent to

forty or fifty nations thrusting interfering fingers into the life's existence of the British Empire ... After we have done our best to fight this war ... I will have no suggestion that the British Empire is to be put into the dock and examined by everybody to see whether it is up to standard.

To British eyes, the proposed 'trusteeships' would just be a façade behind which an informal American economic empire would be erected. As the Colonial Office put it, 'the Americans [were] quite ready to make their dependencies politically "independent" while economically bound hand and foot to them.' Curiously, the trusteeship model did not appear to apply to Hawaii, Guam, Puerto Rico or the Virgin Islands, all *de facto* American colonies. Also exempt was the long shopping list of Atlantic and Pacific island bases for the US Navy drawn up for Roosevelt by the Joint Chiefs of Staff. As Alan Watt, a member of the Australian Legation in Washington, shrewdly observed in January 1944: 'There are signs in this country of the development of a somewhat ruthless Imperialist attitude.' It was the great paradox of the war, as the exiled German-Jewish economist Moritz Bonn noted: 'The United States have been the cradle of modern Anti-Imperialism, and at the same time the founding of a mighty Empire.'*

*

* Nor, significantly, did Roosevelt seem to intend that trusteeship should be the future basis of Russia's vast Eurasian empire. This was what British officials dubbed the 'salt water fallacy': somehow colonies were treated differently if they were separated by sea from those who ruled them.

The wartime alliance with the US was a suffocating embrace; but it was born of necessity. Without American money, the British war effort would have collapsed. The system of Lend-Lease whereby the US supplied her Allies with arms on credit was worth $26 billion dollars to Britain, around a tenth of total wartime output. This was roughly double what Britain was able to borrow from the dominions and colonies. As one American official put it succinctly, America was a 'coming power', Britain a 'going power'. The British officials sent to negotiate with their American creditors in Washington therefore found themselves in the position of humble supplicants. It was a position that did not come naturally to the leading figure in the British delegation, John Maynard Keynes.

Keynes was the greatest economist of the twentieth century, and he knew it. In London everyone – Churchill included – was in awe of his great brain, its brilliance undimmed by the heart disease that would soon kill him. But when he met US Treasury officials in Washington, it was a different story. To the Americans, Keynes was 'one of those fellows that just knows all the answers'. Keynes couldn't stand them either.* He disliked the way American lawyers tried to blind him with jargon – speaking (as Keynes put it) 'Cherokee'. He loathed the way the politicians would answer phone calls in the middle of meetings with him. Above all, Keynes detested the way the Americans sought to take advantage of Britain's financial weakness. In his own stark image, America was trying to 'pick out the eyes of the British Empire'. Nor was he alone in feeling this way. One of his colleagues commented bitterly: 'A visitor from Mars might well be pardoned for thinking that we were the representatives of a vanquished people discussing the economic penalties of defeat.'

These were in fact typical reactions to the rapidly changing balance of power. With few exceptions, the British political elite, unlike the mostly socialist intellectual elite, found it extraordinarily hard to accept that the Empire had to go as the price of victory. In

---

* As he told a friend in 1941: 'I always regard a visit [to the US] as in the nature of a serious illness to be followed by convalescence.'

November 1942 Churchill thundered that he had not become the King's First Minister 'in order to preside over the liquidation of the British Empire'. Even the Labour Home Secretary Herbert Morrison compared the idea of independence for some British colonies with 'giving a child of ten a latch-key, a bank account and a shotgun'. But Britain's own bank account made it clear that the game was up. Once Britain had been the world's banker. Now she owed foreign creditors more than $40 billion. The foundations of empire had been economic, and those foundations had simply been eaten up by the cost of the war. Meanwhile, the 1945 Labour government had ambitions to build a welfare state, which could only be afforded if Britain's overseas commitments were drastically reduced. In a word, Britain was bust – and the Empire mortgaged to the hilt.

When a firm goes belly-up, of course, the obvious solution is for the creditors to take over the assets. Britain owed billions to the US. So why not simply sell them the empire? After all, Roosevelt had once joked about 'taking over the British Empire' from its 'broke' masters. But could the British bring themselves to sell? And – more importantly perhaps – could the Americans bring themselves to buy?

The Transfer of Power

There was something very British about the Suez Canal military base, which covered an area the size of Wales and in 1954 was still home to around 80,000 troops. There were ten lavatories on El Quantara railway station: three for officers (one each for European, Asiatic and Coloured users), three for warrant officers and sergeants of each race, three for other ranks of each race and one for the small number of servicewomen. Here at least, the old imperial hierarchy lived on.

But at the American Embassy in Cairo, the atmosphere was rather different. The ambassador Jefferson Caffery and his political adviser, William Lakeland, were impressed by the young army officers who had seized power in Egypt in 1952, particularly their leader, Colonel Nasser. The Secretary of State, John Foster Dulles, agreed. When Nasser pressed the British to speed up their withdrawal from Suez they did not discourage him. In October 1954 the British at last agreed to begin the phased evacuation of the base; by the summer of 1956 the last of their troops had gone. However, when Nasser proceeded to nationalize the Canal – in which the British government retained the substantial shareholding originally acquired by Disraeli – British restraint cracked. 'What happens here [in Egypt]', Churchill had declared in 1953, 'will set the pace for us all over Africa and the Middle East.' This would prove to be only too true. Convinced that he was dealing with the Hitler of the Middle East, Anthony Eden, now Prime Minister, determined to strike back against Nasser's 'piracy'.

For their part, the Americans could not have been much more explicit about their opposition to a British intervention in Egypt. They had been prepared to exert financial pressure on Nasser by withdrawing their financial support for the new Aswan Dam. But an 1882-style military occupation was another matter: that, they feared, would have the effect of driving Arab states into the Soviet camp. Unilateral action in Egypt or anywhere else, warned Dulles, would 'tear the free world coalition to pieces'. As President Eisenhower later asked: 'How can we possibly support Britain ... if in doing so we lose the whole Arab world?' Such warnings went unheeded. On 5 November 1956 an Anglo-French expedition landed on the Canal, claiming that they were peace-keepers trying to pre-empt an Israeli– Egyptian war.

Nothing could have revealed Britain's new weakness more starkly than what happened next. First, the invaders were unable to prevent the Egyptians from blocking the Canal and disrupting the oil shipments through it. Then there was a run on the pound as investors bailed out. Indeed, it was at the Bank of England that the Empire was effectively lost. As the Bank's gold and dollar reserves dwindled during the crisis, Harold Macmillan (then Chancellor of the Exchequer) had to choose between devaluing the pound – which would, he warned, be a 'catastrophe affecting not merely the British cost of living but also ... all our external economic relations' – or asking for massive American aid. The latter option put the Americans in a position to dictate terms. Only after Eden agreed to leave Egypt unconditionally did Eisenhower arrange a billion-dollar rescue package from the IMF and the Export-Import Bank.

The American refusal to sanction Nasser's overthrow proved to be a mistake. Nasser continued to flirt with the Soviets; indeed, soon it was Eisenhower who was accusing him of trying to 'get control of these petroleum supplies to get the income and power to destroy the Western world'. Nevertheless, Suez sent a signal to nationalists throughout the British Empire: the hour of freedom had struck. But the hour was chosen by the Americans, not by the nationalists.

The break-up of the British Empire happened with astonishing – and in some cases excessive – speed. Once the British had made up their minds to get out, they aimed to catch the first boat home, regardless of the consequences in their former colonies. In the words of the Labour Chancellor Hugh Dalton: 'When you are in a place where you are not wanted, and where you have not got the force to squash those who don't want you, the only thing to do is to come out.'

This had its disadvantages. In their haste to get shot of India, they left behind a chaos that almost undid two centuries of orderly government. Originally, the government had intended to leave India by the second half of 1948. But the last Viceroy, Lord Mountbatten,* indulged his lifelong fondness for acceleration by bringing forward the date for independence to 15 August 1947. He sided openly with the Hindu-dominated Congress against the

* To be precise, Lord Louis Francis Albert Victor Nicholas Mountbatten, 'KG, PC, GCB, OM, GCSI, GCIE, GCVO, DSO, FRS, Hon. DCL, Hon. LLD, Hon. D.Sc., AMIEE, AMRINI' – as he often reminded people. Mountbatten liked to construct genealogical tables plotting his family's royal lineage, using a system designed for pedigree cattle breeders.

Muslim League,* a preference the more surprising (or perhaps not) given Lady Mountbatten's rumoured affair with the Congress leader Jawaharlal Nehru. In particular, Mountbatten put pressure on the supposedly neutral Boundary Commissioner, Sir Cyril Radcliffe – cruelly mocked at the time by W. H. Auden – to make critical adjustments in India's favour when drawing the frontier through the Punjab. The ensuing wave of bitter inter-communal violence left at least 200,000 and perhaps as many as half a million people dead. Many more were uprooted from their homes: in 1951 around seven million people, one in ten of Pakistan's total population, were refugees.

In Palestine too the British cut and ran, in 1949, bequeathing to the world the unresolved question of the new state of Israel's relations with the 'stateless' Palestinians and the neighbouring Arab states.† It was not until after Suez, however, that the dominoes really began to fall.

In the immediate post-war period, there had been various grand designs for a 'new' Empire. The Foreign Secretary, Ernest Bevin, was convinced that the road to domestic economic recovery began in Africa. As A. H. Poynton of the Colonial Office told the United Nations in 1947:

The fundamental objectives in Africa are to foster the emergence of large-scale societies, integrated for self-government by effective and democratic political and economic institutions both national and local, inspired by a

* The Muslim League had been founded as early as 1906 but, under the leadership of Mohammad Ali Jinnah, it became committed to the idea of a separate Muslim state only in 1940.

† Both the Jewish state and Arab nationalism were in some measure creations of British policy during the First World War; but the terms of the 1917 Balfour Declaration had turned out to contain a hopeless contradiction: 'His Majesty's Government view with favour the establishment in Palestine of a national home for the Jewish people, and will use their best endeavours to facilitate the achievement of this object, it being clearly understood that nothing shall be done which may prejudice the civil and religious rights of existing non-Jewish communities in Palestine . . .'

common faith in progress and Western values and equipped with efficient techniques of production and betterment.

There was a new Colonial Development Corporation and an Overseas Food Corporation, and marvellous-sounding schemes for growing groundnuts in Tanganyika and producing eggs in the Gambia. The Crown Agents travelled the world, selling old British trains and boats to any colonial government that could pay and some that could not. There were ambitious plans for the federation of West Indian colonies; of East Africa; of the Rhodesias and Nyasaland; of Malaya, Singapore, Sarawak and Borneo. There was even talk of a new building for the Colonial Office. The old Empire meanwhile continued to attract a steady stream of migrants: from 1946 until 1963 four out of five emigrants leaving Britain by sea went to Commonwealth countries.

This imperial renaissance might have led further if the United States and Britain had made common cause, for American backing was the *sine qua non* of imperial recovery. The first post-war Prime Minister, Clement Attlee, certainly saw the need for it. 'A modest little man with a great deal to be modest about', as Churchill rather unfairly put it, Attlee was nevertheless the more realistic of the two about Britain's future. He recognized that the new military technologies of long-range air power and the atomic bomb meant that 'the British Commonwealth and Empire is not a unit that can be defended by itself ... The conditions which made it possible to defend a string of possessions scattered over five continents by means of a fleet based on island fortresses have gone.' As he argued in March 1946, it was now necessary to 'consider the British Isles as an easterly extension of a strategic arc the centre of which is the American continent more than as a power looking eastwards through the Mediterranean and the East.'

There were in fact many places where the Americans and British successfully co-operated in the post-war period. In Cyprus, Aden, Malaya, Kenya and Iran, British rule was essentially 'underwritten' by the US. This reversal of policy reflected the Americans' growing awareness that the Soviet Union posed a far more serious threat to

American interests and ideals than the British Empire. 'When perhaps the inevitable struggle came between Russia and ourselves,' one American official had observed even before the Cold War began, 'the question would be who are our friends . . . those whom we had weakened in the struggle, or those whom we had strengthened?' Maybe there was something to be said for British imperialism after all. Thus the American General Board of the Navy and the Joint Chiefs of Staff Strategic Survey Committee both agreed that the British network of military bases could provide a useful complement to their own. All this made Bevin bullish:

Western Europe, including its dependent overseas territories, is now patently dependent on American aid . . . [whereas] the United States recognizes that the United Kingdom and the Commonwealth . . . are essential to her defence and safety. Already it is . . . a case of partial inter-dependence rather than of complete dependence. As time goes by (in the next ten to twenty years) the elements of dependence ought to diminish and those of inter-dependence to increase.

It did not happen. On the contrary, Suez revealed that the fundamental American hostility towards the Empire lingered on. And when the Americans exercised their veto, the façade of neo-imperial power collapsed. 'Thinking over our difficulties in Egypt', minuted a world-weary Foreign Office mandarin in the 1950s, 'it seems to me that the essential difficulty arises from the very obvious fact that we lack power . . . On a strictly realistic view we ought to recognise that our lack of power must limit what we can do, and should lead us to a policy of surrender or near surrender imposed by necessity.'

Just as Hitler had predicted, it was rival empires more than indigenous nationalists who propelled the process of decolonization forward. As the Cold War entered its hottest phase in the 1960s, the United States and the Soviet Union vied with one another to win the support of independence movements in Africa, Asia and the Caribbean. What Harold Macmillan called 'the winds of change' when he toured Africa in 1960 blew not from Windhoek or Malawi but from Washington and Moscow. Tragically, they often blew away colonial rule only to replace it with civil war.

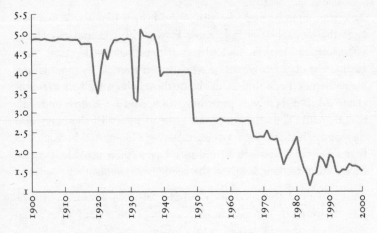

Sterling's crises: dollars per pound, 1900–2000

The bottom line was, of course, the economy. Exhausted by the costs of victory, denied the fresh start that followed defeat for Japan and Germany, Britain was simply no longer able to bear the costs of Empire. Nationalist insurgency and new military technology made imperial defence much more expensive than before. Between 1947 and 1987 British defence expenditure had amounted to 5.8 per cent of gross domestic product. A century before, the proportion had been a mere 2.6 per cent. In the nineteenth century Britain had financed her chronic trade deficit with the income from a vast overseas investment portfolio. That had now been replaced with a crushing foreign debt burden, and the Treasury had to meet the much larger costs of nationalized health care, transport and industry.

It was, as Keynes said, 'primarily . . . to meet the political and military expenditure overseas' that Britain turned to the US for a loan when the war – and Lend-Lease – ended in 1945. But the conditions attached to the loan at once had the effect of undermining British overseas power. In return for $3.75 billion,* the Americans insisted that the pound be made convertible into the dollar within

* The last instalment is due to be repaid in 2006.

twelve months. The run on the Bank of England's reserves this caused was the first of the succession of sterling crises that were to punctuate Britain's retreat from empire: by the time of Suez the pattern was tiresomely familiar. In the early 1950s, Harold Macmillan declared that the choice facing the country was between 'the slide into a shoddy and slushy Socialism (as a second-rate power), or the march to the third British Empire'. After Suez only the first option seemed to remain.

The depreciation of the pound against the dollar was just a symptom of the country's precipitous economic decline: from 25 per cent of world manufacturing exports in 1950 to just 9 per cent in 1973; from more than 33 per cent of world merchant shipping launchings to less than 4 per cent; from 15 per cent of world steel exports to barely 5 per cent. Because she was much less affected by war damage, Britain had emerged from the war as the biggest European economy; by 1973 she had been overtaken by both Germany and France, and very nearly surpassed by Italy. The British rate of growth of per capita GDP between 1950 and 1973 was the lowest in Europe, less than half the German rate. Yet we should not leap to the conclusion that this made a British reorientation away from the Commonwealth and towards continental Europe economically inevitable. That was often how the case for British membership of the European Economic Community was presented. It is true the proportion of British trade with the countries that formed the EEC grew from 12 to 18 per cent between 1952 and 1965. But the share of total trade with the Commonwealth remained substantially larger: though it fell from 45 per cent to 35 per cent, it remained twice as important as EEC trade. It was only after British entry into the 'Common Market' that European protectionist tariffs, particularly on agricultural products, forced a dramatic reorientation of British trade from the Commonwealth to the continent. As so often, it was the political decision that caused the economic change, not the other way round.

What was wrong with the Commonwealth was not so much its declining economic importance to Britain as its growing political impotence. Originally just Britain and the white dominions, the

Remnants of Empire, 2002

Commonwealth was joined by India, Pakistan and Ceylon (Sri Lanka) in 1949. By 1965 there were twenty-one members and ten more joined in the following ten years. The Commonwealth currently has fifty-four members and has become little more than a subset of the United Nations or the International Olympic Committee, its only obvious merit being that it saves money on professional translators. The English language is the one thing the Commonwealth still has in common.

Thus it was that the British Empire, which had effectively been for sale in 1945, was broken up rather than being taken over; went into liquidation rather than acquiring a new owner. It had taken around three centuries to build. At its height it had covered a quarter of the world's land surface and governed around the same proportion of its population. It took just three decades to dismantle, leaving only a few scattered islands – from Ascension to Tristan da Cunha – as mementoes.

Back in 1892 the young Churchill had been all too right to expect 'great upheavals' in the course of his long life. But by the time of his death in 1965 it had become clear that his hope of saving the Empire had been no more than a schoolboy fantasy.

When faced with the choice between appeasing or fighting the worst empires in all history, the British Empire had done the right thing. Even Churchill, staunch imperialist that he was, did not have to think for long before rejecting Hitler's squalid offer to let it survive alongside a Nazified Europe. In 1940, under Churchill's inspired, indomitable, incomparable leadership, the Empire had stood alone against the truly evil imperialism of Hitler. Even if it did not last for the thousand years that Churchill hopefully suggested it might, this was indeed the British Empire's 'finest hour'.

Yet what made it so fine, so authentically noble, was that the Empire's victory could only ever have been Pyrrhic. In the end, the British sacrificed her Empire to stop the Germans, Japanese and Italians from keeping theirs. Did not that sacrifice alone expunge all the Empire's other sins?

Conclusion

Great Britain has lost an Empire and has not yet found a role.

Dean Acheson, 1962

The British Empire is long dead; only flotsam and jetsam now remain. What had been based on Britain's commercial and financial supremacy in the seventeenth and eighteenth centuries and her industrial supremacy in the nineteenth was bound to crumble once the British economy buckled under the accumulated burdens of two world wars. The great creditor became a debtor. In the same way, the great movements of population that had once driven British imperial expansion changed their direction in the 1950s. Emigration from Britain gave way to immigration into Britain. As for the missionary impulse that had sent thousands of young men and women around the world preaching Christianity and the gospel of cleanliness, that too dwindled, along with public attendance at church. Christianity today is stronger in many of her former colonies than in Britain itself.

Sir Richard Turnbull, the penultimate Governor of Aden, once told Labour politician Denis Healey that 'when the British Empire finally sank beneath the waves of history, it would leave behind it only two monuments: one was the game of Association Football, the other was the expression "Fuck off".' In truth, the imperial legacy has shaped the modern world so profoundly that we almost take it for granted.

Without the spread of British rule around the world, it is hard to believe that the structures of liberal capitalism would have been so successfully established in so many different economies around the world. Those empires that adopted alternative models – the Russian and the Chinese – imposed incalculable misery on their subject peoples. Without the influence of British imperial rule, it is hard to believe that the institutions of parliamentary democracy would have been adopted by the majority of states in the world, as they are today. India, the world's largest democracy, owes more than it is fashionable to acknowledge to British rule. Its elite schools, its universities, its civil service, its army, its press and its parliamentary system all still have discernibly British models. Finally, there is the English language itself, perhaps the most important single export of the last 300 years. Today 350 million people speak English as their first language and around 450 million have it as a second language. That is roughly one in every seven people on the planet.

Of course no one would claim that the record of the British Empire was unblemished. On the contrary, I have tried to show how often it failed to live up to its own ideal of individual liberty, particularly in the early era of enslavement, transportation and the 'ethnic cleansing' of indigenous peoples. Yet the nineteenth-century Empire undeniably pioneered free trade, free capital movements and, with the abolition of slavery, free labour. It invested immense sums in developing a global network of modern communications. It spread and enforced the rule of law over vast areas. Though it fought many small wars, the Empire maintained a global peace unmatched before or since. In the twentieth century too it more than justified its own existence, for the alternatives to British rule represented by the German and Japanese empires were clearly far worse. And without its Empire, it is inconceivable that Britain could have withstood them.

There would certainly not have been so much free trade between the 1840s and the 1930s had it not been for the British Empire. Relinquishing Britain's colonies in the second half of the nineteenth century would have led to higher tariffs in their markets, and perhaps other forms of trade discrimination. The evidence for this need not be purely hypothetical; it manifested itself in the highly protectionist policies adopted by the United States and India after they secured independence, as well as in the tariffs adopted by Britain's imperial rivals France, Germany and Russia in the 1870s and after. Britain's military budget before the First World War can therefore be seen as a remarkably low insurance premium against international protectionism. According to one estimate, the economic benefit to the UK of enforcing free trade could have been as high as 6.5 per cent of gross national product. No one has yet ventured to estimate what the benefit to the world economy as a whole may have been; but that it was a benefit and not a cost seems beyond dispute, given the catastrophic consequences of the global descent into protectionism as Britain's imperial power waned in the 1930s.

Nor would there have been so much international mobility of labour – and hence so much global convergence of incomes before 1914 – without the British Empire. True, the United States was always the most attractive destination for nineteenth-century migrants from Europe; nor did all the migrants originate in the colonizing countries. But it should not be forgotten that the core of the US had been under British rule for the better part of a century and a half before the War of Independence, and that the differences between independent and British North America remained minor.

It is also worth remembering that the significance of the white dominions as destinations for British emigrants grew markedly after 1914, as the US tightened restrictions on immigration and, after 1929, endured a far worse Depression than anything experienced in the sterling bloc. Finally, we should not lose sight of the vast numbers of Asians who left India and China to work as indentured labourers, many of them on British plantations and mines in the course of the nineteenth century. There is no question that the majority of them suffered great hardship; many indeed might well have been better off staying at home. But once again we cannot pretend that this mobilization of cheap and probably underemployed Asian labour to grow rubber and dig gold had no economic value.

Consider too the role of the British Empire in facilitating capital export to the less developed world. Although some measures of international financial integration seem to suggest that the 1990s saw greater cross-border capital flows than the 1890s, in reality much of today's overseas investment goes on within the developed world. In 1996 only 28 per cent of foreign direct investment went to developing countries, whereas in 1913 the proportion was 63 per cent. Another, stricter measure shows that in 1997 only around 5 per cent of the world stock of capital was invested in countries with per capita incomes of 20 per cent or less of US per capita GDP. In 1913 the figure was 25 per cent. A plausible hypothesis is that empire – and particularly the British Empire – encouraged investors to put their money in developing economies. The reasoning here is straightforward. Investing in such economies is risky. They tend to be far away and more prone to economic, social and political crises. But the extension of empire into the less developed world had the effect of reducing such risks by imposing, directly or indirectly, some form of European rule. In practice, money invested in a *de jure* British colony such as India (or a colony in all but name, like Egypt) was a great deal more secure than money invested in a *de facto* 'colony' such as Argentina. This was a better 'seal of good house-keeping approval' even than membership of the gold standard (which effectively guaranteed investors against inflation) – though most British colonies ultimately had both.

For all these reasons, the notion that British imperialism tended to impoverish colonized countries seems inherently problematic. That is not to say that many former colonies are not exceedingly poor. Today, for example, per capita GDP in Britain is roughly twenty-eight times what it is in Zambia, which means that the average Zambian has to live on something less than two dollars a day. But to blame this on the legacy of colonialism is not very persuasive, when the differential between British and Zambian incomes was so much less at the end of the colonial period. In 1955 British per capita GDP was just seven times greater than Zambian. It has been since independence that the gap between the colonizer and the ex-colony has become a gulf. The same is true of nearly all former colonies in sub-Saharan Africa, with the notable exception of Botswana.

A country's economic fortunes are determined by a combination of natural endowments (geography, broadly speaking) and human action (history, for short); this is economic history's version of the nature-nurture debate. While a persuasive case can be made for the importance of such 'given' factors as the mean temperature, humidity, the prevalence of disease, soil quality, proximity to the sea, latitude and mineral resources in determining economic performance, there seems strong evidence that history too plays a crucial part. In particular, there is good evidence that the imposition of British-style institutions has tended to enhance a country's economic prospects, particularly in those settings where indigenous cultures were relatively weak because of thin (or thinned) population, allowing British institutions to dominate with little dilution. Where the British, like the Spaniards, conquered already sophisticated, urbanized societies, the effects of colonization were more commonly negative, as the colonizers were tempted to engage in plunder rather than to build their own institutions. Indeed, this is perhaps the best available explanation of that 'great divergence' which reduced India and China from being quite possibly the world's most advanced economies in the sixteenth century to relative poverty by the early twentieth. It also explains why it was that Britain was able to overhaul her Iberian rivals: precisely because, as a latecomer to the imperial race, she had to settle for colonizing the unpromising wastes of Virginia and New England, rather than the eminently lootable cities of Mexico and Peru.

But which British institutions promoted development? First, we should not underestimate the benefits conferred by British law and administration. A recent survey of forty-nine countries concluded that 'common-law countries have the strongest, and French-civil-law countries the weakest, legal protections of investors', including both shareholders and creditors. This is of enormous importance in encouraging capital formation, without which entrepreneurs can achieve little. The fact that eighteen of the sample countries have the common-law system is of course almost entirely due to their having been at one time or another under British rule.

A similar point can be made about the nature of British

governance. At its apogee in the mid-nineteenth century, two features of the Indian and Colonial services are especially striking when compared with many modern regimes in Asia and Africa. First, British administration was remarkably cheap and efficient. Secondly, it was remarkably non-venal. Its sins were generally sins of omission, not commission. This too cannot be wholly without significance, given the demonstrable correlations today between economic under-performance and both excessive government expenditure and public sector corruption.

The economic historian David Landes recently drew up a list of measures which 'the ideal growth-and-development' government would adopt. Such a government, he suggests, would

1 secure rights of private property, the better to encourage saving and investment;
2 secure rights of personal liberty . . . against both the abuses of tyranny and . . . crime and corruption;
3 enforce rights of contract;
4 provide stable government . . . governed by publicly known rules;
5 provide responsive government;
6 provide honest government . . . [with] no rents to favour and position;
7 provide moderate, efficient, ungreedy government . . . to hold taxes down [and] reduce the government's claim on the social surplus.

The striking thing about this list is how many of its points correspond to what British Indian and Colonial officials in the nineteenth and twentieth century believed they were doing. The sole, obvious exceptions are points 2 and 5. Yet the British argument for postponing (sometimes indefinitely) the transfer to democracy was that many of their colonies were not yet ready for it; indeed, the classic and not wholly disingenuous twentieth-century line from the Colonial Office was that Britain's role was precisely to get them ready.

It is a point worth emphasizing that to a significant extent British rule did have that benign effect. According to the work of political scientists like Seymour Martin Lipset, countries that were former

British colonies had a significantly better chance of achieving enduring democratization after independence than those ruled by other
countries. Indeed, nearly every country with a population of at least
a million that has emerged from the colonial era without succumbing to dictatorship is a former British colony. True, there have been
many former colonies which have not managed to sustain free
institutions: Bangladesh, Burma, Kenya, Pakistan, Tanzania and
Zimbabwe spring to mind. But in a sample of fifty-three countries
that were former British colonies, just under half (twenty-six) were
still democracies in 1993. This can be attributed to the way that
British rule, particularly where it was 'indirect', encouraged the
formation of collaborating elites; it may also be related to the role of
Protestant missionaries, who clearly played a part in encouraging
Western-style aspirations for political freedom in parts of Africa and
the Caribbean.

In short, what the British Empire proved is that empire is a form
of international government that can work – and not just for the
benefit of the ruling power. It sought to globalize not just an economic but a legal and ultimately a political system too.

The final question to be addressed is whether anything can be
learned from the British imperial example?

It must be said that the experiment of running the world without
the Empire cannot be adjudged an unqualified success. The post-
imperial age has been characterized by two contradictory tendencies: economic globalization and political fragmentation. The
former has certainly promoted economic growth, but the fruits of
growth have been very unevenly distributed. The latter tendency
has been associated with the problems of civil war and political
instability, which have played a major role in impoverishing the
poorer countries of the world.

Overall, the world experienced higher growth in the second
half of the twentieth century than at any other time. Much of that
was undoubtedly due to the very rapid growth achieved in the
period of reconstruction after the Second World War. According to
the best available estimates, the average annual rate of growth of

world GDP per capita was 2.93 per cent between 1950 and 1973, compared with the miserably low figure of 0.91 per cent for the depressed and war-torn years 1913–50. The entire period from 1913 to 1973 was a time of economic disintegration, however, flanked on either side by periods of economic globalization. These delivered remarkably similar rates of growth in per capita GDP: 1.30 per cent from 1870 to 1913; 1.33 from 1973 to 1998. However, the earlier period of globalization was associated with a degree of convergence in international income levels, particularly between the economies on either side of the Atlantic Ocean, whereas the recent period has been associated with a marked global divergence, particularly as the rest of the world has pulled away from sub-Saharan Africa. There can be little doubt that this is due in part to the lopsided nature of economic globalization – the fact that capital flows mainly within the developed world and that trade and migration are still restricted in many ways. This was less true in the pre-1914 age of globalization when, partly under the influence of imperial structures, investors were encouraged to put money into developing economies.

On the eve of the First World War, imperialism had reduced the number of independent countries in the world to fifty-nine. But since the advent of decolonization there have been sustained increases in that number. In 1946 there were seventy-four independent countries; in 1950, eighty-nine. By 1995 the number was 192, with the two biggest increases coming in the 1960s (mainly Africa, where twenty-five new states were formed between 1960 and 1964) and the 1990s (mainly Eastern Europe, as the Soviet Empire disintegrated). And many of the new states are tiny. No fewer than fifty-eight of today's states have populations less than 2.5 million; thirty-five have less than 500,000 inhabitants. There are two disadvantages to this political fragmentation. Small countries are often formed as a result of civil war within an earlier multi-ethnic polity – the most common form of conflict since 1945. That in itself is economically disruptive. In addition, they can be economically inefficient even in peacetime, too small to justify all the paraphernalia of statehood they insist on decking themselves out in: border posts, bureaucracies and the rest. Political fissiparity – the fragmentation of states – and its attendant economic costs have been among the principal sources of instability in the post-war world.

Finally, although Anglophone economic and political liberalism remains the most alluring of the world's cultures, it continues to face, as it has since the Iranian revolution, a serious threat from Islamic fundamentalism. In the absence of formal empire, it must be open to question how far the dissemination of Western 'civilization' – meaning the Protestant–Deist–Catholic–Jewish mix that emanates from modern America – can safely be entrusted to Messrs Disney and McDonald.

These tendencies provide the best explanation for the failure of history to 'end' with the collapse of the Soviet Empire in 1989–91 and the persistent instability of the post-Cold War world – the most spectacular symptom of which was of course the attacks of 11 September 2001 on the World Trade Center and the Pentagon.

A New Imperialism?

Less than a month after those attacks, the British Prime Minister Tony Blair made a messianic speech to the Labour Party's annual conference at Brighton. In it he spoke with fervour of the 'politics of globalization'; of 'another dimension' of international relations; of the need to 're-order this world around us'. The impending war to overthrow and replace the Taliban regime in Afghanistan, he suggested, was not the first step in the direction of such a re-ordering; nor would it be the last. Already there had been successful interventions against other rogue governments: the Milošević regime in Serbia and the 'murderous group of gangsters' who had attempted to seize power in Sierra Leone. 'And I tell you,' he declared, 'if Rwanda happened again today as it did in 1993, when a million people were slaughtered in cold blood, we would have a moral duty to act there also.' The cases of Kosovo and Sierra Leone were plainly to be understood as models of what could be achieved by intervention; the case of Rwanda as a lamentable example of the consequences of non-intervention. Of course, he hastened to add, Britain could not be expected to carry out such operations on a regular basis. But 'the power of the international community' could 'do it all . . . if it chose to':

It could, with our help, sort out the blight that is the continuing conflict in the Democratic Republic of Congo, where three million people have died through war or famine in the last decade. A Partnership for Africa, between the developed and developing world . . . is there to be done if we find the will.

The nature of this partnership would be a straightforward 'deal':

On our side: provide more aid, untied to trade; write off debt; help with good governance and infrastructure, training to the soldiers . . . in conflict resolution; encouraging investment; and access to our markets . . . On the African side: true democracy, no more excuses for dictatorship, abuses of human rights; no tolerance of bad governance . . . [and] the endemic corruption of some states . . . Proper commercial, legal and financial systems.

Nor was that all. In the aftermath of the attacks of 11 September, Mr Blair declared his desire for 'justice':

Justice not only to punish the guilty. But justice to bring those same values of democracy and freedom to people round the world . . . The starving, the wretched, the dispossessed, the ignorant, those living in want and squalor from the deserts of Northern Africa to the slums of Gaza, to the mountain ranges of Afghanistan: they too are our cause.

Not since before the Suez Crisis has a British Prime Minister talked with such unreserved enthusiasm about what Britain could do for the rest of the world. Indeed, it is hard to think of a Prime Minister since Gladstone so ready to make what sounds remarkably like undiluted altruism the basis of his foreign policy. The striking thing, however, is that with only a little rewriting this could be made to sound an altogether more menacing project. Routine intervention to overthrow governments deemed to be 'bad'; economic assistance in return for 'good' government and 'proper commercial, legal and financial systems'; a mandate to 'bring . . . [the] values of democracy and freedom' to 'people round the world'. On reflection, this bears more than a passing resemblance to the Victorians' project to export their own 'civilization' to the world. As we have seen, the Victorians regarded overthrowing rogue regimes from Abyssinia to Oudh as an entirely legitimate part of the civilizing process; the Indian Civil Service prided itself on replacing 'bad' government with 'good'; while Victorian missionaries had an absolute confidence that it was their role to bring the values of Christianity and commerce to the same 'people round the world' to whom Mr Blair wishes to bring 'democracy and freedom'.

Nor do the resemblances end there. When the British went to war against the dervishes in the Sudan in the 1880s and 1890s, they had no doubt that they were bringing 'justice' to a rogue regime. The Mahdi was in many ways a Victorian Osama bin Laden, a renegade Islamic fundamentalist whose murder of General Gordon was '9/11' in miniature. The Battle of Omdurman was the prototype for the kinds of war the US has been fighting since 1990, against Iraq, against Serbia, against the Taliban. Just as the US Air Force bombed Serbia in 1999 in the name of 'human rights', so the Royal Navy conducted raids on the West African coast in the 1840s and even threatened Brazil with war as part of the campaign to end the slave trade. And when Mr Blair justifies intervention against 'bad' regimes by promising aid and investment in return, he is unconsciously echoing the Gladstonian Liberals, who rationalized their military occupation of Egypt in 1881 in much the same way. Even the widespread feminist disdain for the Taliban regime's treatment of women recalls the way British administrators in India strove to stamp out the customs of *sati* and female infanticide.

In an article published a few months after Mr Blair's speech, the British diplomat Robert Cooper had the courage to call this new policy of 're-ordering the world' by its correct name. If rogue 'premodern' states became 'too dangerous for established states to tolerate,' he wrote, it was 'possible to imagine a defensive imperialism', since: 'The most logical way to deal with chaos, and the one most employed in the past is colonization.' Unfortunately, the words 'empire and imperialism' have become 'a form of abuse' in the 'postmodern' world:

Today, there are no colonial powers willing to take on the job, though the opportunities, perhaps even the need for colonization is as great as it ever was in the nineteenth century ... All the conditions for imperialism are there, but both the supply and demand for imperialism have dried up. And yet the weak still need the strong and the strong still need an orderly world. A world in which the efficient and well governed export stability and liberty, and which is open for investment and growth – all of this seems eminently desirable.

Cooper's solution to this problem was what he called 'a new kind of imperialism, one acceptable to a world of human rights and cosmopolitan values ... an imperialism which, like all imperialism, aims to bring order and organization but which rests today on the voluntary principle'. The precise nature of this 'postmodern imperialism', he suggested, might be extrapolated from the existing 'voluntary imperialism of the global economy', meaning the power of the International Monetary Fund and World Bank, and what he called 'the imperialism of neighbours', meaning the perennial practice of interference in a next-door country whose instability threatens to spread over the border. The institutional locus of Cooper's new imperialism, however, was none other than the European Union:

The postmodern EU offers a vision of cooperative empire, a common liberty and a common security without the ethnic domination and centralized absolutism to which past empires have been subject, but also without the ethnic exclusiveness that is the hallmark of the nation state ... A cooperative empire might be ... a framework in which each has a share in the government, in which no single country dominates and in which the governing principles are not ethnic but legal. The lightest of touches will be required from the centre; the 'imperial bureaucracy' must be under control, accountable, and the servant, not the master, of the commonwealth. Such an institution must be as dedicated to liberty and democracy as its constituent parts. Like Rome, this commonwealth would provide its citizens with some of its laws, some coins and the occasional road.

Perhaps what the Blair speech and the Cooper article both illustrate most clearly is how tenacious the grip of empire remains on the Oxford-educated mind. Yet there is a conspicuous defect in both of their arguments which suggests that idealism has got the better of realism. The reality is that neither the international community (Blair) nor the European Union (Cooper) is in a position to play the part of a new British Empire. This is for the simple reason that neither has the fiscal or the military resources to do so. The total operating expenses of the UN and all its affiliated institutions amount to around $18 billion a year, approximately 1 per cent of the US federal budget. For its part, the European Union's total budget is little more than one per cent of total European GDP; expenditure by national governments accounts for just under 50 per cent. In this respect, both the UN and the EU resemble not so much the Rome of the Emperors as the Rome of the Pope – of whom Stalin famously asked: 'How many divisions has he?'

There is, in truth, only one power capable of playing an imperial role in the modern world, and that is the United States. Indeed, to some degree it is already playing that role.

Bearing the Burden

What lessons can the United States today draw from the British experience of empire? The obvious one is that the most successful economy in the world – as Britain was for most of the eighteenth and nineteenth centuries – can do a very great deal to impose its preferred values on less technologically advanced societies. It is nothing short of astonishing that Great Britain was able to govern so much of the world without running up an especially large defence bill. To be precise, Britain's defence expenditure averaged little more than 3 per cent of net national product between 1870 and 1913, and it was lower for the rest of the nineteenth century.

This was money well spent. No doubt it is true that, in theory, open international markets would have been preferable to imperialism; but in practice global free trade was not and is not naturally occurring. The British Empire enforced it.

By comparison, the United States today is vastly wealthier relative to the rest of the world than Britain ever was. In 1913 Britain's share of total world output was 8 per cent; the equivalent figure for the US in 1998 was 22 per cent. Nor should anybody pretend that, at least in fiscal terms, the cost of expanding the American Empire, even if it were to mean a great many small wars like the one in Afghanistan, would be prohibitive. In 2000 American defence spending stood at just under 3 per cent of gross national product, compared with an average for the years 1948–98 of 6.8 per cent. Even after big cuts in military expenditure, the United States is still the world's only superpower, with an unrivalled financial and military-technological capability. Its defence budget is fourteen times that of China and twenty-two times that of Russia. Britain never enjoyed such a lead over her imperial rivals.

The hypothesis, in other words, is a step in the direction of political globalization, with the United States shifting from informal to formal empire much as late Victorian Britain once did. That is certainly what we should expect if history does indeed repeat itself. Though its imperialism was not wholly absent-minded, Britain did not set out to rule a quarter of the world's land surface. As we have seen, its empire began as a network of coastal bases and informal spheres of influence, much like the post-1945 American 'empire'. But real and perceived threats to their commercial interests constantly tempted the British to progress from informal to formal imperialism. That was how so much of the atlas came to be coloured imperial red.

No one could deny the extent of the American informal empire – the empire of multinational corporations, of Hollywood movies and even of TV evangelists. Is this so very different from the early British Empire of monopoly trading companies and missionaries? Nor is it any coincidence that a map showing the principal US military bases around the world looks remarkably like a map of Royal

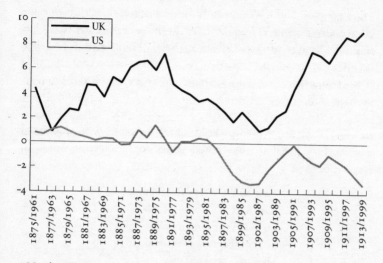

Net foreign investment as a percentage of Gross National Product, UK 1875–1913 compared with US 1961–1999

Navy coaling stations a hundred years ago. Even recent American foreign policy recalls the gunboat diplomacy of the British Empire in its Victorian heyday, when a little trouble on the periphery could be dealt with by a short, sharp 'surgical strike'. The only difference is that today's gunboats fly.

Yet in three respects the process of 'Anglobalization' is fundamentally different today. On close inspection, America's strengths may not be the strengths of a natural imperial hegemon. For one thing, British imperial power relied on the massive export of capital and people. But since 1972 the American economy has been a net *im*porter of capital (to the tune of 5 per cent of gross domestic product in 2002) and it remains the favoured destination of immigrants from around the world, not a producer of would-be colonial emigrants. Britain in its heyday was able to draw on a culture of unabashed imperialism which dated back to the Elizabethan period, whereas the US – born not in a war against slavery, as Mr Blair seemed to suggest in his conference speech, but in a war against the British Empire – will always be a reluctant ruler of other peoples. Since Woodrow Wilson's intervention to restore the elected government in Mexico in 1913, the American approach has too often been to fire some shells, march in, hold elections and then get the hell out – until the next crisis. Haiti is one recent example; Kosovo another. Afghanistan may yet prove to be the next, or perhaps Iraq.

In 1899 Rudyard Kipling, the Empire's greatest poet, addressed a powerful appeal to the United States to shoulder its imperial responsibilities:

> Take up the White Man's Burden–
> Send forth the best ye breed–
> Go bind your sons in exile
> To serve your captives' need;
> To wait in heavy harness
> On fluttered folk and wild–
> Your new-caught, sullen peoples,
> Half devil and half child.
>
> Take up the White Man's Burden
> And reap his old reward:
> The blame of those ye better,
> The hate of those ye guard . . .

No one would dare use such politically incorrect language today. The reality is nevertheless that the United States has – whether it admits it or not – taken up some kind of global burden, just as Kipling urged. It considers itself responsible not just for waging a war against terrorism and rogue states, but also for spreading the benefits of capitalism and democracy overseas. And just like the British Empire before it, the American Empire unfailingly acts in the name of liberty, even when its own self-interest is manifestly uppermost. That was the point made by John Buchan, looking back on the heyday of Milner's imperialist kindergarten from the dark vantage point of 1940:

I dreamed of a world-wide brotherhood with the background of a common race and creed, consecrated to the service of peace; Britain enriching the rest out of her culture and traditions, and the spirit of the Dominions like a strong wind freshening the stuffiness of the old lands ... We believed that we were laying the basis of a federation of the world ... The 'white man's burden' is now an almost meaningless phrase; then it involved a new philosophy of politics, and an ethical standard, serious and surely not ignoble.

But Buchan, like Churchill, detected an heir to this legacy, on the other side of the Atlantic.

... There are on the globe only two proven large-scale organizations of social units, the United States and the British Empire. The latter is [no longer] for export ... But the United States ... is the supreme example of a federation in being ... If the world is ever to have prosperity and peace, there must be some kind of federation – I will not say of democracies, but of States which accept the reign of Law. In such a task she seems to me to be the predestined leader.

Allowing for wartime rhetoric, there is more than a little truth in that. And yet the empire that rules the world today is both more and less than its British begetter. It has a much bigger economy, many more people, a much larger arsenal. But it is an empire that lacks the drive to export its capital, its people and its culture to those backward regions which need them most urgently and which, if they are neglected, will breed the greatest threats to its security. It is an empire, in short, that dare not speak its name. It is an empire in denial.

The American Secretary of State Dean Acheson famously said that Britain had lost an empire but failed to find a role. Perhaps the reality is that the Americans have taken our old role without yet facing the fact that an empire comes with it. The technology of overseas rule may have changed – the Dreadnoughts may have given way to F-15s. But like it or not, and deny it who will, empire is as much a reality today as it was throughout the three hundred years when Britain ruled, and made, the modern world.

Acknowledgements

A book like this is, more than most, the product of a collective effort. Although many of the people I wish to thank here thought they were working for a production company or a channel with the objective of making a television series, they were always contributing towards these printed pages as well.

In the first instance, I would like to thank Janice Hadlow, the head of History at Channel 4, at whose initiative both book and series came into being. Also present at the creation was her deputy, Hamish Mykura, who was originally the Series Producer. At Blakeway Productions, I owe an immense debt to Denys Blakeway, the Executive Producer; Charles Miller, Hamish Mykura's successor as Series Producer; Melanie Fall, the Series Associate Producer; Helen Britton and Rosie Schellenberg, the Assistant Producers; Grace Chapman, the Series Researcher; Alex Watson, Joanna Potts and Rosalind Bentley, the Researchers; Emma Macfarlane, the Production Co-ordinator; Clare Odgers, the Production Manager; and Kate Macky, the Office Manager.

I learned an immense amount about how to tell a story from the three directors who worked on *Empire*: Russell Barnes, Adrian Pennink and David Wilson. I am also indebted to Dewald Aukema, Tim Cragg, Vaughan Matthews and Chris Openshaw, the cameramen; Dhruv Singh, the camera assistant; as well as Adam Prescod, Martin Geissmann, Tony Bensusan and Paul Kennedy, the soundmen.

'Fixers' are crucial figures in any television series: special thanks are therefore due to Maxine Walters and Ele Rickham (Jamaica), Matt Bainbridge (United States), Sam Jennings (Australia), Lansana Fofana (Sierra Leone), Goran Musíc (South Africa), Alan Harkness (Zambia), Nicky Sayer (Zanzibar), Funda Odemis (Turkey), Toby Sinclair and Reinee Ghosh (India).

For various acts of kindness and assistance I would also like to thank Alric, Nasir, the Principal of Lamartinière College, Joan Abrahams, Richard and

ACKNOWLEDGEMENTS

Jane Aitken, Gourab K. Banerji, Rod Beattie, Professor A. Chaterjee, Dayn Cooper, Tom Cunningham, Steve Dodd, Eric Doucot, Tessa Fleischer, Rob Fransisco, Penny Fustle, Alan Harkness, Peter Jacques, Pastor Hendric James, Jean François Lesage, Swapna Liddle, Neil McKendrick, Ravi Manet, John Manson, Bill Markham, Said Suleiman Mohammed, George Mudavanhu, Chief Mukuni, Gremlin Napier, Tracy O'Brian, Adolph Oppong, Mabvuto Phiri, Victoria Phiri, G. S. Rawat, Ludi Schulze, His Excellency Viren Shah, Mark Shaw, Ratanjit Singh, Jane Skinner, Mary Slattery, Iona Smith, Simon Smith, Angus Stevens, Colin Steyn, Philip Tetley, Bishop Douglas Toto, Lieutenant Chris Watt and Elria Wessels.

Writers need good agents; I have been lucky enough to have Clare Alexander, Sally Riley and all at Gillon Aitken, as well as Sue Ayton at Knight Ayton. At Penguin, thanks are due in particular to Anthony Forbes-Watson, Helen Fraser, Cecilia Mackay, Richard Marston and Andrew Rosenheim. Above all, I would like to thank my editor, Simon Winder, whose enthusiasm and encouragement have been above and beyond the call of duty.

Without the support of my colleagues at Jesus College, Oxford, and the Oxford History Faculty, I would not have been able to find the time to write this book and certainly not to make the series. In particular, I would like to thank Bernhard Fulda, Felicity Heal and Turlough Stone.

Finally, many members of my family have helped me to find out more about my own imperial past. I would particularly like to thank my mother and father, Molly and Campbell Ferguson, my grandmother, May Hamilton, my parents-in-law Ken and Vivienne Douglas, and my cousin Sylvia Peters in Canada. Above all, I need to thank Susan, Felix, Freya and Lachlan, who had to soldier on at home – like so many families before them – while Father did his bit for the Empire.

In a venture so collaborative, the scope for human error is inevitably widened. A number of attentive readers kindly wrote to point out slips in the hardback edition. In particular, I should like to thank the hawk-eyed Mr L. W. Haigh. I nevertheless take full responsibility for any mistakes that have survived.

Jesus College, Oxford
July 2003

Illustration Acknowledgements

Photographic acknowledgements are given in parentheses. Every effort has been made to contact all copyright holders. The publishers will be happy to make good in future editions any errors or omissions brought to their attention.

1 Agnes Ferguson with her family at Glenrock, *c.* 1911–21 (by courtesy of Campbell Ferguson)

2 French and Portuguese ships off Buttugar, engraving by Theodore de Bry, for Jacques le Moyne de Morgues, *Navigatio in Braziliam*, 1562 (Musée de la Marine, Paris/The Art Archive)

3 Thomas 'Diamond' Pitt, portrait by John Vanderbank, *c.* 1710–20 (private collection)

4 'The Mast House at Blackwall', by William Daniell, 1803 (© National Maritime Museum, London)

5 'Robert Clive with his Family and an Indian Maidservant', by Sir Joshua Reynolds, *c.* 1765–6 (Gemäldegalerie, Berlin/© Bildarchiv Preußischer Kultbesitz/Jörg P Anders)

6 Eight Gurkhas, group portrait by member(s) of the Ghulam Ali Khan Family, Delhi, *c.* 1815 (The Gurkha Museum, Winchester)

7 'Colonel James Todd Travelling by Elephant with his Cavalry & Sepoys', painting by anonymous East India Company artist, eighteenth century (Victoria & Albert Museum/Bridgeman Art Library)

8 Slaves below decks, watercolour sketch by Lieutenant Meynell, 1844–6 (© National Maritime Museum, London)

9 Sugar plantation in the south of Trinidad, by C. Bauer, *c.* 1850 (private collection/Bridgeman Art Library)

10 'Attack on Bunker's Hill, with the Burning of Charles Town', American School, 1783 or after (Gift of Edgar William and Bernice Chrysler Garbisch. Photograph © Board of Trustees, National Gallery of Art, Washington)

11 'Flogging of the Convict Charles Maher', sketch by J. L., 1823, from *Recollections of Thirteen Years' Residence*, by Robert Jones (Mitchell Library, State Library of New South Wales, Sydney)

12 'A Government Jail Gang at Sydney', by Augustus Earle, 1830 (© National Maritime Museum, London)

13 Slaves in chains, Zanzibar, nineteenth century (Bojan Brecelj/Corbis)

14 David Livingstone, photograph by Maull & Co., *c.* 1864–5 (by courtesy of the National Portrait Gallery, London)

15 An Itinerant Preacher in India, illustration by Anon., nineteenth century (United Society for the Propagation of the Gospel/Eileen Tweedy/The Art Archive)

16 'The Relief of Lucknow 1857: Jessie's Dream', by Frederick Goodall, 1858 (Sheffield City Art Galleries/Bridgeman Art Library)

17 'Passing the Cable on Board the *Great Eastern*', illustration by Robert Dudley from *The Atlantic Telegraph*, by William Howard Russell, 1866 (Science & Society Picture Library)

18 Indian Army with elephants, 1897 (Public Record Office Image Library)

19 Steamships on the Hugli River being loaded and unloaded, Calcutta, 1900 (Hulton Archive)

20 Lord Curzon and His Highness the Nizam at Aina-Khana, the Palace of Maharaja Peshkai, *c.* 1900 (Hulton Archive)

21 Grand procession past the Red Fort during the Delhi Durbar, 1903 (© The British Library)

22 Aurobindo Ghose

23 The victors of Tel-el-Kebir: Scottish troops round the Sphinx, Giza, 1882 (Bettmann/Hulton Archive)

24 Hiram Maxim demonstrating the Maxim gun, *c.* 1880 (© Bettmann/ Corbis)

25 The dead at Omdurman, 1898 (by courtesy of the Director, National Army Museum, London)

26 Churchill bound for England, 1899 (© Bettmann/Corbis)

27 Dead bodies on Spion Kop, Natal, 1900 (Hulton Archive)

28 French cartoon criticizing Boer War concentration camps, by Jean Veber, from *L'Assiette au Beurre*, 28 September 1901 (Archives Charmet/ Bridgeman Art Library)

29 A Spectre in the Light of Day, cartoon from front cover of *Der Wahre Jacob*, 11 September 1900 (AKG London)

30 'Our Allies', French postcard showing English and Hindu soldiers, Nantes, 1914 (private collection/AKG London)

31 T. E. Lawrence, photograph by B. E. Leeson, 1917 (by courtesy of the National Portrait Gallery, London)

32 Sketch of Konyu–Hintok cutting, Thailand, 1942, by Allied PoW Jack Chalker (by courtesy of Jack Walker)

33 Japanese cartoon inciting Indians to throw off British rule, c. 1942 (Imperial War Museum, Department of Printed Books)

34 'Double Nine: Allied Teamwork Wins the Game', Cuban caricature by Conrado Massaguer (© Estate of Conrado Massaguer/Franklin. D Roosevelt Library, New York/Bridgeman Art Library)

35 Colonel Gamal Abdel-Nasser amid crowds during a demonstration against the proposed dissolution of the Revolutionary Council, Egypt, 29 March 1954 (Hulton Archive)

36 Blockade of Port Said during the Suez Crisis, 19 November 1956 (© Hulton-Deutsch Collection/Corbis)

Bibliography

The following is not intended as a comprehensive bibliography of imperial history, which would occupy an excessive number of pages. Rather, it is intended to indicate the principal works on which I have drawn in my research, and to acknowledge my debt to their authors, as well as to provide suggestions for 'further reading'.

GENERAL

Abernethy, David B., *The Dynamics of Global Dominance: European Overseas Empires 1415–1980* (New Haven, 2001)

Brown, Judith M. and Louis, Wm. Roger (eds.), *The Oxford History of the British Empire, vol. IV: The Twentieth Century* (Oxford/New York, 1999)

Canny, Nicholas (ed.), *The Oxford History of the British Empire, vol. I: The Origins of Empire* (Oxford/New York, 1998)

Fieldhouse, David, *The Colonial Empires* (London, 1966)

Harlow, Barbara and Carter, Mia, *Imperialism and Orientalism: A Documentary Sourcebook* (Oxford/ Malden, Massachusetts, 1999)

Hyam, Ronald, *Britain's Imperial Century, 1815–1914* (Basingstoke, 1993)

James, Lawrence, *The Rise and Fall of the British Empire* (London, 1994)

Judd, Dennis, *Empire: the British Imperial Experience from 1765 to the Present* (London, 1996)

Lloyd, Trevor, *Empire: The History of the British Empire* (London, 2001)

Maddison, Angus, *The World Economy: A Millennial Perspective* (Paris, 2001)

Marshall, P. J. (ed.), *The Cambridge Illustrated History of the British Empire* (Cambridge, 1996)

— (ed.), *The Oxford History of the British Empire, vol. II: The Eighteenth Century* (Oxford/New York, 1998)

Morris, James, *Heaven's Command: An Imperial Progress* (London, 1992 [1973])

——, *Pax Britannica: The Climax of an Empire* (London, 1992 [1968])

——, *Farewell the Trumpets: An Imperial Retreat* (London, 1992 [1979])

Pagden, Anthony, *Peoples and Empires: Europeans and the Rest of the World, from Antiquity to the Present* (London, 2001)

Palmer, Alan, *Dictionary of the British Empire and Commonwealth* (London, 1996)

Porter, Andrew N. (ed.), *Atlas of British Overseas Expansion* (London, 1991)

—— (ed.), *The Oxford History of the British Empire, vol. III: The Nineteenth Century* (Oxford, New York, 1999)

Winks, Robin W. (ed.), *The Oxford History of the British Empire, vol. V: Historiography* (Oxford, New York, 1999)

CHAPTER I

Andrews, Kenneth R., 'Drake and South America', in Thrower, Norman J. W. (ed.), *Sir Francis Drake and the Famous Voyage, 1577–1580* (Berkeley/Los Angeles/London, 1984), pp. 49–59

Armitage, David, *The Ideological Origins of the British Empire* (Cambridge, 2000)

Barua, Pradeep, 'Military Developments in India, 1750–1850', *Journal of Military History*, 58/4(1994), pp. 599–616

Bayly, C. A., *Indian Society and the Making of the British Empire* (Cambridge, 1988)

——, *Imperial Meridian: The British Empire and the World, 1780–1830* (London, 1989)

Bernstein, Jeremy, *Dawning of the Raj: The Life and Trials of Warren Hastings* (London, 2001)

Boxer, C. R., *The Dutch Seaborne Empire, 1600–1800* (London, 1965)

Brenner, Robert, 'The Social Basis of English Commercial Expansion, 1550–1650', *Journal of Economic History*, 32/1 (1972), pp. 361–84

Brigden, Susan, *New Worlds, Lost Worlds* (London, 2000)

Carlos, Ann M. and Nicholas, Stephen, 'Agency Problems in Early Chartered Companies: The Case of the Hudson's Bay Company', *Journal of Economic History*, 50/4 (1990), pp. 853–75

Carnall, Geoffrey and Nicholson, Colin (eds.), *The Impeachment of Warren Hastings: Papers from a Bicentenary Commemoration* (Edinburgh, 1989)

Cell, Gillian T. (ed.), *Newfoundland Discovered: English Attempts at Colonisation, 1610–1630* (London, 1982)

Chaudhuri, K. N., *The English East India Company* (London, 1963)

——, *The Trading World of Asia and the English East India Company* (Cambridge, 1978)

Cruikshank, E. A., *The Life of Sir Henry Morgan, with an Account of the English Settlement of the Island of Jamaica, 1655–1688* (London/ Basingstoke/ Toronto, 1935)

Dalton, Sir Cornelius Neale, *The Life of Thomas Pitt* (Cambridge, 1915)

Dickson, P. G. M., *The Financial Revolution in England: A Study in the Development of Public Credit, 1688–1756* (London/Melbourne/Toronto, 1967)

Edney, Matthew H., *Mapping an Empire: The Geographical Construction of British India, 1765–1843* (Chicago/London, 1997)

Ehrman, John, *The Younger Pitt*, 3 vols. (London, 1969–1996)

Exquemlin, A. O., trans. Alexis Brown, *The Buccaneers of America. Comprising a Pertinent and Truthful Description of the Principal Acts of Depredation and Inhuman Cruelty committed by the English and French Buccaneers against the Spaniards in America* (London, 1972)

Forrest, Denys, *Tea for the British: The Social and Economic History of a Famous Trade* (London, 1973)

Fraser, J. Baillie, *Military Memoirs of Lieut. Col. James Skinner, C.B.* (Mussoorie, 1955 [1856])

Hagen, Victor Wolfgang von, *The Gold of El Dorado: The Quest for the Golden Man* (London/Toronto/Sydney/New York, 1978)

Hakluyt, Richard, edited, abridged and introduced by Jack Beeching, *Voyages and Discoveries: The Principal Navigations Voyages, Traffiques and Discoveries of the English Nation* (London, 1985 [1598–1600])

Heathcote, T. A., *The Military in British India: The Development of British Land Forces in South Asia, 1600–1947* (Manchester/New York, 1995)

Hemming, John, *The Search for El Dorado* (London, 1978)

Hossein Khan, Sied Gholam, *The Seir Mutaqherin: or Review of Modern Times: Being an History of India, From the Year 1118 to the Year 1194* (Calcutta, 1903 [1789])

Irwin, Douglas A., 'Mercantilism and Strategic Trade Policy: The Anglo-Dutch Rivalry for the East Indian Trade', *Journal of Political Economy*, 99/6 (1991), pp. 1296–314

——, 'Strategic Trade Policy and Mercantilist Trade Rivalries', *American Economic Review*, 2 (1982), pp. 134–9

Kelsey, Harry, *Sir Francis Drake: The Queen's Pirate* (New Haven/London, 1998)

Kennedy, Paul, *The Rise and Fall of British Naval Mastery* (London, 1976)

Koehn, Nancy F., *The Power of Commerce, Economy and Governance in the First British Empire* (Ithaca, New York, 1995)

Lemire, Beverly, *Fashion's Favourite: The Cotton Trade and the Consumer in Britain, 1660–1800* (Oxford, 1991)

Lindsay, Philip, *Morgan in Jamaica: Being an Account Biographical and Informative of the Latter Days of Sir Henry Morgan, Admiral of Buccaneers, Captain of Privateers . . . also Twice Acting Governor of Jamaica* (London, 1930)

Lyte, Charles, *Sir Joseph Banks: 18th Century Explorer, Botanist and Entrepreneur* (Devon, 1980)

MacInnes, C. M., *The Early English Tobacco Trade* (London, 1926)

Miller, David Philip and Reill, Peter Hanns (eds.), *Visions of Empire: Voyages, Botany, and Representations of Nature* (Cambridge/New York/Melbourne, 1996)

Neal, Larry, *The Rise of Financial Capitalism: International Capital Markets in the Age of Reason* (Cambridge, 1990)

Pagden, Anthony, *Lords of All the World: Ideologies of Empire in Spain, Britain and France, c. 1500–c. 1800* (New Haven, 1996)

Parry, John H., 'Drake and the World Encompassed', in Thrower, Norman J. W. (ed.), *Sir Francis Drake and the Famous Voyage, 1577–1580* (Berkeley/Los Angeles/London, 1984), pp. 1–11

Pearson, N. M., 'Shivaji and the Decline of the Mughal Empire', *Journal of Asian Studies*, 35/2 (1976), pp. 221–35

Pillai, Anandaranga, *The Private Diary of Ananda Ranga Pillai, Dubash to Joseph Francois Dupleix: A Record of Matters Political, Historical, Social, and Personal, from 1736 to 1761*, 12 vols. (Madras, 1904)

Pocock, Tom, *Battle For Empire: The Very First World War, 1756–63* (London, 1998)

Pope, Dudley, *The Buccaneer King: The Biography of Sir Henry Morgan, 1635– 1688* (New York, 1977)

Pope, Peter E., *The Many Landfalls of John Cabot* (Toronto/Buffalo/London, 1997)

Price, Jacob M., 'What Did Merchants Do? Reflections on British Overseas Trade, 1660–1790', *Journal of Economic History*, 49/2 (1989), pp. 267–84

Quinn, David Beers, *England and the Discovery of America, 1481–1620: From the Bristol Voyages of the Fifteenth Century to the Pilgrim Settlement at Plymouth – The Exploration, Exploitation, and Trial-and-Error Colonization of North America by the English* (London, 1974)

Riddy, John, 'Warren Hastings: Scotland's Benefactor', in G. Cornall and

C. Nicholson, *The Impeachment of Warren Hastings: Papers from a Bicentenary Commemoration* (Edinburgh, 1989), pp. 30–57

Rowse, A. L. and Dougan, Robert O. (eds.), *The Discoverie of Guiana by Sir Walter Ralegh, 1596 and The Discoveries of the World by Antonio Galvao, 1601: Historical Introductions and Bibliographical Notes* (Cleveland, Ohio, 1966)

Ruville, Albert von, trans. H. J. Chaytor, *William Pitt, Earl of Chatham* (London, 1907)

Sinclair, Andrew, *Sir Walter Raleigh and the Age of Discovery: The Extraordinary Life and Achievements of a Renaissance Explorer, Sailor and Scholar* (Harmondsworth, 1984)

Williams, Glyn, *'The Prize of all the Oceans': The Triumph and Tragedy of Anson's Voyage round the World* (London, 1999)

Williamson, James A., *The Cabot Voyages and Bristol Discovery under Henry VII* (Cambridge, 1962)

CHAPTER 2

Anderson, Fred, *Crucible of War: The Seven Years' War and the Fate of Empire in British North America, 1754–1766* (London, 2000)

Anstey, Roger, *The Atlantic Slave Trade and British Abolition, 1760–1810* (London, 1975)

Bailyn, Bernard, *The Ideological Origins of the American Revolution* (Cambridge, Mass., 1967)

——, *The Peopling of British North America* (New York, 1986)

Barbour, Philip L., *The Jamestown Voyages under the First Charter 1606–1609, vol. I: Documents Relating to the Foundation of Jamestown and the History of the Jamestown Colony up to the Departure of Captain John Smith, Last President of the Council in Virginia under the First Charter, Early in October 1609* (London/New York, 1969)

Bardon, Jonathan, *A History of Ulster* (Belfast, 1992)

Bauman, Richard, *For the Reputation of Truth: Politics, Religion, and Conflict among the Pennsylvania Quakers 1750–1800* (Baltimore/London, 1971)

Belich, James, *Making Peoples: A History of the New Zealanders from Polynesian Settlement to the End of the Nineteenth Century* (London, 1997)

——, *Paradise Reforged: A History of the New Zealanders from the 1880s to the Year 2000* (London, 2001)

Berlin, Ira, *Many Thousands Gone: The First Two Centuries of Slavery in North America* (Cambridge, Mass., 1998)

Blackburn, Robin, *The Making of New World Slavery: From the Baroque to the Modern, 1492–1800* (New York, 1997)

Boogart, E. Van Den and Emmer, P. C., 'Colonialism and Migration: An Over-view', in P. C. Emmer (ed.), *Colonialism and Migration: Indentured Labour before and after Slavery* (Dordrecht, 1986)

Brogan, Hugh, *The Pelican History of the United States of America* (Harmondsworth, 1986)

Calder, Angus, *Revolutionary Empire: The Rise of the English-Speaking Empires from the Fifteenth Century to the 1780s* (London, 1981)

Calhoon, Robert M., Barnes, Timothy M., and Rawlyk, George A. (eds.), *Loyalists and Community in North America* (Westport/Connecticut/London, 1994)

Campbell, Mavis C., *The Maroons of Jamaica 1655–1796* (Massachusetts, 1988)

Cecil, Richard, ed., Marylynn Rouse, *The Life of John Newton* (Fearn, 2000)

Chiswick, Barry and Hatton, Timothy, 'International Migration and the Integration of Labour Markets', in Michael Bordo, Alan Taylor and Jeffrey Williamson (eds.), *Globalization in Historical Perspective* (Chicago, 2003)

Christie, I. R. and Larabee, B. W., *Empire and Independence, 1760–1776* (Oxford, 1976)

Clark, J. C. D., *The Language of Liberty, 1660–1832: Political Discourse and Social Dynamics in the Anglo-American World* (Cambridge, 1993)

Curtin, Philip D., *Death by Migration: Europe's Encounter with the Tropical World in the Nineteenth Century* (Cambridge, 1989)

——, *The Atlantic Slave Trade: A Census* (Madison/London, 1969)

Draper, Theodore, *A Struggle for Power: The American Revolution* (New York, 1996)

Drayton, Richard, 'The Collaboration of Labour: Slaves, Empires and Globalizations in the Atlantic World, *c.* 1600–1950', in A. G. Hopkins (ed.), *Globalization in World History* (London, 2002), pp. 98–114

Eltis, David, 'Europeans and the Rise and Fall of African Slavery in the Americas: An Interpretation', *American Historical Review*, 98/5 (1993), pp. 1399–423.

Emmer, P. C. (ed.), *Colonialism and Migration: Indentured Servants before and after Slavery* (Dordrecht, 1986)

Engerman, Stanley L. and Gallman, Robert E. (eds.), *The Cambridge Economic History Of The United States, vol. 1: The Colonial Era* (Cambridge, 1997)

Foster, Roy, *Modern Ireland, 1600–1972* (London, 1988)

Frank Felsenstein (ed.), *English Trader, Indian Maid: Representing Gender, Race, and Slavery in the New World: An Inkle and Yarico Reader* (Baltimore/London, 1999)

Galenson, D. W., *White Servitude in Colonial America: An Economic Analysis* (London, 1981)

Gemery, Henry A., 'Markets for Migrants: English Indentured Servitude and Emigration in the Seventeenth and Eighteenth Centuries', in P. C. Emmer (ed.), *Colonialism and Migration: Indentured Labour before and after Slavery* (Dordrecht, 1986)

Grant, Douglas, *The Fortunate Slave: An Illustration of African Slavery in the Early Eighteenth Century* (New York/Toronto, 1968)

Hughes, Robert, *The Fatal Shore: A History of the Transportation of Convicts to Australia, 1787–1868* (London, 1987)

Hunter, James, *A Dance Called America: The Scottish Highlands, the United States and Canada* (Edinburgh, 1994)

Inikori, J. E., 'Market Structure and the Profits of the British African Trade in the Late Eighteenth Century', *Journal of Economic History*, 41/4 (1981), pp. 745–76

Jeffery, Keith (ed.), *'An Irish Empire': Aspects of Ireland and the British Empire* (Manchester, 1996)

Jones, Maldwyn A., *The Limits of Liberty: American History, 1607–1980* (Oxford, 1983)

Jones, Rufus M., *The Quakers in the American Colonies* (London, 1911)

Knight, Franklin W. (ed.), *General History of the Caribbean, vol. III: The Slave Societies of the Caribbean* (London, 1997)

Langley, Lester D., *The Americas in the Age of Revolution, 1750–1850* (New Haven, 1997)

Long, Edward, *The History of Jamaica, or General Survey of the Ancient and Modern State of that Island: With Reflections on its Situations, Settlements, Commerce, Laws and Government* (London, 1970 [1774])

Main, Gloria L., *Tobacco Colony: Life in Early Maryland, 1650–1720* (Princeton, New Jersey, 1982)

Martin, Bernard, *John Newton: A Biography* (Melbourne/London/Toronto, 1950)

—— and Spurrell, Mark (eds.), *The Journal of a Slave Trader (John Newton) 1750–1754, with Newton's 'Thoughts upon the African Slave Trade'* (London, 1962)

Middleton, Arthur Pierce, *Tobacco Coast: A Maritime History of Chesapeake Bay in the Colonial Era* (Newport News, Virginia, 1953)

Newton, John, *Letters to a Wife, by the Author of Cardiphonia* (Edinburgh, 1808)

— and Cecil, Revd R., *An Authentic Narrative of Some Remarkable and Interesting Particulars in the Life of John Newton; Memoirs of Mr. Newton; Forty-One Letters Originally Published under the Signatures of Omicron and Virgil* (Edinburgh, 1825)

Oxley, Deborah, *Convict Maids: The Forced Migration of Women to Australia* (Cambridge, New York, Melbourne, 1996)

Pestana, Carla Gardina, *Quakers and Baptists in Colonial Massachusetts* (Cambridge, 1991)

Quinn, David B., *Explorers and Colonies: America, 1500–1625* (London/ Ronceverte, 1990)

Rice, C. Duncan, 'The Missionary Context of the British Anti-Slavery Movement', in Walvin, James (ed.), *Slavery and British Society 1776–1846* (London/ Basingstoke, 1982), pp. 150–64

Riley, Edward Miles (ed.), *The Journal of John Harrower: An Indentured Servant in the Colony of Virginia, 1773–1776* (Williamsburg, Virginia, 1963)

Rouse, Parke Jr., *Planters and Pioneers: Life in Colonial Virginia – The Story in Pictures and Text of the People who Settled England's First Successful Colony from its Planting in 1607 to the Birth of the United States in 1789* (New York, 1968)

Smith, Abbot Emerson, *Colonists in Bondage: White Servitude and Convict Labour in America, 1607–1776* (Chapel Hill, 1947)

Thomas, Hugh, *The Slave Trade: The History of the Atlantic Slave Trade 1440– 1870* (New York, 1997)

Walvin, James, *England, Slaves and Freedom, 1776–1838* (Basingstoke, 1986)

—, *Britain's Slave Empire* (London, 2000)

Ward, J. M., *Colonial Self-Government: The British Experience 1759–1856* (London, 1976)

Whiteley, Peter, *Lord North: The Prime Minister who Lost America* (London, 1996)

CHAPTER 3

Blaikie, W., *The Personal Life of David Livingstone LL.D. D.C.L.* (London, 1880)

Chinnian, P., *The Vellore Mutiny – 1806: The First Uprising Against the British* (Erode, 1982)

Gelfand, Michael, *Livingstone the Doctor, His Life and Travels: A Study in Medical History* (Oxford, 1957)

Helly, Dorothy O., *Livingstone's Legacy: Horace Waller and Victorian Mythmaking* (Athens, Ohio/London, 1987)

Hibbert, Christopher, *The Great Mutiny: India 1857* (London, 1978)

Holmes, Timothy, *Journey to Livingstone: Exploration of an Imperial Myth* (Edinburgh, 1993)

Jeal, Tim, *Livingstone* (London, 1973)

Liebowitz, Daniel, *The Physician and the Slave Trade: John Kirk, the Livingstone Expeditions, and the Crusade Against Slavery in East Africa* (New York, 1999)

Metcalfe, C. T., *Two Native Narratives of the Mutiny* (London, 1898)

Murray, Jocelyn, *Proclaim the Good News: A Short History of the Church Missionary Society* (London, 1985)

Panigrahi, Lalita, *British Social Policy and Female Infanticide in India* (New Delhi, 1972)

Philips, C. H. (ed.), *The Correspondence of Lord William Cavendish Bentinck: Governor-General of India 1828–1835, vol. I: 1828–1831; vol. II: 1832–1835* (Oxford, 1977)

Ray, Ajit Kumar, *Widows are not for Burning: Actions and Attitudes of the Christian Missionaries, the Native Hindus and Lord William Bentinck* (New Delhi, 1985)

Sen, Surendranath, *1857* (New Delhi, 1957)

Soderlund, Jean R., *Quakers and Slavery: A Divided Spirit* (Princeton, New Jersey, 1985)

Stanley, B., *The Bible and the Flag: Protestant Missions and British Imperialism in the Nineteenth and Twentieth Centuries* (Leicester, 1990)

CHAPTER 4

Allen, Charles, *Soldier Sahibs: The Men who Made the North-West Frontier* (London, 2000)

Allen, Charles (ed.), *Plain Tales from the Raj* (London, 1976)

Baber, Zaheer, *The Science of Empire: Scientific Knowledge, Civilization, and Colonial Rule in India* (Albany, 1996)

Beaglehole, T. H., *Thomas Munro and the Development of Administrative Policy in Madras 1792–1818: The Origins of 'The Munro System'* (Cambridge, 1966)

Bejoy Krishna Bose, Vakil, *The Alipore Bomb Trial, with a foreword by Mr Eardley Norton, Bar-at-Law* (Calcutta, 1922)

Bennett, Mary, *The Ilberts in India, 1882–1886: An Imperial Miniature* (London, 1995)

Bhasin, Raja, *Viceregal Lodge and the Indian Institute of Advanced Study, Shimla* (Shimla, 1995)

Blunt, Sir Edward, *The I.C.S.: The Indian Civil Service* (London, 1937)

Brook, Timothy and Wakabayashi, Tadashi (eds.), *Opium Regimes: China, Britain, and Japan, 1839–1952* (Berkeley/Los Angeles/London, 2000)

Cannadine, David, *Ornamentalism: How the British Saw Their Empire* (London, 2001)

Clive, John, *Thomas Babington Macaulay: The Shaping of the Historian* (London, 1973)

Daumas, Maurice, *A History of Technology and Invention: Progress through the Ages, vol. III: The Expansion of Mechanization 1725–1860* (London, 1980)

Davis, Mike, *Late Victorian Holocausts: El Niño Famines and the Making of the Third World* (London, 2001)

Dewey, Clive, *Anglo-Indian Attitudes: The Mind of the Civil Service* (London, 1993)

Dutton, Geoffrey, *The Hero as Murderer: The Life of Edward John Eyre* (Sydney, 1967)

Endacott, G. B., *A History of Hong Kong* (Hong Kong, 1973)

Frykenberg, Robert Eric, 'Modern Education in South India, 1784–1854: Its Roots and Its Role as a Vehicle of Integration under Company Raj', *American Historical Review*, 91/1 (supplement to vol. 91) (1986), pp. 37–65

Gilbert, Martin (ed.), *Servant of India: A Study of Imperial Rule from 1905 to 1910 as Told through the Correspondence and Diaries of Sir James Dunlop Smith* (London, 1966)

Gilmour, David, *Curzon* (London, 1994)

——, *The Long Recessional: The Imperial Life of Rudyard Kipling* (London, 2002)

Heehs, Peter, *The Bomb in Bengal: The Rise of Revolutionary Terrorism in India, 1900–1910* (Oxford, 1993)

Heuman, Gad, *'The Killing Time': The Morant Bay Rebellion in Jamaica* (London/Basingstoke, 1994)

Hirschmann, Edwin, *'White Mutiny': The Ilbert Bill Crisis in India and the Genesis of the Indian National Congress* (New Delhi, 1980)

Holt, Edgar, *The Strangest War: The Story of the Maori Wars 1860–1872* (London, 1962)

Hutchins, Francis G., *The Illusion of Permanence: British Imperialism in India* (Princeton, New Jersey, 1967)

Irving, R. G., *Indian Summer: Lutyens, Baker and Imperial Delhi* (New Haven, 1981)

James, Lawrence, *Raj: The Making and Unmaking of British India* (London, 1997)

Kanwar, P., *Imperial Simla: The Political Culture of the Raj* (Delhi, 1990)

Kieve, Jeffrey, *The Electric Telegraph: A Social and Economic History* (Newton Abbot, 1973)

Kipling, Rudyard, *Kim* (Oxford, 1987 [1901])

—, *Plain Tales from the Hills* (London, 1987 [1890])

—, *The Man Who Would Be King and Other Stories* (Oxford, 1987 [1885–1888])

—, *Traffics and Discoveries* (London, 2001 [1904])

—, *War Stories and Poems* (Oxford, 1990)

Knight, Ian (ed.), *Marching to the Drums: Eyewitness Accounts of War from the Charge of the Light Brigade to the Siege of Ladysmith* (London, 1999)

Machonochie, Evan, *Life in the Indian Civil Service* (London, 1926)

MacLeod, Roy and Kumar, Deepak (eds.), *Technology and the Raj: Western Technology and Technical Transfers to India, 1700–1947* (New Delhi/Thousand Oaks/London, 1995)

Mehta, Uday Singh, *Liberalism and Empire: A Study In Nineteenth-Century British Liberal Thought* (Chicago, 1999)

Misra, Maria, *Business, Race and Poliitics in British India, c.1850–1960* (Oxford, 1999)

Napier, Lt.-Col. *The Hon. H. D., Field Marshal Lord Napier of Magdala GCB, GCSI: A Memoir* (London, 1927)

— (ed.), *Letters of Field Marshal Lord Napier of Magdala concerning Abyssinia, Egypt, India, South Africa* (London, 1936)

Narasimhan, Sukuntala, *Sati: A Study of Widow Burning in India* (New Delhi, 1998)

Oldenburg, Venna Talwar, *The Making of Colonial Lucknow, 1856–1877* (Princeton, New Jersey, 1984)

Samanta, Amiya K. (ed.), *Terrorism in Bengal: A Collection of Documents on Terrorist Activities from 1905 to 1939*, 6 vols. (Calcutta, 1995)

Seal, Anil, *The Emergence of Indian Nationalism: Competition and Collaboration in the later Nineteenth Century* (Cambridge, 1968)

Spangenberg, Bradford, 'The Problem of Recruitment for the Indian Civil Service during the Late Nineteenth Century', *Journal of Asian Studies*, 30/2 (1971), pp. 341–60

Steeds, David and Nish, Ian, *China, Japan and Nineteenth-Century Britain* (Dublin, 1977)

Sullivan, Eileen, 'Liberalism and Imperialism: J. S. Mill's Defense of the British Empire', *Journal of the History of Ideas*, 44/4 (1983), pp. 595–617

Tinker, Hugh, *A New System of Slavery: The Export of Indian Labour Overseas, 1830–1920* (London/New York/Bombay, 1974)

Tomlinson, B. R., *The Economy of Modern India, 1860–1970* (Cambridge, 1989)

Trevelyan, George Otto (ed.), *The Life and Letters of Lord Macaulay*, 2 vols. (London, 1876)

Waley Cohen, Ethel A. (ed.), *A Young Victorian in India: Letters of H. M. Kisch of the Victorian Civil Service* (London, 1957)

Wong, J. Y., *Deadly Dream: Opium, Imperialism and the 'Arrow' War (1856–1860) in China* (Cambridge, 1998)

Yalland, Zoe, *Traders and Nabobs: The British in Cawnpore 1765–1857* (Wilton, 1987)

CHAPTER 5

Boehmer, Elleke (ed.), *Empire Writing: An Anthology of Colonial Literature, 1870–1918* (Oxford, 1998)

Brailsford, Henry Noel, *The War of Steel and Gold: A Study of the Armed Peace* (London, 1917 [1914])

Davis, Lance E. and Huttenback, R. A., *Mammon and the Pursuit of Empire: The Political Economy of British Imperialism, 1860–1912* (Cambridge, 1986)

Ellis, John, *The Social History of the Machine Gun* (London, 1993)

Ferguson, Niall, *The World's Banker: The History of the House of Rothschild* (London, 1998)

Fieldhouse, D. K., *Economics and Empire, 1830–1914* (London, 1973)

Flint, John E., *Sir George Goldie and the Making of Nigeria* (London, 1960)

Ford, Roger, *The Grim Reaper: The Machine-Gun and Machine-Gunners* (London/Basingstoke, 1996)

Friedberg, Aaron, *The Weary Titan: Britain and the Experience of Relative Decline, 1895–1905* (New York, 1987)

Gallagher, John and Robinson, Ronald, 'The Imperialism of Free Trade', *Economic History Review*, 2nd ser., 6 (1953), pp. 1–15

Goldsmith, Dolf, *The Devil's Paintbrush: Sir Hiram Maxim's Gun* (Toronto/London, 1989)

Headrick, Daniel R., *The Tools of Empire* (Oxford, 1981)

Hobhouse, Emily, *The Brunt of War, and Where it Fell* (London, 1902)

Hobsbawm, E. J., *The Age of Empire, 1875–1914* (London, 1987)

Hobson, J. A., *Imperialism: A Study* (London, 1988 [1902])

Hyam, Ronald, *Empire and Sexuality* (Manchester, 1992)

Imlah, Albert H., *Economic Elements in the Pax Britannica* (Cambridge, Mass., 1958)

Jeal, Tim, *Baden-Powell* (London, 1989)

Lyons, F. S. L., *Ireland Since the Famine* (London, 1982)

MacKenzie, John M., *Propaganda and Empire: The Manipulation of British Public Opinion, 1880–1960* (Manchester, 1984)

—— (ed.), *Imperialism and Popular Culture* (Manchester, 1986)

Markham, George, *Guns of the Empire: Automatic Weapons* (London, 1990)

Marples, Morris, *A History of Football* (London, 1954)

Marsh, Peter T., *Joseph Chamberlain: Entrepreneur in Politics* (New Haven/London, 1994)

Martin, A. C., *The Concentration Camps: 1900–1902: Facts, Figures, and Fables* (Cape Town, 1957)

McCallum, Iain, *Blood Brothers: Hiram and Hudson Maxim – Pioneers of Modern Warfare* (London, 1999)

McClintock, Anne, *Imperial Leather: Race, Gender and Sexuality in the Colonial Contest* (New York, London, 1995)

Moorehead, Alan, *The White Nile* (London, 1971)

Muffett, D. J. M., *Empire Builder Extraordinary: Sir George Goldie – His Philosophy of Government and Empire* (Douglas, Isle of Man, 1978)

Neillands, Robin, *The Dervish Wars: Gordon and Kitchener in the Sudan, 1880–1898* (London, 1996)

Pakenham, Thomas, *The Boer War* (London, 1991)

——, *The Scramble for Africa* (London, 1991)

Platt, D. C. M., *Finance, Trade, and Politics in British Foreign Policy 1815–1914* (Oxford, 1968)

Pollock, John, *Kitchener* (London, 2001)

Roberts, Andrew, *Salisbury: Victorian Titan* (London, 1999)

Robinson, Ronald and Gallagher, John, *Africa and the Victorians: The Official Mind of Imperialism* (London, 1961)

Rosenthal, Eric, *Gold! Gold! Gold! The Johannesburg Gold Rush* (New York/London/Johannesburg, 1970)

Rotberg, Robert I., *The Founder: Cecil Rhodes and the Pursuit of Power* (New York/Oxford, 1988)

Seeley, J. R., *The Expansion of England: Two Courses of Lectures* (London and New York, 1886)

Shannon, Richard, *Gladstone, vol. II: Heroic Minister, 1865–1898* (London, 1999)

Spies, S. B., *Methods of Barbarism? Roberts and Kitchener and Civilians in the Boer Republics: January 1900–May 1902* (Cape Town, 1977)

Staley, Eugene, *War and the Private Investor: A Study in the Relations of International Politics and International Private Investment* (Chicago, Illinois, 1935)

Strachey, Lytton, *Eminent Victorians* (Harmondsworth, 1948 [1918])

Taylor, S. J., *The Great Outsiders: Northcliffe, Rothermere, and The Daily Mail* (London, 1996)

Wynne-Thomas, Peter, *The History of Cricket: From the Weald to the World* (Norwich, 1988)

CHAPTER 6

Aldrich, Robert, *Greater France: A History of French Overseas Expansion* (Basingstoke, 1996)

Andrew, Christopher M. and Kanya-Forstner, A. S., *France Overseas: The Great War and the Climax of French Imperial Expansion* (London, 1981)

Bond, Brian, *British Military Policy between the Two World Wars* (Oxford, 1980)

Brockington, Leonard, 'John Buchan in Canada', in Tweedsmuir, Susan (ed.), *John Buchan by his Wife and Friends* (London, 1947), pp. 267–77

Brook, Timothy (ed.), *Documents on the Rape of Nanking* (Ann Arbor, 1999)

Brown, Anthony Cave, *Treason in the Blood: H. St. John Philby, Kim Philby and the Spy Case of the Century* (London, 1995)

Brown, Judith M., *Modern India: The Origins of an Asian Democracy* (Oxford, 1994)

Buchan, John, *Greenmantle* (London, 1916)

——, *Memory Hold-The-Door* (London, 1941)

Buchan, William, *John Buchan: A Memoir* (London, 1982)

Chakrabarty, Bidyut, *Subhas Chandra Bose and Middle Class Radicalism: A Study in Indian Nationalism, 1928–1940* (London/New York, 1990)

Chalker, Jack Bridger, *Burma Railway Artist: The War Drawings of Jack Chalker* (London, 1994)

Chang, Iris, *The Rape of Nanking: The Forgotten Holocaust of World War II* (New York, 1997)

Charmley, John, *Churchill's Grand Alliance. The Anglo-American Special Relationship, 1940–57* (London, 1995)

Cohen, Michael J. and Kolinsky, Martin (eds.), *Demise of the British Empire in the Middle East: Britain's Response to Nationalist Movements, 1943–55* (London, 1998)

Colvin, Ian, *The Life of General Dyer* (London, 1929)

Conrad, Joseph, *Heart of Darkness* (London, 1973 [1902])

——, *Lord Jim* (Oxford, 1983 [1921])

Daniell, David, *The Interpreter's House: A Critical Assessment of John Buchan* (London, 1975)

Darwin, John, *Britain and Decolonization: The Retreat from Empire in the Post-War World* (Basingstoke, 1988)

DeLong, Brad, *Slouching Towards Utopia: The Economic History of the Twentieth Century, 'Old Draft'* (http://www.j-bradford-delong.net, 2000)

Draper, Alfred, *The Amritsar Massacre: Twilight of the Raj* (London, 1985)

Dunlop, E. E., *The War Diaries of Weary Dunlop: Java and the Burma-Thailand Railway, 1942–1945* (London, 1987)

Ellis, John, *The World War II Databook: The Essential Facts and Figures for all the Combatants* (London, 1993)

—— and Michael Cox, *The World War I Databook: The Essential Facts and Figures for all the Combatants* (London, 1993)

Ferguson, Niall, *The Pity of War* (London, 1998)

Forster, E. M., *A Passage to India* (London, 1985 [1924])

Forth, Nevill de Rouen, *A Fighting Colonel of Camel Corps: The Life and Experiences of Lt.-Col. N.B. de Lancey Forth, DSO (& Bar), MC 1879–1933 of the Manchester Regiment and Egyptian Army* (Braunton, Devon, 1991)

French, Patrick, *Younghusband: The Last Great Imperial Adventurer* (London, 1994)

Gallagher, John, *The Decline, Revival and Fall of the British Empire* (Cambridge, 1982)

Geyer, Dietrich, *Russian Imperialism: The Interaction of Domestic and Foreign Policy, 1860–1914* (Leamington Spa/Hamburg/New York, 1987)

Gilbert, Martin, *In Search of Churchill: A Historian's Journey* (London, 1994)

Gilbert, Vivient Major, *The Romance of the Last Crusade: With Allenby to Jerusalem* (New York, 1923)

Goldsworthy, David (ed.), *British Documents on the End of Empire, The Conservative Government and the End of Empire, 1951–1957 Part I: International Relations; Part 2: Politics and Administration; Part 3: Economic and Social Policies* (London, 1994)

Greene, Graham, *The Heart of the Matter* (London, 1962 [1948])

Hauner, Milan, *India in Axis Strategy: Germany, Japan and Indian Nationalists in the Second World War* (Stuttgart, 1981)

Henderson, W. O., *The German Colonial Empire 1884–1919* (London/Portland, 1993)

Hochschild, Adam, *King Leopold's Ghost: A Story of Greed, Terror, and Heroism in Colonial Africa* (London/Basingstoke/Oxford, 1998)

Inchbald, Geoffrey, *Imperial Camel Corps* (London, 1970)

Kent, John (ed.), *Egypt And The Defence Of The Middle East [British Documents on the End of Empire]*, 3 vols. (London, 1998)

Kershaw, Ian, *Hitler, 1936–45: Nemesis* (London, 2000)

Louis, Wm. Roger, *Imperialism at Bay: The United States and the Decolonization of the British Empire 1941–1945* (New York, 1978)

—— and Robinson, Ronald, 'The Imperialism of Decolonization', *Journal of Imperial and Commonwealth History* 22 (1995), pp. 462–511

Lowe, Peter, 'Great Britain and the Coming of the Pacific War, 1939–1941', *Transactions of the Royal Historical Society* (1974), pp. 43–62

Maugham, W. Somerset, *Far Eastern Tales* (London, 2000)

——, *Collected Short Stories*, 4 vols. (Harmondsworth, 1963 [1951])

Monroe, Elizabeth, *Britain's Moment in the Middle East, 1914–1956* (London, 1981)

Murfett, Malcolm H., Miksic, John N., Farrell, Brian P. and Shun, Chiang Ming, *Between Two Oceans: A Military History of Singapore from First Settlement to Final British Withdrawal* (Oxford/New York, 1999)

Neidpath, James, *The Singapore Naval Base and the Defence of Britain's Eastern Empire, 1919–1941* (Oxford, 1981)

Offer, Avner, *The First World War: An Agrarian Interpretation* (Oxford, 1989)

Overy, Richard, *Why the Allies Won* (London, 1995)

Owen, Geoffrey, *From Empire to Europe: The Decline and Revival of British Industry since the Second World War* (London, 1999)

Perkins, Roger, *The Amritsar Legacy: Golden Temple to Caxton Hall, The Story of a Killing* (Chippenham, 1989)

Pickering, Jeffrey, *Britain's Withdrawal From East Of Suez: The Politics Of Retrenchment* (London, 1998)

Rabe, John, *The Good Man of Nanking: The Diaries of John Rabe* (New York, 1998)

Reynolds, David, *Rich Relations: The American Occupation of Britain, 1942–1945* (London, 1995)

Rhee, M. J., *The Doomed Empire: Japan in Colonial Korea* (Aldershot/Brookfield/Singapore/Sydney, 1997)

Ritchie, Harry, *The Last Pink Bits* (London, 1997)

Schmokel, Wolfe W., *Dream of Empire: German Colonialism, 1919–1945* (New Haven/London, 1964)

Smith, Janet Adam, *John Buchan: A Biography* (London, 1965)

Swinson, Arthur, *Six Minutes to Sunset – the Story of General Dyer and the Amritsar Affair* (London, 1964)

Thio, Eunice, 'The Syonan Years, 1942–1945', in Chew, Ernest C. T. and Lee, Edwin (eds.), *A History of Singapore* (Singapore, 1991), pp. 95–114

Thomas, Lowell with Brown Collings, Kenneth, *With Allenby in the Holy Land* (London/Toronto/Melbourne/Sydney, 1938)

Tomlinson, B. R., *The Political Economy of the Raj, 1914–1947: The Economics of Decolonization* (London, 1979)

Travers, Tim, *Gallipoli 1915* (Stroud/Charleston, 2001)

Trevor-Roper, H. R. (ed.), *Hitler's Table Talk 1941–44: His Private Conversations* (London, 1973 [1953])

Waugh, Evelyn, *Black Mischief* (London, 1962 [1932])

Yamamoto, Masahiro, *Nanking: Anatomy of an Atrocity* (Westport, Connecticut/London, 2000)

Yardley, Michael, *Backing into the Limelight: A Biography of T. E. Lawrence* (London, 1985)

CONCLUSION

Acemoglu, Daron, Johnson, Simon and Robinson, James A., 'Reversal of Fortune: Geography and Institutions in the Making of the Modern World Income Distribution', *NBER Working Paper W8460* (Sept. 2001)

Cooper, Robert, 'The Postmodern State', in Foreign Policy Centre (ed.), *Reordering the World: The Long-term Implications of September 11* (London, 2002)

Edelstein, Michael, 'Imperialism: Cost and Benefit', in Roderick Floud and Donald McCloskey (eds.), *The Economic History of Britain since 1700*, vol. II (Cambridge, 1994), pp. 173–216

Ferguson, Niall, *The Cash Nexus: Money and Power in the Modern World, 1700–2000* (London, 2001)

La Porta, Rafael, Lopez-de-Silanes, Florencio, Shleifer, Andrei and Vishny, Robert W., 'Law and Finance', *Journal of Political Economy*, 106/6 (1998), pp. 1113–55

Landes, David S., *The Wealth and Poverty of Nations* (London, 1998)

Obstfeld, Maurice and Taylor, Alan M., 'The Great Depression as a Watershed: International Capital Mobility over the Long Run', in Michael D. Bordo, Claudia Goldin and Eugene N. White (eds.), *The Defining Moment: The Great Depression and the American Economy in the Twentieth Century* (Chicago, 1998), pp. 353–402

Index

Note: *Italic* page numbers refer to Figures, and to quotations in chapter openings

Abdul Karim ('Munshi') 206
Aborigines, Australia 108–9
Abyssinia 175–8, 222, 234
Acheson, Dean *365*, 381
Adams, John 91
Adams, Samuel 87, 91
Aden 315, 358
administration: India Act (1784) 50–51;
  principles of xxvii, 178, 180, 184,
  369–70, *see also* Indian Civil Service
advertisements 256–7
Afghanistan 144, 174–5; Taliban regime
  373, 374, 380
Africa 113–14, 184, 234–7, 239–40,
  303–4; explorations of 127–31,
  160–62; Livingstone's plans for
  153–61, 162; missionaries to 120,
  153–6; objective for independence
  357–8; Partnership for 374; Rhodes's
  vision for 227, 238–40, 273, 284;
  slaves from 74, 76–9, 113–14,
  115–16, *see also* South Africa; West
  Africa
Africa, Scramble for xxvi, 222, 234,
  239–40, 292; Berlin Conference
  (1884–85) 234–6; France and 229–30,
  232, 233; Germany 234–40
African World Reparations and
  Repatriation Truth Commission xii
agriculture: new crops from Americas
  58; in New South Wales 104, 108

Ahmed Shah Abdali, Afghan leader 28
Aix-la-Chapelle, Treaty of 32
Alexandria 232, 233
Algeria, French 296
Alipore, court case 213
Allahabad, Treaty of 37
Allenby, General Edmund 313
Amboina, Indonesia, massacre (1623) 21
America 2–3, 58–73; British colonies
  (1774) 85, *88–9*; New England
  settlements 61–3, *see also* American
  War of Independence; United States of
  America; Virginia
American Indians 63–6, 101
American War of Independence 84–101;
  British military campaign 97, 98–9;
  Bunker Hill 98; as civil war 94–6;
  constitutional issue 90–94;
  Declaration of Independence 93–4,
  98, 100–101; lessons learned (Durham
  Report) 110–12; Loyalists 95–6,
  99–100; taxation issue 85, 86–7,
  91–2; Yorktown 98–9
Amery, Leo 252, 315, 327
Amherst, Lord 182
Amritsar massacre (1919) 331–3
Amsterdam 18, 23
Ananda Ranga Pillai 31
Anglo-American Telegraph Company
  168
Anglo-Dutch wars 21–2

Angola, Portuguese 234
Anson, George (Admiral Lord) 33, 34
Antarctica 315
anti-Semitism 284
Arabi Pasha 232, 233
Archdale, John 66
architecture, imperial legacy xxii–xxiii,
    211, 215
Arcot 28, 36
Argentina 244
Arnold, Matthew 248
Asia 3, 27; British possessions 241,
    340–41, see also China; India; Japan
Asquith, Herbert 300, 311
Asquith, Margot 207
Atlantic Ocean, winds 9, 25
Attlee, Clement 358
Auden, W. H. 357
Aurungzeb, Mughal Emperor 28
Austin, Alfred 256, 278
Australia 33, 102–110, 194, 315;
    Aboriginal population 108–9; troops
    in World Wars 305, 307–311
Austria-Hungary 298–9, 314

Baden-Powell, R. S. S. 261–2, 266,
    276–9, 292
Baghdad, railway project 302
Bahadur Shah Zafar, last Mughal
    emperor 149, 151
Baines, Thomas 156
Baker, Herbert 215
Balcarres, Lord 83
Balfour, Arthur 287, 315
Balfour Declaration (1917) 357
Balfour Report on Imperial Relations
    (1926) 326
Balkans 231, 314
Baltimore, Lord 66
Bangladesh 371
banks and banking xxiii, 18, 23, 293;
    Rothschild's 223, 233, 285–6
Banks, Joseph 33
Baptist Missionary Society 193
Barbados 72–3
Bargash, Sultan of Zanzibar 236–7, 239

Baring, Sir Evelyn 269, 287
Barker, Lady Mary Anne 263
Barlow, Sir George 145
Barnato, Barney 223
Barrackpur 147, 178
BBC website, view of imperialism xiii
Bechuanaland 224, 240
Bedingfield, Commander Norman 156,
    157
Belgium 231, 234, 236, 240; First World
    War 299–300, see also Congo;
    Leopold
Bengal: administration of 36, 42–3;
    Curzon's proposal to partition
    212–13, 214; Permanent Settlement
    (1793) 51; taxation 37–8, 47–8
Bentinck, William 142–3
Berkeley, Bishop George 34–5
Berlin, Congress of (1878) 231
Berlin Conference (1884–85) 234–6
Berrio, Antonio de 6
Bertie, Francis 290
Besant, Annie 333
Bevin, Ernest 357, 359
bin Laden, Osama 375
Bismarck, Otto von 234, 236, 238
Black Sea 301–2
Blair, Tony, Prime Minister 373–4, 375,
    379
Bloemfontein 279, 281–2
Blunt, Wilfrid Scawen 278
Boer War 274–84
Boers 273–5
Bogle, George 40
Bogle, Paul 193–4, 195
Bombay xxiii, 24, 188
Bonn, Moritz 352
Booth, Charles O'Hara 107
Borneo 241, 358
Bose, Janakinath 190, 205
Bose, Subhas Chandra 205, 346–7
Bosnia-Herzegovina 298
Boston Tea Party 87
Boswell, James 71, 79, 97, 118
Botany Bay 103
Botha, Louis 281

Botswana 368
Bowater, Private Joseph 147, 150
Boys of the Empire 259
Boys' Empire League 259
Boys' Own Paper 259, 292
Brailsford, Henry Noel 284
Branson, James 200, 201
Brazil 118, 244
Brett, Reginald 286
Bright, John xviii
Bristol 5, 6
British Army 247, 305; colonial troops
(World Wars) 305–311, *307*, 311–12,
347; Second World War 338
British Association for the Advancement
of Science 262–3
British Empire: change of attitude to
218–19, 221–2, 247–9, 281, 292–3,
333; compared with other empires
xxiii–xxiv, 234–5, 295, 297; costs and
benefits xvii–xx, xxv–xxviii, 255, 317;
defence costs 247, 255, 327–8, 360,
377; economic benefits and legacy
xviii–xix, 218, 255, 366–70, 371–2;
extent 51–2, 239–41, *241*, 242–3,
340–41; and First World War 302–3;
legacy of xxii–xxiv, xxvii, 216–18,
365–6, 378–80; loss of faith in xvii,
222, 292, 319–24; modern
condemnation of xi–xii; negative
aspects of xvii–xx, xxvi–xxvii, 365–6;
net capital investment in 241, 244–5,
245, 247, 255, 379, *379*; notion of
'Greater Britain' 249, 250–51; origins
and growth of 2, 3–4, 52, 162;
popular Imperialism xvi, 256–7,
258–62, 323–4; relationship of
Dominions with 250–51, 252, 326,
342; retreat from 295, 356–62, 362;
role as globalizing power xx–xxi,
xxiv–xxviii; and Second World War
339; theory of indirect rule 210,
229–30, *see also* colonies;
Commonwealth
British Empire Exhibition, Wembley
(1924) 318–20

British Expeditionary Force 298, 303,
307
British and Foreign Anti-Slavery Society
195–6
British Guiana 79
British Petroleum 316
British South Africa Company 224, 225,
228
Brooks, Colonel Thomas 82
Brown, Samuel Snead 134
Brunel, Isambard Kingdom 168
buccaneers 1–2
Buchan, John xvi, 252, 301, 323,
380–81; *Greenmantle* 300–301
Buller, Charles 110–111
Buller, General Sir Redvers 275
Burke, Edmund 49, 50, 54, 97, 117, 118
Burke, Thomas Henry 253
Burma 347, 371; railway 343–4, 345
Burns, J. D. 305
Burns, Robert, as excise officer 45–7
Burrup, Henry de Wint 155, 157
Butler, Lady 256
Butt, Isaac 253
Byng, Admiral John 33–4

Cabot, John 3–4, 5
Caffery, Jefferson 354–5
Calcutta xxiii, 24, 39, 189, 190; 'Black
Hole' of 36; Governor-General's
palace 51; and Indian nationalism
212–13, 214–15; Victoria Memorial
163, 211
Cambridge, George, Duke of 177, 226
Cameron, Sir Donald 210
Cameroon 234, 236, 240, 303, 315
Campbell, Sir Archibald 40
Campbell, John Talbot (Campo-bell) 80
Campbell-Bannerman, Sir Henry 283
Canada xv–xvi, 34, 254, 347; American
Loyalists in 100, 110; Dominion
status 250, 253; Durham Report
(1839) 111–12; Quebec revolt (1837)
110
Cape Colony 273
Cape Town 166

capital flows 244, 365, 367–8; from India to Britain 41–5; US compared with Great Britain 378–9, 379, *see also* foreign investment

capitalism xx–xxi, xxvii, 139; early Dutch form 18–19, *see also* financial markets

Carey, William 120

Caribbean *see* West Indies

Carlton, Sir Guy 97

Carlyle, Thomas 196

Casement, Roger 296

Catherine (of Braganza), Queen 14, 24

Caucasus, Russian imperialism in 297

Cavendish, Lord Frederick 253

Cawnpore 197, 198; Indian Mutiny 147–8, 151, 152

Central Asia 297

Chalker, Jack 342, 344

Chamberlain, Austen 250, 312

Chamberlain, Joseph 221, 249–51, 252, 262, 292; and Boers 273, 274; and Imperial Preference 287, 326; and Ireland 253, 254–5; view of Germany 288, 289

Chamberlain, Neville 328, 337

Charles I, King 66

Charles II, King 22, 24, 67

Charnock, Job 142

Chiang Kai-shek 351

Child, Josiah 20–21

Childers, Erskine 292, 321

China 165–6, 338–9, 369

Chinsura, Bengal xxiv, 18, 19

Christianity 365

Church of England, missionaries 120

Church Missionary Society 120, 136

Churchill, Lord Randolph 225, 254, 285

Churchill, Winston Spencer xxvii, 295, 333, 355; and American anti-imperialism 351–2, 354; Boer War 275; and First World War 298, 299, 308, 311; at Omdurman 270–72; Second World War 337–8, 348–52, 362–3; view of Germany 289–90

cinema 323

City of London 22

civil wars, modern xxi, 371, 372–3

civilization: as missionary goal 114, 119–23, 135, 375; and US popular culture 378

Clapham Sect 196, 202; anti-slavery movement 116–17, 119; campaign against sati (suttee) 142; and missionary campaigns in India 136–7

Clarkson, Thomas 117

Clive, Robert 36–7, 38, 42

Clough, Arthur Hugh 342–3

Cobden, Richard xviii, xix, xxi

cod fisheries 6, 62

coffee 15–16

Coghill, Lieutenant Kendal 152

Coke, Sir Edward 66

Cold War 359

Coleridge, Samuel Taylor 117

Colonial Development Corporation 358

colonies: direct rule from London 196, 253–4; economic decline since independence 368–9, 372–3; franchise (South Africa) 281; independence 356–8; net investment in 216–18, 255, 368; representative assemblies in 90, 91, 110, 111; troops mobilized (World Wars) 305–312, 307, 347, *see also* emigration

Colquhoun, Patrick, *Treatise* (1814) 51

Columbus, Christopher 2, 3

Combe, George 263

Committee of the Protestant Society 136

common law, institutional systems xxiii, 369

Commonwealth 358, 361; lack of political influence 362; proposals for 326, 342

Company of Royal Adventurers into Africa 20

Company of Scotland 20, 40

Conan Doyle, Arthur 265

concentration camps, Boer War 280–81, 282–3

Congo: Belgian 162, 234, 236, 240, 295–6; conflict in 374

Congo, River 159, 162
Connolly, James 329
Conrad, Joseph, *Heart of Darkness*
 295–6
consumer society, early 12–17
convicts, transportation of 102–5, 106,
 107, 111, 112, 366
Cook, Captain James 33, 34, 102
Cooper, Robert 375–6
Cope, Sir Walter 7
Cornwallis, General Charles, Lord
 50–51, 98–9
corruption 370
cotton 16–17, 131
cricket 85, 261–2, 277
Crimean War 231
Cripps, Sir Stafford 347
Crowe, Eyre 288
Cudjoe, Captain, Maroon leader 81–2
cultural toleration 38–9, 113; in India
 38–9, 133–5, *see also* 'civilization';
 race
Cumberland, Duke of 22
Curzon, George Nathaniel xxi, 207–8,
 209, 210–211, 216, 260; and Delhi
 Durbar 211–12; later years 219;
 proposal for partition 212–13, 214
Cyprus 316, 358

Dale, Sir Thomas 64
Dalton, Hugh 356
Dardanelles 303, 307–8
Darien scheme 40
Darjeeling 181
Darwin, Charles 196
Darwinism 264
Davies, Sir John 56
De Beers Company 223–4, 225, 228
debt *see* financial markets
Defoe, Daniel 12–13, 15, 16, 23, 69
Delamere, Lord 260
Delhi xxiv, 28; government moved to
 214–15, 330; Indian Mutiny 149–50,
 151; Red Fort 27, 28
Delhi Durbar (1903) 211–12
democracy 325, 366, 370–71

'Demos' think tank xiii–xiv
Deppe, Ludwig 303–4
Depression, General 325, 367
Derby, Earl of 167, 176
Dervishes, Battle of Omdurman 270–71,
 272
development, principles for 370
diamonds: India 35, 42; South Africa
 223–4
Dickens, Charles 122, 132, 196
Dilke, Sir Charles 249
Dillon, John 274
diseases: African 114, 155, 303; effect
 on indigenous populations 58, 66,
 108; malaria 124, 156, 160; and
 public health (India) 216–17; on ships
 10, 33, 77–8
Disraeli, Benjamin (Lord Beaconsfield)
 167, 176, 178; Suez Canal shares 231,
 285, 286
Drake, Sir Francis 6, 7, 9
Drayton, Michael 59
Duad Khan, Nawab of the Carnatic 28,
 36
Duché, Jacob 95
Dulles, John Foster 355
Dundas, Henry 40, 49
Dundas, Robert 135
Dunlop, Lieutenant Colonel Edward
 344–5
Dunmore, Lord 101
Dupleix, Joseph François 31
Durban Declaration (2001) *xi*
Durham, John Lambton, Earl of
 110–11
Durham Report 110–12, 252
Dutch East India Company 18–21
Dutch empire xxiv, xxv, 18–24
Dyer, Brigadier-General Rex 331–3

East India Act (1813) 135, 137
East India Company 20–24, 87; Anglo-
 Indian relations 27–8, 134–5; conflict
 with Dutch company 20–22; debt 49;
 employees 25–6, 28, 39–40; granted
 civil administration of Bengal 36;

opium revenues 166, 167; raises native regiments 29, 41, 44; reform (1784 India Act) 50–51; share price 47, 48; wound up 154, 178, *see also* Indian Army

economy: benefits and legacy of empire xviii–xix, 366–70, 372; British India 216–18; consumer 12–17; effect of World Wars on 324–9, 360, *360*, 361, 365; modern globalization xx–xxii, 371–2; Mughal India 27; sterling crisis 360–61, *360*, *see also* financial markets; foreign investment; free trade

Eden, Anthony 355

education: in India 143, 189–90, 200, 214; public schools 259–60, 262

Edward VII, King 211, 226

Egerton, General Sir R. G. 329

Egypt 230, 231–2, 315, 354–5; British protectorate 233; Rothschild Bank and 233, 285–6, *see also* Suez

Egypt, Khedive of 231, 268

Eisenhower, Dwight 355

elites, indigenous xxvi; education of 189–90, *191*, 200; in India 198, 206, 207–8, 209, 212–13, 218

Elizabeth I, Queen 7, 8, 18, 58; and plantation of Ulster 55, 56; and Protestantism 61

Elyot, Hugh 6

emigrants 53–4, 55; as beneficiaries of Empire xiii–xvi, 60–61; and fantasy of 'home' 205–6; Irish 71, 72; Pilgrims 61–3; Scots xvi, 39–41, 71

emigration xxv, 112, 255, 365; from continental Europe 68, 69–70; rate of 68, 69; to Commonwealth countries 112, 358; to supply labour 58, 68–73, *see also* labour migration

Empire Day 252

Empire Marketing Board 327

English language xxiii, xxvii, 82, 362, 366

Entente Cordiale (1904) 289–90

Equiano, Olaudah, slave 77

Essex, Walter Devereux, Earl of 55–6

eugenics 264

Europe 28; balance of power in 230–31; navies 44

European Economic Community 361

European Union 376–7

Evangelical movement 135–6, 139; response to Indian Mutiny 150–51, 152–3

exhibitions, imperial 257

explorations: Africa 127–31, 160–62; survey of India 174

Eyre, Edward 194–7

famines: India xxii, 47–8, 188, 217; Irish xxii, 253

Fanning, David, American Loyalist 96, 97, 100

Farrer, Sir Thomas 201–2

fashion, and consumer economy 16–17

Fashoda incident (1899) 236

Fawcett, Millicent 282

Fenian Brotherhood 253

Ferguson, Adam 117

Ferguson family xiii–xvi

financial markets xxvi, 285–6, 324–5; and Anglo-German cooperation 293; availability of credit 23, 34–5, 46; international debt 325, *see also* banks; foreign investment

financial system: Dutch 18, 22; English adoption of Dutch 23–4, 34

First World War 298–315; as clash of empires 300–303; costs of 315–17, 324; Gallipoli 307–11; imperial troops 305–11, *307*, 311–12; in Middle East 311–14; rise of Germany 288–92

Fisher, Andrew 305

Fisher, H. A. L. 315

Fitzgerald, Oswald 266

Fitzgerald, Richard 106

Fletcher of Saltoun, Andrew 8

football 260

foreign investment 244–5, *245*, 247, 255, 324–5, 368–9; US compared with Great Britain 378–9, *379*

Forster, E. M. 198, 203, 322

Forster, W. E. 171

Fox, Charles James 97

France xxiv, 29, 119, 234, 367; and American War of Independence 97, 98–9; defence spending 328; and Egypt 230, 232, 233; First World War 299, 314, 315; relations with 29, 31–2, 35, 288, 289–90; and Scramble for Africa 230, 232, 234, 236; Seven Years War 32–5; taxation 46, see also French empire

Franklin, Benjamin 86, 91, 92, 94

Franklin, William 95

Fraser, William 41

free trade xx, 129–30, 131, 244, 366; economic benefits of xx, 366–7; extension of 217, 244, 378; role of institutions in xx, 369–70

Freetown, Sierra Leone 115, 120

French East India Company 30, 31

French empire xxv, 30, 31, 244; in Africa 240, 296; in America 101; in India 29, 34, 35; West Indies 30, 34, 83

French Revolution 46

Frobenius, Leo 313

Frobisher, Martin 6, 7

Froude, J. A. 249, 250

Gallipoli campaigns 307–311

Galloway, Joseph 92, 99

Galton, Francis 264

Gambia 7, 74, 240, 358

Gandhi, Mohandas Karamchand (Mahatma) 331, 333, 346, 347

Garraway, Thomas 13

Garvin, J. L. 241

Gates, Sir Thomas 6

General Strike (1926) 325

German Army 272–3, 289, 290

German Colonization Society 236

German empire 234–40, 296–7, 303, 367

German Navy 288–9, 290–91, 304

German South-West Africa see Namibia

Germany 244, 292, 367; ambitions in Middle East 300–303, 311, 312, 313–14; and First World War 298–303; idea of cooperation with Britain 289–90, 335–7; reparations 316–17; rise of 288–9; and Scramble for Africa 234–40, see also German empire; Hitler

Ghana (Gold Coast) 240

Gholam Hussein Khan, Seir Mutaqherin (1789) xvii, 36–7, 41, 42, 47–8

Ghose, Aurobindo 213–14

Gibraltar 30

Gilbert, Humphrey 7, 58

Gingee fort, Carnatic (India) 29, 34

Gladstone, W. E. 253, 254, 374; and Egypt 232–3, 287; and relief of Khartoum 269

global peace 366

globalization: British Empire xxiv–xxviii, 17; modern xx–xxii, 371–2; politics of 373–4

Glorious Revolution (1688) 22–3, 90

Goetze, Sigismund, 'Britannia Pacifatrix' 317

Gogerly, George 137–8

gold 3, 6–7; Matabeleland 223–4, 228; South Africa 273–4

gold standard 247, 324–5, 326

Goldie, George 228–9

Goltz, Field Marshal Colmar von der 294, 302

Gordon, General Charles George 268–9, 270

Gordon, George William 195

Government of India Act (1853) 186

Grace, W. G. 261

Grainger, James, 'The Sugar Cane' 80

Gran Grenada, Morgan's raid on 1, 11

Grant, Charles 136

Granville, Lord 269

Gray, Robert 64

Great Britain 4, 354; concern for indigenous peoples 101, 109, 178, 190–92; condemnation of Amritsar

332–3; constitutional relations with colonies 90–94, 109–12, 196, 253–4; defence expenditure 358, 360, 377; 'Greater Britain' policy 249, 250–52, 260; manufacturing share 288, 361; National Debt 35, 46; policy towards India 154, 163, 178–80; post-war settlement with US 353–4, 360–61; power ceded to United States 354–6, 358; power of Parliament 4–5; reaction to Morant Bay rising 195–6; repatriation of wealth to 41–5, 47–8; and rise of Germany 288–92; and Seven Years War 32–5, 101; threats of other empires 234, 295, 297–8; view of American independence 97–8, 101; view of missionaries 137, 154, *see also* British Empire; Commonwealth; First World War

Great Eastern, SS 168

Great Exhibition (1851) 257

'Great Game' (Afghanistan) 174–5

'Greater Britain', notion of 249, 250–52, 260

Greenway, Francis Howard 105

Grenville, George 86

Grenville, Sir Richard 6

Grey, Sir Edward 290, 350

Gurkhas, in East India Company Army 41

Haggard, H. Rider xvi, 265

Hague Peace Conference (1899) 258

Haider Ali, of Mysore 48

Haiti 83, 380

Hakluyt, Richard (younger) 4–5, 6, 64

Halifax, Lord 334–5, 337

Hallam, Sergeant S.R. 345

Hamilton, Alexander 99

Hamilton, Lady 210

Hamilton, Sir Ian 310

Harmsworth, Alfred *see* Northcliffe

Harrison, John 33

Harrower, John 70–71, 72

Hasan Ethem 311

Hastings, Warren 41–2, 43, 133; as Governor-General 38–9; impeachment of 49–50

Hawke, Sir Edward 34

Hawkins, Sir John 7, 8

Hayls, John 16

Healey, Denis 365

Heber, Reginald, Bishop 137

Heligoland 239

Helmore, Revd Holloway 155

Henderson, Sir Nevile 280

Henley, W. E. 256, 279

Henry VII, King 3, 6

Henry VIII, King 9, 55

Henty, G. A. 256

Herero revolt, Namibia 296–7

Heriot, Thomas 14

heroes, fictional 265

Hicks, Colonel William 268

hierarchy, preoccupation with 93, 208, 209–210, 219

Hirohito, Emperor of Japan 297

Hitler, Adolf xxvi, 297, 334–8, 362

Hobhouse, Emily 281–3

Hobhouse, Leonard xviii

Hobson, J. A. xviii, 283–4

Hodson, William 151

Home Government Association (Ireland) 253

homosexuality 265–7

Hong Kong 166, 305

Howe, General William 98

Hudson Bay Company 20, 22, 65

Hughes, William M. 316–17

Hugli (Hooghly) River, Bengal 17–18

human rights: Congo 295–6; Japanese empire 339

Hume, Allan Octavian 205

Hunt, G. W. 257

Hunt, Dr James 262–3

Husayn ibn Ali, Sharif of Mecca 312

Hyderabad 28, 44

Ilbert, Courtenay Peregrine 199

Ilbert Bill, and White Mutiny 199–203, 204

immigration: from colonies 54, 365; into US 112, 367, 379

Imperial British East Africa Company 229

imperialism 238–9, 249–50; critical view of xiii, xvii–xviii; modern 376–7; other forms xxiv, 296, 297–8; popular 256–7, 258–62, 323–4; Radical critique of 283–4, *see also* Congo; Dutch empire; French empire; German empire; Japanese empire; Spanish empire

Imphal, Battle of 347

indentured labour 68–73, 102, 367

India 16–17, 36–7, 39–40, 252; alternatives to British rule 218, 347; Amritsar massacre (1919) 331–3; British cultural influence 39, 142–4, 145, 146; British legacy in 216–18, 366; campaigns to modernize 139, 140–44; Crown administration (after Mutiny) 154, 178–9; education system 143, 189–90, 191, 200, 214; extent of British rule 51, 172–3, 174; in First World War 305–7, 330; French possessions in 29, 30, 34, 35; imperial economy 216–18; independence 356–7, 369; industry 197–8, 216; legal system 199–200; missionary movement in 135–44, 153; Mughal Empire xxiv, 27–9; principles of administration of 50–51, 178, 180; racial tensions 197–205; railways 169–70; romantic view of 206, 208; in Second World War 346–8; Simla 181–3, 201, 211, *see also* Bengal; Calcutta; East India Company; Indian Army; Indian Civil Service; Indian Mutiny; Indian nationalism

India Act (1784) 50

Indian Army 147, 170–71, 179–80; Abyssinia expedition 176–8; at Delhi Durbar 212; East India Company regiments 29, 41, 44, 47; First World War 305–7, 330; mutiny at Vellore (1806) 145, 146; native troops 170–71, 247; Second World War 346–8; significance of religion in 146, *see also* Indian Mutiny

Indian Civil Service 50–51, 180, 186–9, 375; examination for 185–7, 190; incorruptibility of 50–51, 217; and Simla 180–84; size of xxvi, 163, 184–5, 191; uncovenanted staff (Indians) 189

Indian Mutiny (1857) 145–53, 168; Evangelical response to 150–51, 152–3; retribution for 151–2

Indian National Congress 205, 212–13, 330

Indian nationalism 205, 218, 295; and Amritsar massacre 331, 333; Quit India campaign 346–7; terrorism 213–14

Indonesia 19, 21

Industrial Revolution 164

infanticide (female), in India 139–40

institutions: 'common law' xxiii, 369; importance to free trade xx, 369–70; representative assemblies 90, 91, 110, 111; survival of parliamentary xxvii

intermarriage: in India 39, 40–41, 133–4, 203; in Latin America 63; miscegenation 81, 203–4

International Monetary Fund 356, 376

Iran 316, 358, 373

Iraq (Mesopotamia) 303, 306, 311–12, 315, 317, 375

Ireland 55–7, 329–30; direct rule from Westminster 252–3; Easter Rising (1916) 329; Home Rule 253–4, 297; radical nationalism 253–4; Unionism 254

Irish: as emigrants 71–2; transported as convicts 102, 103, 107

Irish Free State 348

Isandhlwana (1879) 276

Islam 39, 267, 301, 302, 373

Israel, state of 357

Itagaki, General Seishiro 343

Italy 297, 314, 328; colonies in Africa 234, 240

Jamaica 1–2, 12, 196; Maroon population 81–3, 195; Morant Bay uprising (1865) 192–7; sugar plantations 11, 72, 79–80
James I, King 56–7, 61
James II, King, as Duke of York 22, 67
Jameson, Leander Starr 274
Jameson Raid 276
Jamestown, Virginia 60–61, 64, 66
Japan xx, 5, 245; in Second World War 342–6, 348
Japanese empire xxiv, 297, 329, 339, 343, 366
Jardine Matheson 166
Java 18–19
Jefferson, Thomas 93, 94, 100–101
Jerusalem 313
'jingoism' 171, 257
Jinnah, Mohammad Ali 357
Johnson, Samuel 1, 43, 71, 97, 100
justice 374, see also law
Jutland, Battle of 304

Kartar Singh, Signalman 306
Kemal Ataturk (Mustafa Kemal) 308
Kennedy, Charles Pratt 181
Kenya xiv–xv, 240, 358, 371
Keswick, J. J. J. 199–200, 201
Keynes, John Maynard 324, 326, 353, 360
Khalifa, the (Mahdi's heir) 270
Khartoum, siege of 268–9
Kimberley, diamond mines 223–4
Kimberley, Lord 200, 210
Kingsford, J. D. 213
Kipling, Lockwood 206
Kipling, Rudyard 182–4, 198, 247; on ICS 185; on Ilbert Bill 202; Kim 175; 'Recessional' 219; 'The Man Who Would be King' 38; 'The White Man's Burden' 380; as 'voice of Empire' 258; and Wembley exhibition 318
Kiralfy, Imre 257
Kirk, Dr John 156, 157–8, 236–7, 239
Kisch, H. M. 188

Kitchener, General Herbert Horatio (Lord) 266, 269–70, 272, 308; Boer War 279, 280–81
Korea, Japanese rule in 297, 343
Kosovo 373–4, 380
Kuruman, Bechuanaland 122, 124–5
Kut el Amara, siege of 312
Kuwait 316
Kwai, River xxiv, 343

Labouchere, Henry 284
labour: indentured 68–73, 102, 367; shortages in early colonies 58, 68, see also slavery
labour migration xxv, 324, 365; from India 217, 367
Ladysmith, Natal 275, 279
Lakeland, William 354–5
land: expropriation of 63–6; grants to settlers 56–7, 60, 66–7, 106; as source of royal patronage 66–7; tenure xxiii, 51, 139
Landes, David 370
Latin America 58, 63, 244, 245, see also Brazil; Spanish empire
Latin Monetary Union 247
law: Indian legal system 199–200; rule of xxiii, 197, 367, 369
Lawrence, Henry 146, 148
Lawrence, T. E. 312–13, 315, 321–2
Lebanon 315
Lee, Arthur 71, 219
Leicester, Robert Dudley, Earl of 55
Leopold II, King of the Belgians 162, 234, 236, 240, 295
Lesseps, Ferdinand de 230
Levant Company 20
Lexington, 'battle' of 84, 85, 92–3
Liberal Party: and Boer War 283, 284; and First World War 289, 290, 299–300; and Imperialism 249–50
Liberalism 138–9, 196, 201–2, 207
Liberia 222
liberty xxiii–xxiv, xxv, 54, 366; American War of Independence and 84, 85, 100; and Durham Report 111,

liberty – *cont.*
  112; and indentured labour 68–9, 70;
  inscription (New Delhi) 215;
  settlement of Australia and 104–5;
  and slavery 78–9, 100–101
Liman von Sanders, Otto 302
Lipset, Seymour Martin 370–71
literature, popular 256, 292
Littleton, Edward 80
Liverpool, slave trade 76, 118
Livingstone, Charles 156
Livingstone, David 114, 117, 153–4,
  159–60, 196; campaign against
  African slavery 128–30, 159; as
  explorer 127–31; as missionary
  123–6; *Missionary Travels* 132–3;
  plan to open up Africa 154–61, 162
Livingstone, Mary 126, 157
Livingstone, Zambia 160
Lloyd, George 210
Lloyd George, David 283, 301
Lobengula, Matabele chief 223–4
Locke, John 64–5
Loewe, Ludwig 273
Logan, Patrick 107
London, commodity market 15–16
London Missionary Society 120, 122,
  155–6; Livingstone and 123–4, 127,
  132–3; view of Indian Mutiny 153
Londonderry 57
Long, Edward 79, 80–81
Louis XVI, King of France 97
Low, David, 'Colonel Blimp' 322–3
Lucknow: rebuilt by Napier 179–80;
  siege of (1857) 148–9, 152
Lugard, Frederick 210, 229–30
Lusitania, SS 304
Lutyens, Sir Edwin 182, 215
Lytton, Lord 209–10, 218

Macartney, Sir George 35
Macaulay, Thomas Babington 152,
  189–90, 212
Macaulay, Zachary 116, 119, 136
Macdermott, G. H. 257
Macdonald, Hector 266–7, 271

Machonochie, Evan 187–9, 208–9, 212,
  217
Mackenzie, Charles Frederick, Bishop
  156, 157
McLaren, Kenneth ('The Boy') 266
Macmillan, Harold 355, 359, 361
Macquarie, Lachlan, Governor of New
  South Wales 105–7, 108
Madagascar 240
Madras xxiii, 24, 28, 32, 48
Mafeking, siege of 276–9
Magdala fortress, Abyssinia 175, 177
Mahdi, the 267, 268, 270, 272, 375
Mainodin Hassan Khan 149, 151
Makalolo tribe 126, 129
Malaya 184, 241, 342, 358
Malthus, Robert 111
Manning, Frederic 307
Manning, George 82
Mansfield, Lord 92, 101
maps 10, 171, 174
Marathas 28, 48, 51
Mariners Mirrour, The 10
marriage: in early American colonies 63,
  64, *see also* intermarriage
Marsden, Samuel 120
Marvell, Andrew 53
Marxism, view of imperialism xviii
Mary I, Queen 55
Massachusetts 62–3, 90
Massachusetts Bay Company 62–3, 64
Massey, William Ferguson 348
Matabeleland 223–6, 227–8
Maugham, W. Somerset 263, 322
Maxim gun 224–5, 229, 274; adopted
  by Germany 273, 289; at Omdurman
  271, 272
Maxim, Hiram 226–7
Maxwell, Hugh 197, 198, 199, 202
Maxwell, John 40–41
Meath, Earl of 252
Medway, Dutch attack in 21
Meerut, Indian Mutiny 147
Mehmet Ali, Egyptian leader 230
mercantilism 21
Merchant Adventurers 19–20

Mesopotamia *see* Iraq
Methodism 117, 120–21
Mexico 7, 350, 369, 380
Middle East: Britain and 312–16; German ambitions in 300–303, 313–14, *see also* Iran; Iraq; Ottoman Empire
Mill, John Stuart xx, 138, 196
Milner, Alfred 251–2, 262, 273, 274; and Boer War 278, 282, 283
Minto, Lord 260
miscegenation 81, 203–4
missionary societies xxv–xxvi, 120–21, 371; in Africa 154–5, 160; civilization as goal 114, 119–23, 375; equivalent to NGOs xxvi, 114, 120, 139; in India 135–44, 153; reaction to Indian Mutiny 151–3, 154, *see also* London Missionary Society
Mitra, Pramathanath Mitra P. 213
Moffat, Robert 125
Moltke, Helmuth von 299
Moluccas 19
monarchy, English 4
monetary system, global 247
monopoly trading companies 18–21, 26
Montagu, Edwin 315, 330, 333
Montgomery-Massingberd, General Sir Archibald 328
Morel, Edmund 296
Morgan, Sir Henry 1–2, 11–12
Morley, John 258
Morocco 245, 290
Morrison, Herbert 354
mortality rates 73; among missionaries 121, 155–6; among slaves 77–8, 77, 80; Boer War 276, 280, 282; First World War 303, 324; in India 42, 170–71; in Japanese camps 346; West Indies 72–3
Morton, J. B. 322
Mountbatten, Earl 356–7
Mughal Empire xxiv, 27–9
Munro, Thomas 135
Munster, Ireland 56, 57
Muscat 316

Muscovy Company 20
music hall 257
Muslim League 357
Mussolini, Benito 297, 335
Mysore 44, 48, 51, 208–9

'nabobs' 43–4
Namibia 234, 240, 296–7, 303, 315
Nanking, fall of (1937) 338–9
Napier, General Sir Robert 176–8, 179–80
Narragansett Indians, Rhode Island 65
Nasser, Colonel Gamel Abdel- 355
National Africa Company 228
nationalism: Arab 312–13, 314; colonial movements 295; Indian 205, 212–14, 295, 330–31, 333; Irish 253–4, 329–30, 333; and political fragmentation 372–3; radical 251; Young Turk 311
Nauru 315
navigation, art of 9, 10
Navigation Acts (1651 and 1660) 21, 90
Nehru, Jawaharlal 205, 333
Nehru, Motilal 205
Neill, Brigadier-General 151
New Caledonia, French 296
New Delhi 214–15, 330
New England 62–3, 85
New Guinea 241, 315
New Royal African Company 22, 76
New South Wales 105–7, 109
New York (New Amsterdam) 21, 67, 90
New Zealand 120–21, 261; Maoris 108, 120–21; troops in First World War 305, 307–311
Newbolt, Henry, 'Vitai Lampada' 262, 267
Newfoundland 6, 62
Newport, Christopher 7, 11
Newton, John, slave trader 73–4, 76–9, 117
Ngami, Lake 127, 130
Nigeria 228–9, 239, 240
Nile, source of 158–9, 162
Norfolk Island 107

North, Lord 87, 91, 92
Northcliffe, Lord (Alfred Harmsworth) 257–8, 292
Northcote, Sir Stafford 177
Nyangwe, massacre at 159
Nyasa, Lake 157, 158
Nyasaland 240, 358

O'Dwyer, Sir Michael 331, 332
oilfields, Middle East 316
Oliver, Peter 53
Oman 316
Omdurman, Battle of (1898) 267, 375
O'Neill, Hugh, Earl of Tyrone 56
O'Neill, Shane 55
opium trade 166, 167
Opium Wars (1841 and 1856) 165–6
Orinoco River 7
Orwell, George 294, 320, 327
Osborne House 164–5, 167, 206
Ottoman Empire 230, 286–7, 314, see also Egypt; Turkey
Oudh 44, 48, 49, 148–9, see also Lucknow
Overseas Food Corporation 358

Pacific, British possessions 241
Page, Walter 350
Paine, Thomas, Common Sense 93
Pakistan 357, 371
Palestine 315, 357
Pall Mall Gazette 258, 267, 269
Palmerston, Lord 158, 166
Panama 2, 11, 40
Park, Mungo 127
Parnell, Charles Stewart 253–4
Pearl Harbor (1941) 349
Pearse, Patrick 329
Pearson, Karl 264, 288
penal system 102–5
Penn, William 67–8, 81
Pennsylvania 67, 117
Pentagon, 11 September attacks 373
Pepys, Samuel 16
Persia see Iran
Peru 7, 369

Peshawar 151, 152
petitions 118, 136–7
Petty, William 20
Philadelphia, Christ Church 94–5
Philby, Harry St John Bridger 321
Philby, Kim 321
phrenology 263
Pickering, Neville 266
Pilgrims, emigration to America 61–3
Pinto, Isaac de 35
piracy 7–9
Pitt, Thomas 'Diamond' 26, 32; acquisition of diamond 42, 43; as Governor of Fort St George (Madras) 28
Pitt, William (the elder) 32–3, 35, 43, 72, 92
Pitt, William (the younger) 50, 117
Plassey, Battle of 36
Playfair, Lieutenant Colonel William 143–4
Pocahontas 64
Pocock, Sir George 34
Poland, Russian rule in 297
political fragmentation 372–3
Pondicherry xxiv, 30
population: of American colonies 63, 65–6, 68, 86; Germany 288; India 27, 190, 191; of modern countries 372–3; native American 64
Portobelo, Panama 2, 11
Portsmouth, naval base 164–5
Portuguese, and art of navigation 9
Portuguese empire xxv, 3, 63; in Africa 240
Portuguese slave trade 74, 119, 129
Powhatan Indians 64, 66
Poynton, A. H. 357–8
press xxvi; popular 257–9
Price, John Giles 107
Price, Roger 155
privateers 2, 8
protectionism 42, 287, 324, 326, 366–7; American 217, 367
Protestantism xxiii, xxvii, 4, 61
Puritans 61–3

Qatar 316
Quakers 67, 117
Quebec 34
Quiberon Bay 34

race: growing problem of 192–3, 194–5, 197–205; informal segregation (India) 198–9; scientific theories of 262–5, *see also* Jamaica
Radcliffe, Sir Cyril 357
Raikes, Charles 154
railways 169–70, 297, 343–4, 366; Anglo-German projects 289; Berlin to Baghdad 302; Burma 343–4, 345; Rhodes's Cape Town to Cairo scheme 227
Ralegh, Sir Walter 6, 7, 14, 56, 58
Ralegh, Wat 8
rape, fear of 203
Reade, Winwood 262
Redfern, William 105
Reformation 4, 61
Reibey, Mary 107
Relief Fund for South African Women and Children 282
religion *see* missionary societies; Protestantism; Puritans; Quakers
religious revival 116, 193
religious tolerance 68, 134–5
reparations, modern claims for xii–xiii
republicanism 93, 329–30
Revere, Paul 84
Rhode Island 65, 91
Rhodes, Cecil 221, 222–8, 230, 266, 292; relations with Rothschild 223–4, 225; view of Germany 288; vision for Africa 227, 238–40, 273, 284
Rhodes Scholarships 227
Rhodesia 225, 240, 305, 358
rifles 271, 274–5
Ripon, George Robinson, Marquess of 198–9, 200–201, 202, 204–5
Roanoke Island 58, 59
Roberts, Earl 279–80
Roe, Sir Thomas 27
Rolfe, John 64

Roman Catholic Church 121
Ronalds, Francis 168
Roosevelt, F. D. 348–52
Rosebery, Earl of 285–6
Rothschild, Alfred de 286
Rothschild, Ferdinand de 285
Rothschild, Nathaniel de, Lord 226–7, 233, 273, 286; and Rhodes 223–4, 225, 283, 285–6
Rothschild Bank 223, 233, 285–6
Rothschild family 293
Royal African Company 20, 22
Royal Air Force 337–8
Royal Geographical Society 126, 127
Royal Navy 44–5, 44, 164–6, 170, 247, 290–91, 316; British West Africa Squadron 115, 118–19, 165; Dreadnoughts 247; expansion of 9–10, 32–3; First World War 304, 308; naval and coaling stations 245–6, 247; Second World War 339
Royal Niger Company 228
Ruskin, John 196, 221
Russia: expansion of 174, 297, 352; and First World War 298–9, 300, 314; as imperial rival 288; trade 20, 302, 367, *see also* Soviet Union
Rwanda 373–4

Said, Edward, *Orientalism* xvii
St Leger, Sir Warham 55
Saki (Hector Hugh Munro) 292
Salisbury, Marquess of 171, 206, 238–9, 249
Santo Tomé 8
sati (suttee) 139, 141–4
scholarship, in Indian culture xxii, 38–9
science 33, 262–5
Scotland 30, 40
Scots: as emigrants xvi, 39–41, 71; transported as convicts 103
Scott, Paul 198, 203
Scout movement 292–3
scurvy 10, 33
Searight, Kenneth 267

Sechele, Bakwena chief 125–6
Second World War 338–48; America and 348–52; cost of 353–4, 360–61
Seeley, John Robert, *The Expansion of England* 248–9
Serampore 135
Serbia 299, 373, 375
Seringapatam 51
Seven Years War 32–5, 36, 85–6, 101
Shangani River, Battle of 224–5
Sharp, Granville 117
Sheridan, Richard 50
ship building and design 9–10; improvements 33; steam ships 165, 166, 169
ships: convict 103, 105; slaving 76, 79, 117
Shire, River 157
Siam (Thailand) 245
Sidgwick, Adam 156
Sierra Leone 114–15, 240, 373–4
Sierra Leone Company 116
silk 16
silver, South American 6, 7
Simla 181–3, 201, 211
Singapore 305, 339, 342, 358
Skinner, James, Skinner's Horse 41
slave ships 76, 79, 117
slave trade 74, 76–84, 77, 83–4, 114; abolition of 101, 115, 118–19, 159, 375; claims for reparations for xii–xiii; Zanzibar 128, 159, 236–7
slavery 162, 366; campaign for abolition of 116–18; economic case for 74; legacy in Jamaica 192–3, 195–6; Livingstone's mission to end 128–30, 159; in United States 100–101, 118
slaves: emancipation of 101, 115, 118; rebellions 81–2; sexual exploitation 80–81; on sugar plantations 79–80
Sleeman, William 140–41
Smith, Adam xvii, xviii, 48, 92, 117
Smith, Colonel Francis 84
Smith, Captain John 60, 62, 64
Smith, Captain Robert 133–4, 144

Smuts, General Jan xxi, 350
Social Darwinism 264–5
Society for the Abolition of the Slave Trade 117
Society for the Promotion of the Christian Gospel (1698) 120
Society for the Propagation of the Gospel (1701) 120
Somaliland 240, 316
Somme, Battle of the 306
Sorabji, Cornelia 263
South Africa 223–5, 281; Boer War 274–84; gold 273–4; missionaries in 121
South Sea Company 20
Soviet Union 297–8, 356, 358–9; collapse of 372, 373, *see also* Russia
Spain 8, 55, 56, 119
Spanish empire xxv, 2–3, 4, 58, 63, 240, 369; English raids on 1–2, 6, 7–8, 11
Spanish Succession, War of 30
Spenser, Edmund 56
spice trade 3, 19, 21, 23–4
Spion Kop, Battle of 275–6
sports, team games 260–62
Spurgeon, Charles 151
Stalin, Joseph 297–8, 351
Stamp Act (1765) 86, 91
Stanley, Henry Morton 160–62
states: independent 372–3; international intervention 374–5; limited xxiii, xxvi; self-determination 351–2
Stead, William Thomas 258, 268
Sudan 237, 240, 267–73, 316, 375; Battle of Omdurman 267
Suez Canal 230, 354
Suez Canal Company 231–2, 285, 286
Suez crisis (1956) 355–6
sugar 11, 13, 72; use of slaves 74, 80–81
sumptuary laws 16
Surat, near Bombay 19, 20, 24
Sydney, Australia 103, 105–6
Sydney, Sir Henry 55

Tagore, Rabindranath 213
Tagore, Satyendernath 190
Taiping rebellion (1863–4) 268
Tanganyika 210, 315, 358; German
 territory 234, 236, 238, 240, 297
Tanganyika, Lake 161
Tanzania 371
Tasmania 107, 108–9
taxation 5, 46–7, 86; of American
 colonies 85, 86, 91–2; Dutch system
 18; India 37–8, 47, 216, 218
tea 13–14, 86–7
team games 260–62
technology 166, 168–9, 171, 249;
 German 304; industrial 164; military
 33, 165, 328–9, 352
Tel-el-Kebir, Battle of 233
telegraph 168–9, 169, 175–6, 366
Tennyson, Alfred, Lord 196, 256
Terry, Samuel 106–7
Tewfiq, Khedive of Egypt 232
textiles 16–17, 19, 24
Thackeray, W. M., Vanity Fair 43–4
thagi (thuggee) 139, 140–41
Thatcher, Dr James 94
Theodore (Tewodros), Emperor of
 Abyssinia 175, 177
Thomason, James 140
Thomson, James 9, 76
Thornton, Henry 116
Thornton, Richard 156
Threlfall, William 121
Tiedemann, Major von 272
Tighe, George 277
Tipu Sultan, of Mysore 48, 51, 145
Tirpitz, Admiral Alfred von 288, 291
tobacco 13, 14–15, 60–61
Togoland 234, 240, 303, 315
'Tory-entalism' 205–20
tourism, East Africa 260
Townshend, Charles 86, 94
Townshend, General Charles 311–12
trade xviii–xx, xxv, 245, 254–5;
 Caribbean 72; with Commonwealth
 361; and consumption 12–17; with
 India 17; protectionism 42, 217, 287,

324, 326, 366–7, see also free trade;
 spice trade
Trans-Siberian Railway 297
Transjordan, British mandate 315
transportation of convicts 102–5, 106,
 107, 111, 112, 366
Trevelyan, Charles 143
Trichinopoly, siege of 36
Trinity House, Deptford 10
Trollope, Anthony 109
Trotha, General Lothar von 296–7
Trucanini, last Tasmanian Aborigine
 109
Trucial States 316
Tucker, Josiah 92
Turkey 230, 231, 245, 311; and
 Gallipoli campaign 307–11; German
 ambitions in 301–3
Turnbull, Sir Richard 365

Uganda 240
Ujiji, Lake Tanganyika 161
Ulster, plantation of 55–7
Underhill, Edward 193
United Concessions Company 224
United Nations 377
United States of America 95, 110, 111,
 217, 367; conception of empire
 350–51, 352; defence spending 378;
 foreign investment 324–5; foreign
 policy 375, 378–80; hostility to British
 Empire 350–51, 358–9; imperial
 responsibilities 380–81; imperialism
 compared with British model 377–80;
 Lend-Lease 353, 360; and Second
 World War 348–52; slavery in
 100–101, 118; and Suez crisis 355–6;
 supremacy of 354–6, see also
 America; American War of
 Independence
Universities Mission to Central Africa
 155

Venezuela 11
Vereeniging, Treaty of (1902) 281
Versailles, Treaty of 315–16

Victoria Falls 130–31, 159

Victoria, Queen 163–4, 167–8, 176, 219–20, 222; Diamond Jubilee 219, 240; Empress of India 206; on Gordon 269

Vietnam 297

Vincent, Matthias 26

Virginia: colonization of 58–61, 72; colony of 6, 7, 69–70, 90; Jamestown 60–61, 64, 66; mortality rate 72

Volkner, Revd Carl S. 121

Wahabbis, Islamic sect 267

Wahunsonacock, Powhatan chief 64

Wakefield, Edward Gibbon 111

Waller, Edmund 14

Walpole, Horace 51

Warburg family 293

Warren, General Sir Charles 275

Warrior, HMS 165, 166

wars: civil (modern) xxi, 372–3; and imperialist sentiment 256, 258, 264–5; small 51, 66, 366, *see also* American War of Independence; Boer War; and World Wars

Washington, George 86, 99

Wateson, George 10

Watt, Alan 352

Waugh, Evelyn 322

Wedgwood, Josiah 117

Weingott, Alex 309

Weingott, Sam 309–310

Welles, Sumner 351

Wellesley, Richard, Earl of 51

Wembley, British Empire Exhibition 318–20

West Africa 21, 222, 240, 348; slave trade 74–5

West Indies 75, 306–7, 358; French sugar islands 30, 34, 83; mortality rate 72–3; piracy in 1, 7–8, 11; slave population 118, *see also* Jamaica

Western Samoa 315

Westminster, Statute of (1931) 326

White, John 59

White Mutiny (1883) 199–203

Wickham, R. 13

Wilberforce, William 116, 136

Wilhelm II, Kaiser 302

Wilkie, Wendell 351

William III of Orange, King 22–3

Williams, Henry 121

Wilson, Henry 303

Wilson, Horace H. 144

Wilson, Lady Sarah 278

Wilson, Woodrow, US President 315, 350, 380

Winant, John G. 349

winds, influence on trade 9, 25

Winthrop, John 63, 65

Wodehouse, P. G. 293

Wolfe, General 34

Wolseley, Sir Garnet 233, 269

Woolf, Leonard 320

World Bank 376

World Conference against Racism, Racial Discrimination, Xenophobia and Related Intolerance (2001) *xi*, xii

World Trade Center, 11 September attacks 373

Wrong, Professor George M. *xi*

Wyatt, Sir Francis 64

Wylie, Macleod *113*

Younghusband, Francis 321

Zambezi River 127, 130, 156–8

Zambia, economy 368

Zambian Highlands 131, 154, 156, 159

Zanzibar 236–8, 239; slave market 128, 159, 236–7

Zimbabwe 371

Zulu Wars 276